SAVING
THE CITY

SAVING THE CITY

The Challenge of Transforming
a Modern Metropolis

DANIEL SANGER

Véhicule Press

Published with the generous assistance of the Canada Council for the Arts, the Canada Book Fund of the Department of Canadian Heritage, and the Société de développement des entreprises culturelles
du Québec (SODEC).

Cover design and title page type by David Drummond
Set in Adobe Minion by Simon Garamond

Dépôt légal, Library and Archives Canada and the
Bibliothèque national du Québec, third trimester 2021.

LIBRARY AND ARCHIVES CANADA CATALOGUING IN PUBLICATION

Title: Saving the city : the challenge of transforming a modern metropolis /
Daniel Sanger.
Names: Sanger, Daniel (Daniel K.), author.
Identifiers: Canadiana (print) 2021024044X | Canadiana (ebook)
20210240733 | ISBN 9781550655803
(softcover) | ISBN 9781550655889 (HTML)
Subjects: LCSH: Projet Montréal. | LCSH: Political parties—Québec
(Province)—Montréal. | LCSH: City
councils—Québec (Province)—Montréal. | LCSH: City planning—
Environmental aspects—Québec
(Province)—Montréal. | LCSH: City planning—Political aspects—
Québec (Province)—Montréal. | LCSH:
Montréal (Québec)—Politics and government—21st century.
Classification: LCC JS1761.3.A2 S26 2021 | DDC 320.9714/28—dc23

Published by Véhicule Press, Montréal, Québec, Canada

Distribution in Canada by LitDistCo
www.litdistco.ca

Distribution in the U.S. by Independent Publishers Group
ipgbook.com

Printed in Canada on FSC certified paper.

CONTENTS

Preface

I FIRST THOUGHT OF WRITING a book about Projet Montréal around 2015 or 2016 when I felt that I was done working for the political party and for the city of Montreal and that it was perhaps time to return to my previous life: writing and journalism.

The book I had in mind originally was quite different, more about what I knew best, our experience running the borough of Plateau-Mont-Royal. In particular, how our buckle-your-seatbelts approach—deliver as best as possible the bold changes we promised in the 2009 campaign, weather the inevitable storm and let the voters decide four years later—had proven successful. It would be something of an optimist's guide to municipal politics; how to be re-elected with ever-larger majorities without compromising or triangulating or obsessing on a daily basis about "comms" and public relations. Instead, working full out to improve a city and letting actions speak for themselves.

Then, of course, in 2017 Projet Montréal got elected city-wide and the story got bigger and my time working with the party for the city was extended. And the book which came out of it all evolved into something of a hybrid: a chronicle of the party as well as a discussion of how we transformed the Plateau.

For those looking for better models of municipal governance, as well as different ways of doing politics, this book can be of interest. Certain things, it's true, set Montreal apart. Few other cities in Canada have political parties at the municipal level, something which tends to lead to much more wholesale, regular renewal at City Hall. Councillors can't rely on simple name recognition and local support to get re-elected; they also usually need to be on the right team. Also, like many other cities across Quebec and Ontario, Montreal went through a merger two decades ago to create a governance structure that better reflected the reality of its growth. But the city merged in its own distinct way. To be specific, it went through a protracted merger-demerger process in which 28 municipalities became one, only to subsequently become 16 again. Come 2006, the city of Montreal was about twice the size, with 50 percent more people and, very importantly, a system of *arrondissements* or boroughs.

The borough system allowed for something which municipal activists in the city (and elsewhere) had been clamouring for since the 1960s: significant local control over the development of (and thus life in) their neighbourhoods. It is something that, in the pursuit of uniformity, rationalization and economies of scale, the mergers pushed ever more out of reach in many cities, including Toronto and Ottawa. And it was something which led to a certain amount of controversy and derision in Montreal, where initially critics only saw duplication, overlap and inconsistencies, especially when one borough saw and did things differently than its neighbours or the central city.

With the years, however, the virtues of the borough system have proven their value, allowing for finer tuning of projects and policies by people closer to the ground in Montreal's various neighbourhoods. It has also allowed boroughs to act as little laboratories for different initiatives which would have been unlikely to make it through the central city machinery but nonetheless prove successful and end up replicated across the city. It is not a system for centralizers or strongman mayors who thrive on control but it is a system which seems to work. It is also one which allowed Projet Montréal to show its stuff, rather than simply backseat driving from the opposition benches.

Those who believe cities can be effective agents of social and environmental change will find important lessons in what we did, and how we did it. At its core, however, the story about Projet Montréal is, like all stories, a human one, one of personalities and visions, of good luck and bad decisions, and that is what I have sought to tell.

Chapter 1

The autumn of 2017 was a glorious one in Montreal. Sunny days were warm but never stifling. The evenings crisp, but not cold. About half as much rain as usual—enough to keep the grass green and rinse the dust from the city's streets but not extinguish the residual glow of August.

The fine weather was reflected in the mood of the citizenry. Sure, Donald Trump had been elected the year before and his narcissism and vulgarity threatened, well, everything, but there was nothing we could do about that. Up here, all was as well as could be. The province's economy had never looked so good, unemployment and interest rates were lower than ever, Montreal was a—even *the*—global "it" city. Not in the contrived way as it had been 50 years earlier during Expo 67. Rather, in a more quiet and substantial way, as a beacon of social peace, prosperity and quality of life that was almost Scandinavian, but better, due to its extra helping of diversity and cultural dynamism.

As autumn advanced, the leaves turning and the days shortening without the typical grey drizzle of the season, there was no more optimistic cohort of the Montreal population than the candidates and *militants* of Projet Montréal. It was, after all, a municipal election year and the political party, which for 13 years had gotten used to being described as out-of-touch, single-issue or simply radical, which had started out as little more than a pressure group to bring back tramways, and which just a few months earlier had been given no real chance of winning, suddenly looked as if it might do just that.

Mayor Denis Coderre, who after being elected four years previously had been expected to remain in office for at very least two—and perhaps three or four—mandates, didn't seem very interested in keeping the job. Famous for being an omnipresent glad-hander, gripping and grinning his way to high office whether as a federal minister or major metropolitan mayor, he had led a grumpy, oddly passive campaign, expecting to be re-elected in spite of a record void of any fresh ideas or coherent vision.

Meanwhile, Projet Montréal had a new look. It was moving away from the features that had seen it grow steadily, but too slowly, over the previous three elections. No longer led by its founder, Richard Bergeron—brilliant as ice, and about as warm too, incapable of clicking with most of his caucus let alone the electorate—it was a kinder, gentler party. Its new leader was Valérie Plante, she of the quick smile and full laugh, who wore bright coloured dresses rather than blue or grey suits, and seemed to actually be a real human being rather than a caricature of a Duplessis-era ward boss, like Coderre, or an aloof professor like Bergeron.

Plante had been elected party leader less than a year earlier. It was a divisive leadership campaign which saw the caucus go one way and the membership another. But it was the membership who decided and Plante had done well to keep the party from splitting in the aftermath. Still, no one had any real faith she could become mayor, at least not in November 2017. First elected in 2013, she had been an unremarkable councillor and, during the leadership campaign, had often been unsteady. So much so, in fact, that a member of the Coderre administration admits there was "great joy" when the party chose her. "Her knowledge of the files was not very deep. Her ability to communicate a message was not particularly praiseworthy," he says. "So there was great satisfaction when we saw that she was elected."

Politics, however, is not something one is born good at. Like most everything else, it can be learned. Plante's arc of improvement was spectacular, both during the leadership campaign and afterwards, as she had to firmly but gently impose her authority while winning over members of the caucus who had opposed her. Nonetheless, she remained little-known by the Montreal population through the spring and well into the summer of 2017. Then came a cheeky mid-August advertising blitz which seized the public imagination. It was a simple image: Plante, her arms crossed, something between a smirk and a sneer on her face, accompanied by the words *L'homme de la situation. Valérie Plante. Mairesse de Montréal*—"The man of the hour. Valérie Plante. Mayor of Montreal." The colour scheme was sober—white, grey and black—leavened by a touch of turquoise-teal. Any hippie green and NDP/Québec Solidaire orange were studiously avoided. The impact was as desired; people talked about the poster and its boldness, and they talked about Plante.

From the campaign's official start in late-September, the party went from strength to strength. At the same time, Coderre's campaign not only failed to launch but found itself ever more on the defensive for ill-conceived projects meant to highlight the city's 375th anniversary: the Formula E electric car race through the city's downtown, as if the annual F1 race wasn't enough; the incomprehensibly costly concrete stumps scattered around Mont-Royal Park, as if all the wood ones were too old-fashioned; the urban rodeo, as if Montreal was Calgary. The circus part of Coderre's "bread and circus" strategy was exploding in his face and just making him grouchier.

With good reason. Coderre had led in the polls in June—43 to Plante's 29 percent—but the gap was closing by late September when just 5 percent separated him and Plante. With under two weeks to go, a Projet Montréal victory was looking possible: Plante and Coderre were tied at 38 percent. Even if Coderre polled better among people who said they would "definitely vote" and those who typically turned out in greater force—homeowners and the elderly—Plante clearly had momentum. With a week to go, a poll put her in the lead.

Election day on November 5th brought typical autumn weather. Rainy and cool, windy and grey. The get-out-the-vote operations for both parties, having already done what they could to maximize advance polling turnout, swung into action. It had taken Projet Montréal several general and by-elections, to fully appreciate the importance of strong advance-poll and E-day efforts. It had taken it even longer to make them happen. By 2017, however, with abundant volunteers and hard-won experience—not to mention reliable voter tracking software—everything seemed to be working. Voters who, over weeks of phone and door-to-door canvassing had been identified as definite or likely supporters, even the *indécis*, were casting ballots.

Still, there was little letting up before the polls closed at 8 pm. Even in the Plateau-Mont-Royal, where the re-election of borough mayor Luc Ferrandez and his Projet Montréal team had been a foregone conclusion before the campaign started, the councillors were out in the streets encouraging people to vote until after dark. Alex Norris was outside the Société des alcools on Rue St-Denis but found that most people he accosted were from out of borough or even outside Montreal. "It wasn't really worthwhile, but I wanted to take advantage of the last hours to maximise the turnout. City-wide, we were far from certain." Mile-End councillor Richard Ryan was distributing flyers outside the PA supermarket on Ave du Parc and found himself being teased by friends amused by his zealousness and his literal interpretation of the every-vote-counts maxim.

For his part, Ferrandez didn't take a break from getting out the vote until he started being threatened in the early evening. "I was knocking on doors where people told me, 'Look, if there is one more person who bangs on my door or phones me from Projet Montréal, I'm going to burn down your damn electoral headquarters and I'm gonna smash you in the face.' It was crazy. At one point we were doing too much, way too much."

So he went back to his apartment, which was just a few hundred metres from the headquarters on Ave Mont-Royal, had something to eat and got ready to go down to La Corona, where the Projet Montréal troops from across the city were to gather.

On the other side of the mountain, in Côte-des-Neiges–Notre-Dame-de-Grâce, victory was much less assured. Along with boroughs such as Ahuntsic-Cartierville, Villeray-St-Michel-Parc Extension, and Mercier–Hochelaga-Maisonneuve, it had been identified as a populous, central borough in which the party had to make a breakthrough in order to win the city mayoralty. Although I was a Plateau resident, and political employee of that borough, Côte-des-Neiges–Notre-Dame-de-Grâce was where I had been working the entire campaign. My line, only half joking, was that having transformed the Plateau over the two previous mandates, it was time to export the revolution. Since Valérie Plante had convinced Sue Montgomery, an old friend of mine from my journalism days, to run for mayor of Côte-des-Neiges–Notre-Dame-de-Grâce, I decided to work on her campaign. It had been more hit-and-miss than the campaign in the Plateau, where we had held all the seats since 2009 and the councillors were experienced and knew the issues inside and out. In Côte-des-Neiges–Notre-Dame-de-Grâce the slate was much more of a mixed bag—two sitting councillors who didn't much care for each other, three aspirants with limited knowledge of the municipal scene and little to no profile, and Sue. On top of that we were up against three old political pros, who had all served multiple mandates in city council, the National Assembly, or both.

In candidates' debates, Sue would often get laughs and score cheap points by accusing her adversaries of "mansplaining," covering up the fact that her grasp of the issues and familiarity with Montreal municipal politics was woefully shaky. Still, her smiling, joking persona was, like Valérie's, a welcome relief from the stiff, straight men in suits. Not to mention, she was on the team with momentum; in Montreal elections people almost invariably vote the ticket. Rare is the district or borough which will vote for one party locally and another city-wide.

On election day we considered one district a slam dunk, another likely and a third, probable. The other two were Hail Marys and the borough mayoralty was anybody's guess. As darkness fell, those keeping track of the numbers said we had to urgently concentrate our energies on the Côte-des-Neiges district of Magda Popeanu, a party stalwart from the earliest days, its former president and, since 2013, one of our sitting councillors. Our supporters there, it seemed, weren't braving the cold drizzle and going out to the polling stations. So at about 6:30 PM, we fanned out across the district and went knocking on doors of supporters who appeared not to have voted yet. I found myself on streets I didn't know with names I had never heard before—Dornal, Fulton—urging people to go out in the rain to a nearby school or church basement to do their bit for municipal democracy. Most assured me they would; I am quite certain none did. Eventually, it was time for us to head to La Corona as well.

In the Mercier–Hochelaga-Maisonneuve district of Tétreaultville, those analyzing the polling had more encouraging news. It looked like Suzie Miron would finally be elected, on her third kick at the can. Born and brought up in the district, Miron had never lived anywhere else. This was where she had raised her children. It was also where, in 2009, she had lost her patience with the city councillor's indifference to her community's call for a sports centre to be built. At a borough council session in August, she went to the microphone and made her case for the project, as she had before on several occasions, without much hope the administration in place would make it happen.

After returning to her seat, she was approached by two members of Projet Montréal and asked if she might consider running for the party. "They were looking for a candidate for Tétreaultville and they really wanted a woman," Miron remembers. She didn't know the party but was open to the idea; she had been considering running as an independent. She went home, Googled it, and liked what she read. On September 1st, she joined the party and became a candidate.

She came in second but was still beaten handily in that first election, losing by 15 percent to the incumbent. In 2013, she came in second again, but by only 1.4 percent or 161 votes, while the incumbent came in fourth. All the while she remained actively involved in the party organization, first locally and then on the *conseil de direction*. She had worked to transform it from a male-dominated party of "urbanism geeks and transportation freaks" to something more rounded, with more women—something more human. With Valérie Plante replacing Richard Bergeron as leader, she felt that 2017 might just be the year. "In 2013 there were people who told me, 'I'm voting for Coderre because your leader, I can't handle him.' Richard wasn't working for me, not at all. He was just too weird for people."

She took an unpaid leave of absence from her job at Hydro-Québec as early as the utility would allow—the moment the campaign officially began—and she hit the streets. "From the end of September until November 5th, I went door-to-door every day. I would begin at 10 AM and I would stop when it was dark. I was doing it all the time."

Among the rules of political campaigns: do not go door-knocking unaccompanied, and do not waste your time doing so during the work hours of the weekday. Miron ignored both. "In my district there are a lot of older people and there are people who work from home," she explained. As election day drew closer, Valérie Plante brought her snowballing popularity to the district on several occasions in support of Miron. It was recognition of the dedication she had shown to the party, of Miron's support during the leadership campaign and, especially, of the fact that if the party was to win Mercier–Hochelaga-Maisonneuve, it would have to win Tétreaultville. She was there again on E-day, accompanying Miron on visits to polling stations.

Miron didn't do any door-to-door that day. Instead, after the tour of polling stations she worked the phones and by the early evening she was feeling more confident than ever. She headed to La Corona too.

Plante hadn't gone out of her way to support Giuliana Fumagalli, the party's candidate for mayor of Villeray St-Michel–Parc-Extension, during the campaign. If anything, it was the opposite—even if the borough was as important to win as Mercier–Hochelaga-Maisonneuve. Fumagalli was a newbie to the party. A customer service clerk with Canada Post who was active in the union and housing groups, she had only decided to run on Mother's Day; better that than spending the campaign complaining about the candidates. But her knowledge of municipal politics was limited and she knew that she probably wouldn't go anywhere running as an independent.

"So, I called Projet Montréal and told them I wanted to run as mayor and they said 'Sure, just send us your CV.'" She wasn't told, she says, that she would have to win a nomination race; she just thought she was the party's candidate and put a team together.

As summer progressed, other possible mayoral candidates came forward and the party cooled on Fumagalli, her rough-cut brashness and her hardline politics. She was urged to run elsewhere, to cede the nomination to someone with more financial and managerial expertise, and told "You don't fit the portrait." She refused. "I'm from Parc Ex and I'm full legit. I ain't running anywhere else."

She tried to win the party over. She ditched her steel toe boots and work clothes from her days at the Canada Post sorting plant. "I went to buy myself a suit, with a belt, the whole thing. I wanted to looked like a candidate, like *the* mayor. So I put on my high heels, make-up, the whole shebang." It didn't work. The calls kept coming, from the party president, its director-general. "Everybody called me and I said no."

Eventually, it was the August 28th nomination meeting. In her effort to win the party over, Fumagalli had gone on a membership-selling blitz—"to my Italians, my Greek neighbours, all the Pakistanis of Parc Ex"—and made sure as many as possible came out to support her. Even if other candidates had supported her opponent, Fumagalli won. The party had to accept her, if not with a smile.

Like Miron, she took a leave-without-pay from her regular job and campaigned constantly. There were "weird feelings" at group events with the other candidates but that didn't stop her from attending. By election day, she was exhausted, mentally and physically. Still, she toured the polling stations in her borough, initially accompanied, but at the end, alone.

At the second to last polling station, she was asked who she was and what she was doing there. She told them she was the Projet Montréal candidate for mayor. "Huh? You're not Valérie Plante!" she was told. Discouraged, she walked out into the November evening darkness "and there was this gust of wind, huge, like you could almost see it, and I remember thinking, 'this is the wind of change.'"

In her car, she burst into tears, thinking "Shit, I'll never win. They don't even know who I am." So she called up a nun she knew and said, "Just talk to me." The nun consoled her, saying they would still love her even if she lost.

At John F. Kennedy High School in St-Michel, the last polling station, the welcome was warmer. A man she didn't recognize greeted her with a huge smile. "He walks out and I follow him." It turned out to be the singer Marco Calliari whom she had run into earlier in the campaign. "I don't know this guy but he's so friendly that I ask him, 'Can you just give me a hug, please, because this is very hard.'"

Feeling a bit better, she went home, put on some fresh clothes and went to the hairdresser's where she got done up. Then it was on to the Corona.

Never had there been such a line-up at a Projet Montréal event. By shortly after 8 PM, the line stretched up Rue Notre-Dame Ouest, past the fancy décor store next door, past l'Gros Luxe Sud-Ouest, the small apartment building, the empty lot, the antiques store and the Starbucks at the corner and then down Rue Vinet. People for 150 metres or more, two or three abreast.

Most were long-time supporters and volunteers and the reflex of many candidates and inner-circle staff was to go to the back of the line. It seemed impossible, however, that everyone would get in so that would likely mean spending the evening on the sidewalk. Finally the call went down the line that candidates were to go to the front.

By now the mood of feverish excitement in the line-up was evolving into elation as early results came in showing Valérie ahead and with a lead which just kept growing. Crucial must-win boroughs were all trending Projet while those considered in the bag showed almost unimaginable double digit leads. The wave many of us had been feeling was cresting with perfect timing. And magically, the line-up started moving and soon we were inside.

The last time anywhere near as many Projet Montréal members and supporters had found themselves in a room like this had been 11 months and one day earlier when Valérie Plante had won the party leadership at the Théâtre Olympia. The day had begun tense and ended more so, with some councillors refusing to join Valérie on stage after she was declared the winner. At least one had to be restrained and led outside after blowing his lid when a long-time supporter urged him to show a little grace and accept the results.

The atmosphere inside the Corona couldn't have been more different. There was hugging, smiling and cheering as borough after borough was conquered. The Sud-Ouest, where we all were, was won by more than 40 percent; Rosemont–La Petite-Patrie and the Plateau by more than 30 percent. Those were no surprise; the party already held them. Then the smaller boroughs: Outremont and Lachine by 15 percent, Île-Bizard–Ste-Geneviève by 6 percent. Finally the big boroughs which were crucial for the party to win: Mercier–Hochelaga-Maisonneuve, 10 percent; Villeray–St-Michel–Parc-Extension 8 percent; Ahuntsic–Cartierville 5 percent; and, lastly, Côte-des-Neiges–Notre-Dame-de-Grâce, by 4 percent, a reversal from earlier in the evening when the party and Sue had trailed.

One by one the teams in each borough took the stage to cheers. Speeches were made, some eloquent, some stumbling, all greeted with unbridled enthusiasm. Then it was Valérie's turn. "375 years after Jeanne Mance, the founder of the city, Montreal finally has its first woman mayor," she shouted to applause. "We led a historic campaign."

To less applause, she added, "We have an enormous amount of work to do over the next four years." It wasn't something everyone wanted to hear, even if we all knew it was true.

Chapter 2

Montreal is a rarity for having political parties at the municipal level. In most cities in Quebec and Canada, it is simply individuals who run for mayor and councillor. They may be associated with a provincial or federal party because of past activities—perhaps they were a provincial cabinet minister, ran unsuccessfully for a federal seat or are a well-known activist or organizer. Or they may choose to not-so-subtly affiliate themselves with a party by their choice of red, orange, blue or green for their posters and campaign literature[1]. But only in very few municipalities are they actually running for a specific municipal party officially sanctioned by a provincial electoral commission.

Even then, it is something of a stretch to treat the majority of municipal parties which have existed in Montreal—from Jean Drapeau's Civic Party to Équipe Denis Coderre—as true political parties. More often than not, they have simply been convenient vehicles to win and hold on to power; clusterings of candidates around a mayoral hopeful, united by little more than the desire for a seat on city council and the salary and prestige that go with it.

In this way, there is a symbiosis. The mayoral hopeful is able to suggest there is a movement, even a groundswell, in support of their candidacy and be guaranteed a cast of deferential supporters hanging on their every word and nodding vigorously at campaign events and press conferences. Meanwhile, the candidates for council get to attach themselves to a known commodity, even someone perhaps labelled

1 Red = Liberal; orange = NDP; blue = Tory; green = Green.

a star, who they hope will sweep into power, carrying them along. If elected, the councillors will be first in line for positions on the executive committee, on standing committees, and a wide variety of municipal bodies such as transit authorities, regional commissions and police pension boards. Almost all of these come with substantially more salary and prestige, without necessarily requiring much work. In turn, the mayor is insured a means of imposing discipline, because as easily as these posts and perks are distributed, they can be taken away. Errant councillors can even be kicked out of caucus and, next election, party benediction can be withdrawn from a councillor who votes, or steps, out of line frequently enough.

The trappings normally associated with political parties at the federal and provincial levels—conventions, policy debates, local riding associations, nomination meetings, and coherent party structures independent (at least nominally) of the party leader and elected representatives—have, in general, been absent from the Montreal municipal scene.

In the 70-odd years that municipal parties can be said to have existed in Montreal, there have really only been two which, in any comprehensive way, fulfilled these criteria: the Montreal Citizen's Movement (RCM/MCM) and Projet Montréal. Both were founded as leftist, grassroots parties with a wide swath of green, calling for things like better (even free) public transit, more social and affordable housing, and greater municipal democracy and transparency. Both required years of dedication and activism by party faithful before finally being elected, city-wide, in the fourth municipal election they contested. Both counted as their strongholds, in the early, most challenging years, the Plateau-Mont-Royal and Rosemont-La Petite-Patrie neighbourhoods, central neighbourhoods with a history of progressive politics. The two parties were similar enough that Projet Montréal has sometimes been called the MCM 2.0 and the MCM has been called the proto-Projet.

That said, the two parties could hardly have had more different origin stories.

The MCM was the concerted creation of a broad variety of political, community and social groups which, in the spring of 1974, joined together in reaction to Jean Drapeau's populist authoritarianism. Four years earlier, many of the same groups had been united under the banner of the FRAP—le Front d'action politique—and had had the misfortune of being a leftist coalition with more than its fair share of *indépendentistes* running a campaign against Drapeau in the middle of the October Crisis. Several of their candidates and activists were thrown in jail under the War Measures Act and federal cabinet minister Jean Marchand accused them of being a front for the FLQ. Drapeau himself went a step further, assuring Montrealers that, "If the FRAP is elected, blood will flow in the streets of Montreal!"

Universal suffrage had recently been instituted in Montreal, extending the franchise beyond simply property owners and leaseholders to all residents over 18. The number of Montrealers who could vote had virtually doubled and a disproportionate number of new electors were tenants and younger citizens. Still, in a crowded field, Drapeau was re-elected with 92 percent of the vote. His closest opponent—one of six—won 3 percent. Every single council seat went to candidates from Drapeau's Civic Party. The FRAP was, predictably, devastated and discouraged.

By 1974, however, the shine was beginning to come off Drapeau and his administration. His imperiousness and disdain for accountability had only increased with wall-to-wall control of City Hall; famously, Drapeau didn't hold a single press conference between the 1970 and 1974 elections. "Everything that people were angry about in 1970, they were still angry about in 1974," remembers Sam Boskey, a FRAP activist and later MCM councillor. "Drapeau was still in power. There was still no transparency and no public involvement in decision-making at City Hall." Meanwhile, the urgent need for order that accompanied the October Crisis had passed, the glow of Expo '67 was an ever more distant memory and the huge cost overruns, corruption and chaotic organization of the 1976 Olympics were beginning to come to light. The community and social groups got together again, this time without the aggressive acronym. They were now the Rassemblement des citoyens de Montréal: the Montreal Citizens' Movement. It would take 12 years before they finally came to power, but they get credit for making municipal democracy in Montreal worthy of the name.

Among other things, they introduced standing commissions, public consultations on major projects and issues, and a real public question period.

Projet Montréal, for its part, wasn't created in reaction to a mayor, like Drapeau, with super-sized ambitions, a proclivity for demolishing and steamrolling, both figurative and literal, and an allergy to being questioned or contradicted. Instead, it emerged out of an impatience for change and a desire for action rather than noble intentions and unfulfilled promises. More specifically, it was born from the serendipitous meeting of a driven but disaffected urban planner intent on bringing tramways back to the streets of Montreal and a small community group seized with the quixotic idea of pedestrianizing Avenue Mont-Royal in the Plateau.

By 2003, Richard Bergeron hadn't been at the *Agence métropolitaine de transport,* at the time the transportation planning authority for the Montreal region, for more than a few years but it had been long enough for him to become frustrated by the political inertia of his adopted city. Many considered it a fact of life, part of the new urban reality that had come with the long hangover—which included multi-billion-dollar cost overruns—which followed the Olympics debacle. For Bergeron, however, it was but another obstacle to overcome in a life full of them.

Bergeron was born in 1955 to young, working-class parents in Alma in the Lac St-Jean region and had a childhood worthy of a Dickens novel, complete with heavily handicapped mother, alcoholic father and years in a warehouse-like orphanage run by nuns, some nice, others nasty, followed by indentured servitude on local farms. He nonetheless cruised through school effortlessly at the head of his class, and did well enough studying math and pure sciences in CEGEP to be accepted to study architecture by both Laval University in Quebec City and l'Université de Montréal.

Bergeron chose Laval but the spring preceding his first semester he moved to Montreal from Alma to work as a taxi driver. During that summer, Bergeron was smitten, especially by the Plateau where he found an apartment on Rue Fabre near Laurier for $68 per month.

Quebec City and Laval became for him just a place to study as he spent all his weekends and holidays in Montreal behind the wheel of his cab.

Bergeron wasn't particularly "a car guy" but he did come of age in North America during a period when the car was not just king, but something to be worshipped. He was no stranger to the cult. A car for Bergeron in the mid-70s was freedom, power, virility and much, much more. His father had given him and his brother a small Peugeot 204 as a starter car when he was 17. It was totalled within a couple of months and replaced initially by various motorcycles. Bergeron was rarely able to resist pushing the vehicles to their maximum and beyond. As a taxi driver, a sideline Bergeron kept up throughout his architecture studies, his aggressiveness did not subside. He suggests he forsook automobile ownership when he realized that, behind the wheel, he would always be a danger to the public. "[B]ecause I can't change my nature or modify my genetic code," he would later write, "the only alternative was to renounce cars." Today he says his renunciation was more poetic: epiphany, or satori, that occurred on the side of a road in Guinea-Bissau in 1984. His motorcycle had broken down not far from a small village and a colleague he was travelling with went off on his own motorbike to find a mechanic. Bergeron expected the villagers, at least the kids, to come over and see him, perhaps beg for something.

"During the hour and a half, two hours it lasted, no one came to talk to me. No one even looked at me. It was a real lesson in humility followed by the question, 'Who am I, here?' And from that little experience, which was almost nothing, I learned a great lesson. They taught me what my place was."

It led him to question western consumer culture in a way he never had before: "Those people there had nothing. Objectively, they had nothing. But they are proud, they are noble and they are well. Sure, infant mortality is high. Sure, lots of things. But as a way of life it was breathtakingly beautiful, peaceful and noble. And that is where my reflection began."

He returned to Canada shortly thereafter. "By the time I was getting off the plane I had decided never to own another car for the rest of my life."

Returning to study urbanism at UdeM, Bergeron, in his telling, took over, or at the very least made himself indispensable in the department. "I wrote all the research projects for all the profs. I filled out all their grant applications. I became their equal and I was still doing my master's. I still didn't have my degree."

Soon enough, however, he did have his diploma and went out in the private sector work force, getting a job in Montreal with Daniel Arbour et Associés which at the time was Lavalin's in-house urbanism division. He only lasted a year before going back to l'Institut d'urbanisme. "Since I was already thinking about it when I was doing my master's, I enrolled in my doctorate."

Bergeron was expected to take at least three or four years to complete his dissertation and received funding to do so. Course work included, he had it pretty much wrapped up after barely two years. He kept busy in different ways. He taught as a sessional lecturer. He had a business named Hypothèse which helped students with term papers—as often as not, writing them. Then when he learned that Montreal's Co-operative Housing Federation, or *la Fédération des coopératives d'habitation de l'île de Montréal* (FÉCHIMM), was looking for a new director-general, he applied for the job.

Bergeron had a certain familiarity with the world of co-ops—he lived in one in Hochelaga-Maisonneuve at the time and had worked with them in Guinea-Bissau—but he was far from an expert. Not that he would have dreamed to admit as much.

"He was an odd bird, a one-of-a-kind," recalls Pierre-Alain Cotnoir, a veteran pollster and political peripheral in Montreal's progressive and *indépendentiste* circles, who at the time was on the board of FÉCHIMM. "Not an ounce of self-doubt. The first words out of his mouth when he came in for the interview were that we would be lucky to have him and stupid not to hire him."

An odd bird. A one-of-a-kind. Cotnoir was far from the only person to have such an impression of Bergeron, whether on first encounter or repeated exposure, and Bergeron freely admits to rubbing many people the wrong way.

"Objectively, I was irritating, arrogant, much too sure of myself. In everything," he says. Was it, as with many, over-compensation for deep insecurity? One way or another, Bergeron rarely failed to make an impression, good or bad. In the case of FÉCHIMM, it was at least good enough to get the job and for two turbulent years he ran the organization. He earned the enmity of many more-established co-ops which had paid off their mortgages and had low operating costs—and therefore low rents—by arguing for the creation of a fund to which they would have to contribute and which would help to finance new co-ops.

Less controversially, but more notable insofar as it telegraphed his nascent ambition to transform all of Montreal and not just its housing co-ops, was a brief he wrote along with Cotnoir which was tabled in the name of FÉCHIMM to a provincial commission. *The Working Group on Montreal and Region*, commonly known as la Commission Pichette, was set up in 1991 at the request of the City of Montreal which at the time was in fiscal crisis. The commission—which, among other initiatives, is considered by many to have led to the forced municipal mergers of 2001, when the 28 different municipalities on the island of Montreal were amalgamated—was mandated to propose governance structures which were both simpler and stronger for the city and region.

Bergeron and Cotnoir's brief was a 20-page analysis of how the car-oriented development of the preceding decades had weakened the city, prompting families to flee to the suburbs, and, as often as not, off the island. It was a trend that had to be reversed or the city would die, they argued (adding of course that housing co-operatives could play a crucial role in the renaissance of a new, family-friendly Montreal).

Cotnoir, like many, was impressed, astounded even, by Bergeron's "capacity to analyze and process information," but his intransigence made him difficult to work with in a job which required more than a little diplomacy. "He was definitely out of the ordinary with social shortcomings," is how Cotnoir describes Bergeron at the time.

He was gone after two years but by then he had his doctorate.

Between 1993 and 1996 Bergeron picked up contract work here and there: a sessional lecturer at Laval University in Quebec City and then at UdeM's Institut d'Urbanisme and UQÀM; doing studies for various government departments. The transformation of his adopted city, Montreal, became increasingly his singular focus. His timing was good.

As in so many other cities, the administrative structures of Montreal had always lagged behind its growth. Into the 1990s, what people considered Montreal was really a patchwork of different municipalities which, at best, were poorly coordinated, and at worst worked at cross purposes. From 1970, the Communauté urbaine de Montréal had provided a certain coherence as far as emergency services and public transport were concerned, but when it came to planning and urban development the member municipalities were reluctant to relinquish any authority.

Imposing reform was politically easier for a Parti Québécois provincial government than a Liberal one. Any changes would inevitably generate disgruntlement, especially in the heavily anglophone municipalities on the western half of the island of Montreal—the bedrock of Liberal support in the province. The PQ had little to lose by angering them; the party had always been anathema.

Under René Lévesque, the party had already made some progress in containing the free-for-all that was urban development until the mid-1970s. In 1978 there had been Law 90, strictly limiting zoning changes for agricultural land, both as a means to contain rampant urban sprawl and ensure that the most fertile land in the province remained dedicated to growing crops. In 1979, it adopted the first provincial law on planning and urbanism, creating rural municipal authorities and requiring them to conform to various standards in terms of planning and consultation. Underlying it all was a 1977 moratorium on the building of any new autoroutes, which contributed to sprawl.

The 1980 referendum defeat took the wind out of the PQ's sails, however, and the party's electoral calculus was amended by a fundamental fact: those leaving Montreal to live in the off-island suburbs were to a large degree francophone, the PQ's base. Tying the hands of the municipalities that many of them lived in or aspired to, could cost them seats.

A decade and a half later, the PQ was back in power and ready to take another crack at it, if with a narrower focus—the Montreal region alone. In 1996 Lucien Bouchard's government created a new ministry called the Ministère de la metropole, which was tasked with the responsibility of ensuring the coordinated economic, social and cultural development of Montreal. It was a tiny ministry, made up of barely a dozen full-time employees with, it turned out, very little clout compared to the bigger, more established players such as municipal affairs, transport, and industry and commerce. Still, its mandate was full of promise for Bergeron who was hired as a consultant to do a series of studies.

Bergeron felt radical steps had to be taken to get more people living in Montreal—he felt the downtown core needed 100,000 more people and the island somewhere between 500,000 and 750,000 to fully reach their potential. One study proposed "nationalizing" all land within a kilometre of every metro station. Properties which were well-used would be released from the order; the rest would be expropriated. "Everything which is abandoned, everything that is wasted space, everything which is just parking—all of that would be transformed."

Bergeron felt that with the municipal mergers on the horizon, the PQ government would be able to achieve what Lévesque failed to do. "I was certain. I really believed we were doing something that would be meaningful. We had a chance to change things, to completely change the way Montreal had been developing. And I was one of the most important linchpins in the process. It was incredibly intoxicating."

Around the cabinet table, however, the ministry didn't carry much weight and indeed within two years the reason for its very existence was being questioned. In the 1998 election campaign, the Liberals promised to eliminate it. They weren't elected—the PQ returned with a solid majority—but Bouchard still rolled the Ministère de la métropole in with municipal affairs.

The move didn't have much of an impact on Bergeron. By then he was consumed with the culmination of a side project he had been working on for several years: the publication of *Le livre noir de l'automobile.* He had been working on the book for four years before it was published in early 1999 and it showed. The book is a painstakingly exhaustive—and exhausting—400-page exposé of the cost in human life and injuries from car accidents around the world. Filled with charts and graphs, it rails against the tendency to build cars that are ever heavier, ever faster and ever more dangerous, at least to those not inside the vehicle.

Bergeron chose to publish the book himself rather than compromise with an editor who might have found it too long, too dense, and too didactic. One result of this was that the book generated little attention. It did, however, provide him with a meticulously researched if highly opinionated calling card which, perhaps remarkably, did not cause him problems getting contracts from government bodies. It also wasn't an obstacle in his being offered a full-time job in early 2000 at the *Agence métropolitaine de transport* (AMT) which had been set up a few years earlier to plan and coordinate public transit service among the numerous municipalities and transit authorities of the Montreal region. Even if its mandate was much broader, the AMT had been focused since its creation in 1997 on a relatively minor component of the public transit supply: improving the suburban train network in the Montreal area.

Bergeron had little interest in suburban trains—"a suburban train is a tool of urban sprawl," he says—so as a "strategic analyst" with a great deal of autonomy within the AMT, he turned his interest towards an old public transit option that was new again.

The last tramway had disappeared from the streets of Montreal in the late summer of 1959—around the time that Bergeron was being consigned to the orphanage—but in his travels he had come under the spell of urban light rail and was aware of the tramway revival underway around the world, especially in Europe. Even if Montreal has winter, even if, built as it is around Mont Royal, it is far from flat, even if car culture reigns supreme, Bergeron became convinced that a modern tramway was needed to save the city.

The AMT's founding president Florence Junca-Adenot was an easy sell: she was originally from Bordeaux and was familiar with the ambitious tramway project underway there and appreciated the need for "a technological choice between the metro and buses."

For Bergeron, the tramway quickly became key to his plans to curb sprawl and add hundreds of thousands of people to the population of the island, either by convincing them not to decamp for the off-island suburbs or simply by attracting them to a more dense, re-invigorated, less car-centric city.

He threw himself into trying to persuade municipal and provincial leaders—and pretty much anyone else who would listen—

that *le néo-tramway*, as some called it, was the future of urban mobility, in Montreal as elsewhere. Not the clattering and rickety contraptions some still remembered from their youth or old movies, sharing the roadway with cars and trucks and, as often as not, either stuck in traffic or jamming it up. Rather, the sleek, smooth and quiet tramways with low floors and easy access, racing along dedicated tracks past gridlocked cars, with priority passage at intersections and comfortable seats. The kind that had begun popping up not just all over Europe but in Asia and even the United States.

For Bergeron, the tramway would attract people who turned up their noses at crowded, grubby, lurching buses and at a cost which was a fraction of expanding the metro. It would be an attractive "intermediate technology" to a population which for decades had been told that cars meant freedom, convenience, and success.

Bergeron wrote reports and proposed tramway routes. He organized one-on-one meetings, he gave presentations and he took part in conferences. He blueskied cost breakdowns and financial plans which projected huge long-term savings for the city and province. He preached the tramway gospel to anyone who would listen, whether they were in a position of influence or not. Any possible convert to the cause was worth a conversation.

Finally, through the AMT, Bergeron organized a trip, a *mission ministérielle*, to three cities in France—Bordeaux, Paris and Lyon—and to Amsterdam to look at their public transit and, in particular, their tramways. On the junket were Junca-Adenot, several employees of the Ministère des Transports du Québec (MTQ), representatives of different transit authorities as well as Claude Dauphin, a Montreal executive committee member and the president of the Société de transport de Montréal (STM). Serge Ménard, then minister of Transport, joined the delegation at two or three stops for various meetings and protocol events.

Even if their paths had crossed on various occasions, Ménard kept getting Bergeron's name wrong and calling him Gérard, which for a man with Bergeron's pride was hard to take. "It drove me crazy," he says. Just as bad was Ménard's lack of interest in anything but how the various transit projects and authorities were financed.

Relations between the two men were frayed almost beyond repair when, not long after their return from Europe, Bergeron called up the environment reporter for *Le Devoir*, Louis-Gilles Francoeur, and essentially dictated two long pieces which he describes as "If I were the transport minister" articles.

The first article dealt with what needed to be done to bring public transit in Quebec's major cities up to par; the second dealt with inter-city transport of people and freight. Both quoted Bergeron and his writings extensively and exclusively and proposed radical action in order to allow Quebec to meet its targets under the Kyoto Protocol. In particular, Bergeron called on the province to overhaul its taxes and registration fees for cars and trucks, charging more—much more—for less energy efficient vehicles. The proceeds—$2 billion dollars per year, he calculated—would go into a fund to pay for new infrastructure and public transport, from high-speed inter-city trains to, of course, new tramway systems.

Were it a proposal from an academic or the Green Party, it would have been par for the course. Coming from an AMT bureaucrat, it constituted backseat driving of the first order, calculated to enrage the provincial government, in particular Ménard. Which it duly did.

After the first article appeared, Florence Junca-Adenot went to Bergeron's office and said, "I just got off the phone with the minister. He is demanding that I fire you."

Bergeron asked precisely what Ménard had said. "Did he use the words *câlisse* and *tabernak*?"

"Yes, and many others," she replied.

Bergeron then told her she would probably hear more of the same the next day, when the second article was due to appear.

Junca-Adenot succeeded in mollifying Ménard—or at least convincing him that firing Bergeron would be counter-productive and make everyone look bad—and Bergeron escaped with a dressing-down. The minister didn't seem to bear a grudge a few weeks later when Bergeron handed in his report on *Le Nouveau Tramway*. He fully expected Ménard to sit on it and let it collect dust on a shelf. Instead, Ménard read the 64-page document within a day or two, told Junca-Adenot he thought it was excellent and greenlit its publication.

Bergeron set to work on another report: *L'économie automobile du Québec*. His collection of facts and figures was compelling: public transit authorities in the Montreal region were being forced to move millions more passengers every year while seeing their funding decline by millions of dollars, an obviously unsustainable situation; spending on new vehicles by Quebecers had climbed by almost 5 billion dollars—over 50 percent —in the previous five years, with, of course, corollary increases in spending on fuel; of every new dollar spent by Quebec households, 63 percent went on their cars and only 37 percent on food, furniture, leisure activities and the like. Since Quebec produced neither automobiles nor fuel, one out of every two dollars spent on expenses related to automobiles went towards create jobs and economic prosperity outside the province, a bleed of a staggering $21 billion dollars annually.

The report was written against the backdrop of the US-led invasion of Iraq—which most Quebecers saw as an oil-driven asset grab—making it that much more pertinent. It also coincided with a change in provincial government. In April 2003, Jean Charest's Liberals dislodged the Parti Québécois, which in the eyes of many had grown tired after being in power for two mandates and three premiers.

The change in government meant a major change for Bergeron: in November of 2003, Charest replaced Florence Junca-Adenot at the AMT with Joël Gauthier. Whereas Junca-Adenot had been eminently qualified for the position, Gauthier's nomination was pure patronage; he had been a top bagman and director-general of the PLQ and had helped engineer Charest's election.

When Junca-Adenot learned of her dismissal, she called Bergeron into her office and told him that he had three days to publish *L'économie automobile du Québec* or else all bets were off. She couldn't ensure that her successor would allow it to see the light of day. It was published that Friday. At the end of the following week, Bergeron's first under the new boss, Gauthier invited him into his office. "Now I'm going to pay for it, I thought," says Bergeron.

Instead, Gauthier broke out the cigarettes and booze and praised Bergeron's report. He said everyone in government had read it. "Unanimous—it's excellent," Bergeron remembers Gauthier saying.

"We're not like the Péquistes. Péquistes talk and talk and talk and talk and talk. It makes for nice documents but nothing gets done." The new Liberal government, he suggested, might not be effusive about the report publicly but would take action on it, and Bergeron says some of his proposals, in particular surtaxes, were adopted in the 2004 provincial budget. "They were small measures," he says, "but better than nothing."

More significantly, that Friday evening cinq-à-sept in Gauthier's office became a regular ritual for the two men. Fuelled by whiskey, wine and tobacco, Bergeron mentored Gauthier about transportation planning while Gauthier mentored Bergeron in politics. "We became accomplices like you wouldn't believe," Bergeron recalls.

The arrangement between the two men was an enjoyable way to end the week. For Bergeron, however, it was particularly useful because, in the previous months, the strategic analyst had decided it was time for him to become a political organizer.

Bergeron's job at the AMT had always been, to a large degree, what he wanted it to be; self-guided on a par almost with a university professor. A regular activity of his after the ministerial mission to Europe had been to give conferences about tramways, the new generation that was appearing in cities around the world, and how they were an answer—*the answer*—to Montreal's public transport woes.

Part of his spiel was that, politically, implementing a tramway would not be an easy task, especially among older people who could recall the tramways of yore, their unreliability, and the way they blocked traffic and caused congestion as private cars proliferated. For the tramway to return to a city's streets, it needed a "champion" and this champion had to be the city's mayor. As Alain Juppé had been in Bordeaux, as Catherine Trautmann had been in Strasbourg, as Jean Drapeau had been for the metro in Montreal.

During the question period at the end of one conference, a woman stood up and said "Monsieur Bergeron, it is clear that you should be the champion of the new tramway in Montreal!"

To this, Bergeron replied, "The champion has to be none other than the mayor of the city. As far as I know, I am not the mayor of Montreal!"

The line drew some laughter, but the questioner was not deterred. "So you are not mayor of Montreal? Well then, become the mayor!"

The remark may have been offhand and to a large degree in jest, but Bergeron says it got him thinking. Not so much about becoming mayor himself, but starting a political movement—not shouting from the sidelines, but actually being in the midst of the action making things happen.

A few days later, he says, he found himself in intense discussion with colleagues from the AMT, venting as usual about all the things that needed to be done but which were not happening. One colleague had heard the rant one time too often. "Richard, you are always criticizing things," Bergeron remembers being told. "If you are that unhappy with the situation, you shouldn't be working here. You should be in politics."

"That's when it really hit me," Bergeron says.

Chapter 3

Around the same time, a small group of community activists in the Plateau-Mont-Royal was also arriving at the conclusion that they would have to start their own political movement if they wanted to see any real change happen on their streets. It was late 2002, and a half-dozen active members of *Mont-Royal Avenue Verte* wanted a radical transformation of the main east-west commercial corridor of the Plateau to make it more focused on "active" and public transit. They weren't pushing for full pedestrianization—there still had to be room for public transit and delivery vehicles—but they wanted a dramatic reduction in the space given over to private automobiles, especially through the elimination of parking spaces, with a corresponding increase in room for pedestrians and cyclists.

The Plateau had long been known for its political and social activism. On the municipal level, however, things had been relatively quiet since the MCM had come to power in 1986. The MCM was, in many ways, the Plateau's party, the Plateau's people, and even if the neighbourhood had not necessarily seen all the improvements that had been hoped for, there had been some progress. There certainly hadn't been any project such as the razing of the avenue of trees in the middle of Boulevard St-Joseph, or the autoroute Berri, as had occurred under Drapeau, to bring people to the barricades.

By the mid and late 1990s, however, the MCM was both out of power and unrecognizable to many of its early *militants* after repeated splinterings and defections. City Hall again seemed deaf to the neighbourhood's concerns. At the same time, ever more of the ever-increasing number of cars in the Montreal region seemed to be transiting through the area on their way to and from downtown. With no autoroute like the Décarie, they were supposed to travel on the arteries—du Parc, St-Urbain, St-Laurent, St-Denis, Papineau, De Lorimier, Iberville, Sherbrooke, St-Joseph—which was bad enough, given that these were shopping streets, or residential or both. Increasingly, however, transit traffic was detouring to smaller, local streets to avoid congestion on the arteries, or clogging up collectors such as Mont-Royal, Christophe-Colomb and Rachel. Small groups of citizens and neighbours began meeting and mobilizing in church basements, living rooms and kitchens to talk about what needed to be done.

There was Huguette Loubert who lived on Rivard between Roy and Duluth, a favourite "rat-run" for motorists who raced up Berri from downtown and then used it to make their way over to St-Denis. There was Gabriel Deschambault who had seen his stretch of Christophe-Colomb between Parc Laurier and Parc Lafontaine become a thoroughfare between Ahuntsic and the Centre-Sud for thousands of commuters, including many hospital, TVA, and Radio-Canada employees. Both were lifelong residents of the Plateau who had witnessed firsthand a deterioration in the neighbourhood's fabric—not to mention the peace and tranquility—as cars took up more and more space.

Then there were people like Christian Boulais and Luc Ferrandez. They were Quebecers who had travelled widely, been inspired by neighbourhoods they had visited, especially in Europe, and then, returning to Montreal, been seduced by the Plateau.

The scale of their ambitions varied. Loubert was focused on the Plateau as a whole. Deschambault seemed only concerned with reducing the number of cars on his street. Boulais and Ferrandez, meanwhile, wanted to transform the entire city, starting with the Plateau. Boulais' group, *La rue pour tous*, concentrated on getting transit traffic off local streets and reducing the speed limit on them from 50 km/hr to 30 km/hr. Ferrandez, for his part, wanted to do everything.

A Montrealer who had grown up in Ahuntsic, Ferrandez had gone to Paris to study at l'*École des hautes études en sciences sociales*, returning in 1990. Ferrandez had no formal training in urbanism or design but he was a quick study and read and researched tirelessly. He was also an excellent communicator with a rare capacity to inspire, unlike many of the early apostles of traffic-calming and enlightened urbanism who were generally short on political and, often, social skills. Ferrandez was so different, so smooth and slick, that some regarded him with suspicion. At least one or two thought he might even be a spy, a sort of *agent provocateur*, for the MTQ, as he focused more and more of his energy on generating opposition to the province's plans to transform Notre Dame into an autoroute in order to bring cars more quickly into downtown Montreal from the East End. The fact that Ferrandez seemed to have no end of cash—at the time he was a well-paid consultant at Hydro-Québec and spent freely and generously—only contributed to the suspicions about him.

Some in his new circle of acquaintances liked the idea of a new autoroute serving the South and East of the island; the better to keep transit traffic off other streets, they felt. Ferrandez, however, could not have been more opposed. "We cannot build another autoroute on the banks of the river," he insisted. With the project on the drawing board, destined to go ahead unless a movement against it could be mobilized, it consumed more of Ferrandez's time.

Before becoming utterly focused on Notre-Dame, however, Ferrandez had founded a traffic-calming group, the blandly named, and short-lived, *Association montréalaise pour l'apaisement de la circulation,* and its members had drawn up a list of projects to work on. Another one, no less ambitious than stopping the planned autoroute, was the pedestrianizing of Avenue Mont-Royal.

The idea had occurred to other people over the years and recently, it had become the cause of Claude Mainville and Marie-France Pinard, a couple who had moved to the Plateau two years earlier. He was an engineer who had grown up in modest circumstances in Montréal-Nord, the son of a clerk from The Bay and a sales woman from Birks. Like Bergeron, he had put himself through university driving a taxi. She was a microbiologist, who came from a wealthy but unhappy family in Ville-Mont-Royal, the daughter of a Liberal minister—but had fled its pampered confines forever at 17. "I gave the finger to everyone in the family," she says.

In the 1970s and 1980s, the two had both been involved with the Workers Communist Party—she openly, he more discreetly—and their paths had crossed on occasion but they had only gotten together in 1993. "We were both in a bar cruising," Pinard says. "We clicked immediately."

Mainville was newly separated and living in Vieux-Longueuil with his three children. Within two months, Pinard and her son had left their apartment on the island and moved in. She was soon working with him at the small air-quality monitoring company he had started. The company had its offices on Sherbrooke Street, near Parc Lafontaine, and every workday morning saw them stuck in traffic along with tens of thousands of other commuters from the South Shore. One morning in 2000, halfway across the Pont Jacques-Cartier, they had enough.

"As usual we were stuck in traffic," Pinard remembers. "Claude looks at me and says, 'Are you sick of being in a gas chamber?' I said, 'Yes, I can't take it anymore.' We sold our car two months later. It was over. We moved into Montreal."

The couple rented an apartment on St-André near Laurier Park and would go to work and do their shopping on foot, quickly becoming radicalized pedestrians. Marie-France fought for and won a pedestrian crossing at the intersection of her street and Boulevard St-Joseph, which a few decades earlier had been one of the Plateau's most elegant avenues, with a wide median of mature trees down the middle, before it was transformed into a six-lane thoroughfare.

Then, in the spring of 2002, they turned their attention to Avenue Mont-Royal, where they did most of their shopping. Mainville had always had severe asthma and was extremely sensitive to air pollution, a condition which had led to his air-quality monitoring business. Frequently, he had to give himself several blasts off his inhaler as he carried his groceries home. One day, after pausing to use his pump on the street, he had another idea for Pinard. "Hey—what do you think of getting a petition going to get rid of cars from the street?" she remembers him suggesting.

She wasn't keen. "I said, 'Are you nuts? Not only will you have to do that out here on the sidewalk when already you can barely breathe but you will have to shout! You'll make yourself sick. And if we get a hundred people to sign it, we'll be lucky. You'll be a laughingstock.'"

Mainville's suggestion got a more enthusiastic response when he took it to a meeting of Ferrandez's *Association montréalaise pour l'apaisement de la circulation.* Soon, several members of the committee had signed onto the campaign, and it had a name—*Mont Royal Avenue Verte*—and, by March 2002, they were working on the wording of the petition's text.

A key member was Sébastien Gagné, who had come to know Ferrandez years earlier through their parents. He had travelled the world for several years after getting a university degree in mathematics and returned to Montreal around the time AMAC was holding its first meetings. Others were Martin Audet and Jean Ouimet. Mainville, however, remained the chief organizer, composing a battle-plan, with headings such as *mission, objective, strategy,* and allocating tasks to various members.

"He was passionate," Gagné says of Mainville. "For a fairer, greener world. He was really ahead of his time. And he spoke well and incisively. He reminded me a lot of the union leader Michel Chartrand," who, it so happened, had been Mainville's mentor when he had worked at the CSN.

By May, the group was setting up a stand on Mont-Royal—a small table, a chair or two, a parasol, a pile of pamphlets, copies of the petition and some pens. The petition was clear about favouring the transformation of Mont-Royal, "into a pedestrian street between Frontenac and du Parc with efficient and ecological public transport service and facilities for cyclists, rollerbladers, skateboarders and pedestrians." All it asked for, however, was for the public to be consulted on the future of the street.

It only took a few minutes to get the hundred signatures that Pinard had feared would be the total collected. After a few weekends devoted to the task, usually outside the Mont Royal metro station but sometimes on other street corners along the three kilometres of Mont-Royal concerned, more than 5,000 people had signed and the idea was generating media interest.

The group planned to present the petition at the Plateau borough council sometime in the fall. But Helen Fotopulos, who presided over the council—this was during the four-year period when boroughs existed but the position of borough mayor did not—poured cold water on the idea before the petition came close to being tabled. "It is very nice. We can also dream that there is no snow in winter and sign a petition to make it so!" she told a reporter for *La Presse*.

The head of the Mont-Royal merchants' association, Michel Depatie, was diplomatic in the media, saying "People are allowed to dream" but suggesting that impact studies alone would cost millions. Behind the scenes, however, he lobbied vigorously against the idea, using his back channel to the local councillors and City Hall to ensure it would not go anywhere. And on the ground, he was aggressive to the point of physical assault.

"The merchants hated us," remembers Pinard, who quickly enough joined her spouse and his new allies in collecting signatures. "One day we were collecting signatures. By then we had about 10,000. And Michel Depatie storms over, red with rage, and hisses, 'Don't come collecting signatures on our street. You are going to kill business.' And he comes up to me and shoves me."

Fotopulos's doubts didn't necessarily need to be reinforced by the merchants' anxieties. "We already had Prince-Arthur and that was a headache for all sorts of reasons," she remembers. There were additional snow removal and garbage collection complications but it went well beyond that. Commercially, the pedestrianization of Prince-Arthur between Boul. St-Laurent and Laval in the early 1980s had been successful to start with but two decades later the street was a bad cliché. What had been a corridor of charming hippie boutiques and small restaurants had turned into a stretch of oversized eateries all serving the same menu, and empty for most of the week and all winter. This was due to bad zoning rather than the banning of cars—no limits had been placed on the number of restaurants or their size—but it was still a lesson in unintended consequences.

Architect Owen Rose had recently graduated from McGill when he came across Mainville and Pinard collecting signatures for Mont Royal Avenue Verte (MRAV) in the early fall of 2002. He not only signed the petition but quickly became one of the core organizers. "I thought it was the coolest idea," says Rose, who grew up in B.C. before moving to Montreal. "It was about putting people before cars."

He remembers being shocked and insulted by Fotopulos's attitude. "It was an icy slamming of the door." The group was not discouraged, however. They not only kept collecting signatures of citizens but also solicited the support of a long list of organizations. Before long, Greenpeace, Équiterre, the Confédération des syndicats nationaux, Transport 2000, le Conseil régionale de l'environnement de Montréal, Cyclo Nord-Sud, l'Association québécoise de lutte contre les pollutions atmosphériques and Vivre en ville were backing the project, insofar as it concerned the idea of a public consultation.

In late fall, when the petition had 18,000 signatures—significantly more than had voted for Fotopulos or her entire Plateau team in the municipal elections the year previously—the MRAV committee decided it was time to present it to the borough council. They organized a small, festive demonstration with horns and drums to greet the councillors when they arrived. Then, during question period, Pinard formally asked to table the petition.

"We had boxes and boxes of paper. 18,000 signatures. 90 percent of them from the Plateau," she remembers. "And Fotopulos says to us, 'We don't govern by petition.'"

Her highhandedness infuriated Mainville, says Pinard. "Claude goes up to the mic after me and says, 'You have brought it on yourselves—this is your last mandate. We are going to start our own party!' It wasn't true. We hadn't done anything at that point. He was just being a loudmouth. He was so enraged by her reaction. But that is when the idea of a political party was planted. That evening."

Until then, the energetic campaign for MRAV had been fuelled by the summer sun and the enthusiasm of the pedestrians on "l'Avenue," as it is called. With Fotopulos's rebuff just as winter was arriving, "we had a down," in the words of Pinard.

Part of that "down" had to do with conflicting strategies within the group. Mainville and Pinard were for immediate, direct action. "We were coming from a party on the hard left," Pinard says. "Our position was direct action: you don't get anything unless you are in the streets. Forget it. They won't listen to you. You need to put the pressure on."

Indeed, the evening they tabled the petition, they proposed occupying the council room after Fotopulos gave them the brush-off. Others, dismissed the suggestion. "Forget it, we're not a gang of savages," Pinard remembers Sébastien Gagné saying.

"The dominant tendency," that of Gagné and Jean Ouimet, urged moderation and reasoned argument. "Claude always had his fist in the air," Gagné says, adding that this likely led to some of the media portraying the group as "radical extremists" even though all they were asking for was public consultations.

The divisions didn't keep the group from meeting every Monday evening, or from continuing to collect signatures, but the refusal to hold consultations on Mont-Royal led to a loss of steam and direction. They certainly weren't actively following up on Mainville's threat to form a political party to unseat Fotopulos and her team.

As the summer of 2003 approached, the group planned different activities. Mainville and Pinard liked die-ins, where a group of pedestrians would occupy an intersection and bring traffic to a halt by lying prone on the asphalt, and critical mass bike parades in which dozens of cyclists rode together. "That was our way of pushing, to make people understand that it was stupid that the street be entirely dedicated to cars," says Pinard.

Gagné, for his part, was more interested in education and to this end organized a series of four lectures in late May and early June. There would be urbanist Jean Décarie talking about public space, heritage expert Dinu Bumbaru on urban planning, Louis Drouin of the direction de santé publique on urban health and a certain Richard Bergeron on public transit.

The conferences were at Le Placard, a small café on Mont-Royal East near des Érables, and on the Tuesday night when Bergeron appeared to give his presentation about tramways, members of the group were immediately transfixed by his vision. "We were all there and we were like, 'This guy is a rock star! This guy is a rock star!'" remembers Rose.

Pinard remembers Bergeron saying that for Montreal to build a tramway, it needed a mayor to champion the cause. "So when it was over, Claude and I, without talking to each other, immediately had the same idea: we went up to him to say, 'Mr. Bergeron, you are that champion. What are you waiting for to start a political party?'"

Bergeron, for his part, remembers Mainville approaching him and asking, "Where do you plan to go with all this?"

"I said, 'It's simple—I am thinking of starting a political party.' And he said, 'Wow! I think we need to talk.'"

Phone numbers were exchanged and before long Bergeron was meeting with the group at Mainville and Pinard's apartment on St-André. "We realized we were in the same situation," says Rose. "Richard had arrived at the conclusion he had done all he could within the AMT. And we had concluded that if we wanted to push the idea of Mont-Royal Avenue Verte, we had to get political."

The way Rose describes it, fireworks went off all around, but the real connection, it seems, was between Bergeron and Mainville who he says "came together extremely rapidly." Whereas Mainville and Ferrandez never got along—"two alphas" is how Pinard describes their mutual aversion—he and Bergeron were sufficiently different and complementary to appreciate each other without feeling threatened. "They made a nice combination. And they were both loudmouths."

The regular meetings on St-André soon included Bergeron and were less about Mont-Royal Avenue Verte and more about the new political party they were going to create. When weather permitted, they would meet in the back garden; when it was cold or rainy, inside. Before long, they were discussing what the party should be called.

"We had trouble finding a name. A lot of trouble," remembers Pinard. "We couldn't agree. Everyone had their own opinion. There were so many suggestions."

It was Bergeron who proposed "Projet Montréal" and it was eventually agreed upon, more because it was the best of a bad list of names and everyone was tired of the discussion than because of any great enthusiasm for it. "I don't find it an attractive name," says Pinard 16 years later. "It's banal."

Banal or not, the name gave the party a concreteness it didn't have before and it went from an idea to something to get off the ground, up and running, within a year if it was going to get anywhere close to achieving its goal. That goal, of course, was winning power at the next municipal election, in 2005.

Chapter 4

Bergeron had spoken with people with more political experience than him about starting a party from scratch. Each had warned him that it would be a long, difficult, thankless task which would almost certainly end in failure. At very least, he should prepare to spend a long time in the wilderness and expect to compromise his principles—or even sell his soul—to get anywhere close to power.

One of these people was Pierre-Alain Cotnoir, his old acquaintance from FÉCHIMM, who told him that a new progressive party was an excellent idea. Cotnoir, a longtime Péquiste, had been asked to consider taking over the leadership of the MCM in the late 1990s, but instead ended up proposing that, to beat Pierre Bourque, the party should merge with a coalition of suburban mayors to form what eventually became Union Montréal.

The two met at Librairie Olivieri on Côte des Neiges. Cotnoir knew Bergeron, a man of action, wanted to change the world but "was becoming frustrated because his reports and studies were collecting dust on shelves." Building a party, he warned, was easier said than done, however. "I suggested he go for it, but told him to be prepared to spend 10 years in opposition."

Gauthier, at the AMT, gave him similar advice, and tried to coach him through the ABCs of political organizing. At their end-of-the-week sessions in Gauthier's office, he tried to make the neophyte understand that true grassroots parties created in church basements and around kitchen tables were a thing of the past, if indeed they ever existed. It wasn't a question of building a party up from nothing, Gauthier said, but of plugging into and creating alliances with pre-existing political networks.

Bergeron enjoyed "the Fridays around the ashtray and the bottle of scotch" but he didn't take Gauthier counsel. "I would tell him everything and he would say, 'Richard, that is not how you do politics.' And I would answer, 'Joël, I have told you a hundred times: my entire life, whatever I was doing, there was a standard way of doing things before and then it changed once I arrived. And it will be the same with politics.'"

Even when Gauthier offered to introduce him to potential donors, Bergeron wasn't interested. "Above all, I don't want to meet the people you want to introduce me to," Bergeron says he replied with a smile. "I don't want their money."

Still, for whatever reason, Gauthier encouraged Bergeron's mission to the point where not only was Bergeron spending virtually all of his time at the AMT working on Projet Montréal, but others at the organization were openly working on it too. "At one point it seemed everyone at the AMT was helping me. Everyone. The logo was conceived by AMT's designer," says Bergeron. "I had Joël Gauthier's complete support in creating Projet Montréal."

By the end of 2003, Mainville was drafting the statutes for the new party and Bergeron was ringing prospective candidates. The first person he contacted was Michel Labrecque, who at the time was the director-general of Vélo Québec and ran the Montréal en lumières festival for Spectra. The two positions, as well as regular Radio-Canada appearances, gave Labrecque a profile that many felt made him a natural for municipal politics and, in particular, a progressive party with an emphasis on public and active transport. Bergeron and Labrecque had lunch at Café Cherrier and Bergeron says he got nothing but encouragement. He says he received similar support from others he approached, including Josée Duplessis, at the time an environmental consultant with strong ties to the PQ, who was active in the eastern Plateau.

Members of environmental and community organizations such as Équiterre, Vivre en ville, Transport 2000 and the Centre d'écologie urbain were also enthusiastic about the plan to start a new party, to the point that a preliminary organizing meeting was set up for February, 2004 at le Centre St-Pierre on Panet St. south of Ste-Catherine—where, incidentally, the MCM had been born 30 years previously.

They printed up flyers and even bookmarks. In the days prior to the meeting Bergeron and his colleagues from the AMT joked about the possibility that no one would show up to the meeting. "I had three buddies from the AMT who said to me, 'We'll come along just in case no one shows up. Then at least there will be four of us and we'll get a laugh out of it.'"

Their moral support was appreciated but unnecessary; when Bergeron arrived, it was a full house of about 20 people. "When I entered the room, all the seats were taken." He did have reason to be disappointed, however—Labrecque was a no-show. "It was counting on him the most," he says. "I was really disappointed because if there was one person who let me believe that he would be up for it, it was him."

Still, the level of interest and support was such that if Bergeron, Mainville, Pinard and Rose—the core group at this period—needed any more encouragement, this was it. It was time to file for official party status with the Directeur général des élections du Québec. They did so on March 8th. Bergeron was listed as party leader, Mainville as official agent. The party-to-be's official address was Bergeron's home on de la Gauchetière; it listed a total of $405 in financial assets.

Bergeron says he only put himself down as party leader because there was no one else; he had no intention, he maintains, of actually being the party's candidate for mayor of Montreal on November 6th, 2005. "I saw myself as the person who started the movement, gave it life. But I wasn't thinking of a full-time political career for myself." However, given the force of Bergeron's personality, the specificity and depth of his vision, and his admitted stubbornness—the fact that he *always* knew best—it was unthinkable to others that he not be the leader. For someone like Labrecque who might have been interested in a leadership role within the nascent party, Bergeron's character and style, combined with his central role in the venture, was not an added attraction. In fact, it was just the opposite.

Although Bergeron didn't see himself as the party's candidate for mayor, he didn't exclude running as a councillor. Mainville, on the other hand, had absolutely no interest in running for office, even if he was very comfortable with a microphone in his hand and had a human warmth and charisma that Bergeron lacked.

So the two men's plan in 2004 was to obtain party status, spend the summer and early fall getting the word out and signing up members, and hold a founding convention in early November, a year pretty much precisely before the municipal election. In that time, credible candidates for office, including for mayor, would present themselves, they hoped.

To this end, Bergeron undertook a conference tour of Montreal's boroughs, promoting the new party and expounding on the ambitious future he foresaw of tramways and densification. Mainville would accompany him—and afterwards let him know how he had to do better next time. "For Claude, my conferences were always too long. The ideal meeting for him was a fifteen-minute talk and then discussion for an hour and a half. I would say, 'But no, if people don't have material to ask questions about, what questions do you want them to ask?' We had a product to sell."

Their differing approaches underlined the stark contrasts between the two men—Mainville, unfailingly grassroots for whom *le peuple* knew best and should be allowed to decide; Bergeron, the professor with little faith in the wisdom of the masses.

"Mainville adhered to the viewpoint that change came from below towards the top. But without really even wanting it, because I am the way I am, I think the change is going to come from me. The theory of the leader, that change comes from above," Bergeron remembers. "It sometimes led to conflict and arguments."

It was the first sign of a disconnect that was to plague Bergeron for the next decade, for as long as he was leader of Projet Montréal. He headed a staunchly democratic party whose members were overwhelmingly left-wing but he had little time for the Left. If he was going to be a politician, however, Bergeron would have to learn to be diplomatic, to be tolerant, to listen to the lecturing and hectoring. Or at least pretend to. "I ended up hardened," he says. "You block your ears, you let them talk, you nod your head and then you turn and leave."

The party received official recognition on May 28th, 2004 and within two days had generated media interest. *Le Devoir* set the tone with an enthusiastic article with an alarmist headline: "An anti-car party." Bergeron was described as "an intellectual overflowing with diplomas" who knew the city intimately, having driven a taxi over 100,000 km on its streets. He was quoted saying he was taking the leap into politics out of frustration. Quebec, he said, specialized in "producing the most beautiful reports in the world, founded on the best principles, but which never result in concrete action."

The party's plans for tramways, pedestrianizing Ste-Catherine Street, lowering speed limits and slashing car use were reported with enthusiasm. "The philosophy of PM can be summed up in four words: fairness and sustainable development," it announced.

Over the summer the party continued to generate media attention, sometimes short articles in community papers announcing an upcoming conference by Bergeron ("Projet Montréal Wants To Be Known"), sometimes because Bergeron was increasingly on the speed dials of reporters and could generally be relied on for a good quote ("The car is a machine to kill the city and create suburbs"), and sometimes with opinion pieces that Bergeron wrote for *La Presse* or *Le Devoir*.

The membership grew with each conference and each article and with the efforts of Bergeron and other true believers who distributed pamphlets outside metro stations. By October it had surpassed 100 members. Early that month, *La Presse* columnist Rima Elkouri wrote a flattering and encouraging curtain-raiser for the founding convention, which was scheduled for November 7th. Even if, like other journalists, Elkouri might have been put off by Bergeron's braggadocio—which, together with his political naiveté, undermined his credibility—she gave him the benefit of the doubt. It was clear there was an appetite for a green, grassroots municipal party with big and bold ideas, and not just among those attending Bergeron's conferences, but also journalists. "Friends from the 450, buckle your seatbelts. The time has come for the revenge of the 514," she wrote, invoking the area codes for Montreal's off-island suburbs and the downtown.

Much of the summer and early fall of 2004 was devoted to organizing the founding convention, with Bergeron's home as the operation's headquarters. His young daughter Nadianeh and wife Amina stuffed envelopes while he made phone calls, trying to generate media interest or coax well-known Montrealers into attending. There were four he was confident would show up and give the convention a legitimacy and cachet it might otherwise lack: Louise Harel, who as a PQ minister had overseen the municipal mergers but was now bored in opposition and known to be contemplating running for mayor of Montreal; Steven Guilbeault, who as a founder of Équiterre and, at the time, the head of Greenpeace Quebec, was one of the province's best-known environmentalists; Amir Khadir, the doctor who at the time was a representative of l'Union des Forces Progressistes[2] and Michel Labrecque.

There was a full house at the Centre St-Pierre on the afternoon of Sunday, November 7th, but only one of the four showed up: Khadir. With Claude Mainville presiding over the event, he gave a speech. There was music. Then Bergeron, compensating for the no-shows, gave what would become something of a specialty during his political career: a long, elaborate discourse which was more lecture than stemwinder: informed, insightful and intelligent, but infuriatingly long and inappropriate to the circumstances.

On housing issues Bergeron said a *régistre des loyers* was an absolute imperative to keep landlords from hiking rents illegally between tenants. In a nod to the Left, he spoke of the need for more democratic participation, perhaps through *conseils de quartiers*, what some of the old MCMers used to half-jokingly refer to as "Soviets." And, of course, he spoke at length about public transport. Three weeks previously the *Office de consultation publique de Montréal* had come out with a report which took a very similar line to that of the nascent party. Car ownership in Montreal was growing at seven times the use of public transit and much faster than the population. Radical action was needed. Bergeron spoke of the need for more investment in buses and the metro, a reduction in the cost of a monthly pass from $59 to $40 and, certainly, the party's signature issue, the tramway. He portrayed new generation tramways as a silver-bullet solution to the city's transport and traffic challenges. A fraction of the cost of the metro, more attractive to ride and faster than buses, appropriate for most every neighbourhood.

---

2 UFP always had two spokespeople, one male, one female.

It was music to the ears of his audience who, to a large degree, had come to the convention because of Bergeron's tramway vision, and were happy to describe themselves as transit geeks. They were also overwhelmingly male, an issue the party was conscious of when it came time to deal with the *poutine*—the nuts and bolts—of the founding convention, the election of a board of directors and the creation of various committees.

So when a young woman who had come to the convention on a whim, after being invited by a classmate who happened to be the son of Claude Mainville, volunteered her time and energy, she was welcomed enthusiastically. Émilie Thuillier was in many ways typical of much of the early membership of Projet Montréal—and atypical for membership of a political party in general. She had never belonged to another party and wasn't even that interested in politics. What interested Thuillier was how the city worked, and how it didn't. She had done a BA in geography and was finishing up a master's; her thesis was on the sustainable development plans of different cities and how to measure success in their implementation.

Even if she had never been politically active, Thuillier had been an organizer at CEGEP and university, active with groups like Amnesty International. "Shy but sometimes with the desire to give my opinion," is how she describes herself at the time. So when the call went out at the congress, she was happy to put up her hand and was soon party vice-president.

Political posturing and bluster weren't completely absent from the congress. Bergeron said the new party would be irresistible to some sitting councillors, especially those who had been elected with the MCM but now served with the governing *Union des citoyens de Montréal* (UCCIM). He promised a real breakthrough in the 2005 municipal election. "We will undoubtedly elect a bunch of councillors and maybe even snag a borough mayoralty," he announced. Bergeron stressed that the party was for all Montreal and all Montrealers, countering a perception already emerging that it was a party of a privileged few in central neighbourhoods with good access to public transit, shops within walking distance and no need for daily use of a car. "We are portrayed as the leftist intellectual party in the Plateau," he said. "But it's in the Plateau where there is the least to do."

Bergeron's bravado didn't extend, however, to the first electoral challenge the party would face—a by-election to replace a pair of UCCIM councillors who had had to resign after pleading guilty to extorting $75,000 from a developer in return for a zoning change. The by-election was in the forcibly merged suburb of St-Laurent.

Voting day was barely a month after the convention and the party did manage to field Roger Gagnon, an electrician at Bombardier who was a regular candidate for lost causes (such as the PQ) in the area. He knocked on doors, handed out pamphlets and was unfailingly good-humoured. "A pearl. Solid gold," Bergeron remembers, bestowing two of his highest compliments. Still, Gagnon only received 473 votes, enough for a measly 3 percent. UCCIM, the party of Mayor Gérald Tremblay, easily held on to the seat.

Chapter 5

No one was aware of it at the time, but in the 18 months leading up to the creation of Projet Montréal, there were various developments in provincial politics which would prove hugely important to the party ever having a chance to flourish and take power city wide. The catalyst for these developments was the decision of Jean Charest's Liberals to promise, during the provincial election campaign of early 2003, that they would allow formerly independent municipalities—which had been forced to become part of the *une île, une ville* Montréal—to "de-merge" if their residents so desired.

It was an undertaking made largely to satisfy the Liberal Party's West-Island base; some Liberals suggest Charest made it in the heat of the moment at a big campaign rally at Fairview Shopping Centre. "It wasn't a policy decision taken by the party as a whole," says Joël Gauthier, then director-general of the party. "We were very surprised by it at the headquarters." Robert Libman, who as mayor of Cote-St-Luc had fought vigorously against the mergers but since their implementation was in charge of urbanism on Montreal's executive committee, was also shocked by the political improvisation—even amateurism—of Charest. "He didn't need to make the promise to get the support of the people to whom it was directed."

Certainly, it was an undertaking that few powerbrokers in the party wanted to deliver on. Yes, there had been any number of reasons to oppose the mergers, whether on philosophical or historic grounds or simply for practical reasons. *One island, one city* had a nice ring to it but there was virtually no evidence to suggest the mega-city would bring better services to citizens at a reasonable cost. The hugely complicated merger paperwork was complete, however; it was done, and allowing it to be undone would have meant re-opening a Pandora's box of problems which had been closed for barely a year. Finally, as Libman appreciated, the political payoff for making such a promise was negligible; the Liberals would easily coast to crushing victories on the West Island without such a pledge.

The original merger legislation for Montreal had created the borough system in an attempt to address some of the grievances of the municipalities slated to be subsumed by the mega-city. The system, it was argued, would allow for local control over issues best decided locally while the monthly borough councils would provide a venue for citizens to hold their representatives to account without having to make the trip all the way to Montreal City Hall and in more welcoming, less imposing venues.

For Westmount, Ville-Mont-Royal, Pointe-Claire and the other formerly independent suburbs, the powers delegated to the boroughs were risibly insignificant compared to those they had formerly enjoyed and the new arrangement remained entirely unacceptable. However, for neighbourhoods like the Plateau, Rosemont-La Petite-Patrie, Mercier-Hochelaga-Maisonneuve, Le Sud-Ouest and Côte-des-Neiges–Notre-Dame-de-Grace, being given the status of borough and the powers that came with it was something entirely new, at least since they themselves had been independent municipalities before being absorbed by Montreal in the 19th and early 20th centuries.

It was a measure of local governance for which many in the central neighbourhoods had long yearned. That it came as part of a wider centralizing effort spearheaded by Pierre Bourque, a mayor for whom consultation was anathema and who was clearly nostalgic for the simple authoritarianism of the Drapeau era, might have been ironic but so what?

Bourque never got to be mayor of the *une île, une ville* Montreal. The island-wide election of November 2001 was won by a strange-bedfellows alliance of suburban mayors and opposition councillors who banded together to fight Bourque and his centralizing ambitions. The new party UCCIM, which would eventually be rebranded as Union Montréal, recruited a genial former provincial cabinet minister to lead it, Gerald Tremblay.

In the 2001 campaign, Tremblay undertook to delegate more powers to the boroughs if elected. It was hardly a priority in the first half of his mandate and it is easy to understand why: virtually everyone working for the city, from the mayor down to the blue-collar workers, were busy enough just setting up and rendering operational the 27 new entities. This was especially true for the nine which had previously been part of the City of Montreal and were entirely new creations—Ville-Marie, Le Plateau-Mont-Royal, Rosemont–La Petite-Patrie, Villeray–St-Michel–Parc-Extension, Côte-des-Neiges–Notre-Dame-de-Grâce, Ahuntsic–Cartierville, Le Sud-Ouest, Mercier–Hochelaga-Maisonneuve and Rivière-des-Prairies–Pointe-aux-Trembles.

These were the biggest boroughs in the new city, with between 70,000 and 160,000 people, whereas many of the former-suburbs-turned-boroughs had 20,000 residents or fewer, so the stakes were that much higher. Organizational structures had to be put in place; staff had to be transferred; dozens of new directors and *chefs de divisions* had to be named. In some boroughs, such as the Plateau, office space had to be scouted out and rented. "It was a bit of a zoo," remembers Fotopulos.

Even if the former suburbs could easily have handled more responsibilities, and in most cases were bristling to have them, it was unrealistic to expect that the brand-new boroughs needed more power at a time when many employees were, figuratively speaking, still figuring out where the washrooms were.

That was not a consideration, however, after Charest and the Liberals were elected and found themselves immediately under pressure from their faithful to push forward with allowing the municipalities forcibly merged by the PQ to "de-merge." Few members of the new provincial government actually liked the idea, and virtually no one sitting around the executive committee table at Montreal's City Hall wanted to un-do the mega-city. Yes, half of the executive committee members were former suburban mayors who had gone to the barricades to fight against the forced mergers of their municipalities by Louise Harel and the PQ. But now it was a *fait accompli* and they had interesting new jobs with considerable, wide-ranging powers, and, in most cases, generous salary increases to boot.

A strategy was developed between the offices of the mayor and the premier. Somewhat more sophisticated than simply carrot-and-stick, it could be described as carrot, fence and stick. As a first step, more responsibility would be delegated to the boroughs. On the financial front they were given a small power of taxation—not full as some members pushed for—and the right to draft their own budgets, rather than having the central city impose one. They were also given more say over staffing. Finally, the position of borough council president would be eliminated and replaced by borough mayor, who would be elected by the residents of the borough and not simply nominated by fellow councillors. That was the carrot.

The fence was the rules governing the de-merger vote. From the start, it was decided that the normally accepted standard—50 percent plus one of the votes cast—could not apply. For a time, it appeared that the law would require that 50 percent plus one of all eligible voters would have to get out and cast a ballot in favour of demerging—an extremely high threshold given that turnout in municipal elections frequently doesn't exceed 40 percent. Eventually it was agreed that at least 35 percent of all eligible voters would have to vote to de-merge. To even ensure a vote was held, de-merger proponents would have to get 10 percent of eligible voters to sign a petition calling for a referendum.

Finally the stick: any municipality which voted to de-merge would pay for it. They would be required to belong to the *Communauté métropolitaine de Montréal* as well as the *Conseil d'agglomeration* and the cost for shared services such as police, fire protection and public transport would be onerous, as much as half of a municipality's budget.

Despite this cocktail of inducements, barriers and disincentives—not to mention the fact that their political leaders overwhelmingly opposed de-merging—15 municipalities voted to leave Montreal of *une île, une ville* in late June of 2004. Except for the micro-municipality of Montreal-Est—population less than 4,000—and Ville Mont-Royal/Town of Mount-Royal, they were all west-end or West Island. Not to mention, in general, well-off and anglophone.

In the end, the de-mergers, which came into effect on January 1st, 2006, siphoned off 12.5 percent percent of the population, and gave the balance of power to the central neighbourhoods. The voters taken out of the equation were not only more likely to be well-heeled and anglophone; they were also more conservative, car-dependent and less inclined to be the least bit interested by a new municipal party which was all about better public transit, traffic calming and densification.

Over the following decade, Projet Montréal would broaden its platform and diversify its program. It developed nuanced policies involving cultural development, social housing and public security, to mention a few. But it is safe to say that the party would still have struggled to get traction in the municipalities which chose to de-merge. The likelihood of Projet Montréal ever being elected city-wide in an *une île, une ville* Montreal: somewhere between zero and negligible.

The delegation of new responsibilities to the boroughs, extended in an effort to keep the ex-suburbs from de-merging, would also play a key role in Projet Montréal coming to power. These responsibilities gave the boroughs more latitude and independence in their management of day-to-day operations—such as garbage collection, snow removal, street cleaning and park maintenance—as well as in projects—anything from bike paths, zoning or parking policy and prices—and of course budgeting and fiscal planning. No borough took full advantage of these new powers for several years, almost as if no one fully appreciated the extent of the decentralization that had taken place. In 2009, however, when Projet Montréal won control of its first borough, the Plateau, that changed and the party was given an opportunity to show off the kind of administration it might offer.

That being said, all this was far from the imaginations of Richard Bergeron, Claude Mainville and others as they worked on setting up the party in 2004 and, after the founding congress in early November, putting a team together for the election in November 2005.

The congress had generated extensive and positive media coverage. A *Le Devoir* profile of Bergeron compared him to "Red Ken" Livingston, the left-wing mayor of London who had recently introduced a congestion charge on cars and trucks entering the central core of the British capital; a *La Presse* feature portrayed him as a brilliant and diligent public servant driven to make the leap to politics by frustration at "political inaction." It quoted him describing himself as an expert in writing reports "that almost no one read before they ended up lost on a shelf."

These stories helped to bring in yet more members, including several who would become pillars of the party for the next decade. One of the most notable was Patrick Cigana, who due to his good humour and basic decency, would become one of the most appreciated *militants* in Projet Montréal for the next 15 years. Like Thuillier, he had grown up in a home where politics was not a regular subject of conversation and had never been a member of a political party before. "I joined as a citizen who wanted tramways and better public transportation in Montreal," he remembers. "I said, 'This is what we need,' and I went to the website and sent in my $10."

A couple of months later, in March 2005, Cigana got a call from a man called André Allard inviting him to a meeting to set up an ALA—an *Association locale d'arrondissement*—for Rosemont-La Petite-Patrie. ALAs are Projet Montréal's municipal version of riding associations, a basic building block of the party, a tool for recruiting members, raising money, and organizing events. At election time, they are especially important, playing an indispensable role in recruiting and nominating candidates and mobilizing volunteers to staff the cam-paign, whether it be handing out pamphlets or going door-to-door and making phone calls.

Setting up ALAs had been one of the party's main objectives for 2005, in a list drawn up by Claude Mainville and endorsed by the party's steering committee, the Comité de direction provisoire. It hadn't been going smoothly. Meetings had been scheduled and then cancelled, then re-scheduled and cancelled again. At the time not a single ALA had yet been officially created, and if Projet Montréal was to "undoubtedly elect a group of councillors and maybe even snag a borough mayoralty," as Bergeron had predicted, it would need ALAs at very least in the Plateau and Rosemont-Petite-Patrie, if not in three or four other boroughs.

There were about a dozen people at the March 20th meeting and Cigana didn't volunteer for an official position and the responsibilities that would go with it. He had a young child which was responsibility enough. He says, "I knew that if I was were going to get involved, I would go all in. That's the way I am." He left the meeting expecting to be convened until another in the following weeks as the party ramped up its preparations. No news came until June when another member of the ALA phoned him: André Allard had defected to Vision Montréal. The party was desperate—it needed someone to coordinate the ALA and run the campaign in Rosemont. Cigana stepped up, later adding candidate in the district of Vieux-Rosemont to his list of tasks in the 2005 campaign.

While the new party with its ambitious vision and idealism was successful in attracting many earnest and intelligent neophytes who had never imagined themselves joining a political party, it was less successful in recruiting experienced organizers to join its ranks, let alone any stars who might immediately have given it legitimacy and standing in the media. Louise Harel, who Bergeron had hoped to recruit to lead the party, had, of course, blown off the founding convention. Another who showed no interest in joining the party was André Lavallée, a well-respected former MCM councillor and member of the executive committee.

Then there were those involved in municipal politics on a day-to-day basis, whose livelihood depended on backing the right horse in the race for mayor; they didn't want anything to do with Projet Montréal. Snowdon councillor Marvin Rotrand was considered a good bet to defect: he paid steady lip service to progressive issues and despite being a councillor for two decades and having got in on the ground floor with UCCIM he still hadn't won a place on the executive committee. But at a meeting with Bergeron, Rotrand was nakedly contemptuous and the two men ended up disagreeing on virtually everything.

Even if long-time activist journalist and union organizer Paul Cliche had joined the party shortly after its creation, as did André Cardinal, a former councillor for the MCM in the Plateau in May, 2005, it seemed that Projet Montréal was not going to be as irresistible to progressives and defectors from other parties as Bergeron and others had expected.

There were other problems as well. The party found itself in a financial hole very quickly. The founding congress had brought in $817 but the by-election in Ville St-Laurent had cost $7,100—$15 for each of the 473 votes obtained. Meanwhile the fundraising cocktail had been a bit of a bust—only 22 people showed up when at least 50 had been expected. Within two months of its creation, the party was $10,000 in the red.

The tensions between Bergeron and Mainville were also a recurring theme. Now that he represented Projet Montréal and not just himself, the Comité de direction provisoire (CDP) told Bergeron that any opinion piece or news release had to be submitted for its approval before being sent to the media. The leader also had to learn to drone on less at the various conferences he was invited to address as well as at the meetings that the party organized. Twenty minutes maximum, he was told, then open up the floor to questions. And perhaps a word or two in English, otherwise the party couldn't be expected to go anywhere in the West End.

Finally, there were the webpage and internet headaches. In March 2005, four months after the party was created, Google searches for "projet montréal" still weren't bringing up the party's page. And when people were actually able to get to the site, there were chronic problems for those wanting to join the party, contribute money or even send messages to its officials. Meanwhile the CDP member responsible for IT often didn't show up for meetings and, because he was renovating his apartment, was frequently without a reliable internet connection.

These could have been considered growing pains for a young party and there was a silver lining: membership was constantly if slowly increasing, even though media coverage of Projet Montréal had dried up. By early March there were 340 members, triple the number six months earlier, and more were signing up every week. Beyond members, many of whom could be relied upon to volunteer during the campaign, the party would also need contenders for the November election. But hopes for a star candidate—whether to run for mayor of Montreal in Bergeron's place, mayor of a borough or even simply as councillor—had faded by the spring. Everyone Projet Montréal was courting seemed also to be wooed by UCCIM and Vision.

The 2001 election had not been that close. Gerald Tremblay had won 49 percent of the vote for mayor while Pierre Bourque had received 44 percent. But much of Tremblay's cushion came from areas of the West End and West Island—now de-merged—which voted 70 percent, 80 percent or even higher in UCCIM's favour. Meanwhile, the vote-rich central boroughs, often with populations of more than 100,000 people, had overwhelmingly supported Bourque and Vision. So Tremblay and UCCIM needed a new strategy to win in 2005, one which leaned less on grumpy suburban mayors.

UCCIM decided to strike an alliance with a traditional adversary: the Parti Québécois. Pierre Bourque and Vision had generally been able to count on the PQ vote and PQ machine in previous elections. But Bourque had alienated the party, especially its left wing, through his decision to run for the conservative nationalist Action démocratique du Québec in the 2003 provincial election while still leader of the opposition at City Hall. Exploiting this opportunity, UCCIM struck a deal with several PQ riding associations in central Montreal in which the PQ would activate the party machine in support of Tremblay and his team in return for being allowed to designate candidates to the UCCIM slate.[3]

Louise Harel offered up a political attaché, Christine Mitton, who had electoral ambitions and who she seemed happy not to have in her employ anymore. Mitton was placed to run for city council in the eastern Plateau. Another PQ MNA nominated Josée Duplessis, the environmental consultant who had been an enthusiastic supporter of the idea of Projet Montréal, to run for the new position of borough councillor.

UCCIM also went after several candidates with name recognition, progressive bona fides, and even a bit of star power in the central neighbourhoods, as well as PQ connections. These included André Lavallée and Michel Labrecque. Projet Montréal made a play for Labrecque as well. But given that UCCIM's chances of re-election were much greater than Projet Montréal's chances of winning, and

3 UCCIM, as with most municipal parties other than the MCM and Projet Montréal, had no formal nomination process for its candidates. Rather, the leader and the party's brain trust drew up a slate on their own, sometimes in consultation with sitting councillors, sometimes not.

also perhaps because it was led by a polished former cabinet minister rather than a headstrong political neophyte, there wasn't much of a competition.

While UCCIM won the bidding for Labrecque's star candidacy, the party did not accede to one of his requests. Labrecque lived in the eastern Plateau and wanted to run in his home district—De Lorimier. As he puts it, he decided to get into politics to work locally. "I didn't want to save the world. I just wanted a stop sign at the corner." But De Lorimier, of course, was promised to Mitton.

So after final vetting and a conversation with Tremblay, UCCIM took the path of least resistance. With Fotopulos being upgraded to the new position of borough mayor—or at least candidate for—there was a vacancy in the western half of the Plateau. "They told me, 'You're replacing Helen in Mile-End,'" Labrecque says. It was a convenient decision for the party and an acceptable solution for Labrecque. For Projet Montréal, however, it would turn out to be monumental and possibly fundamental to its survival.

Chapter 6

As spring turned to summer and the election drew closer, Projet Montréal's search for candidates with name recognition proved fruitless and Bergeron's bravado waned. In June he was already saying that the election would be a "coronation" for Tremblay. A few weeks later, he was scaling down the number of candidates the party would put forward in the election and how many seats it could hope to win. Rather than candidates for all 105 elected positions, Projet Montréal would field 40 or so; rather than "lots of councillors" and perhaps even a borough mayoralty, the party was aiming for five council seats. "Less than that, and we are not credible afterwards," he said. "And the important thing is to ensure that there *is* afterwards."

By this time, Bergeron had accepted that he was going to have to be his party's candidate for mayor and that the one star candidate who seemed prepared to run for Projet Montréal wasn't going to be allowed to.

Candidates for mayor in Montreal usually also run for city council in a district of their choosing, in tandem with what is known as a *co-listier*. If they win the mayoralty as well as their district, the *co-listier* is the councillor for the district. If they lose the mayoralty but win their district, then they sit in council as leader of their party. Not even Bergeron expected to win the mayoralty, so his *co-listier*'s chances of being elected to council were effectively nil. Perfect for a faithful supporter who nonetheless was not interested in becoming a city councillor—someone like Amir Khadir.

Khadir, however, was the spokesman for the Union des forces progressistes (UFP)—later to evolve into Québec Solidaire—and the executive of the party didn't want him doing double-duty. The rationale was that there were provincial by-elections expected and the campaigns might overlap. But there was also almost certainly concern that an association with Bergeron or the young party might end up embarrassing the UFP somehow. So instead of Khadir, Carl Boileau, the young coordinator of the Plateau ALA, would run as Bergeron's *co-listier*. Their district: De Lorimier, against Christine Mitton.

The party had also lost its candidate for mayor of the Plateau, a teacher and Caisse Populaire administrator by the name of André-Bernard Guévin. In his case, Claude Mainville was the back-up, although considerable arm-twisting was required. Mainville's health was getting worse and he was neither interested in undertaking a six-week campaign of door-knocking and hand-shaking nor becoming mayor of a complex borough. Marie-France Pinard was even less in favour of the idea.

Eventually, Bergeron took Mainville out for a sandwich, and, as they sat on a bench, told him, "Claude, you don't have a choice about it. We need a name to put on the ballot and we are putting yours."

"And if I win?" Mainville asked.

"Don't worry. You won't win," Bergeron answered. "I am not asking you to win, I am asking you to put your name on the ballot."

Finally, Mainville relented. "Ok, as long as I won't win, you can put my name."

The other candidates who volunteered or were dragooned into running in the Plateau were a mixture of eager true believers and compliant *poteaux*—or "posts" (candidates with no expectation of winning who only run to help the party compete in as many districts as possible and thereby appear more thriving than it actually is). The borough council candidate in De Lorimier was Émilie Thuillier. She too required convincing by Bergeron. "After all, I am a pretty shy person," she says. "The thought of seeing my photo everywhere—no, no, no way. That didn't interest me at all."

Then someone, she doesn't remember who, said to her: "Émilie, you participated in drawing up the program. You voted for it, you're involved, you are motivated. Now you are going to take it all, your vision of the city, and give it to someone you don't really know and tell them, 'Take this message to the voters?' And say this person is elected, well, you still don't know their values or what decisions they might make, even with the program. Why do you need an intermediary between you and the voters when you have a vision for the city and can clearly express it?"

"That made me think," Thuillier remembers. In any case, she didn't have an excuse not to run: she had just finished her master's degree and had no job lined up.

After the Plateau, Rosemont was the most fertile ground for Projet Montréal. It too had a mix of the earnest and dedicated and those just there to fly the flag. The candidate for borough mayor, who would take on UCCIM's formidable André Lavallée, was Marc-André Gadoury. Gregarious, quick-tongued and politically ambitious, Gadoury got the nod not because of his devotion to the cause—rather, he was always seen as something of an opportunist—but because he had already run in an election. No matter that it was for the Green Party in the riding of Chateauguay and he received less than 4 percent of the vote; it still meant that he had more campaign experience than virtually anyone else. Meanwhile, in the district of Vieux-Rosemont, Patrick Cigana ran because there was no one else who was game for it. In other boroughs, the situation was similar: the occasional enthusiastic and determined member willing to give it their all despite having effectively no chance, surrounded by those who had, with varying degrees of reluctance, agreed to take a bullet for the young party but wouldn't break a sweat campaigning.

In some cases, candidates required a great deal of convincing but, once convinced, jumped in with both feet. Such was the case with Magda Popeanu, who in due course would become the party's president, Bergeron's closest collaborator and a member of the city's executive committee. In the spring of 2005, however, she was simply a Snowdon resident who was fed up with the neglect of the district, which straddles the open wound that is the Décarie expressway. "I was so revolted by the dirty sidewalks, the garbage, the traffic that I went to the borough council and they were incredibly arrogant."

So along with another Snowdon resident Popeanu founded a residents' association and invited all the party leaders to her house. Bergeron accepted the invitation, as did Bourque and both tried to recruit her to join their parties. "But Richard fascinated me with his ideas for the tramway. I'm a lover of tramways."

Still, Popeanu wasn't prepared to run as a candidate when Claude Mainville called her up and began coaxing her. She reminded him that she hadn't been in Canada very long. Having immigrated to Montreal from Romania in 1992, she still had a pronounced accent, and felt that being a woman was a handicap. "But finally he convinced me."

The party was only able to drum up two other candidates in the borough, a teacher and union activist and a student. That was better than boroughs such as Outremont, Lachine, or St-Léonard where Projet Montréal didn't field any candidates whatsoever, as well as Île-Bizard-Ste-Geneviève, where only one candidate would end up running: Bergeron's wife, Amina Ouaqouaq.

In Mercier–Hochelaga-Maisonneuve the party fielded a complete slate but only after Éric-Alan Caldwell agreed to run for mayor two days before the deadline for candidacies. Caldwell had grown up on a farm in Estrie and moved to Montreal in 2000 after, among other things, planting trees out west and cutting cane with indentured Haitian workers on sugar plantations in the Dominican Republic. His first apartment in the city was just metres from Rue Notre-Dame and he says his laundry would smell of diesel when he brought it in off the line. When he learned of the plans to turn it into an autoroute, he threw himself into the community opposition movement.

At the time, all established parties at the municipal, provincial and federal levels supported the initiative. "There was only Richard Bergeron who was against it," Caldwell says. So he signed up with Projet Montréal and went to the initial meeting to create the party's Association locale d'arrondissement in the borough. "There were only three of us there and one of the other two had serious mental health problems."

In the end, the party was able to head into the 2005 campaign with 71 candidates, out of 104 possible, considerably more than the 40 Bergeron was anticipating a few weeks earlier. Many of them may have been *poteaux* but it was still a respectable number for a party which hadn't existed a year earlier, was led by a little-known transport planner, and which had been spurned by all the stars it had tried to recruit.

A solid slate of candidates didn't necessarily make for a well-organized and serious Projet Montréal campaign, however. Rather, it was every candidate, or at least every borough, for itself. "It was artisanal," is the euphemism Caldwell uses. In 2003 the Charest Liberals had run on the slogan, *We're ready!* "In 2005 my joke was that our slogan should be, *We're not ready, not in the least!*" says Caldwell.

UCCIM, meanwhile, was gearing up to run as professional a campaign as Montreal municipal politics had ever seen. By mid-September, when the campaign officially got underway, the party was coming out with a new release every day, alternately pitching its platform and blasting its opponents—in particular, Vision, which of course it saw as the bigger threat. These allowed it to determine, to a large degree, the narrative of the campaign, which could be boiled down to sensible, responsible administration of the city, nothing flashy, nothing unpredictable. There were very few ambitious promises or undertakings, beyond a tramway (or light rail, since tramway was already Bergeron's political trademark) on Ave du Parc, 15,000 social housing units and $10,000 to young families to help them buy homes in the city and keep them from decamping for Terrebonne or the South Shore.

More emphasis was placed on the $500 million dollars that Tremblay promised for getting rid of potholes, on the *tidiness squads* that he would create to clean up the downtown and on the 311 telephone service that would spare citizens the Kafkaesque runaround they often got trying to get in touch with various city services.

The party made some missteps. Its slogan "Go Montréal" was seen by some as confirmation that that UCCIM didn't care about Montréal being primarily a francophone city, but this was off-set by Vision's gaffe of only distributing pamphlets in English in Côte–des-Neiges–Notre-Dame-de-Grâce.

Pierre Bourque's campaign never seemed to get off the ground. Within a few days of the kick-off, two of his candidates had withdrawn for personal reasons. A few days later it was revealed that various others were actually paid-up members of UCCIM and had wanted to run under its banner but been rebuffed. In many ways, this simply underscored the permeability and fluidity of political parties at the municipal level in Montreal—at least nine UCCIM candidates had been councillors with Vision themselves. Still, it sent the message that Tremblay's was the A team.

But a bombshell—one which would ripple through municipal politics for the next decade—hit UCCIM on October 1st, when *The Gazette* published the first of a series of exhaustive investigative articles revealing that the city had given contracts to 94 percent of the 300-odd businesses whose owners and directors had contributed money to UCCIM. Vision was not spared either as the articles revealed Bourque's party had itself benefitted from donations from the bosses of various real estate, roadwork, legal, and other firms doing business with the city.

Bergeron and Projet Montréal jumped all over the article as proof that the established parties were active participants in a system which, if not necessarily corrupt in the eyes of the law, was at least rotten. In contrast to its usual, minimalist news releases—the longer the release, the bigger the bill, after all—the party issued a lengthy denunciation of the financing of UCCIM and Vision. "We are of the opinion that the population of Montreal is entitled to a little more respect," said Bergeron. "It wants a real democracy. Certainly not a mayor controlled by lawyers, consultants, construction firms, engineers, architects, automobile dealerships and real estate developers.

"There is only one way to expose this and ensure Montreal's culture of nepotism changes, and that is to elect Projet Montréal," he continued, calling for the Directeur générales des élections du Québec to launch a special investigation "to determine the scope of the ramifications of this system of payback for friends of these parties."

Tremblay himself called for an inquiry—after the election—but vigorously denied that there was any connection between the donations and the awarding of contracts. Certainly, however damning, the evidence was all circumstantial and there was no contract which was shown to have been accorded because a donation was made. Tremblay also went on the offensive, launching a complaint to the Conseil de presse du Québec against *The Gazette* and its reporter, Linda Gyulai.[4]

Bergeron accused Tremblay of shooting the messenger and said "the leader of UCCIM is trying to turn an ethical debate into a

4 The complaint was rejected—in April 2006, five months after the election.

legal dispute… After all, the population wants a City Hall which has credibility and integrity and is upstanding."

Still the issue was easy enough to deflect, not least of all because Vision, in a glass house, was reluctant to join in the attack and, probably, because the exposé was in *The Gazette* rather than in *La Presse* or on Radio-Canada. Even if its fundraising methods would ultimately be the downfall of UCCIM/Union Montreal and of Tremblay himself, the damage done by this early exposé was minimal.

The rest of the campaign went UCCIM's way, with the party bringing everything back to potholes, cleanliness and responsible management, and ensuring that the voters not get too worked up by anything. Two-thirds of the way into the campaign, there had still not been a single poll showing which party stood where in popularity, whereas at the same stage in 2001, six had been released. Even in Quebec City, which was in the middle of its own campaign, three polls had come out. The explanation from the head of a polling firm: "If the media haven't ordered any polls, it is because they are not interested in the campaign and take for granted Gérald Tremblay will be elected."

A few days after that, François Cardinal wrote a column about the campaign with a headline that said it all: "Zzzzzz…" He suggested Bourque and Tremblay were each trying to be more boring than the other but "one must also look at the parties' programs, which are about as lacking in audacity, imagination and ambition as the annual report of a firm of accountants."

Projet Montréal, Cardinal acknowledged, suffered no shortage of interesting ideas. But, displaying an elitist streak, he said that as long as Bergeron "is surrounded by a bunch of nobodies" the party wasn't worthy of much consideration. "We are not born unavoidable and essential; we become it," he continued, justifying what was the central frustration for Projet Montréal in the election: the lack of media interest and attention.

As often as not, no journalists showed up at the party's news conferences. If more than two or three came out, it was considered a smash hit, even if it only resulted in a news brief or a single paragraph added to a longer article which focused on UCCIM or Vision. The logical extension of this was that when it was time for the two televised candidates' debates—the first in French and the second in English—only Tremblay and Bourque were invited. Neither received very good reviews. The English debate, one journalist observed, "unfolded in the greatest cacophony." Bergeron was left to comment over the phone from his living room.

On the ground, going door-to-door, it was an entirely different campaign. City council districts in Montreal tend to have populations of between 30,000 and 35,000. This translates to anywhere between 10,000 and 20,000 residences, depending on household size. Which itself translates to an almost insurmountable amount of stair-climbing and door-knocking for the serious candidate who wants to connect with as many voters as possible.

Émilie Thuillier found this out quickly going up and down the streets of the eastern Plateau doing door-to-door, an electoral task which she initially dreaded but grew to love. Her plan at first was to knock on every door in De Lorimier and win people over with the strength of the Projet Montréal vision, but after an evening or two she realized that doing it that way, and spending as long as she needed at every door, she would only get one side of a single block done per evening.

She learned that brevity was key and that voters identified through telephone canvassing as likely to vote and possibly for Projet Montréal were to be focused on. Sometimes no selling of the party's program was necessary. "The door would open and the person say, 'What party are you with?' and I would try to explain, Projet Montréal, this and that, very concisely. Then they'd say, 'It's Tremblay? It's Vision?' And I would answer, 'No! No! It's a whole new party. It's Projet Montréal.' And the people would say, 'Okay, great! I'll vote for you.' And I would say, 'I can explain to you what we are all about.' 'No, no, that's okay. I don't want Tremblay, and I don't want Vision, so I'll vote for you. Thanks.' It was pretty fun to do door-to-door with that vibe."

More often, however, it was just trying to talk to as many people as possible between 6 PM and 9 PM, the time between when they got home from work and when it was to late to ring any doorbells. The trick was to read their moods and inclinations and say the right thing in response, keeping it brief, and moving on to the next door.

Thuillier had to work with Carl Boileau, the *co-listier* for Bergeron in the same district, but they were like oil and water. Boileau describes the 2005 campaign as "slapdash" and "the worst time of my life" in terms of lack of sleep and just being overwhelmed, all the time. "Everything had to be done." Posters, website, organizing meetings, herding volunteers, and of course, doing the door-to-door. Thuillier, he says, used to think he was high sometimes because he was so exhausted and had such bags under his eyes.

Boileau analyzed, poll by poll, past electoral results for the district at the municipal, provincial and federal levels, as well as census data from Statistics Canada, and says he used it to determine where Projet Montréal was most likely to find its support, such as concentrations of younger voters. His De Lorimier colleagues, however, remember his door-to-door strategy for different reasons. "I did door-to-door with him several times and I always had to say to him, 'Carl, be serious, we're not doing this so you can cruise women,'" laughs Bergeron. "He wasted a lot of my time."

With no outside polls to work with and minimal in-house *pointage*, the Projet Montréal team in the Plateau was convinced throughout the campaign that its best chances lay in the district of Jeanne-Mance where two former MCM veterans were facing off for city council—Michel Prescott for UCCIM and André Cardinal for Projet.

Bergeron says he never expected to win himself, whatever the brave face he showed to his team and the confident predictions he made publicly. That is not to say he didn't enjoy the campaign. "I had an absolute ball," he says. "I really didn't expect it. The frenzy of being in the middle of it. It was really fun and motivating." As much as anything, he remembers his job being that of a cheerleader, always being optimistic and confident. "My responsibility was to convince the others that it was possible. What you really think, you're not required to say out loud."

There were candidates, however, who sincerely thought they had a chance to be elected. "I was there to win," says Carl Bégin, the candidate in the Rosemont district of Étienne-Desmarteau. "I was naive and idealistic and seduced by Richard's rationality." Such hopefulness was, however, rare. "In 2005 we were there to get the magic number," says Patrick Cigana, the candidate in Vieux-Rosemont and the borough campaign director, referring to the 15 percent of the vote which qualified the candidate and party to be reimbursed 50 percent of their campaign costs. Those costs were not considerable—the campaign in Rosemont cost a total of $4,000 according to Cigana—but for a party as impoverished as Projet Montréal, it was nonetheless significant.

Getting the magic number was important for other candidates, who neither had much in the way of cash to spare nor flush social networks that might fund their campaigns and thus had to bankroll much of the costs themselves. Certainly, the party as a whole was not in a position to help out: the total campaign costs for 2005 were less than $70,000 whereas UCCIM spent over $2 million and Vision $1.85 million. On a per candidate basis, that worked out to about $1,000 for Projet Montréal and about $20,000 for the established parties.

"I didn't have any support from the party. None whatsoever," remembers Magda Popeanu, "Because there wasn't any. There was no infrastructure."

Popeanu's colleague running in the Notre-Dame-de-Grâce district, a teacher named Jeff Itcush, a brought his own organization and "infrastructure" to the campaign from the union for which he was a vice-president, but he wasn't about to share. Popeanu recalls a frosty reception when she and a friend paid a visit to Itcush's campaign headquarters.

The only poll of the 2005 campaign was released a week before voting day and didn't provide much joy or encouragement for anyone other than Gérald Tremblay and his UCCIM team. It gave him 47 percent support with only 27 percent for Pierre Bourque and Vision. "Richard Bergeron, of Projet Montréal, would have received a meagre 4 percent of the vote," read the *La Presse* article about the poll. Some 53 percent of the people polled said they had little or no interest in the election; barely half knew when it was to take place. For many of those running or volunteering for Projet Montréal in its first campaign, the election couldn't come fast enough after the disheartening poll.

Because of its diversity—linguistic, cultural, economic—Montreal is a notoriously difficult city to poll. Sample sizes need to be larger and more balanced, the analysis of the variables more nuanced than in other, more homogenous cities, such as Quebec. The cost of commissioning a poll rises proportionately as does the possibility of the polling firms ending up embarrassed. While the 2005 poll was more accurate than those carried out at the end of the 2001 campaign—which predicted a Bourque victory—they were way off for Projet Montréal.

When the vote-counting was finished in the wee hours of November 7th, Richard Bergeron had received more than double the support that had been predicted for him little more than a week earlier—even if he was still in the single digits. Still, his 8.5 percent was close enough for Bergeron to declare a sort of victory in front of a jubilant crowd of roughly one hundred supporters at the Centre St-Pierre. "Phase one is over and it was conclusive: we have become a credible party," he said. "It will allow me to hold my head high."

More importantly, Projet Montréal actually won a city council seat and it was Bergeron himself who was elected. His margin of victory was slim—270 votes, less than 3 percent—and would not be confirmed for several weeks after UCCIM called for a recount. At the borough council level, the result was even tighter—only a handful of votes separated Emilie Thuillier and Josée Duplessis—and a recount was also required. In that case, however, it was Thuillier who ultimately came up short.

In the Plateau as a whole, the party did very respectably, finishing ahead of Vision in every race. The only candidate to get less than 30 percent of the vote was, to his great relief, Claude Mainville, who had not campaigned at all and had no desire to be elected.

The results in Rosemont were also encouraging for Projet. The party came in third with at least 15 percent of the vote and as much as 23 percent in four of the five races.

Elsewhere in the city, results were mixed. In Côte-des-Neiges–Notre-Dame-de-Grâce, both Magda Popeanu and Jeff Itcush hit the magic number although the third candidate Trevor Hanna came in sixth in a field of six with less than 5 percent of the vote. Only five candidates other than Hanna received less than 5 percent of the vote, among them Bergeron's wife, Amina, the *poteau* running for the mayoralty of Île-Bizard–Sainte Geneviève.

All this occurred at the end of a campaign which, judging by the turnout, had left Montrealers as uninspired and disinterested as any in decades: only one in three Montrealers who was registered to vote did so, the lowest participation since 1966 when Montreal was essentially a one-party state. Jean Drapeau won that election with 94 percent support while well over half the councillors won by acclamation.

Chapter 7

IF PROJET MONTRÉAL wasn't exactly a big winner, Vision and Pierre Bourque were clearly the big loser. Before the vote, Bourque had said he had no interest in being leader of the opposition for another four years and would resign if Vision was not elected to power. After conceding defeat, however, he changed his tune. "I am a man of my word," he told reporters, "I am here to stay." The next day he was unsure; he needed a few days to reflect.

Bergeron correctly saw Bourque's vacillating as evidence that Vision was rudderless and weak, so his bluster returned. He told reporters that now that Projet Montréal had proven itself credible, the party would resume courting councillors elected with the other parties who had been tempted to join Projet but hadn't been convinced of its viability. "We will go and ask them, 'Remember that chat we had a while back? Well, maybe now is the time to finalize things,'"

Vision councillors would come over because their ship was clearly sinking, he explained, while many UCCIM councillors would feel lost in the crowd. Even if being on the winning team was fun, those who didn't get appointments to the executive committee, to boards such as the STM or commission presidencies, would soon enough grow disaffected. "Lots of people will get bored in [Tremblay's] administration," said Bergeron, suddenly the political schemer. "There are too many people and not enough jobs."

Even if Bergeron had nothing to offer potential *transfuges* or floor-crossers, either at the city or borough level, Tremblay did perhaps have a problem in that regard. His overwhelming victory—54 percent versus 36 percent for Bourque—included 15 of 19 borough mayoralties and 47 of the 65 seats in city council. There were certainly one or two backbench councillors whose values, or at least whose discourse, were well-reflected by Projet Montréal. Exhibit #1 in this regard was Josée Duplessis.

Her running for UCCIM had been seen by Projet founders as naked opportunism and a great betrayal. "Josée said to me, 'Oh Owen, I am now at the age where I need a system in place and a secretary to answer the phone. I am past the point of building something from scratch,'" remembers Owen Rose. "Fine if she didn't have the time or energy to build a new party, but she was going over to join Helen Fotopulos who we had established was the devil!"

"Nice container with nothing in the way of contents. And she's an *arriviste*," sneers Marie-France Pinard, almost 15 years later.

Bergeron, however, was more understanding, or perhaps had learned quickly that it rarely pays to bear a grudge in politics. "Josée came to me beforehand to apologize," he remembers. She was a single mother with a very young child and needed security which she felt was more likely to be found running with UCCIM rather than Projet Montréal. "You can be reckless," Bergeron remembers Duplessis telling him. "You've got a good job at the AMT, a job for life."

After his win was confirmed, Bergeron did indeed plan to continue on at the AMT. Over the previous two years, he had juggled many tasks—setting up a new party, teaching part-time, working at the transportation agency, and not to mention running a campaign. He felt he could easily handle, as many city councillors did, holding down a full-time job in addition to his duties as an elected official. There was also a financial aspect. Montreal has an abundance of city councillors—65 compared to Toronto and Ottawa, which have 25 and 23 respectively—but they are paid about half as much.[5] In 2005, Bergeron could have expected to make approximately $45,000 along with a tax-free expense account of about $13,000. His AMT salary was significantly more, somewhere in the neighbourhood of $80,000. So, Bergeron planned to take a page from the book of Pierre Bourque and

5 They also don't have any staff directly allocated to them whereas in Ottawa councillors each receive almost $300,000 for staff while in Toronto it is over $500,000.

donate his city salary to charity while continuing to work for, and be paid by, the AMT.

Joël Gauthier was not opposed to the idea. "Richard is a smart guy and is very hard-working. He was a good employee." Board members of the AMT felt otherwise. "There was enormous pressure," to get rid of Bergeron from André Lavallée, who after his election as mayor of Rosemont–La-Petite-Patrie had been named to the executive committee in charge of transport and as such had a seat on the AMT board.

In mid-December, Bergeron was called into Gauthier's office and presented with two possible scenarios. He could quit the AMT and receive four months of salary as well as other benefits, for a total of about $35,000, he remembers. Or he could take a leave of absence for the four years of his mandate.[6] "I was floored," Bergeron says. "I had my legs cut out from under me. I really wasn't expecting it."

Bergeron refused both offers and, in mid-February, took the case to the Commission des normes du travail, alleging, not incorrectly, that his firing was politically motivated. "Initially, Projet Montréal, it was fun and a breath of fresh air," he told *Le Devoir*. "But once I was elected, the party became a threat." He also turned on Gauthier, who had been so indulgent of him over the previous two years when Bergeron, by his own admission, would routinely show up for work at 11 AM after an evening event the day before, put in a few hours work (as often as not on Projet Montréal files) before leaving at 3 PM for another party function. Gauthier, he said dismissively, was simply "a political tool put there to serve the government in place."

The official AMT line for why Bergeron couldn't do the two jobs simultaneously was conflict-of-interest. The transit agency was responsible for the whole Montreal region, not simply the city of Montreal or even the island, but also Laval, Longueuil and dozens of other municipalities in the greater Montreal area. The interests of each had to be considered as impartially as possible in the AMT's studies, planning and proposals. As a city councillor, it would be Bergeron's

6 Gauthier says this offer was eventually extended to as long as Bergeron was an elected official; anytime he quit politics or was defeated he could have had his job back.

obligation to put the priorities of Montreal first and foremost and thus, the AMT argued, the jobs were inherently incompatible.

Bergeron felt he would no more be in a conflict-of-interest than, say, a councillor who also worked as a real estate agent and was called upon to vote on zoning changes. It wasn't the strongest argument and when the dispute came before the commission—Bergeron having refused multiple efforts by the AMT to settle it amicably—he blew his case with one comment. Asked whether being a Montreal city councillor wouldn't cause him to prioritize the city's interests over those of other municipalities, he said he had always done so anyway in his time at the AMT so it wouldn't change anything. "I lost the case on that answer," he remembers. He also lost what might have been a fair settlement. "Where personal finances are concerned, I'm a real idiot."

Bergeron's pigheadedness was certainly bad for his bank account but it was good for Projet Montréal; the party was now the singular focus of his abundant energy and ambition. He threw himself into his new job as a city councillor and leader of a young party with the same fervour as his previous endeavours.

Even before his victory was officially confirmed, Bergeron had shown up at the Plateau Mont-Royal council where the borough budget was being adopted. Since he had yet to be sworn in, he was barred from sitting with the other councillors, but that didn't stop him from expounding, during the public question period, on the need to consult the public on how to spend their money. Fotopulos heard him out for a minute or two before telling him question period was for questions, not lectures, and that, anyway, the spending decisions had already been made.

At his first appearance in city council a few days later, Bergeron, by now sworn in, called on Tremblay to include him in the delegation of 15 Montreal councillors named to sit on the agglomeration. He said that since Projet Montréal had received more than 120,000 votes in the election, it was only fair. It was an interesting argument and the position would have not just earned Bergeron a generous salary bump but also another forum in which to hold forth. Still, Tremblay was having none of it.

Two days later he was going after Tremblay about the introduction of a special pothole tax which had outraged Montrealers when it was announced by the re-elected UCCIM administration in the city budget tabled shortly after the election. The next week he was back on the subject of taxes, calling on Tremblay to include the opposition in the preparation of a new budget since the previous one had been withdrawn. The week after that he was challenging the administration on bus and metro ticket prices.

At every opportunity available, Bergeron was barging into the spotlight and towards the microphone, with an interesting take on city issues and a novel (if frequently unworkable) proposition. The approach got him attention at City Hall: Tremblay and Executive Committee president Frank Zampino did promptly sit down with him and hear his proposals for the budget after he asked to be consulted in December. It also made him a favourite of journalists, for whom he was both a breath of fresh air and a reminder of the MCM during its finest moments, when it was in opposition and full of bold, ambitious ideas, before it was weighed down by the actual responsibilities of administering the city.

The Gazette's Linda Gyulai followed Bergeron on and off for six months to write a flattering three-part, 8,000-word profile of him, his party and his early days in office. Gyulai, who had been covering municipal politics since the 1980s, portrayed Bergeron as a brilliant and driven Cartesian visionary; the party as a grassroots collection of young idealists and experienced activists. Together, she suggested, they heralded a new dawn in Montreal municipal politics.

Bergeron "was ambitious, all right, but his ambition wasn't power," Gyulai wrote. "He had ideas, and he was going talk about them for the next four years, until he and his team could make them happen."

Henry Aubin, a *Gazette* columnist and editorial writer who had been covering Montreal city politics even longer than Gyulai, was also excited by Projet Montréal and its leader. In various columns, Aubin praised Bergeron's intellectual rigour and fresh ideas. Bergeron was "a fine city councillor" with whom "council is becoming a more interesting place," Aubin wrote in the spring. Later, he began a column about Bergeron with the words, "Stop the presses: The leader of a Montreal municipal party is not treating voters as dolts."

Bergeron and the party certainly had reason to feel optimistic about their prospects and their central mission in the months after the election: on a trip to Paris in February, Tremblay announced that Montreal would soon be getting its tramways back. He mentioned three routes, including Ave du Parc, which Bergeron had studied and proposed while at the AMT, as well as Rue Notre-Dame East and one linking the Peel Basin with the downtown. All three would converge on Boul. René-Lévesque and the first would be running within four years, Tremblay said.

Even if some Projet Montréal members were outraged by Tremblay appropriating the central plank of their platform, Bergeron could only rejoice. "This may be the beginning of a new era, a new way of life in the city. The return of the tramway will allow the population to reappropriate much of the public space that was given over to the automobile when the tramways disappeared," he said, adding that the impact on Montreal would be as significant as that of the metro 40 years earlier.

The party, and its *raison d'être*, were on a roll.

Two months later, however, it hit a bump which knocked it off course and from which Bergeron's reputation would never fully recover. By the time Projet Montréal was being created, *Le livre noir de l'automobile* was already several years old and Bergeron was thinking that it might be time to write another book. After all, a book, whether it be a memoir or an extended essay, is a time-honoured calling card for any politician with big ambitions. Publisher Michel Brûlé of *Les éditions Intouchables* felt likewise and commissioned Bergeron to write a follow-up to *Le livre noir*. His stipulations: no charts or graphs, much less data, more prose and opinion. And time its release to coincide with the municipal election campaign.

Bergeron left the writing of the book until virtually the last minute. Finally, with Brûlé threatening to cancel his contract, Bergeron sent Amina and Nadianeh to Morocco for a month and sat down at the keyboard. In one day alone he says he wrote 35 pages or 16,000 words. The book was finished and handed in to *Les Intouchables* well before his wife and daughter returned. *Les Québécois au volant* was published in October 2005, in the middle of the election campaign, but generated little attention. No one seems to have read it carefully at all.

In mid-April, however, Patrick Lagaçé, then a *Le Journal de Montréal* reporter, made it deep enough into the book to come across the paragraph on page 104 in which Bergeron questioned the attacks of September 11th, 2001. "We all saw ad nauseum two airplanes crash one after the other into the Twin Towers of the World Trade Center in New York," he writes, adding, "That is the only event of which we are certain." The two other plane crashes that day—one into the Pentagon, the other in a field in Pennsylvania—didn't happen, he suggests, because "no one saw the least bit of airplane wreckage. I am personally the sort who cannot believe that two 60 tonne-aircraft can vaporize. It just may be that on the 11th of September, 2001, we were simply witnesses to a titanic act of state terrorism."

As controversial, even outlandish, as they are, the remarks are made in an almost offhand way, in a sequence in which Bergeron is holding forth about the need of the United States to ensure a steady supply of oil, given that it was consuming 21 million barrels a day, 45 percent more than 20 years earlier. And they are logically inconsistent since Bergeron is suggesting that the U.S. needed the Pentagon and Pennsylvania crashes to justify invading Iraq—as if the World Trade Center attack would not have been enough. It is not hard to imagine that Bergeron composed the paragraph during one of his all-day-and-much-of-the-night writing binges. Or that, as he boasts, the editor barely changed a comma when reviewing the text.

None of this concerned journalists, however, when the *Journal* broke the news that Bergeron was a "truther." He didn't help his cause when, grilled by reporters, he wouldn't budge from his position. "There are good reasons to ask questions … I stand by what I wrote entirely," he told *Le Devoir*, refusing even to acknowledge that by promoting such a conspiracy theory, he might hurt Projet Montréal and his own nascent political career. "It is certain that if I were in the backwoods of Missouri or Mississippi, it is possible that my political career would be finished. But not here. Our critical reflexes in regards to the Bush administration are sufficiently honed that we can accept to discuss certain things."

Bergeron, of course, was wrong. The truther tag would stick to him, like gum on his shoe, for the rest of his political career, as confirmation to many Montrealers that while he might have good ideas for the city and lead a dynamic party, he just wasn't mayor material. The episode also made it clear to the members and *militants* of Projet Montréal that however great Bergeron's contribution to the party was, however significant his assets and expertise, he came with drawbacks.

Chapter 8

In the early months of 2006, with one councillor elected and, its membership was sure, many more to come, the party leadership worked to develop a functioning structure and clear guidelines to ensure that the party did not become a one-man show.

Some of the old tensions between Mainville and Bergeron had returned, with Bergeron sometimes sending out communiqués or taking positions on issues without first running it by the Conseil de direction (CD).[7] The CD would meet Wednesday evenings at party headquarters—the ground floor of Bergeron's house on Rue de la Gauchetière—and Bergeron often found himself being chastised for improvising policy or firing off news releases, including a nine-page opus regarding his dismissal from the AMT, without submitting it to the CD to vet beforehand.

Such tensions between party members and the party's elected representatives were hardly unique to Projet Montréal. Indeed, they occur more frequently than not with grassroots parties. In the case of the MCM, they came close to destroying it. Six months after its founding in 1974, the party elected 18 councillors to City Hall, an explosive start which in hindsight was too much, too soon. It quickly fell into internecine squabbling between members who felt the party should be a more or less conventional political party, albeit with a radical agenda, and those who felt it should be a revolutionary social movement with a focus on enlightening and mobilizing the masses.

7 It had ceased being the Comité de direction provisoire shortly before the 2005 election.

In the words of one journalist, the party was "more interested in bringing down the capitalist system than seizing power at City Hall."

Internally there were prolonged, bitter debates about the role of councillors and to what degree they should be allowed to speak for the party. The most hardline felt that councillors should be little more than conduits for relaying the positions of their local organizations; that all questions should be resolved by grassroots committees before being communicated to the caucus and councillors. Needless to say, this was unworkable, not to mention unpopular among many of the elected councillors. By 1978, five had left the caucus, with two of them setting up the more centrist Groupe d'action municipal (Municipal Action Group, or MAG). In the municipal election that year, the MCM saw its caucus reduced to a single member with its mayoral candidate finishing third behind the MAG leader. The MAG also elected only a single councillor, Nick Auf der Maur, who dismissed the MCM as "snarky theoreticians... They want to reform the world. We want to reform the city."

With only one elected councillor and a much less ideologically insistent membership, Projet Montréal wasn't going to face the same internal turmoil. The prospect of conflict was also reduced when Claude Mainville, his asthma worsening, and Marie-France Pinard moved out of Montreal to Val-David. For all intents and purposes, Bergeron was left alone as the intellectual founder—and director—of the party. Mainville was replaced as party president by Magda Popeanu who challenged Bergeron less than her predecessor, not least of all because, having grown up in Ceauşescu's Romania, Popeanu was as skeptical as Bergeron about some of the left-wing positions Mainville, Pinard and others pushed to have included in the party discourse.

Bergeron's excesses were also contained somewhat by the party's first employee, Émilie Thuillier, who was hired soon after the election to do everything Bergeron didn't have the time or inclination to do but also served as something of a mollifying influence. Among Thuillier's day-to-day tasks were party communications with members, helping to build up and coordinate the ALAs, and backstopping Bergeron with his council preparation, as well as essentially all of his constituency work.

Les cas de quartier—neighbourhood cases—are an essential part of a councillor's work and can easily take up almost all of his or her time. A *cas de quartier* can be virtually anything—a request for a speedbump or a stop sign at the corner; a complaint about neighbours who put their garbage out at the wrong time or rowdy patrons at a nearby bar; citizens venting about increased taxes, lack of parking, bumpy streets or scofflaw cyclists; homeowners at their wit's end trying to negotiate the city rules and labyrinthine bureaucracy governing building an extension, redoing the façade or replacing their decrepit front balcony.

Many councillors take pride in being on top of all the *cas de quartier* in their district and knowing as many residents as possible by name and address, even phoning them on their birthdays. Bergeron never even pretended to be interested in or concerned about De Lorimier's *cas de quartier*. He left the retail politics to others. Being councillor for De Lorimier was useful because it allowed him to lead Projet Montréal from a seat within the city council chamber. That was the extent of it.

His lack of interest in the affairs of his district, even the Plateau at large, didn't win him any respect from the other councillors in the borough. His attendance at the regular meetings between councillors and borough directors was spotty; if he showed up, he was usually late and hadn't often read the documents to be discussed. "Richard was completely out-to-lunch on many issues," remembers Fotopulos. "He was a very bad councillor to begin with and didn't get any better."

Bergeron doesn't dispute it. "I never took care of my constituents, directly or immediately." His job, as he saw it, was building the party city-wide and as quickly as possible, not nurturing it in districts which had already proven themselves receptive. An opportunity to do this presented itself in early May 2006 when Pierre Bourque finally announced his resignation from city politics, as leader of Vision Montréal and as councillor for the eastern Rosemont district of Marie-Victorin.

There had been rumours that he was going to quit on several occasions in the previous months and each time Bergeron had tried to coax various Vision councillors to cross over to Projet Montréal. "Wait until he actually does quit," they had responded, "then we can talk." A few added that UCCIM had been sniffing around the Vision caucus making overtures to assorted councillors as well.

Once Bourque did resign, Bergeron realized that he still had nothing to offer prospective *transfuges* and, try as he might, no Vision councillors were going to quit a ship which, even if sinking, was still a ship rather than something more akin to an inflatable dinghy which could very easily deflate entirely in the three and a half years before the next municipal election.

So the only other option open to Bergeron and the party was to try and win the by-election which, in due course, was set for September 24th. By mid-June they had found a candidate who they felt could win it for them. Kettly Beauregard had been the Vision councillor for the district from 1994 until 2001, while Pierre Bourque was mayor of Montreal. Elected as Bourque's *co-listière*, she was Montréal's first Black city councillor and was immediately named chair of the important public security commission. After two years in the job, she was made a junior member of the executive committee, responsible for cultural relations. She was considered a staunch Bourque loyalist until 2001 when, again elected in tandem with the Vision leader, she had to step aside for him, since he hadn't been re-elected as mayor.

Days after the election, she claimed Bourque promised her a job as an attaché at an annual salary of $57,000 but never paid her anything. Eventually, in early 2003, she sued him for almost $85,000 in back pay and damages. The suit's timing was odd: it came as Beauregard and Bourque were both preparing to run as candidates in the provincial election a few weeks later, she for the Parti Québécois in a staunchly Liberal riding in Montreal's North End, he for the Action Démocratique in the less predictable East End riding of Bourget. Neither candidate seems to have been helped by the legal action and the publicity it brought. Beauregard came in second but with fewer than half the votes of her Liberal adversary while Bourque came in a distant third.

Beauregard then ran as an independent for the 2005 municipal election in her old riding against Bourque and the *co-listière* who had succeeded her.[8] It was her turn to finish third but she didn't give up trying to get her job and district back. When, a few months later,

8 City councillors can run for provincial or federal office without resigning, as Bourque did in 2003. If elected, of course, they then must quit.

Projet Montréal needed a candidate in Marie-Victorin, she offered her services.

The party threw all it had into the campaign. New members had signed up since its encouraging showing the previous November and everyone, no matter what borough they lived in, was urged to do anything—hand out flyers, go door-to-door, make phone calls—for Projet's candidate in eastern Rosemont. She might not have shared the party's vision any more than that of Vision, she may not have cared more for tramways than highways, for human-scale neighbourhoods and bike lanes than high rises and big box stores, but this was electoral politics and Beauregard was wearing Projet's green and blue.

Hopes were riding high on the day of the by-election as supporters and by-election workers, including Claude Mainville down from Val-David, filled the campaign headquarters. Early results justified the enthusiasm. With one-third of the votes counted, Beauregard was ahead by a slim margin—.5 percent—over her UCCIM adversary, Carle Bernier-Genest, considered a rising, progressive star in the party. Vision was already out of the game. With two-thirds of the vote, her lead had grown to 3.3 percent.

But the trick to any election is getting your vote out. It is especially true in by-elections, when the participation rate is almost invariably much lower than in general elections, and getting out the vote involves ensuring that as many supporters as possible vote in the advance polls, the BVA or *bureaux de vote par anticipation.* Projet Montréal didn't have the machine that UCCIM had, or even that of Vision, to mobilize supporters. When the BVA vote came in, the results were "catastrophique" as the campaign director told the crowd. The air went out of the room, if not the dinghy. "You just have to laugh," Mainville told a discouraged supporter. "It has become so tragic that if you take it seriously, you give up."

Beauregard and Projet got more than twice the number of votes the party's candidate had received less than a year earlier and more than four times the share of the vote but she nonetheless ended up losing to Bernier-Genest by more than six percentage points, 37.6 to 31.5 percent. Projet Montréal still had only one councillor elected out of 105.

It wasn't long before the party would get another chance. A year after the by-election in Rosemont—a year during which the Tremblay administration tabled an ambitious, 20-year, $8-billion-dollar transit plan but spent much of the time defending its proposal to change the name of Ave du Parc to Boulevard Robert Bourassa—the first corruption scandal hit UCCIM. (Or rather Union Montréal; the party underwent its own, smoother name change in May 2007.)

It was small-time but nonetheless damning. Outremont mayor Stéphane Harbour was a handsome up-and-comer in the party. He had done a stint on the executive committee in charge of urbanism and sat on various commissions. If on the bland and entitled White-male side, his political future seemed bright within the Liberal/ Union Montréal universe. Then two internal city reports pointed to "irregularities" at Outremont's City Hall.

On the one hand there were the cases of scotch charged to the borough and consumed by Harbour, his colleagues and cronies in the "piano bar" reception room of the attractive white building on Côte-Ste-Catherine. Nothing actually illegal but it looked terrible: the second smallest borough in the city with, by far, the largest alcohol tab, not all of which went for receptions or public events.

On the other hand, there was the minor-league fraud, which was illegal and which years later would see Harbour sentenced to house arrest after he pleaded guilty. Harbour, who was making $110,000 per year, felt the borough should pay for his English lessons but didn't want to have to ask borough council to approve a motion to that effect, as would have been required. So instead he had his chief of staff and the borough director claim the $1,800 cost as their own, which was allowed since they were employees and not elected officials. They then passed on the money to Harbour.

Making it worse was Harbour's resistance to coming clean and, then, his blaming it all on the chief of staff and borough director. Despite his fervent denials and protestations, he was quickly cut loose by all his allies as the media went to town on the scandal. Within a month he had resigned and a by-election for a new mayor for the borough was underway by Halloween 2007.

The Union candidate was Marie Cinq-Mars, who had been a

borough councillor with Harbour, and was a well-known member of the community. Meanwhile, Projet Montréal found someone who couldn't have had a better profile. Jean-Claude Marsan was a founder of Héritage Montréal, a pillar of the architecture and planning department at the Université de Montréal and one of the city's most respected commentators on urbanism. He also had a political past which added to his lustre: he had been in on the founding of the MCM in 1974 and had run as a candidate in Rosemont that election. The Union/Liberal machine was nonetheless able to mobilize its forces and on December 16th, just as the first major snowstorm of the winter hit the city, almost half the votes cast went to Cinq-Mars. Marsan came a respectable second with 37.5 percent. Bergeron was still the lone Projet Montréal councillor at Montreal City Hall.

In the fall of 2007, the Tremblay administration also successfully navigated the sudden, surprise departure of Benoît Labonté, the mayor of the downtown borough of Ville-Marie and member of the executive committee responsible for culture. Labonté had been a top advisor and chief of staff to federal Liberal cabinet ministers, including Paul Martin, before taking over the leadership of Montreal's Chamber of Commerce. Along with Lavallée and Lebrecque, he had been one of Tremblay's star recruits in 2005, a sign that the UCCIM/Union Montréal bench was strong and deep and capable of renewal.

Out of politics or in, Labonté did little to hide his ambition and he made no effort to disguise his desire to succeed Tremblay as mayor. When, shortly after Bourque's resignation and barely six months into his second mandate, Tremblay announced he would run for a third, Labonté wasn't thrilled. He also came to understand that his naked ambition hadn't done much to endear him to his colleagues, several of whom cultivated hopes themselves of replacing Tremblay, if more discreetly. Given that the caucus was riven by factions and rivalries, Labonté appreciated relatively quickly that winning the necessary support to take over the leadership of the party would be almost impossible. So in September 2017, just before Stéphane Harbour's world fell apart, Labonté quit Union Montréal and the executive committee, citing Tremblay's lack of leadership as his main reason.

Few people saw the departures as indicative of any sort of crisis with the party. Instead they accepted Tremblay's portrayal of Labonté as a petulant under-performer. "He has just shown us today that his personal ambitions are more important to him than culture and the downtown."

Halfway through its second four-year term, Tremblay's administration appeared as secure as could be hoped for, and, in all likelihood, given the disarray of Vision Montréal and the not-ready-for-primetime Projet Montréal, cruising towards a third mandate. Indeed, in early January in a column about what to expect in 2008, Henry Aubin wrote that Tremblay was as secure in power as Jean Drapeau had been in his heyday. A few weeks later, Aubin was extolling Tremblay's "two scandal-free terms."

He perhaps hadn't been reading *Le Devoir* closely enough. In mid-December, the paper published a front-page exposé regarding a conflict of interest in the rewarding of the biggest contract in the city's history, the installation of 30,000 water meters in industries, businesses and institutions across the island. The engineering firm hired by the city to manage virtually all aspects of the awarding of the $355 million dollar contract was, it turned out, a business partner of the firms in the consortium which won the bid. In the following days, things just got murkier when *Le Devoir* revealed that the top city official involved in the awarding of the contract had left the city to work for the same engineering firm.

The opposition at City Hall was soon asking questions and demanding that the contract's signing be delayed. The union representing Montreal's blue-collar workers as well as the environmental group *Eau Secours* followed suit. Within a few weeks, however, a lid was put on the controversy, at least for the rest of 2008. At the request of Vision's interim leader Noushig Eloyan the province's municipal affairs minister, Nathalie Normandeau, had looked into the awarding of the contract: there was no "concrete and factual element" for believing that the winning consortium had received any preferential treatment," her ministry reported in mid-February.

Richard Bergeron and Projet Montréal had not jumped on *Le Devoir*'s revelations with the same fervour as Vision. It may have been simply because Eloyan got to it first and Bergeron didn't want to be seen as endorsing Vision or blindly following their lead. It may also have been because the rationale behind the installation of water meters across the island was a good one in the eyes of the party, ensuring, as it would, a more responsible use of a precious, if abundant, resource, while diversifying the city's revenue stream.

Bergeron did, however, raise questions a few months later when the politician who would end up at the centre of the water-meter scandal took the city by surprise by announcing he was quitting politics to work in the private sector. Frank Zampino had been a pillar of UCCIM/Union since its creation and had been the president of the executive committee for as long as Tremblay had been in power. The power of a president of the executive committee varies from mayor to mayor, depending on their leadership style. Under Tremblay, it was widely understood that Zampino ran the show and that the mayor was as much front-man or figurehead as anything else. One former Union councillor compared the Tremblay-Zampino relationship to that of George Bush and Dick Cheney.

Tremblay was teary-eyed when meeting the media after Zampino announced his resignation and said he had been blindsided by the decision of his righthand man. "Normally, I see things coming but this one, I really didn't," he said. "I cannot hide the fact that I sincerely regret this decision."

Bergeron did not join in the chorus of homages to Zampino's steady management and fiscal responsibility. He called Zampino's decision "nebulous" and wondered "if there is not something fishy behind it."

"Zampino was at the heart of projects which have raised the most questions," Bergeron continued, mentioning the development of Griffintown and plans to develop a shopping centre in the northeast of the city but making no reference to the water-meter question. "There is perhaps something there, not to mention the fact that he oversaw the spending of billions of dollars."

Certainly, on the surface, the timing of Zampino's resignation was odd. If a councillor or mayor quits or dies more than a year before a general election, a by-election must be held to fill the position. If it is less than a year, the post is simply filled at the city-wide vote. Zampino's explanation for quitting when he did was that he didn't want to wait until he was 50 before embarking on a new career. But he was only 48 when he stepped down and, if he was really the faithful soldier and public servant he made himself out to be, he could have waited six months to save the city the hassle and expense of a by-election.

Zampino's departure prompted one of two by-elections held in September 2008. His job, as mayor of the borough of St-Léonard, was barely worth contesting by Projet Montréal, especially after former mayor Michel Bissonnet announced that he wanted to return as the Union candidate. Zampino had won with 78 percent of the vote; Bissonnet would almost certainly do better.

The other by-election was for a city council seat in the Ahuntsic district, the councillor for which had died in mid-April. There, Projet Montréal felt it might have a chance. The party had won 15 percent of the vote in 2005 on the most shoestring of campaigns. Three years later it was a more organized and mature party and it had a candidate who could be counted on to campaign tirelessly and stay on message. Émilie Thuillier had moved to the district in 2006 and her experience running for the De Lorimier borough councillor position in 2005 had convinced her she actually did want to be an elected official. When she raised her hand and said she would like to be the party's standard-bearer in Ahuntsic, the enthusiasm was widespread. She might not have had the name recognition of Jean-Claude Marsan or even Kettly Beauregard, but in the two and a half years that she had been Projet's only employee, she had proven reliable, competent and hard-working. There would be no surprises with her.

Voting day was September 21, and the campaign officially began in early August, but the three parties all announced their candidates in June. Vision was first out of the gate hoping to capitalize on the attention it was getting for having just installed its new leader. Benoît Labonté had initially planned to start his own party when he quit the Tremblay administration. Then, according to someone close to him at the time, he realized that not only would it be "a shit ton of work" but that a four-way race in 2009 would favour the incumbent. So he made nice with Vision—or at least some of its divided leadership—and soon enough he was their new leader.

The Vision candidate was Hasmig Belleli, a founding member of the party and a councillor from 1994 until 2005, when she had lost to Pierre Lapointe (himself a Vision veteran before crossing over to UCCIM). Union's candidate was Michel Hamel, a former head of the borough's merchants' association, the president of the local Optimist Club and active in various other community groups. For Projet, things were little trickier. Thuillier had taken a few weeks to decide; she knew she wanted to have children in the near future and wondered whether becoming a city councillor and mother in quick succession was compatible. After discussions with Bergeron and others close to her, she decided to go for it and the party was only too happy to have her.

Even though the campaign got going in high summer, Thuillier didn't lack for volunteers. "Members from all the boroughs came to work on the campaign. It was fantastic. I felt like the whole party was behind me." Thuillier lived and breathed the campaign even more than most candidates: the headquarters were at her house and everything ran out of there, from the storage of signs and pamphlets to planning meetings, volunteer training, and tabulation of the door-to-door and telephone canvassing results.

The canvassing suggested it would be close and Thuillier felt like she had a chance. On election day, however, it was clear that she and Projet couldn't compete with the name recognition of her two adversaries or the electoral machines of Union and Vision. In the end, Belleli squeaked past Hamel by 59 votes. Thuillier got 27 percent but was still more than 500 votes behind Hamel.

With a general election a year off, the victory in Ahuntsic, however slim, gave Vision a bump while signalling to Union that re-election would not necessarily be a cakewalk. But any honeymoon for Labonté would be brief.

Labonté's takeover of Vision, even if uncontested, had never generated unequivocal enthusiasm among the party's caucus or membership. His main selling card was his capacity to get under Tremblay's skin and his connections to the corporate world. Beyond that, many suspected he was interested in Vision name and war-chest but not its human resources. Certainly, he didn't win the caucus over with a style which was both insecure and superior. "He wore Hugo

Boss jeans to a Walmart party," was how one councillor expressed it. On top of that, he was a poor communicator in group situations while highhandedly imposing plans and policies without consulting caucus.

Even before the late summer by-elections, the defections began. First to go were his chief of staff and the party's director-general. The departures were construed by many as predictable house-cleaning, inevitable when a new leader makes a party his own. When, however, later in the fall, a parade of other senior party members and two councillors followed suit, it was clear there was a real problem. The first councillor to go was Claire St-Arnaud, a Vision veteran who was also the leader of the opposition in council and caucus president. She was followed by Pierre Mainville, a councillor from Ville-Marie whose departure meant that Labonté lost his majority on borough council. Perhaps most telling was the departure of Robert Laramée, also a Vision councillor from early days who had been the party's candidate for mayor of Ville-Marie in 2005, losing to Labonté. He had then gone on to become director-general of the party and in that position had been integral, along with Saint-Arnaud, in recruiting his former adversary to lead Vision. "The arrival of Mr. Labonté rejuvenated the party for a little while but he is not the team player and unifier I had thought he was," Laramée said.

In the midst of these departures, an issue which would preoccupy many at Projet Montréal on and off for much of the next year, was raised: whether the party should enter into some sort of alliance, or even merge with Vision. It was an idea that Henry Aubin had put forth several months earlier saying Labonté and Bergeron were possibly complementary opposites: one a staunch federalist, the other a sovereigntist (or at least it seemed; he was, after all, a unilingual francophone from Lac St-Jean); one a smooth, impeccably bilingual managerial type, the other an ideas man who required reining in, not to mention, polishing. Bergeron had initially shut the door on the idea, but in early October, Aubin was at it again, quoting Labonté saying he was "very, very open" to the idea. Bergeron, for his part, acknowledged that he had had some informal discussions with Labonté about the idea and that he was no longer as opposed to it as before. The following day, *The Gazette* published an unsigned editorial endorsing the idea.

Superficially, it was easy to see the political attractiveness of the proposal. As things stood, the two parties split the opposition vote and Union, even if it received only 40 percent or so of the vote, could easily be returned to power with another crushing majority. The results of the three by-elections that Projet Montréal had fought seriously had led Bergeron to believe that his party was competitive in the more central districts while Vision could get more support in peripheral boroughs. If some sort of alliance, perhaps a non-aggression pact in certain parts of the city, could be negotiated, he felt that Union might be vulnerable, that this particular unfairness of the first-past-the-post system might be countered.

In 2007 Bergeron had mused about the desirability of proportional representation at the municipal level, and how under such a system Projet Montréal would have won 9 seats in 2005. He had also been forthcoming about how much of the job of a mayor—the *protocolaire*, the representation, the grip-and-grins and public appearances—didn't interest him at all. This seemed to be an extension of such reflection, with Bergeron wanting to re-make the system before he or his party was even a real player in it.

If Bergeron, the political ingénue, was intrigued by the idea of a merger or alliance, others in Projet Montréal were appalled by it. Paul Cliche wrote an op-ed in *Le Devoir* and gave interviews to whoever asked saying such a move would be suicide for the young party. Vision "is a conservative party which many feel is an extension of the Civic Party of the autocrat Jean Drapeau. In contrast, Projet Montréal is a young progressive party a bit like the MCM was before it came to power," he wrote. In other words, the two had nothing in common except an adversary—not a good basis for an alliance.

Cliche lauded Bergeron's intelligence and idealism but lamented his innocence. "Idealist, he is not savvy enough to defend himself against certain political tactics. We can well imagine what would happen if such an alliance was victorious. Bergeron would certainly be named to the executive committee by the new Mayor Labonté. But the main reforms proposed by Projet Montréal would quickly be put aside."

He wrapped up with a not-at-all-veiled warning to Bergeron: "It is high time that Mr. Bergeron remember that he has no mandate from the party to explore such possibilities with Mr. Labonté. Projet Montréal is a democratic party and it is up to its members to determine its future."

Other senior members used similarly strong language to call Bergeron into line. It was the first internal Projet Montréal split to make its way into the media and, just slightly more than a year before the election when the party should have been out recruiting candidates, the timing was awkward. Bergeron understood this quickly enough. "I will never, never renounce the heart of our platform," he told reporters, effectively putting an end to the flirting, at least for the time being. Vision and Union, he said, were cut from the same cloth while Projet Montréal was created to change the fabric of municipal politics.

Chapter 9

A YEAR BEFORE THE 2009 election, I realized that Projet Montréal was, as I would tell friends, the natural ruling party of the Plateau. I decided to get involved.

I came to the party because of a NIMBY traffic issue: cars were using my block on Avenue de l'Esplanade as a shortcut, or rat-run, between two major arteries and every morning during rush hour there was a line of cars bumper-to-bumper over 300 metres or so, waiting for the light at the corner to change. I wrote a long email to Helen Fotopulos proposing possible solutions such as allowing left turns from one artery to the other. I also suggested other measures for keeping transit traffic off residential streets, including changing the direction of one-way streets from one block to another. These were known as *têtes-bêches* in French, and I had seen how effective they were when living in the Annex area of Toronto and while visiting other central residential neighbourhoods in various big cities.

The response I received weeks later from her political attaché was somewhere between underwhelming and insulting; the main element I remember was his insisting that I refer to traffic engineers as "traffic-calming engineers." Otherwise, he wouldn't talk with me. It all seemed to confirm an opinion many in the neighbourhood had of the Fotopulos administration: that it talked a good line, was happy to commission studies and hold consultations, but found any excuse to avoid actually implementing change.

Certainly that seemed to be the case with a local campaign to have a stop sign installed in front of our local primary school. It seemed like such a simple thing—it *was* such a simple thing—but residents had been demanding it for a decade or more and still the city had not installed one. Rue Bernard had been completely torn up and re-built at a cost of millions of dollars, with wider sidewalks, curb extensions and elevated intersections, partly with an eye to calming traffic. But they still hadn't been able to plant a stop sign on Bernard at Waverly.

My frustration with the traffic problems in the Mile-End led me to attend, with a neighbour, a meeting at La Maison d'Aurore, a venerable social service organization in the eastern Plateau. Several months earlier, Isabelle Gaudette, a community organizer there, had organized a photo competition with the theme *Ce que vous déplaît de votre quartier*— or "what bugs you about your neighborhood." When most of the entries had to do with cars and traffic, she decided to set up a committee which would propose changes to the borough. In 2006, the Fotopulos administration had promised to produce a traffic and mobility plan—in official jargon, a *Plan de déplacement urbain* or PDU—based on community consultations for the Plateau, but since then nothing had happened. When overtures from Gaudette's comité de circulation were also met by silence, they decided to draft their own PDU, the PDU-Citoyen. The meeting my neighbour and I attended was to develop proposals for it.

Residents from all over the Plateau were present, some with very specific concerns involving just their street or nearby intersection, others with more ambitious visions of reducing the speed limit to 30 km/hr, massively expanding the bike path network, and, of course, keeping transit traffic—cars and trucks passing through the Plateau—off local streets as much as possible.

Richard Bergeron arrived late and spoke on various points but only when asked to comment; he knew it was a community event and politicians pushing their product weren't welcome. If I had heard of Projet Montréal before then I hadn't paid much attention; my interest in Montreal municipal politics had diminished and then disappeared after the MCM was elected and, a few years later, I moved away from Montreal. My interest hadn't returned when I came back to the city; the Bourque years, the merger and de-merger debates, and then Tremblay—there seemed to be little vision or ambition to transform the city in a sustainable, greener way.

If Bergeron's brief interventions were interesting, even inspiring, they didn't come close to being as compelling as those of the bearded guy whose name I didn't catch. Speaking with passion, authority and humour, he made a lyrical appeal for making the Plateau an urban paradise by reducing the space given over to cars whether for roadway or parking, greening and beautifying all manner of public domain, planting trees, and making the commercial corridors more attractive. My reaction was immediate: why is this guy not our mayor? He seemed, however, to be a simple citizen and it was Bergeron and Projet Montréal which were the political option available.

In the days following I read the party's program and anything I could find about it. It confirmed to me that this was the party which should be governing the Plateau and all of Montreal. Perhaps it was time to actually buy a party membership card and become a *militant*?

Even though I come from a politically active family, I had never belonged to a party before and had never expected to join one. On the one hand, it was considered incongruous with being a journalist; on the other, I had never come across a party which I could embrace wholeheartedly. Federally, I was somewhere between Green and NDP; provincially, something of an anglo orphan, more likely to vote Québec Solidaire than Liberal or PQ. On the municipal level, since the disappointments and decline of the MCM, I had simply lost interest.

Projet Montréal seemed to be a reason to plug back in, and more than ever. Part of it may also have been time of life. I had two young children, I owned a building, I had gotten to know my neighbours and the local merchants. I was putting down roots, becoming part of the community and increasingly concerned with what was happening locally, in the corner of the world I circulated in on a daily basis, rather than nationally or internationally, places I might simply visit on increasingly rare trips abroad.

Like going to a bar, a movie or for a hike, I thought getting involved with Projet Montréal would be more fun to do with a friend and I had the perfect person in mind. I had known Alexander Norris for 20 years at that point, since before he moved to Montreal to work at *The Gazette*. By 2004, we had both burned out on daily newspaper journalism and were doing other things—me, magazine articles and true crime books; him, contracts of different sorts, including teaching journalism and research for TV documentaries.

In the fall of 2008, however, I had heard a worrying rumour: Alex was considering applying for a job doing corporate communications for Air Canada. A worse fit for both him and the airline was hard to imagine. A much better fit, I thought, would be city councillor. So I called him up and pitched him the idea of running for Projet Montréal in November 2009. Even if he didn't know the party much better than I did, he didn't need convincing. A weekend or two later we were attending our first Projet Montréal event and soon enough we were regulars at the Plateau ALA meetings, along with Carl Boileau and Guillaume Vaillancourt, a former school commissioner who had taken over as ALA co-ordinator and was seen as a possible candidate for borough mayor.

As I saw it, the priority during the winter and spring of 2009 was recruiting good candidates and that is what I put my energy into. With Bergeron in council and often in the media, Projet Montréal had grown steadily since the 2005 election and various members who would become pillars of the party had signed up. These included François Limoges and Peter McQueen, who had joined in 2006, Craig Sauvé in 2007, and Sylvain Ouellet who made it a New Year's resolution for 2008 to become an active member of the party. All of them, sooner or later, would become city councillors. But as was clear from the first Projet event that Alex and I attended the party at the time was overwhelmingly male. The party needed more women, both as candidates and members, and some of the first people I tried to recruit to run in the Plateau were Isabelle Gaudette, of La Maison d'Aurore, Colleen Thorpe of Équiterre and artist Isabelle Anguita, who at the time was one of the main organizers of the Comité des citoyens du Mile End. Even if all of them shared Projet Montréal's vision, none of them were interested; partisan politics seemed to repel them.

Richard Ryan, the other main coordinator at the Comité des citoyens du Mile End was less averse to the idea when I mentioned it to him. He wasn't a woman but as a community organizer both professionally for a CLSC in Terrebonne and in our own neighbourhood, I felt he would make a good candidate for Mile-End. I didn't know it at the time but he had actually been a Projet member from early days and then, working on Amir Khadir's campaign in 2007, he caught the politics bug. When, on December 8, 2008, Khadir was finally elected for the riding of Mercier which covers much of the Plateau, it confirmed change was possible. Richard was still a bit insecure about being a candidate himself, feeling that he wasn't experienced enough. But after I suggested he run, and several others did likewise, that was all the encouragement he needed.

The last person I recruited for the 2009 campaign was another old friend, Christine Gosselin. I knew her through my brother, who had been in the same doctoral program as her in comparative literature at the University of Toronto. When, in the mid 1990s, she moved back to Montreal to finish her thesis, Christine and I became good friends. We wrote a film script together, made preserves, and went to shows. Perfectly multi-lingual, tremendously learned and very hard-working—not to mention a lot of fun—she had never had a job which challenged her after opting out of the academic world. Financially she didn't really need gainful employment. She did, however, seem to need a calling or a mission and when I phoned her one day and suggested she consider running in Rosemont, or at least help out on the campaign, she didn't need to be asked twice.

During the 2005 campaign, Christine had campaigned for Union Montréal—a neighbour and friend of hers at the time was Isabel dos Santos, the borough councillor for the Jeanne-Mance district—and even done some door-to-door with Helen Fotopulos. During that campaign, however, she had heard Bergeron being interviewed on the radio and thought to herself, "Wow! This is the party I should be working for."

My call had reminded her of that. Within a few days Christine had phoned Patrick Cigana. The next day, her birthday, they met for coffee and he asked her to run immediately. She ticked off almost all the boxes—intelligent, gregarious, committed to the party's vision, perfectly fluent in French and English (not to mention Italian), a resident of the borough. Most importantly, two of Rosemont's four districts still lacked candidates and the party needed at least one woman on its slate.

Rosemont is a big borough, wider than it is tall, stretching from Ave du Parc more than seven kilometres east to Lacordaire, beyond the Village Olympique. The farther east one goes, the farther from the Orange Line, the more conservative, car-centric and suburban it becomes—and the less welcoming to the ideas of Projet Montréal. The two most promising districts were already spoken for by men who had been with the party for several years, François Limoges and Marc-André Gadoury. Christine opted for the district of Vieux-Rosemont which included the commercial artery of Rue Masson and the new residential developments in the old Angus railyards.

In the Plateau the distribution of districts and posts was more complicated, partly due to the arcane manner of determining how Montreal's borough councils are composed. All boroughs have mayors, who preside over their local councils and sit in city council. The biggest boroughs in Montreal, those with four or more districts, only have city councillors. But boroughs with populations of about 110,000 or less have both city and borough councillors—unless they are Outremont or Île-Bizard—Sainte-Geneviève, in which case they only have borough councillors, in addition to the mayor. This is to ensure representation at city council that is approximately proportional to population while also guaranteeing that each borough council has at least five members. As I used to remark, it has all the particularities and idiosyncrasies of a system that has been in place for hundreds of years, such as the Swiss cantonal system, even if it was only devised in 2003.[9]

With a population of 104,000, the Plateau has three districts, so a city and borough councillor for each. Richard Bergeron and the party were very keen on Alex Norris's candidacy and it was assumed he would go up against long-time MCM councillor (and brief leader)

9 LaSalle, for reasons I have never understood, has two borough councillors per district which means that voters there cast five ballots on election day: for mayor of the city, mayor of the borough, city councillor and two borough council candidates. In Ville-Marie, on the other hand, voters only cast two ballots: for mayor of the city and city councillor, since the mayor of the city is now automatically mayor of Ville-Marie. In all other boroughs voters have three or four ballots to cast.

Michel Prescott, who had overseen the party's absorption into UCCIM, in the Jeanne-Mance district. Covering the southwest corner of the borough, including the Milton-Parc/McGill Ghetto area, it was where Alex had lived for all but a few months of his 20 years in Montreal. It also was home to most of the borough's Portuguese population which made it an especially good fit given Alex's fluency in the language.

Bergeron, it was assumed, would run again in De Lorimier, and a woman by the name of Piper Huggins, a former organizer and staffer with the NDP, was to run in Mile-End. Huggins wasn't very present in the fall and winter of 2008–2009—she had been badly hurt in a cycling accident, resulting in a broken leg, and was convalescing. When I finally met her in the late winter, she was very pleasant but underwhelming as a candidate. Her French was not anywhere near as good as an effective councillor's needed to be and she lacked assertiveness and vigour. Bergeron, I surmised, probably liked the fact that Huggins had worked for the NDP and would be able to tap into its network of supporters more than he thought she would be a good candidate or councillor.

Then, in April, Bergeron convinced Josée Duplessis to quit the Fotopulos administration and become Projet's second councillor. The circumstances of her changing parties depend on who one speaks to. According to other members of the Plateau team, Duplessis, uncertain that Projet was a sure bet in De Lorimier, only agreed to jump when she was told that if she didn't come over then Projet Montréal would run Nimâ Machouf, the dynamic, warm wife of Amir Khadir, against her for the seat. Given that Union Montréal was being buffeted by scandals and resignations at the time and Duplessis had won by all of nine votes in 2005 against an unknown candidate, it was a convincing threat.

Duplessis' version is more complicated. She says she had progressively lost faith in Union, both the Fotopulos administration as well as that of Tremblay, and had been particularly shocked by a fundraising cocktail in St-Leonard organized by Frank Zampino where guests left "wads of bills" in a container by the door. "I went to that thing and remember that I wasn't even able to get through the door, so sick to the stomach it made me," she says.

She had also had health issues which compelled her to take an extended break in early 2009 during which time she says she decided not to run again. When word got out among her constituents, however, she says she was bombarded by phone calls and emails pleading with her to stick with it, whether as an independent or another party. "No one told me, 'Go to Projet Montréal,'" she recalls. "People said to me, 'Run again. Choose your party and we'll follow you.'"

Duplessis says her working relations with Bergeron had always been good and the party had grown and matured since 2005 so that when he proposed that she run again but under the Projet Montréal banner, she agreed. The announcement was made on April 26th, her 40th birthday.

Whatever the actual circumstances of her joining Projet Montréal, Duplessis didn't come cheaply. She would cross the floor if Bergeron would change districts in order to allow her to rise a rank and become a city councillor. It meant an increase in prestige and about $20,000 more in salary for Duplessis. Bergeron accepted without any hesitation. He didn't have any attachment to De Lorimier or even the Plateau; his only real interest was seeing Projet Montréal running the city.

Initially Bergeron planned to run in his home district, Saint-Jacques, in the downtown Ville-Marie borough, where he lived almost in the shadow of City Hall. Saint-Jacques includes Old Montreal, Chinatown, the Gay Village and much of the Centre-sud; it is as politically unpredictable as it is diverse and soon enough Bergeron realized it would be too much of a gamble. Instead he opted to run in the district directly north: Jeanne-Mance.

This led to a shuffling of candidacies. Everyone agreed that Alex Norris was a stronger candidate than Piper Huggins, so it was decided he would become the city council candidate in Mile-End. Huggins couldn't be the borough council candidate in the district, however—running two anglos in a neighbourhood that was 60 percent francophone was a non-starter. Anyway, Richard Ryan (who, despite his name, is a pretty much unilingual francophone) had stronger connections and a better network in Mile-End than Piper. So she would run as borough council candidate in Jeanne-Mance in tandem with Bergeron, a good mix in terms of gender and language. Nimâ Machouf, who was not really interested in being elected but was very keen to do anything to help the party, would run as Bergeron's *co-listière.*

Duplessis' partner in De Lorimier would be Carl Boileau, Bergeron's *co-listier* from 2005. Bergeron had helped Boileau win an internship at city hall in Paris after that election and upon his return, Boileau had resumed his activities with the Plateau ALA. The only member of the team who had actually grown up in the Plateau, Boileau worked as an exterminator and brought a certain authenticity to the team. I always got along with him but others found his lack of organization and rigour infuriating. Still, he was the longest serving member of the ALA and the party was not yet in a position to be picky, even in the borough where it was strongest.

Chapter 10

As spring advanced towards summer, the one position remaining to be filled on Projet Montréal's slate in the Plateau was the most important one: the party's candidate for borough mayor. Many of us had assumed it would be Guillaume Vaillancourt, who as a school commissioner between 1998 and 2007 had become vice-president of the Commission scolaire de Montréal. He had taken over the ALA co-ordinator duties when Carl Boileau went off to Paris and injected a structure and level of organization which had been sorely lacking previously. He devoted three or four evenings a month to the party with as many ALA members as he could round up. One evening would be dedicated to recruiting new members and to phoning people whose memberships had lapsed and urging them to renew. Another would be spent dealing with ALA business, increasingly preparing for the 2009 campaign. And the first Monday of the month would be reserved for attending borough council meetings and doing his best to put the Fotopulos administration on the spot during the public question period. Occasionally there would also be a social event, a picnic or a potluck, or perhaps a conference and group discussion about affordable housing, densification, bike paths or, of course, tramways.

The real hope, however, was that Michel Labrecque would also turn his back on Union Montréal and come over to the party with which almost everyone felt he would be a better match. There was reason to expect it might happen. The fall and winter of 2008-09 had seen a series of scandals rock Tremblay's administration. In October, the vice-president of his executive committee, Côte-des-Neiges councillor Francine Senécal, had abruptly quit to take up a position as the directrice-général of the Cégep de Vieux-Montréal. The timing was strange and a possible explanation soon appeared in a series of exposés in *La Presse* regarding the Société d'habitation et de développement de Montréal (SHDM), of which Martial Filion, Senécal's husband, was the director-general. The Faubourg Contrecoeur scandal, as it was known, involved SHDM having sold an immense swathe of city property, the size of 75 football fields, to a developer with close ties to the Montreal mafia for a fraction of its municipal assessment. It provided months of headlines as other media jumped on the story: Filion was suspended and eventually fired; Senécal's job offer at the Cégep du Vieux was retracted; suspicious fires destroyed buildings and offices; other questionable land sales to mobbed-up developers were revealed.

At the same time, the water-meter scandal returned with a vengeance when Zampino was hired as a vice-president of one of the companies in the consortium which won the contract. It was also disclosed that, while executive committee president, he took vacations on the yacht of construction company boss Tony Accurso, who was quickly becoming the face of municipal corruption in the city.

In a matter of months, the administration which *The Gazette* had lauded for being scandal-free a year earlier, had become synonymous with crookedness. Many people, in the Plateau and elsewhere, wondered how long straight-arrows like Labrecque would be able to stomach staying with Union. The defection of Duplessis to Projet Montréal led some people to expect that Labrecque would soon follow. Duplessis herself expected as much. She says she had discussions about switching over "with Richard and with Michel. It's certain he was thinking about it. He was between, 'I'll quit' or 'I'll go over to Projet.'"

Labrecque tells a different story. He says he was hugely frustrated by the difficulty of moving projects forward in the Plateau—whether it was the *Plan de déplacement urbain* or the stop signs on Bernard—because of a toxic work environment in the borough offices coupled with contempt and disregard towards the elected councillors from some of the most senior staff. The trouble stemmed overwhelmingly from the borough director, Johanne Falcon, and her public works director, Gilbert Bédard.

At one point, Labrecque says he was so furious that he phoned up the city's head of human resources to push for Falcon's transfer. "I said, 'My dear sir, I don't know you but I am furious. And if you don't find a solution, we will fire her at borough council.' He said, 'You can't do that!' And I said, 'Just watch me. We will do it by resolution.'"

The resolution never happened. Instead Labrecque says he began thinking of not running for re-election himself. But not before he organized a meeting with Duplessis and the two other Plateau borough councillors, Isabel dos Santos and Eleni Fakotakis, and later, went to meet Gérald Tremblay at City Hall.

Duplessis' defection reinforced the message that there were serious problems in the Plateau, at least to Union Montreal brass. If the message had been missed by the general public, it wasn't for long. Even if there were no scandals on the scale of Faubourg Contrecoeur or the water meters, Fotopulos and her borough operation soon began receiving their share of negative press.

In early May, it was revealed that Fotopulos had attended a Canadiens' game in the luxury box of an engineering firm which received city contracts—and whose senior staff contributed generously to the party. Two weeks later, *La Presse* carried an extensive report about the poisonous work environment in the Plateau, based on numerous complaints from borough employees past and present and an investigation by the city's Ombudsman. Johanne Falcon was accused of having instituted "a regime of terror" with "a management approach that relies on fear, distrust, and lack of respect and collaboration." This had led to "low morale among staff, an abnormal number of employees leaving to work in other boroughs and much psychological trauma for many of them, whether they are white collar employees, professionals or directors."

Indirectly, it was a harsh condemnation of Fotopulos's management, and it offered an answer to a question so many citizens had about the borough: "Why did it seem nothing ever got done?" The answer: the borough operations were completely dysfunctional.

On May 12th, the Plateau ALA had held its nomination meeting for all the councillor positions. Municipal campaigns are often won with shoe leather, persistent door knocking and shaking as many hands as possible at block parties and street fairs. Even if election day was still almost six months away, the plan was to get candidates, especially those in winnable districts, in place well in advance to give them the whole summer to campaign.[10] The event was at the Fraternité des policiers et policières' hall beside the Laurier metro and was largely a formality; none of the nominations were contested. Each candidate would deliver a two-minute speech and then the 50-odd people present would enshrine them as the party's standard bearers.

There wasn't much of a show to steal but the MC for the evening, a bearded and smiling man with a discourse which was at once intelligent and amusing, inspiring and urgent, did so with ease and elegance. It was the same guy I had seen six or eight months earlier at La Maison d'Aurore. Few people in the room knew him before the evening began but by its end, they knew that Luc Ferrandez was the answer to the question that was on everyone's mind: who would make a good candidate for mayor of the Plateau if Labrecque didn't come over?

In early 2004, Bergeron had tried to recruit Ferrandez to embark with him and Mainville on the creation of Projet Montréal and Ferrandez had listened with interest. The two had got to know each other after Ferrandez had attended a couple of Bergeron's presentations in the late 1990s or early 2000s during which Bergeron preached the gospel of densification, public transport and Transit Oriented Development, or TODs. "He was a breath of fresh air in an arid world," says Ferrandez. "He was the first to say that the city was important. He was my hero. He was the hero of everyone who wanted to transform the city."

Their visions diverged dramatically in some respects. Ferrandez remembers Bergeron's discourse as being excessively technical, all about transport and density, with no poetry or greenery or humanity to it. "He wanted towers everywhere," Ferrandez says, including on top of the Mont-Royal metro station. Bergeron, he says, had little to no interest in social dynamic or "mixity"—how the design of the city could influence the interactions of its inhabitants. Ferrandez, for his part, was convinced that making the city green and its public spaces beautiful was as important as good public transit. He also believed

10 Rosemont had held its nomination meeting six months earlier, almost a full year before the election.

the low-rise, high-density design of the Plateau, Centre-Sud, St-Henri and other neighbourhoods built between 1880 and 1920 was hugely preferable to apartment towers. It led to children playing in alleyways, people on their front balconies, shovelling their walks, greeting their neighbours, all of which added up to community.

These differences, however, were not why Ferrandez did not sign up when Bergeron tried to recruit him to the cause of Projet Montréal in early 2004. "He said 'I'm starting a political party,'" Ferrandez remembers the conversation going. "'With who?' I asked. And he listed off a gang of nobodies and crackpots. 'It'll never work,' I told him."

Bergeron, of course, wasn't deterred by Ferrandez's naysaying. Blind to the challenges he faced and his own shortcomings, Ferrandez says "he was absolutely certain he would be the next mayor of Montreal. There was no doubt in his mind." If he had to do it with a gang of "nobodies and crackpots," at least to begin with, so be it.

Earning in the neighbourhood of $1,500 per day as a consultant for Hydro-Québec, Ferrandez revolved in a wealthier and more corporate orbit than most of those who were working to get Projet Montréal off the ground. And between 2005 and 2009, he contributed money to the party and occasionally attended its events. But that is as far as it went. If he had any interest in running for city council in 2009, he kept it to himself. He didn't stop re-imagining Montreal, however. Once the Autoroute Notre-Dame battle was won, Ferrandez devoted his urbanistic energy to a study of Mont Royal and put together a presentation which was impressive enough that he was hired part-time by the city division with the mandate to protect and promote the mountain.

As the 2009 election approached, Ferrandez began thinking about becoming a Projet Montréal candidate, largely because of pressure from Josée Duplessis. First, however, he wanted to get a better idea of who the ALA members were. MCing the nomination meeting was the perfect opportunity for that. Both sides were convinced.

Ferrandez made the announcement that he would be the party's candidate for mayor of the Plateau on May 21st, at a press conference held on the grass in Parc Lafontaine. Richard Bergeron and most of the other candidates were there to support him as was Ferrandez's mother.

In a short speech and in answer to questions from the two or three journalists present, he laid out his vision for the borough, especially when it came to investing in parks and public space, and reducing the room given over to cars in the Plateau without cutting parking for residents. He also stressed how he was up to the task of transforming the culture of the borough bureaucracy. "I was a specialist in managing change for seven years with Hydro-Québec," he said. "Diverging points of view and crisis management, I've been there."

The press conference went smoothly and unremarkably—the way it was supposed to for the introduction of a new political hopeful—until towards the end when Bergeron was asked about the party's hopes of recruiting Michel Labrecque for the job he had just announced was being filled by Ferrandez. Rather than saying that time had run out, Bergeron said he still hoped Labrecque would make the leap. "He said he is in reflection mode about his political future until the end of the month. We are not closing the door to him. I hope he hears this message one last time."

It could have been taken as anything from a lukewarm endorsement of Ferrandez to an implicit disavowal of him and the remark left most people confused, not to mention aghast at Bergeron's hamfistedness. Ferrandez, for his part, laughed it off but, inside, was insulted and seething, not least of all because his mother had been there to witness Bergeron's faux pas.

Whatever the case, the Labrecque question became moot a little more than a week later when, on June 1st, Fotopulos held her own press conference to announce that she would not be running again for mayor of the Plateau. Accompanied by Labrecque and Tremblay, it was announced that Labrecque, who had been named head of the Société de transport de Montréal (STM) six months earlier, would be Union's candidate for Plateau mayor and if he won would do both jobs.

The press conference was all smiles and love but few people bought the act. Fotopulos, who has always maintained that she was not pushed out, nonetheless acknowledges that "somebody was out to get me" and that there wasn't any "team spirit" on the Union team, either in the Plateau or beyond. "I wasn't enjoying myself anymore," she adds. "And anyway, already it was not looking good in general for us in the Plateau."

Meanwhile Labrecque maintains that he also intended to quit politics and only agreed to run again to repay a "debt of honour" he owed to Tremblay dating from the early 1990s, when he was at the helm of Vélo Québec and Tremblay was a provincial Liberal cabinet minister. "He helped us get La Maison des cyclistes up and running and so I was indebted to him. So I went to see him and I told him, 'I will run'... I didn't know then that it would be for mayor. And then Tremblay went to see Fotopulos, and told her I wanted to run and that he would like her to run in another borough." Fotopulos was soon named as Union's candidate in the district of Côte-des-Neiges, where she had lived for years despite being councillor and then mayor of the Plateau, after Francine Senécal's departure.

Within Projet Montréal, Union's musical chairs were seen as Machiavellian manoeuvring by Labrecque. It was thought he had convinced Josée Duplessis to jump to Projet by leading her to believe he would soon do likewise. Then, instead of following her lead, he used her defection, and the subsequent negative media attention on her and the borough administration, to convince Tremblay to pull the plug on Fotopulos so he could become borough mayor.

Labrecque laughs at the suggestion that he might have been so conniving. Like Fotopulos, he says the writing was on the wall in the Plateau and that he never expected to win. Indeed, at his meeting with Tremblay at which he accepted to run again, he says he told the mayor that he considered his chances of being elected virtually nil. "I didn't say zero, but pretty much."

Chapter 11

If the machinations within Union were preoccupying Projet Montréal in the Plateau in the spring of 2009, it was negotiations with Louise Harel, and then with Vision Montréal, which were the main concern of the party as a whole.

Harel had resigned from the National Assembly in the fall of 2008 and within weeks, was making plans for how to become mayor of Montreal in November of 2009. During the winter she ran into Guillaume Vaillancourt, the co-ordinator of the Plateau ALA, at a gymnastics event where his daughter was competing. Harel was there to watch her grandchild. The two knew each other through Harel's daughter who had been a school commissioner alongside Vaillancourt. Harel was aware that he was active in Projet Montréal and, sitting down beside him, she began sounding him out about running for mayor. "I told her that she couldn't just announce her candidacy six months before the election and expect to win," Vaillancourt remembers. "She needed a structure, a machine, a party."

Vaillancourt thought Harel might be the ticket to power for Projet Montréal and says he then tried to broker a meeting between her and Bergeron. Bergeron, however, not only refused to meet with Harel, he refused to discuss the possibility of giving over the leadership of the party to her. When Vaillancourt had first joined the party two years previously, he says Bergeron still spoke of himself as the *défricheur*, the set-up man, the person who would get Projet Montréal up and running but—conscious of his shortcomings politically, socially and temperamentally—almost certainly not lead it to power. "But in 2008 he began to believe in himself as that person as well," says Vaillancourt.

If that was the case, Bergeron had other reasons to be skeptical of Harel. There was the contempt she had shown towards him and the party at its founding. There was also the fact that for much of Montreal she was seen as not only an unreconstructed sovereigntist but also the minister who had imposed the still-contentious mergers on the city and region. The public dressing down that Bergeron had received from influential members of the party for entertaining the possibility of a merger with Vision was also still fresh in his memory.

Still, if he refused to meet with Harel in early 2009, it didn't stop Bergeron from meeting again with Benoît Labonté at Magda Popeanu's house in Snowdon. Harel, it was clear, was shopping around for a party and Labonté, whose failure-to-launch and subsequent internal battles as Vision leader had left him severely wounded politically, saw her as a saviour. "Labonté came to see us because he had promised Louise Harel the complete package: Vision Montréal plus Projet Montréal," says Popeanu, who was Projet Montréal's president at the time.

Bergeron was characteristically blunt with Labonté, she recalls. "Richard told Benoît Labonté very clearly, 'Look here, I can do a merger or a deal with whoever you want as long as you are not in the picture yourself.' He didn't want to be associated in any way with Labonté and for that, you have to give it to Richard. He showed real acumen."

In Projet Montréal's inner circle, the idea of recruiting Harel to replace Bergeron as leader prompted diametrically different reactions. Some, who felt the main strength of the party was its capacity to appeal to environmentalists, progressives and the urbanistic-minded of all stripes, felt that Harel, who had always put Quebec independence ahead of Montreal, would destroy what was essentially a delicate coalition. These included Craig Sauvé, a West Islander who had moved to St-Henri at 17, come to the party via the NDP, and become Projet Montréal's second paid employee in 2008. The party, he felt, would lose both its purity—some of which derived from it not being closely tied to a provincial party—and any chance to appeal to non-francophones. "It was a massive stress for me. The closest I have ever come to a breakdown," he remembers.

Patrick Cigana also saw no political benefit to it. At the time, it was felt that Projet's best potential for growth was in the boroughs along the metro's Orange line—Ahuntsic–Cartierville, Villeray–St.-Michel–Parc Extension, Côte-des-Neiges–Notre-Dame-de-Grâce, le

Sud-Ouest, Ville-Marie as well as, of course, the Plateau and Rosemont. "I don't think Louise Harel will win us a single vote west of Boulevard St-Laurent," Cigana told Bergeron and others.

Some, however, saw Harel as Vaillancourt did: immediate credibility that would catapult what was often dismissed as a fringe party into the conversation and make it a legitimate contender in November. These included François Limoges who had joined the party in mid-2006 with political experience that few other members could claim. Limoges had grown up poor and friendless in eastern Rosemont. "Très reject," in his words, he would amuse himself by jumping on the metro and exploring different parts of the city. At Cégep, he found a milieu and camaraderie in student politics and caught "the bug." Then, after graduating, he saw a television interview with Sammy Forcillo, at the time the vice-president of Pierre Bourque's executive committee. Limoges was so appalled by Forcillo's answers—"populist, vague, disappointing"—that the next day he looked up the MCM in the phone book and went and signed on.

The party had seen better days—"I wasn't the only person under 30 years old; I was the only person under 50 years old," remembers Limoges—but it still had considerable resources and could draw 500 people to its general council meetings. Limoges served on the MCM's equivalent of a *conseil de direction* and, despite the endless internecine squabbling that was tearing the party apart, "I loved those years. I learned an enormous amount," he says.

Soon, however, there was virtually nothing left of the MCM. The attendance at general council meetings had dwindled to a few dozen, and so Limoges left. For the next few years "I remained very interested in the municipal scene but was an orphan." He did a spell—"by accident"—as president of the Bloc Québécois' youth wing but says he was always more interested in what was going on his street corner than another endless conversation about sovereignty.

Finally, in May 2006, he went to a Projet Montréal general council and "fell in love immediately." He was very impressed by Bergeron "but it was really the group as a whole which blew me away. I listened all day and I saw in the room an authenticity in people's interventions that I had never seen before," he remembers. "I was like, 'That's where

I want to be. With that gang there.' There was a combination of naiveté and noble intentions. I had never seen so much raw good will, without personal ambition, calculation or hypocrisy."

Within no time, Limoges was on Projet Montréal's *conseil de direction* and, even if he regularly butted heads with Bergeron, had garnered an influence within the party due to his experience and his eloquence at the microphone and around a meeting table. By early 2009, Limoges says he was increasingly aware of Bergeron's political limitations and thought Harel could help change the "alien, oddball, weird image" of Projet Montréal. "I found it a legitimate undertaking," he says, citing Harel's reputation as a progressive. "Even if I appreciated Richard, we could see that he had gone as far as he could go in the polls and with the media."

Because of his connections in sovereigntist circles and his enthusiasm for the idea, Limoges was delegated by Popeanu to negotiate with Harel's emissaries. No progress was made through the late winter and spring; there was little sense of urgency and neither side wanted to appear desperate to strike a deal. Harel was also continuing to discuss joining Vision with Labonté and other members of that party. Vision was considered by most the bigger prize; a poll that spring gave it 21 percent support, just slightly behind Union with 26 percent. Projet was at 10 percent. Limoges, however, had the impression that Harel would have preferred to take over Projet Montréal, since it didn't have the baggage or skeletons in the closet that Vision did.

Her ideal scenario, however, was to assume control not just of one party but of both. That, of course, was not going to fly with Bergeron or others in Projet Montréal, at least as long as Labonté was still in the picture. After all, until 18 months earlier, Labonté had been a senior member of Union Montréal, and the rumours of corruption were swirling around him as they were with others still with the Trembly administration. "We knew that Labonté was up to his neck in the collusion scandals of Union Montréal. He was Gérald Tremblay's heir apparent," says Limoges.

In May, Harel's supporters began to apply pressure. There was an influx of new members to Projet Montréal, as there often is in the months leading up to an election. In this case, however, many of them were young Péquistes and seemed to report to Frédéric Lapointe, the Harel associate with whom Limoges had discussed some sort of collaboration. "Lapointe was the chief scout. He was telling them what to do."

They showed up as observers at *conseil de direction* meetings and many attended the late May weekend congress in St-Henri where the party program was debated. The show of force was not appreciated by many Projet faithful but Bergeron was still under pressure from some in the party, including his new recruit Josée Duplessis, to strike some sort of deal with Harel.

Luc Ferrandez was also contacted by Harel's camp to pressure Bergeron into stepping aside for the PQ *védette*. After discussing it with Bergeron and receiving his encouragement, Ferrandez met with Harel at his apartment on de Lanaudière to try and work out a deal. After several hours of discussion he felt he had a workable arrangement. In the style of Québec Solidaire, Bergeron and Harel would be co-chefs of Projet Montréal and, were the party to be elected, Harel would serve as mayor for the first mandate while Bergeron presided over the executive committee. The second mandate, the roles would be reversed—as long as the alliance held and the party was re-elected.

Ferrandez phoned Bergeron with the details. After a brief conversation Bergeron said he would think about it and get back to Ferrandez with his response. Instead, Ferrandez says that within an hour Bergeron had sent an email to all Projet Montréal members saying that he opposed any alliance with Harel or Vision.

Ferrandez was astonished and chalked it up to Bergeron's "misplaced pride." He and others continued to press Bergeron to work out an arrangement with Harel. So just a few days after writing to the party membership that "the candidacy of Louise Harel for mayor of Montreal is not desirable," Bergeron asked for a meeting and went to her house on June 1st, before the Plateau's monthly borough council meeting.

"I said that if we both ran and fought each other, Gérald Tremblay would win. Because we would divide the opposition vote," Bergeron remembers. He insisted on remaining leader of Projet Montréal but would renounce running for the mayor's job and urge all Projet

Montréal supporters to vote for Harel if she ran as an independent. If Benoît Labonté would do the same thing, he said, her victory was all but guaranteed without the two parties having to merge. "That is my offer," Bergeron says he told her as he left to go to borough council.

By the time council was over in the late evening, Harel had told various media that Bergeron was willing to step aside and let her take the helm of Projet Montréal but that she had refused. Journalists were waiting to scrum Bergeron as he left to head home. "It shows to what degree she was vicious and untrustworthy. After we had agreed not to talk about it publicly," he says.

The leak further poisoned what was already a difficult, even toxic negotiation. The announcement two days later by Harel and Labonté that she was taking over Vision should have completely killed the idea. It didn't.

In mid-June Bergeron and Popeanu met with Guillaume Vaillancourt, Frédéric Lapointe and another Péquiste at Vaillancourt's home in a co-op in Milton-Parc. "They were super aggressive," remembers Popeanu. "They tried to intimidate us" by saying that with Harel in the race, Projet Montréal would fare even worse than it had in 2005. The Harel camp's proposal was that Bergeron support Harel for mayor and run for Plateau mayor himself. Ferrandez, it seemed, was expendable, in their calculations.

"Richard left the meeting very troubled," Popeanu says, and they spent more than two hours on the corner of Sherbrooke and Ste-Famille discussing what to do. "Finally, Richard said, 'No, no—I won't give up my place. We will campaign for the mayoralty of Montréal.'"

Even then efforts to force some sort of arrangement continued, if without Bergeron's blessing. Two conditions encouraged this: the appreciation that even with the almost daily revelations of Union Montréal's crookedness, the party would likely win a three-party race, especially one in which it was seen as the only federalist option; and Bergeron's relatively weak support as leader within his own party.

Bergeron was immensely respected and appreciated for having been the motivating force behind Projet Montréal's conception. The man who didn't know better, who didn't have the political smarts to know that he was embarking on a fruitless venture, so he went ahead and did it anyway. Still, few in the party felt that he had the stuff—the charisma, the personality, the capacity for collaboration and compromise—to win the mayor's job. There were also those who worried that if he did somehow become mayor, he would be a disaster.

So Limoges met with Lapointe and others on several more occasions over the summer but to no end. Harel's position had also hardened. "Their line was, 'You can join us. You can melt into Vision Montréal and we can let you have your own little club within it,'" Limoges recalls. "It wasn't serious. It was really arrogant. They were convinced Louise Harel would sweep the city." They were impervious to understanding a basic fact of Montreal, Limoges says: the anglophone and allophone vote is significant enough that it is fundamentally a federalist city.

By late August, the idea of any kind of deal with Harel and Vision—whether it be a merger, an alliance, a non-aggression pact in certain boroughs or districts—was well and truly shelved. Guillaume Vaillancourt and various others who had pushed for the idea from within, including Lapointe and Hadrien Parizeau, the grandson of the premier who had worked with Émilie Thuillier in Ahuntsic, quit Projet Montréal to join the Vision of Louise Harel. Vaillancourt was announced as Vision's candidate for mayor of the Plateau.

Chapter 12

THE CLARITY PROVIDED BY a straight three-party race was a relief for many, especially those running or organizing campaigns in more federalist and diverse parts of the city. Harel's Péquiste past and role in the forced mergers—not to mention the fact that she didn't speak English—immediately excluded Vision from any consideration whatsoever by many in the English community. "Among public figures, perhaps only Mom Boucher could make Tremblay look so good in comparison," *The Gazette* wrote in an editorial. "We can't imagine a more damagingly divisive candidate, or mayor." In a year which had seen an endless cascade of negative coverage of Gérald Tremblay's administration, Harel's candidacy was excellent news for Union Montreal's re-election chances, the paper noted.

There were, of course, a few anglophones who greeted Harel as a prospective saviour for a city faced with a crisis of confidence in its civic administration. These included lawyer Julius Grey and former MCM councillor Robert Keaton. In general, however, Harel's takeover rendered Vision an impossible option for most anglos. This was clear immediately to Karim Boulos, the much-appreciated Ville-Marie borough councillor who had followed Labonté out of Union and later to Vision. He knew that running with Harel would be the kiss of death, and quit to run as an independent.

Within Projet Montréal, people like Craig Sauvé, Patrick Cigana and Alex Norris, who had argued against any alliance with Harel and Vision, felt the party had dodged a bullet. Cigana remembers summing up his reaction as simply, "I'd rather lose now and stand a chance in 2013 than sign a pact with the devil."

Resisting electoralist temptation allowed Projet to credibly cast itself as the fresh, clean party of ideas against two tired and compromised machines. And with the frontrunners being a former PQ minister and a former Liberal minister, it permitted the party to adopt a "neither sovereigntist nor federalist, we're Montrealers" narrative when required.

Not that many were making such calculations going into the election. The party might have been four years older than when it ran in its first election but it was still very much a seat-of-the-pants operation. Its headquarters were still in a converted bedroom on the ground floor of Bergeron's home; it still only had two employees, both young and relatively inexperienced, who shared all of $50,000 in salary budget between them; and if some planning for the election had got underway in late 2008 or early 2009, it was uncoordinated and haphazard well into the summer. No campaign manager or DOC—*directeur de campagne*—was ever named, let alone months in advance; instead the task fell to Craig Sauvé. He was, after all, the party employee not running for a seat in council himself.

Still, like a slow-growing vine, the party had quietly, almost imperceptibly grown between 2005 and 2009, not only strengthening its main trunk in the Plateau and Rosemont but extending its reach beyond the central districts. Often it just involved individuals who joined the party because they found it reflected their values and were keen to take a run at elected office. There was Jean-François Desgroseilliers who would join Émilie Thuillier as a candidate in Ahuntsic and come within a whisker—98 votes, 1.1 percent—of winning. There was John Symon in Lachine, who would run unsuccessfully in 2009 and 2013 only to lose the nomination, in 2017, in the district he had patiently cultivated. And there was Peter McQueen, probably the most calculated and single-minded of new recruits, running in the Notre-Dame-de-Grâce district of CDN-NDG.

Peter had been the only familiar face at the first Projet Montréal event I had attended with Alex Norris in November 2008. He was someone I had met at parties, a friend of friends from Concordia University, who I knew to have done well investing in real estate in the Plateau and elsewhere in the late 1990s but had sold out early, around 2005, convinced the market had peaked. By then, he had moved to lower NDG, the St-Raymond neighbourhood south of the tracks, and started a family while getting involved in community and cycling groups, including the le Monde à bicyclette.

McQueen had joined Projet shortly after the 2005 election and worked on the unsuccessful by-elections of 2006, 2007 and 2008. All the while, however, his main interest was laying the groundwork for his own 2009 campaign. "Right from the start, I was in with an agenda," he says. "My agenda was to be the candidate, win, take down Marcel Tremblay," his councillor, and the mayor's brother "and change some shit here in eastern NDG. Right from the start. Everything I did was aiming for that goal."

In the provincial elections of 2007 and 2008 McQueen ran for the provincial Green Party—not with any expectation of winning but rather "to get my name recognition up." He became known as Green McQueen and was in perpetual campaign mode. "And not quietly. Get names, get email addresses, go to every public event you can go to," is how he describes his strategy, adding, with perhaps a certain understatement, "Some people might have thought I was a bit obnoxious."

McQueen's candidacy is one that would in all likelihood have been torpedoed had Harel taken over Projet Montréal or the party had formed an alliance with her and Vision. His district is 50 percent anglophone and 18 percent allophone; the Liberals tend to receive between 60 percent and 80 percent of the vote in provincial elections whereas if the PQ breaks 10 percent it's considered an excellent showing. Just as McQueen's candidacy escaped damage by an association with Harel, it benefitted from controversy over two megaprojects underway in his corner of the city: the building of the English superhospital and the planned demolition and rebuilding of the Turcot Interchange.

Nowhere, however, was the Turcot project as big a concern as in the Sud-Quest borough, where it brought in a flood of members to Projet Montréal, which, as with l'autoroute Notre-Dame, was the only political party to present a coherent, alternate vision.

One of these new members was Sophie Thiébaut, a community worker who by the spring of 2009 was spending much of her time mobilizing the neighbourhood against plans to rebuild the interchange in a virtually identical manner. Her work, and the cost and scale of the project itself, generated a groundswell of opposition—and soon resulted in Thiébaut being out of a job. "For the community group I worked for it was just too much. They found that they could no longer control me, that I was beginning to have political opinions which were too entrenched," she remembers. "So they fired me."

Virtually the same day she was dismissed she was approached by Craig Sauvé and asked to run. "I had a bit of notoriety," she says. It took Thiébaut almost two months to say yes; she had only lived in Canada for three years at that point so had never voted municipally and Projet Montréal was little known in St-Henri, Point-St-Charles, Ville-Émard and the other neighbourhoods which make up the Sud-Ouest.

Once she did commit, however, she was a serious candidate in a district which had a history of grassroots mobilization and activism. The MCM contingent from the Sud-Ouest, including former councillor Marcel Sévigny, had been among the least compromising in the party and Thiébaut and Projet tapped into some of this energy. "It was a very active campaign. I wasn't just a sweet community worker."

As with the ALAs in the Plateau and in Rosemont- La Petite-Patrie, the party in the Sud-Ouest came out with a local platform, proposing specific initiatives and interventions which a Projet Montréal borough council would implement. Going a step further than the Plateau or Rosemont, the Sud-Ouest produced theirs after a small public consultation. "We could claim to have a local version of the Projet Montréal platform linked to local issues, " Thiébaut says. "At the time, that set the bar high for their Union and Vision opponents. We scored points with this approach."

Eventually, Projet Montréal would manage to present candidates for every seat in every borough across the city in 2009 but it still had to resort to using *poteaux*—or candidates in name only—"all over the place," says Sauvé. These were frequently party members who lived in the Plateau, Rosemont or another central neighbourhood who ran in boroughs where Projet had little or no profile or organization, such as Anjou, LaSalle, or Verdun.

Richard Bergeron's wife Amina didn't have to run anywhere, but the party was still sufficiently short of candidates that well into August, the party was looking for a credible candidate to run for mayor of Outremont. We had tried to recruit two CBC semi-celebrities: Dennis Trudeau, who had retired a few years earlier, and Anne Lagacé Dowson, who had taken a leave of absence to run for the NDP federally the year before and then been fired by the broadcaster. Neither had much time for Richard Bergeron nor any real enthusiasm to run; Trudeau spent some of the discussion railing against the recently constructed bike path on Côte-Ste-Catherine—the kind of project a Projet Montréal candidate should be enthusiastic about. Lagacé Dowson felt too burned by her 2008 federal campaign to run again and, anyway, seemed keener about Louise Harel becoming mayor than Bergeron.

Finally, the party was desperate enough that Magda Popeanu phoned me up to inform me that it had been decided that I should be the candidate for mayor of Outremont. My immediate reaction was to laugh, which didn't go over very well with Magda, who as party president was also presiding over the electoral committee. But not only did I not have any interest in running—anywhere—I was also aware that my profile was a terrible fit for Outremont: an anglophone whose French was still fairly shaky, who hadn't grown up in Montreal and who lived on the wrong side of Ave du Parc, only venturing to the borough to visit friends, buy bread, or play hockey or tennis. I was also entirely invested in the campaign in the Plateau, for which I had decided to put aside a book project and work full-time until the election. Happily, the party conscripted a much more appropriate candidate in Étienne Coutu, a young architect who had gone to Collège Stanislas and lived on the right side of Parc, if not quite in Outremont, and would quite quickly become one of Bergeron's closest collaborators.

By then the Projet Montréal campaign on the Plateau was well underway and well organized, certainly in comparison with the central campaign. We had hired a full-time campaign manager in July, Guillaume Cloutier, a young grad student who had recently moved to Montreal after a year backpacking around Europe. There he had been struck by the extent and efficiency of public transport as well as the way many cities and even villages accommodated pedestrians with car-free zones and *rues piétonnes*. In comparison, Montreal "was nowhere" and when his elder brothers told him about Projet

Montréal, he signed up. Then, when his supervisor in the political science department said that managing a municipal campaign could count as the internship that all students had to do, he became the campaign manager.

Guillaume didn't have much on-the-ground political experience, and was also skeptical of Luc Ferrandez as a candidate because he was so polished and well-dressed, and therefore so unlike everyone else in Projet Montréal. "Was he an opportunist?" he remembers wondering. "I didn't want Projet Montréal to become hijacked by people who show up at the last minute, who know the inner workings of politics well and then take the thing over."

Their working relationship didn't get off to a good start when Cloutier, following "the little handbook 101 for candidates," ordered Ferrandez to begin doing his door-to-door in mid-July when most of Montreal was on vacation. "Luc was really mad at me," Cloutier says. "He came back, brought me the pamphlets and said, 'I knocked on twenty doors. Only one person answered and the guy was having a beer. He didn't give a shit. It's 30 degrees.'"

In Rosemont, Marc-André Gadoury had been going door-to-door since March, trying to spend as little time as possible with each voter, just shaking hands and conveying the message that he was there and he was active. He would eventually become something of a legend in the party, claiming to have knocked on every door in his district two if not three times in that campaign. For their part, François Limoges and Christine Gosselin had been at it since about May, if at a less disciplined and tireless pace. Ferrandez, however, decided that other candidates could keep the door-to-door for themselves; it just wasn't an efficient use of limited time.

Still, he needed an unmediated way to connect with voters, beyond standing outside a metro station or supermarket and handing out pamphlets. So Ferrandez came up with the idea of *partys de trottoir*—sidewalk parties—and had his father and sister help him outfit a bike trailer with a collapsible screen, a projector, a computer and a battery. The plan was to hold impromptu conferences, along with a PowerPoint presentation and question-and-answer sessions as well as a bottle or two of wine, on street corners and in parks several evenings a week, reaching dozens of people at a time, getting them out of their houses and talking to each other. In the presentation, Ferrandez would outline his vision for the Plateau, showing images from other cities, inspiring people, coaxing them to imagine the neighbourhood differently. With more trees and greenery, less of the city devoted to cars and parking, more investment in and concern for public space—all helping to encourage community and a richer civic life.

The concept didn't impress Guillaume Cloutier. "I just rolled my eyes. I said, 'Dude, okay, if you're going to do this, do this,'" he recalls. "I just gave up, saying, 'He's going to do the campaign his way.'"

The *partys de trottoir* were, of course, a hit and helped create a buzz for the Plateau campaign that couldn't have been bought or duplicated by any amount of door-knocking and pamphlet distribution. They also got Ferrandez his first real media exposure when Rima Elkouri devoted a column to him shortly after the official start of the campaign. She had initially intended to do a piece on Alex Norris and his decision to jump from journalism to municipal politics but Alex, an old acquaintance of hers, suggested that Luc and his street corner parties were a better story, not to mention one which would boost the whole Plateau team and not just Alex.

"I was wrong," Cloutier says. "I learned a lot as a political organizer. That politics 101, straight politics, is not all there is. We're not reinventing the wheel, but we have to think outside the box a bit." What Cloutier calls "a more creative vision, a more artisanal was of doing the campaign" manifested in other ways. Richard Ryan organized a screening of Bruno Dubuc's *La fin de néandertal* one evening outside a café on Rue St-Viateur. The recently released film chronicles the early days of Projet Montréal and compares the relative merits of political organizing and community mobilization.[11] "It was a bit long for a campaign event," Ryan says.

Later in the six-week campaign, we all pitched in to organizing an Artists for Projet Montréal concert at the Sala Rossa. The original idea for the show may have been mine but it was hardly a remarkable brainwave; the logic was that the Plateau, with arguably the highest

11 It is now available for viewing free on Youtube.

density of artists in Canada, had a population sensitive to the concerns of the cultural community. If a whole bunch of artists were endorsing the party, we felt it would sway a disproportionate number of votes. We weren't able to attract any big names—I remember Jean Leloup, who was a neighbour of ours and friend of my son, looking at me with indulgent bemusement when I asked if he might be interested in playing a benefit for a political party. Rather, our headliners were musicians Paul Kunigis, Marie-Marine Lévesque and Ève Cournoyer along with comedian Christian Vanasse of the Zapartistes.

At very least, the show generated a couple thousand dollars for the campaign. How well it worked in winning us votes, however, I have no idea. Certainly better than another initiative: our attempt to interest McGill University students living in the Milton Parc area in getting out and voting for us. Two basic truths of municipal politics, and indeed politics in general, is that property owners vote in greater numbers than renters and older people vote more than young. This handicapped Projet Montréal insofar as many of its policies were aimed at benefitting renters, public transport users, as well as cyclists and pedestrians. McGill students, many just in Montreal for as long as it took to get their degree, barely voted at all, even if many had the right to. Yet even after printing up specific pamphlets aimed at anglo university students and distributing them outside the Milton Gates every afternoon for most of a week, turn-out among McGill students was abysmal.

The Milton-Parc neighbourhood makes up part of the Jeanne-Mance district, where Bergeron was running but hardly campaigning, given that he was concentrating almost exclusively on the city-wide mayoral race. It was nonetheless the most important district in the city to win, given that it would allow the party leader to, at very least, maintain a presence in city council. On paper, with a more diverse and transient population, it was probably the most challenging district in the Plateau for Projet Montréal. Certainly, the incumbent, Michel Prescott, who had been the district's councillor for 27 years, suggested as much when he heard Bergeron was to be his opponent.

"But why are you running in Jeanne-Mance?" Bergeron remembers Prescott asking him. "You have no chance! Are you no longer interested in politics? You're an important person in municipal politics.

Christ, I'll beat you too easily. Running against me—that's the equivalent of resigning from politics! You still have time to reconsider."

Prescott's bluff had no effect on Bergeron. Still, in order to assure his victory, the central campaign did pitch in by helping with polling in the district in order to identify possible sympathizers and win them over. Such polling—or *pointage*—is a basic part of political campaigns but one which was largely absent from the 2009 Projet Montréal effort. No specialized software was acquired to organize the polling. Rather, the party simply worked off spreadsheets supplied to all the parties by the election authorities and any lists of possible or probable sympathizers lent—officially or unofficially—by parties at the provincial and federal levels, specifically the NDP and Québec Solidaire.

Locally, the Plateau campaign also assigned a disproportionate number of volunteers to do door-to-door in Jeanne-Mance compared to the other districts in the borough given that the main candidate was not on the ground much at all. The number—and energy—of the volunteers in the Plateau was an early indication that the campaign was indeed headed for success. There wasn't a coordinated recruitment drive and trying to determine precisely how word gets out is a useless endeavour because it is rarely exactly the same for two people. But several factors had a big impact. Municipally, it was the first election in which Facebook played a role and the Projet team in the Plateau was way ahead of Union and Vision in exploiting its potential. "Carl Boileau strongly recommended I get on Facebook and told me to say yes to all the friend requests, just bring them all in," Alex Norris remembers.

There was no organized strategy to speak of. Rather, each candidate simply used social media as they saw fit at a time when the idea of Web 2.0, as it was known, was still fairly novel. As Norris puts it, "By ourselves we developed our own personalities, just doing our own posts, unfiltered by any kind of central party mechanism or strategy. We just said what we thought and promoted our cause in our own words. I remember being surprised by how many likes and reactions and comments we got because we were engaging with the public and it generated buzz."

Facebook inevitably brought people through the door of campaign headquarters to volunteer, just as it directed them to where Luc was giving a *party de trottoir*. Volunteers also came because of the constant deluge of negative press regarding Union and, later in the campaign, Vision, leaving Projet Montréal, by default, the only untarnished option in a campaign in which integrity quickly became the central issue.

The pent-up desire for change in the Plateau—which had been crucial in my own involvement and that of others on the team—was also important in encouraging citizens who otherwise weren't politically active, to come out and help the campaign in whatever way was possible.

Reduced to their essentials, the actual discourse of the three parties in the Plateau was remarkably similar: increased constraints on cars and traffic, more space for pedestrians and cyclists, more investment in parks and greenspace—these were the motherhood and apple pie of the 2009 Plateau campaign, the virtue no one could object to. Projet's slogan in the borough, however, insisted on action: *Nous allons le faire! We will do it!* The candidates and campaigners were not shy in stressing that we felt that there had been adequate studies and consultations about what needed to be done. What remained was actually imposing the changes, or, in good franglais, *realizing the interventions*. The fact that we had specific examples for what we would do across the borough also had a major impact with voters.

We couldn't deny that the Fotopulos administration had brought concrete improvements to the Plateau—the elimination of the interchange at des Pins and Parc, the sidewalks on St-Laurent and Bernard, not to mention various regulatory measures—but these had been both few and far between and flawed in execution or final result.[12] We were proposing smaller scale projects which would have an impact on more people closer to where they lived, shopped or where their kids went to school. And we had a list.

---

12 Why, for example, did the remade Ave du Parc have to be four—even three—lanes in each direction between des Pins and Mont-Royal? It just encourages speeding and further divides Mont-Royal from Parc Jeanne-Mance.

In most campaigns the first real challenge involving *bénévoles* is the night of the first sign blitz. According to the law governing elections, signs on public property are only permitted as of midnight on the first day of the official campaign although in reality as of nightfall the previous evening is acceptable. This means that as soon as it gets dark there is usually a scramble by all the parties to get their posters into the most prominent positions on the best lamp standards at the busiest intersections around the city.

In mid-August 2009, however, in what was a vain attempt to change the developing narrative of the campaign and position themselves as greener than the rest, Union Montréal announced it would not be printing and putting up election signs anywhere in Montreal for environmental reasons.[13] Louise Harel, not wanting to be out-manoeuvred, impulsively announced Vision Montréal would do likewise.

At Projet Montréal there was no discussion. We felt our environmental bona fides were solid enough already and that we had nothing to gain from such greenwashing. On the contrary: we had everything to gain by getting our name out and our ideas and candidates talked about since the party was still relatively little known.

So under the tutelage of Carl Boileau's father, who not only had decades of experience putting up campaign signs for the PQ but also owned an old pick-up truck, we had the field to ourselves and the rush of getting it all done on the first evening was nowhere near as urgent as usual. "We were the only ones with signs," remembers Alex Norris, "and it kind of made up for some structural disadvantages we faced being the poorest of the three parties."

What they saved on printing and postering costs, Union and Vision spent on advertising, whether on radio ads, the sides of buses or wherever. Respectively they spent $871,000 and $502,000 on *publicité* that election, out of total election expenditures of just under $1.5 million each. Projet Montréal meanwhile spent just $117,000

---

13 The signs are made of plastic and could of course end up in landfills even if coroplast is entirely recyclable.

on advertising, which included the signs, on total expenses of $246,000.

The party certainly needed any visibility it could generate. A poll in early May had put it at a measly 10 percent in voter preference—barely above the 8.5 percent it scored in the 2005 election. The comparison wasn't entirely valid since Vision only scored 21 percent, Union Montréal only 26 percent and more than 40 percent of respondents either didn't have an opinion or were none-of-the-above. Still, it indicated that the party's main challenge was getting on people's radar. And in an election which was shaping up to be all about corruption and sleaze, as something more than a one-issue tramway party.

After the Projet Montréal policy convention in St-Henri in May 2009, Bergeron announced some of the party's campaign promises. Yes, there would be the 30 kilometres of tramway within three years as well as 10,000 new social housing units in the first mandate. But he also stressed measures to ensure greater transparency and minimize collusion and corruption. Open executive committee meetings, less out-sourcing—especially to the firms of consulting engineers which so often seemed central to any collusion—and a reduction in the maximum permissible annual donation to municipal political parties from $1000 to $300. This last undertaking was directed squarely at Union Montréal: of the $1 million the party had raised in 2008, more than half had come from people donating the maximum $1,000. Projet Montréal, meanwhile had raised a total of $50,000 in 2008.

But it was the endorsement in August from a man who *The Gazette* called "a pan-Canadian icon of probity" which, above all, helped Projet Montréal position itself as the upright alternative, the party which didn't run on dirty money and could be relied on to clean up the way business was done in the city.

An active environmentalist, Cym Gomery, the daughter of Judge John Gomery, had got involved with Projet Montréal in 2007 or 2008 and, about a year before the election, had become a regular at the party's executive meetings. By late spring, she had indicated an interest in being the party's candidate in the western NDG district of Loyola. As corruption and questionable political financing began developing into the central issues of the campaign, the obvious question presented itself: might her father, who had become a household name across Canada for his investigation just a few years previously of the sponsorship scandal which rocked the federal Liberal governments of Jean Chrétien and Paul Martin, be interested in endorsing Projet Montréal?

It was a Hail Mary request: even if Gomery had retired in 2007, judges are usually extremely reticent about taking public political stands. To a certain surprise, however, Cym relayed back the word that her father would be happy to discuss the possibility. So a few days later, Craig Sauvé and Richard Bergeron were driving south out of Montreal to Gomery's farm not far from the American border. They found him on his knees in the garden. Over apéritifs on the patio, they popped the question: would he endorse the party and Bergeron for mayor? Perhaps even join the campaign in some capacity?

Gomery had a few questions about certain positions Bergeron had taken and declarations he had made. But he was quite quickly convinced that the party was serious, and not only because it had already undertaken not to accept anonymous donations of more than $25,[14] to publish on its website the name of anyone who gave $100 or more within 24 hours of the contribution, and to investigate any donation of $250 or more to ensure than the donor was not only contributing his own money[15] but doing it without any expectation of favour or benefit. After an hour so of pleasant discussion, Gomery said yes, he would be happy to make his first-ever foray into partisan politics, endorse Bergeron and Projet Montréal, and even become honorary chair of the party's fundraising campaign.

---

14 Provincial law allowed anonymous donations of up to $100 which made for a major loophole in the law since it essentially allowed someone to contribute as much $99.99 as often as they liked. One Union Montreal event in St-Léonard in 2008 brought in $47,960 in anonymous donations.

15 Since only individuals who are allowed to contribute to political parties in Quebec—not companies, unions or institutions of any sort—a fairly common means of skirting the law was for a business to reimburse employees for donations to politicians or parties the business wished to finance.

A press conference was hastily organized but the news was too good to contain; it had been leaked to *La Presse* and *The Gazette*. Henry Aubin called it the "biggest boost" the party had ever received, coming as it did "at a time when ethics at City Hall have never been more at a premium. Sleaze appears rampant. Mayor Gerald Tremblay's administration is the subject of four current police investigations of questionable practices."

Beneath a photo of Bergeron and Gomery in shirtsleeves, sitting around a table, smiling like old friends, *La Presse* quoted the retired judge sounding distressed about the state of affairs in Montreal. "I have spent my entire life in this city but I am worried and troubled. Montreal is in decline. Public integrity seems to be imperilled."

To the inevitable question about whether he wasn't just doing it to help his daughter get elected, Gomery said he shared Projet Montréal's concerns regarding urban planning and the environment. Lamenting that the "city has abandoned itself to the automobile," he said, "The biggest issue facing not only the city but the world is the climate crisis, and Projet Montréal seems to be the only party that has focused attention on it."

Gomery's imprimatur gave the party a credibility it had lacked among journalists and commentators. It didn't, however, seem to be extend to voters' enthusiasm for Bergeron, who was persistently dogged by his comments on 9/11 as well as the popular consensus that, however interesting and detailed his ideas, he just wasn't mayoral material. In a September poll taken before the official start of the campaign, Bergeron was the preferred choice of 14 percent. On the surface, this seemed a modest improvement on the party's May numbers. But this poll eliminated the undecideds and don't-knows: Harel was at 41 percent and Tremblay at 38 percent.

Such numbers justified what can be considered the kiss-of-death for candidates who hope to be dark horses but end up as also-rans: not being invited to leaders' debates. This is what happened at the first debate of the campaign, hosted by Jean-Luc Mongrain on LCN on Sept. 23. As a consolation prize, Bergeron got a one-on-one with Mongrain the next day.

By then, however, things were beginning to break the right way for Bergeron and Projet Montréal. On Sept. 21, the auditor-general produced a 170-page report into the water-meter contract and summed it up succinctly: "Too fast, too big, too expensive." Urging the city to cancel the contract, he didn't point the finger at anyone specifically but did question the "close links" between the firms which won the contract and people at the city.

After a tumultuous, last council session before the campaign officially began, Tremblay did cancel the contract and fired the city's two top civil servants. It was vindication for Bergeron who had been calling for the contract to be cancelled since May (even though, like virtually all other members of council, he had voted for its adoption less than two years earlier).

A new poll, taken in the days following the release of the report, brought good news to Bergeron and Projet Montréal: they were now the favoured option of 20 percent of voters and seemed to be the sole beneficiaries of the growing popular disgust at the way business was done. Harel and Vision had stalled and, at 40 percent, even possibly slipped a bit; Tremblay and Union were down to 35 percent.

On the ground, in the boroughs, there were other signs that a combination of hard work and good luck might also pay off by late September. In Ahuntsic, Émilie Thuillier was in the midst of her second campaign in just over a year and beginning to feel that this time she might end up on top. Her campaign had been rattled in the summer by the defection of two of her main organizers to join Harel and Vision, one of whom would end up running against her.

Still, the Vision candidate who had won the 2008 by-election had decided to change districts so the added challenge of running against an incumbent wasn't an issue for Thuillier; meanwhile, the Union candidate in that vote, who had come in a very close second and was appreciated locally, wasn't running again. Instead, Tremblay had convinced Diane Lemieux to run on his team for the district. But if the former PQ minister was considered a heavyweight in provincial politics, the district was far from a sure thing for a Péquiste, and Lemieux didn't have the local traction Thuillier had built up. "People recognized me. More and more, I was 'Émilie' and not just another candidate who wanted to get elected." Thuillier, of course, also didn't have to carry the Union and Vision baggage her opponents had, which was becoming heavier by the day.

In NDG, Peter McQueen was feeling that his campaigns with the Green Party in 2007 and 2008 were paying off. He had raised enough money to rent a small commercial space on Sherbrooke Street as a headquarters, and it gave his campaign visibility and credibility. His constant glad-handing and his manic energy attracted volunteers, including many from outside his district and even his borough. "Mine became the campaign to work on for young anglo lefties," he remembers. "Everyone wants to work on a winning campaign and mine was the most promising."

In going door-to-door, McQueen found that he and Projet Montréal got a good reception; Richard Bergeron, not so much. "Too many people were too negative about Richard Bergeron and I had to disassociate myself," he says. "No question. And the people who were against him were not just one kind of people." McQueen found that many Jews tended to be cool towards Bergeron because "of the weird line in his book," not to mention the fact that he had converted to Islam, if only to marry Amina. "And of course, drivers were against him." So McQueen learned to fold the leaflets he distributed in such a way that Bergeron's face wasn't visible.

By early October, the task of getting Richard Bergeron elected mayor didn't look like it was going to be accomplished. It wasn't that the election campaign as a whole wasn't generating interest or attention. On the contrary, with the multiple scandals and the distinct slates, it had captured Montrealers' attention in a way few elections had in years. It wasn't that Bergeron was not getting exposure. Since his late September poll results, he was now being invited to all the debates—and there were many. On culture, on the environment, on the economy; on radio, in front of a chamber of commerce, in a TV studio.

It was more that, from the start, Bergeron seemed to be considered little more than a bit player, an interesting addition to the cast, who added colour and a bit of quirk, but not a real contender like Harel or Tremblay. People found his style—didactic to the point of lecturing, even sermonizing—hard to take. "You don't have a monopoly on virtue!" was a line Harel used to good effect in more than one debate. "We're not in a university lecture hall," was another.

A full-page profile by Michèle Ouimet in *La Presse* on October 5 did nothing to improve matters. It portrayed Bergeron as a vainglorious crackpot. Brilliant, perhaps; a visionary, possibly; uncorrupted by politics-as-usual, certainly. But not necessarily the kind of person one wanted to run their city of two million. The interview with Ouimet had gone sideways when Bergeron accompanied her to the door after 90 minutes. As she was putting on her boots, he lit a cigarette and remarked that he smoked to stay healthy. How exactly does that work? Ouimet asked. Bergeron explained that smoking diminished his lung capacity, which kept him from running as fast as he might otherwise, which meant he didn't injure himself. "I have theories about everything," Bergeron went on. Which, of course, opened the door to Bergeron's ideas about September 11th, 2001, a theory from which he didn't exactly back down.

The leader's campaign, which had pinned much hope on the profile, convinced it would be favourable, perhaps even vault Bergeron into contention, was left even more hobbled.

The campaign's comms team was part of the problem. It was of a piece with the rest of the campaign: inexperienced, disorganized and undisciplined, if full of goodwill. Bergeron had hired a communications director, Militza Jean, who turned out to have very little, if any, background dealing with the media. Other communications people were young and talented but had minimal political experience. Perhaps the most effective role was played by Sylvain Ouellet, who wasn't able to be too active in the campaign because he was working for Équiterre. Still, every day before going to bed and then early in the morning he would put together a comprehensive press review which would be emailed to everyone working on the campaign.

But there was no one giving Bergeron the coaching he required nor fine-tuning the party's message in such a way to allow it to better connect with voters and be taken more seriously by reporters. Increasingly, this was apparent to some in the party, among them Alex Norris. "Richard Bergeron, notwithstanding all his strengths, was capable of committing serious gaffes on a regular basis," he says.

"It was felt by some of us that anything that could professionalize the operation and protect us from going off the rails would be a good idea."

Étienne Coutu, who was working full-time on the campaign after quitting his architecture job in August, felt similarly. A few years earlier, Coutu had been active in the PQ and had worked to get André Boisclair elected leader. He had stayed close enough to him that after Boisclair quit politics, Coutu was comfortable phoning him up to discuss the general amateurism of the Projet Montréal campaign and ask Boisclair for the phone number of one of his former advisors, Joël Simard-Ménard.

Simard-Ménard had been the PQ's communications director before becoming Boisclair's press attaché but had found himself on the outs with the party when Pauline Marois took over. He was at loose ends and before long was meeting Coutu and Norris at a restaurant on Boul. St-Laurent. Bergeron, who had been encouraged to attend, didn't think a political professional was necessary; to a certain extent he seemed to oppose the idea on the basis that it would erode Projet Montréal's purity.

Coutu and Norris were immediately impressed by Simard-Ménard but of course the final call would have to made by Bergeron; Simard-Ménard would need unfettered access to him and his agenda, and the two men would have to have some sort of chemistry. So the next day Simard-Ménard accompanied Coutu to a press conference in the Sud-Ouest where Bergeron was announcing a party proposal which would encourage more diversity among city suppliers.

Calling for firms which met certain diversity thresholds to be awarded extra points when time came for their bids to be evaluated, it would have constituted something of an affirmative action plan for suppliers owned and/or staffed by minorities. It was a characteristic Projet Montréal proposal for the time: thought-out, complex, nuanced. The kind that Bergeron had pledged to stop making in March of 2008 while in opposition because, he said, too many of his good ideas were being appropriated by the Tremblay administration or by Vision. Instead he would save them for the election campaign.

It was also a characteristic Projet Montréal press conference for the time: no journalists showed up. Bergeron gave the press conference to a room of Projet Montréal candidates, supporters and staff, and an inscrutable guy leaning against the wall: Simard-Ménard. After it came to a mercifully rapid conclusion, Coutu approached Bergeron and said, "A fiasco, eh? Come here, I have someone for you to meet."

The two men went out to lunch. As Bergeron recalls, they spoke first about the press conference. "Joël says to me, 'I think I know politics. I'm just going to explain your mistakes from this morning to you.' And he spends half an hour tearing me down. I was like, 'You're right, you're right, you're right.'"

Then Simard-Ménard went on to analyze an interview Bergeron had given to Michel C. Auger earlier that morning, underlining "the incredible amateurism of our approach."

Finally, it was time to look forward, at least as far as what was on the agenda for later in the afternoon. "Then he asks me, 'Give me five pieces of advice for *Tout le monde en parle*,'" Simard-Ménard remembers.

It was October 15th, the election was just over two weeks away, and Bergeron, along with Harel and Tremblay, had been invited to be a guest on the hugely influential talk show. The show is recorded on Thursdays but only broadcast on Sunday evenings—to an audience of almost invariably more than a million people, sometimes as many as two million. Simard-Ménard had spent two full days preparing Boisclair for his appearance on *Tout le monde en parle*; with Bergeron "we had 45 minutes in front of a smoked meat sandwich." His main points: Repeat, repeat, repeat—since the show is edited, they will take your best word choices; don't just look at the host—look at the other guests too; and, above all, be prepared for hard questions about his views on 9-11 and his conversion to Islam.

Bergeron refused to believe that Guy A Lepage would ask him about what he saw as insubstantial issues; surely he would concentrate on Bergeron's ideas for densifying Montreal, improving public transit with the tramway, or eliminating collusion and corruption involving city contractors.

In the green room before the show's taping, Bergeron was surprised and impressed at how Simard-Ménard seemed to know everyone. He also got a kick from the look on Louise Harel face when she learned that

Simard-Ménard was now working for Projet Montréal. But it was when Guy A Lepage asked him his first question that Bergeron appreciated the full value of his new hire: he asked him not only to explain his views on the 9/11 attacks but also why he had converted to Islam.

"Joël brought professionalism in extremis to the 2009 campaign," says Bergeron, a point echoed by many. "He immediately took control of the campaign. I didn't listen to him all the time because it's not in my nature to listen. It takes spontaneity from time to time. But we really needed him."

For his part, Simard-Ménard was half-shocked, half-amused by the amateurism of the campaign. "It was 100% half-assed. It was phenomenal to what extent it lacked organization," he says. Still, he was impressed by the quality of people involved, whether as candidates or volunteers, and charmed by their earnest dedication. "Everyone was of such good faith. Everyone was so motivated to work and participate. And there were really good, smart people involved."

Immediately following Simard-Ménard's arrival, Projet Montréal got the biggest boost of its campaign—though it had nothing to do with him. *Le Journal de Montréal* had locked out its journalists in January but that hadn't stopped them reporting. Instead they published their work on a website called ruefrontenac.com, after the street in the Plateau where *Le Journal* has its offices.

On October 16th, the day after the *Tout le monde en parle* taping but before its broadcast, journalist Fabrice de Pierrebourg came out with a blockbuster: Benoît Labonté had met with Tony Accurso in March 2008 and solicited $100,000 to finance his campaign for the Vision Montréal leadership.

Labonté initially denied everything, but under a cascade of corroborating reports, he quickly folded. Within a few days he was gone, from his position as Harel's lieutenant, then from Vision, the campaign, and politics as a whole. Harel and other party candidates, who at first defended him, were left squirming; Bergeron, who for months had been urging journalists to look into Labonté's fundraising, was triumphant.

Harel had been leading in the polls all campaign but not comfortably, and a poll taken just before the Labonté exposé but released afterwards showed an even tighter race: 37 percent for Harel and 36 percent for Tremblay, well within the margin of error. Bergeron and Projet Montréal had crept up to 23 percent. With Vision now looking as compromised as Union when it came to questionable fundraising practices, Bergeron was increasingly being looked at by journalists as the only uncorrupted option.

"Of the three candidates, he's the only one with a fresh face, new policy ideas, and an approach to clean political financing that shines," Henry Aubin wrote on October 22nd. "He's the virgin in the whorehouse."

"Richard Bergeron may be an original surrounded by neophytes," wrote Michel David in *Le Devoir* the same day, "but he is now the only one whose closets contain no skeletons and he also benefits from the backing of Mr. Clean himself, Justice John Gomery."

By then, Simard-Ménard had already determined that the best way to ensure that Projet Montréal catch up to the wounded Union and Vision campaigns was to bring out "Mr. Clean" again. Gomery, he told the party, was an under-used asset. He had been trotted out in mid-August and then not seen again.

"Before Joël, we didn't call journalists," recalls Sylvain Ouellet. "We issued a press release and that was it. With Joël we understood that you could call journalists in advance to promote your story. And later, if there was a journalist who really talked nonsense, you could phone him up and tell him off."

Bergeron and Gomery called on the Quebec government to set up a commission of inquiry to look into political financing in Montreal. Bergeron also suggested a commission—perhaps the same one—to look into price-fixing in the municipal construction contracts. The provincial government had already promised to close a loophole which allowed businesses to donate to leadership campaigns but that was a band-aid measure, Gomery said. "When a patient is sick, we don't begin treatment until we know the nature of the sickness," he said. "I don't think we know the extent of the sickness that is affecting our political institutions."

A few days later, Gomery was at Bergeron's side again at another press conference, at which Projet Montréal opened its books to journalists, revealing the names of all the people who had contributed to $167,352 that the party had raised that year. Everyone who had contributed $250 or more had been contacted by the party's official agent, former Université de Montréal law professor Jacques Boucher, and told that there would be no favours in return, Bergeron said. "I challenge Gérald Tremblay and Louise Harel to commit to the same thing."

Gomery, meanwhile, went after Tremblay and Harel as if it were he who was running for mayor. "Being as charitable as possible to Mr. Tremblay, one must conclude that he is guilty of wilful blindness. He didn't see what he should have seen," he said, adding, "I think Ms. Harel's party is suffering from the same problems. Frankly, there is no alternative. We must elect Richard Bergeron."

By then, increasing numbers of Montrealers were coming to that same conclusion. *La Presse* published its final poll of the campaign on October 30th, the polling having taken place over the two preceding days. "It's complete suspense" read the headline. Given the margin of error of plus or minus 3.5 percent, the three candidates were in a dead heat. Importantly, however, Harel was still in first place at 34 percent, and Bergeron was now at 32, while Tremblay was down to 30.

It was the first hint all campaign that the party actually had a shot at winning. Bergeron took it as validation of his conviction that taking power at City Hall wouldn't necessarily require the decade or so that Pierre-Alain Cotnoir, André Cardinal and others had warned was inevitable. "A lot of people would say, 'It's going to take a long time.' I would reply, 'It might be instantaneous,'" Bergeron says. "My job is not to look ahead twelve years. My job is to convince people that tomorrow morning everything is possible."

After all, there was a principle which governed much of his life, and certainly his political career: "A rule one moment may well be entirely invalidated the next."

Simard-Ménard was less sanguine. On the contrary, the poll filled him with apprehension. "I was like, 'Gang, we're in trouble! If we get elected, we're in deep shit! There's no one ready to take power in Projet Montréal. Nobody, nobody, nobody!'"

On the ground, the final poll was a boost but didn't change things: we were in the final sprint. We just had to finish the race, and get the vote out. In the Plateau, there were those like Richard Ryan and myself who had been confident of a wall-to-wall victory from the start and nothing had occurred during the campaign to make us doubt it. Just the opposite. Not that Ryan had found campaigning in Mile-End a breeze.The population was "politically aware" and each person required persuading. Winning a single vote was rarely a case of 30 seconds on a doorstep; more often, it was 30 minutes of reasoned discussion on a street corner. "I learned never to push too hard," Ryan says. By the end of the campaign, however, he had enough of those conversations to not just be confident of victory, but convinced.

Alex Norris, on the other hand, running in the same district, had always assumed he would lose. Perhaps it was his nature—or maybe his long experience with the NDP—but even the last poll didn't reassure him that getting elected in the Plateau was a good bet. With the election on Sunday, November 1st, the last day of campaigning fell on Halloween. Rather than go trick-or-treating with his kids or stay home giving out candy, Norris spent the evening knocking on doors he hadn't made it to earlier in the campaign. If someone wasn't home or answering, he painstakingly wrote out personalized messages to them and attached it to a campaign pamphlet. "My focus was eking out a victory for myself," he remembers. "Notwithstanding all the scandals, Union Montreal seemed entrenched in the Plateau and it seemed unimaginable that they would be defeated that year—until it actually happened."

A political campaign never has as many volunteers as it does on election day. Supporters who earlier in the campaign were too busy or lazy to help put up signs or go door-to-door or contribute to telephone polling, emerge from the woodwork and offer their services to get out the vote. This can involve phoning up supporters to urge them to vote, knocking on the doors of people who aren't answering their phones, driving voters to the polls, or even minding someone's children while they go to cast their ballot. As the day progresses, volunteers are required to run the "bingo sheets" from polling stations back to the campaign staffers so they can verify which supporters have yet to vote—that way, they can be called or visited once again.

With municipal elections often decided by a few dozen votes or fewer, the task of pulling each and every vote acquires a life-and-death urgency. Similarly, making good use of all the volunteers available becomes of capital importance; after all, that volunteer you can't immediately think of a job for might end up being the person who later gets out the crucial vote that pushes your candidate over the top.

Once the polls close it is time for the hardcore volunteers to go to the polling stations to observe the vote-counting. I found myself in the basement of a church in the De Lorimier district and it quickly became clear that my optimism hadn't been misplaced. The Projet candidates were outpolling those of the other parties by a significant margin, with every second vote cast in their favour. Before long, I received a call from Guillaume Cloutier telling me not to bother wasting any more time in the basement of St-Stanislas-de-Kostka; the Élections Montréal numbers coming in from across the borough confirmed the same trend. It was time to celebrate, first at the Plateau headquarters on Rue St-Denis, and then later at Le National on Rue Ste-Catherine Est. The party had finally out-grown the Centre St-Pierre.

Chapter 13

PROJET MONTRÉAL SWEPT the Plateau easily, each candidate winning at least 10 percent more of the total vote than their nearest rival, which in all cases was the Vision Montréal representative. City-wide, however, the news ended up being much better for Union Montréal than the last polls had suggested. Gérald Tremblay finished with 38 percent of the vote and his party was left in control of 13 of the city's 19 boroughs. Its candidates won 39 of 65 city council seats and another 31 of 39 borough council positions.

Harel received almost exactly what the last *La Presse* poll had forecast: 33 percent. It was Projet Montréal and Bergeron for whom the last poll turned out to be just a mirage. Bergeron received just over a quarter of the votes for mayor of Montreal, a respectable third place. With a higher turnout than in 2005, it meant he received significantly more than three times the number of votes as in 2005.

Much more importantly, by the end of the evening, Bergeron had a real caucus: besides himself, nine other Projet Montréal candidates for city council had been elected along with four borough councillors. In Ahuntsic, there was Émilie Thuillier who edged out Diane Lemieux by 120 votes—but there was also the surprise victory of Pierre Gagnier to the borough mayoralty. Gagnier was a veteran of Montreal municipal politics and had done stints in various parties including Drapeau's Civic Party, the short-lived Parti municipal de Montréal, and Vision Montréal. For both Gagnier and Projet it was a marriage of convenience: he needed a banner under which to run, the party needed a candidate. No one was under any illusion that Gagnier shared Projet's vision or priorities. "We said yes without doing any research on Gagnier because we were convinced that we had no chance of winning the mayor's office," remembers Thuillier.

Then, moving south on the Orange Line, there was François Limoges and Marc-André Gadoury in Rosemont–La Petite-Patrie. Limoges won his district handily by Plateau-like numbers—more than 15 percent. The victory was sweetened by the fact that the Vision candidate who finished a distant second was Harel advisor, Atïm Léon, who had been among the most aggressive in predicting Projet Montréal's demise if it didn't merge with Vision. Still, Gadoury's 141-vote victory was more impressive in many ways; he beat former PQ minister Rémy Trudel with a shoe-leather campaign while François Croteau, at the time a doctoral student in urbanism and the Vision candidate for borough mayor, won a tight three-way race.

Croteau was an accidental mayor. A matter of days before the official start of the campaign, he was invited to a fundraiser hosted by Vision's youth wing at a bar on Rue Beaubien Est. Croteau was broke and wasn't going to go, until a friend said a $10 donation was fine and that he would lend him the money. At the fundraiser Croteau mentioned to a pair of Harel's aides that he would be happy to advise her on urbanism issues in the borough. One of them went off to share this with Harel and she came over to join the group.

"But it's you!" she said when she was introduced to Croteau.

"It's me what?" he asked.

"It's you who we need to be our candidate for mayor of Rosemont–La-Petite-Patrie!"

He answered something to the effect of, "Why not?" and that was all it took. "She didn't know I existed before we'd met, and three minutes later, I was running for mayor," Croteau remembers. No one at Vision wanted to take on André Lavallée,he says. "Everyone thought he was unbeatable."

Croteau, who later admitted he had followed much of the campaign on TV from the comfort of his couch, had predicted he would win by 3 percent and almost nailed it: his margin of victory was 2.8 percent. Patrick Cigana, Projet's candidate for the mayor's job, came in a close second, and after the fact was criticized for not putting enough effort into winning. "I thought I was going to the slaughterhouse," he remembers.

In the Plateau, of course, Projet won the borough handily with margins as large as 20 percent but it was in the Sainte-Marie district of Ville-Marie that the party scored its most crushing victory. There the candidate was Pierre Mainville for whom, like Gagnier, Projet Montréal was little more than a party of convenience. He had been elected for Vision in 2001 and 2005, back when it was under Pierre Bourque's leadership, but never clicked with Benoît Labonté and had quit the party in the fall of 2008. Still, he hoped to keep his city council job, which he managed to carry out while also working as a technician at Radio-Canada.

Few expected him to win, however, until the Rue Frontenac exposé and Labonté's abrupt withdrawal from the campaign, which came too late for Vision to put forward another candidate. Sainte-Marie was never particularly hospitable terrain for Union Montréal and Mainville won the district with 65 percent of the vote. Union managed only 20 percent.

Farther east, in Mercier–Hochelaga-Maisonneuve, the Harel Effect expressed itself with a vengeance. The Vision candidate for mayor, former Bloc Québécois MP Réal Ménard, who had initially agreed to run for Tremblay until Harel convinced him it was a bad idea, won with more than 52 percent of the vote, double that of the Projet candidate. Projet's city council candidates in the borough also came in second in their races, and with between 26 and 30 percent of the vote but still well behind the Vision victors. It would be another four years before MHM elected its first Projet Montréal councillor.

In the Sud-Ouest, Sophie Thiébaut came out on top in a three-way race for her borough councillor position. Steeve Lemay, running for city councillor in the same district as Thiébaut, kicked himself for having stopping campaigning about halfway through the race. "Steeve could have won," says Thiébaut. "At a certain point during the campaign, he gave up. He stopped believing in it."

Next door, across the old Rivière St-Pierre and up the Falaise St-Jacques, Peter McQueen had never given up campaigning in over-drive. He scored a surprisingly comfortable victory against two strong opponents: by almost 10 percent points over school commissioner Marie-José Mastromonaco, who ran for Union, and by almost 20 percent over UQAM urbanism professor David Hanna, representing Vision. In the district of Côte-des-Neiges, Magda Popeanu, who had worked on the central campaign more than her own, and then had the added challenge of running against Gérald Tremblay and his *co-listière* Helen Fotopulos in her district, came in second-place with a respectable 34 percent of the vote. Meanwhile, in the unpredictable Loyola district, Cym Gomery, the judge's daughter, came in third with less than 20 percent of the vote.

The celebrations at Le National went long and late. It wasn't like the NDP victory parties I remember my parents taking me to as a child, where what we were celebrating was simple survival. Projet Montréal hadn't taken City Hall but few had actually expected such an upset might really occur; fewer still felt the party was ready for it. We weren't even the main opposition; Vision had elected 16 city councillors and four borough councillors. We had, however, won complete control of a showpiece borough along with councillors in five others. It was organic, manageable growth, markedly different from that of the MCM which, at the same point in its history, was suddenly reduced to one seat.

Most of the the new Projet Montréal caucus on the steps of City Hall, November 2, 2009.

I made it home shortly before sunrise, time enough for an hour or two of sleep before driving up to the Laurentians to visit a house I had been asked to write about for an architecture magazine. Alex Norris, Richard Ryan and the other newly elected councillors stayed up all night celebrating. They then reconvened the following day for a photo on the steps of City Hall, posing around a bicycle.

Few observers shared the jubilation of the new Projet Montréal caucus and inner circle. Depending on their politics, the re-election of Tremblay and Union Montréal was either the least bad result (according to *The Gazette*) or evidence that the crooked Liberal machine still had a stranglehold on Montreal. "One can now say that shame has a city," Michel David wrote in *Le Devoir*. "Union Montreal had the means to 'get out the vote' and the job was well done. But angry voters should not need to be held by the hand to go out and vote. If the population is indifferent, why should the hustlers and schemers be ashamed?"

Channelling Jacques Parizeau, David said Tremblay's victory was thanks to "the massive support he received from the non-French speaking electorate. Many will conclude that in the eyes of some, the mafia is still better than the separatists."

During the campaign, as the scandals and opprobrium rained down on his administration and party, Tremblay had acknowledged the need for change and a fresh start. He hadn't, however, gone so far as to echo Bergeron's promise that, if elected mayor, he would invite members of the opposition parties to sit on his executive committee. For Bergeron, it was an effort to soften the edges of his party, which was still seen by many as a gang of radical, anti-car environmentalists, and by others as inexperienced idealists with their heads in the clouds and no administrative or managerial depth.

A few days after the election, however, Tremblay had a change of heart and decided that he would make place for one Vision councillor and one Projet Montréal councillor on the executive committee. It wasn't because Tremblay was short of councillors; he still had a substantial majority in council. Three of his brightest lights had, however, gone down to defeat. Without Labrecque, Lavallée or Lemieux and their progressive bona fides on the executive committee, it would be hard to make the case that he had learnt his lesson, that his administration was chastened and changed. And who knows? The representatives from Vision and Projet might just bring in some valuable ideas and expertise.

That is a charitable way of explaining Tremblay's decision to bring in councillors from the other parties, a decision which did not go over well at all with the Union caucus. After all, for them it meant two fewer seats around the table, and the attendant perks and prestige, not to mention the likelihood of leaks.

The more cynical way of explaining it is that Tremblay's apparent openness was an effort to neutralize the opposition. A basic, non-negotiable condition of sitting on the executive committee was to support all its decisions and positions however much one might disagree. This enforced solidarity would be conveyed by the council's seating plan: the Vision and Projet members of the executive committee would not sit with their own caucuses but in the front rows of the Union section.

There was never any question who in the Projet caucus would sit on the executive committee: Tremblay wanted the party leader himself and Bergeron wanted the job. Still, before accepting he presented the idea for discussion to the first meeting of the new Projet Montréal caucus. It was soon enough after the election that the meeting was held at the campaign headquarters at Ontario and Papineau which still had not been packed up and vacated.

Given that the idea of having a politically diversified executive committee had been initially put forth by Projet Montréal in the last weeks of the campaign, it was hardly surprising that the caucus was overwhelmingly supportive. Especially since Bergeron was being offered dossiers right up his and the party's alley: urbanism and *mise en valeur du territoire*—development of territory.

"I was the only one who disagreed," remembers Alex Norris. "I said we would essentially lose our leader and he would be co-opted because he would have to defend the administration and we would be left leaderless. At a time when we had to establish our identity as a political force at City Hall."

Bergeron appealed to Norris to rally to the position of the majority; he wanted approval to be unanimous. Instead, Alex demanded a vote.

Only after he saw that his arguments had failed to sway any other councillors, did he rally. It was a sign of things to come with the new city councillor from Mile-End: forceful, articulate and often unpopular arguments coupled with an intransigence which dismayed, even infuriated many colleagues. Even if, on many occasions, they admitted after the fact that he was right.

Just as there was no doubt the Projet delegate on the executive committee would be Bergeron, there was never any consideration that the Vision member would be Harel. Her party as a whole took a more skeptical approach to what *The Gazette* breathlessly described as a "revolution in how the city is governed." They saw it more as a "lobster trap" which would snare the party into supporting the administration, or at very least, defuse criticism.

When Vision eventually agreed to give it a try, Tremblay rejected the first candidate Harel put forward, Pierre Lampron, a senior Vidéotron executive who she had coaxed into running on the promise that he would be the president of the executive committee. Eventually, they settled on Lyn Thériault, who had been the mayor of Mercier–Hochelaga-Maisonneuve before ceding the candidacy to Réal Ménard. She was given the dossier of social and community development, the family and the elderly.

Tremblay reserved for himself the presidency of the executive committee, a clear signal that he intended to be more hands-on going forward. He also left Sammy Forcillo and Luis Miranda, two senior councillors and fixtures of past executive committees about whom rumours were swirling, out in the cold. Promoted were two perceived straight arrows: Alan DeSousa, mayor of the borough of St-Laurent and Michael Applebaum, mayor of Côte-des-Neiges–Notre-Dame-de-Grâce.

Jobs were also found for his defeated bright lights: Diane Lemieux became his chief of staff at City Hall while André Lavallée became his chief of staff in the Ville-Marie borough. For his part, Michel Labrecque was able to stay on as STM president.

In the offices of *la deuxième opposition*, as their caucus would be known for the next four years, Projet Montréal was also hiring. For the first time, they had a real office—a suite of rooms on the ground floor of City Hall which, in lieu of windows, had a glass wall looking out on to the main corridor. Unsurprisingly, it would be referred to as the Aquarium.

Each elected representative is allotted a budget for research and other purposes and parties typically pool their resources to pay for staff. Having elected 14 councillors, Bergeron suddenly had a budget to work with and promptly hired Joël Simard-Menard as his chief of staff. For virtually everyone in the party, it was a no-brainer. Joël was not a true believer—he took pleasure in teasing many of us for cycling year-round, not eating meat, and asking where the compost bin was kept. Still, no one questioned his political smarts or know-how, let alone his contribution to the campaign, even if the party's final score had as much to do with Vision's meltdown as anything. "There was Richard before Joël Simard-Menard and there was Richard after Joël Simard-Menard," says François Limoges. "Joël really helped Richard become a better politician."

Beyond that, the two men clicked on a personal level. Some of it may have had to do with them both being *bluets* long transplanted from the Lac St-Jean region. Or maybe it was because they were smokers whose mutual solidarity was reinforced by frequent cigarette breaks outside City Hall, whatever the weather. Their bond also probably stemmed from the fact they were both outsiders in the Projet Montréal of 2009. For Simard-Menard, this was a given; he was a political mercenary brought in for a specific task. For Bergeron, it was more difficult to explain. He had founded a party not because he sought a political career or thousands of followers but because no other party pushed the projects he felt were important. But after a few years, the party, which he had ended up leading because no one else was interested , had evolved into something which didn't resemble him very much at all. Certainly, it was still based around a shared vision of tramways (or at very least, improved public transit), increased density, and containing urban sprawl. Increasingly, however, other issues associated with the party left him indifferent and aghast. Subsidizing cloth diapers or crusading against systemic racism were not positions Bergeron ever expected the party to get behind.

Patrick Cigana recognized this early on and remembers asking Bergeron before the 2009 election, "How does it feel being the leader of a green, left-leaning party when you are neither?" Bergeron, he says, just smiled in acknowledgement that the observation was just. Cigana adds that Bergeron's hostility towards cars was based on their huge cost to the Quebec economy, which he put at $25 billion per year, and their inefficient use of public space. "Richard never spoke of pollution, or greening, or beautification," Cigana says. "And he used climate change because it was a convenient argument against cars."[16]

Trusting him as he did, Bergeron delegated other hiring decisions to his chief of staff and Simard-Menard immediately hired the person who had brought him into the party, Étienne Coutu and, soon after him, Sylvain Ouellet. There wasn't much time to get comfortable in their new offices or decide in which drawer to stick the post-it notes and erasers: there were three councils to prepare for before the end of the year and at least half the caucus had never sat in city council before.

16 Bergeron's antipathy to cars is nuanced by a great appreciation for their technological sophistication. He is probably the only person in Projet Montréal to not only buy *Le Guide de l'auto* every year but actually read it cover to cover.

Chapter 14

In the Plateau, Ferrandez also wasted no time in taking matters in hand. The day after the election—and still two weeks before being officially sworn in—he met with Isabelle Cadrin, the borough's director of culture, sports, leisure and social development. She was filling in for Johanne Falcon, since her departure on sick leave six months earlier.

The meeting had an odd dynamic. In many respects, it was a job interview for Cadrin since it was openly understood that Falcon would not be returning, that the borough needed a new director and that it was Ferrandez's decision who would get the job. But Ferrandez was also after information from Cadrin.

For hours, Ferrandez asked Cadrin question after question about the borough, its organization, operations, finances, and, of course, the workplace atmosphere. Her responses were detailed and solid, neither sugar-coated nor disingenuous. It was clear that she had followed the campaign closely and understood the changes that Ferrandez and the Projet Montréal team wanted to bring to the borough. She was direct about which she felt were feasible and which she considered far-fetched. At the end of the afternoon, Ferrandez was impressed enough with her answers and attitude that he told her she had the job permanently.

It was perhaps rash and impetuous, characteristics Ferrandez displayed often enough, but it was a good bet. Over the next eight years, Ferrandez and Cadrin's close collaboration—he challenging her to re-imagine how the borough delivered services and what its priorities should be; she reining him in and helping make our team's projects happen, whether by finding financing or mobilizing the human resources—transformed the Plateau on multiple levels. Most obvious to residents and visitors, this involved curb extensions, bike paths, sidewalk widening, and the planting of thousands of new trees as well as the elimination of various streets in order to expand parks. Almost as profound and all but invisible to anyone not working at the borough or city, was the institutional transformation of the borough as a workplace. It took years and went no more smoothly than many other changes, but in time the Plateau became a relatively functional and efficient place to work, at least by City of Montreal standards.

As Alex Norris remembers, "Luc knew that if we wanted to get anything done, we had to be on good terms with the civil service and develop a respectful relationship with them where our roles were properly circumscribed but where a clear vision was set on our part. He set the stage for a really effective working environment between elected officials and the civil service which lasts to this day."

In the fall of 2009, however, this was all a long way off and, by no stretch of the imagination, a guaranteed thing.

Luc had mentioned on a couple of occasions during the campaign that if he won, he wanted me to work for him as a political attaché. My intention had been to go back to my life as a freelance journalist and writer after the campaign. In the previous years, I had written a book about Quebec's biker war and ghostwritten the autobiography of a professional organized crime infiltrator. Both had done well financially[17] and I was deep into the research for my next book, the true story of a group of suburban Montreal teenagers who broke into a semi-abandoned house and discovered more than $2 million cash. They got away with the money but not without having to deal with intimidation by Russian thugs, kidnappings by a Haitian street gang and parents who wanted the loot for themselves. And that was just the start of it. It was a great story but I was near my fill of true crime writing and felt the need to do something more substantial, to contribute to society—however clichéd it sounds. I also missed the social interaction of actually *going* to work in an office or newsroom, as opposed to

---

17 As one publisher told me, "I love these books! They can be complete shit but they still sell really well!"

working from my desk, at the other end of the apartment, often in my pyjamas. I thought that working on the campaign for a couple of months might be enough of a break, but it only whetted my appetite for more. Making new friends and working with old ones on a political campaign was more fun than going through court records and trying to get taciturn police and prosecutors to talk. With the team elected wall-to-wall in the Plateau, there was suddenly the added attraction of power and being in a position to enact the change we had been calling for. So I told Luc that I was keen on working for him for two years, at which point I planned to return to my suburban teenagers.

Guillaume Cloutier and Christine Gosselin were hired in similar positions; our start date was January 4th, 2010. By then, the councillors and Luc had had a meeting with the borough directors alone and a second with the directors and selected senior staff. At the first, the directors gave the new councillors the basic information about the borough and its operations: the organigram, the different departments and divisions, budgetary basics and the like. "It was a fabulous meeting," says Richard Ryan. "They arrived with big binders and Isabelle [Cadrin] opened the meeting by saying 'We read your platform and Mr. Ferrandez's blog. There are lots of things we can accomplish together. There are others which are not in the borough's jurisdiction. But we understand your vision.'"

The atmosphere, he says, was one of relief and enthusiasm. "They seemed so relieved, breathing again, happy after all the trash they went through before with Falcon and Fotopulos, the war between the mayor and borough director."

The second meeting was not held at the borough offices on Ave Laurier but rather at the Mile-End library, later renamed la Bibliothèque Mordecai Richler, on Ave du Parc in order to accommodate not only the five borough directors but also various *chefs de divisions.* At this meeting, Ferrandez delivered a modified version of his *party de trottoir* presentation. "It was the first big moment where he was transmitting to the civil service what his overall vision was," says Alex Norris. "It was a really effective event because it allowed people to visualize what he had in mind rather than talking in platitudes. Specific ideas with specific plans which gave us legitimacy to act quickly."

Mingling with the borough staff after this meeting, Alex began chatting with Guy Ouellet, at the time director of *Aménagement urbain et services aux entreprises*—Urban planning and business services. He asked Ouellet whether the borough had the authority to ban billboards on its territory. Ouellet said that in theory it did and told Alex that the annual revenue the massive signs brought into the borough was negligible, perhaps $1,000 per billboard. Between the lines, he made clear he would be happy to try to ban the signs even if the advertising companies would fight tooth and nail against the by-law on grounds that it compromised their freedom of expression and that of their clients. Thus began a 10-year battle to get rid of all commercial billboards in the Plateau which finally ended with the Supreme Court refusing the billboard companies' request to appeal.

Between the getting-to-know-each-other sessions and the blue-skying, there was also more immediate, less pleasant business to attend to. At his first meeting with Cadrin, Ferrandez had been made aware of the dire financial position the borough was in. "We don't even have money to buy the paint," she told him when he spoke of improving street marking.

One reason: the winters of 2007 and 2008, which had each seen more than three metres of snow fall on Montreal, 60 percent more than average. Snow had not been removed from sidewalks for weeks at a time because crews and machinery had to be dedicated to keeping the streets clear. For children, it was a dreamworld, the sidewalks more and more like paths through a forest as snowfall after snowfall dumped another 20, 30 or 50 centimetres on the city. For the elderly or those with any mobility problems, it was confinement by climate. For the borough's finances it was back-to-back disasters, as the annual operations budget was blown by the extra costs in overtime and emergency snow removal contracts.

Boroughs are not legally permitted to run deficits. Nevertheless, the Plateau had no choice but to borrow money from the central city and pretend, through some accounting fiction, that it wasn't a debt. So when Projet Montréal took over in late 2009, not only was there no money in the kitty and the central city was holding a $4 million IOU which had to be paid back. Not an easy task, when the annual budget was only about $50 million and, even then, the borough was severely underfunded in many respects.

After another lengthy meeting between councillors and directors, Ferrandez announced a radical reform of snow removal practices, just in time for winter. With the aim of saving money to both pay back the central city and, fingers crossed, generate a little bit extra for the myriad projects our administration had in mind, Ferrandez declared that the borough would wait until 15 centimetres of snow had fallen rather than just 8 centimetres before ordering a *chargement*—the hugely expensive operation of removing the show and trucking it away—and if it was the weekend, well, everyone would just have to wait until Monday for the *chargement* to begin. "There will no longer be snow removal at any cost," he said.

Richard Bergeron was more emphatic. The preoccupation with snow removal had become "a real hysteria," he said. "And this hysteria stems from the dependence on the car. Is it really that urgent to have snow removal employees working at double time on weekends just so that traffic can run smoothly on Monday morning?"

For the media, which was eager for evidence that Projet Montréal was indeed as radical as its caricature, this was red meat, the first volley in the war on cars and their owners. To some, the bearded Ferrandez might as well have been a modern-day Trotsky or Guevara, a portrayal he didn't exactly resist playing into in the following months and years.

Financially, however, the move could have been that of the most cost-cutting fiscal conservative. Over two years, the borough was able to save almost $7 million in snow removal costs, paying off its debt to the central city while putting money aside for new projects.[18] Ferrandez's happiness at being perceived as a revolutionary extended to his dealings with the borough directors. Richard Bergeron remembers a meeting

18 Years later, Ferrandez says there was another motive behind the decision to relax the snow removal criteria. "Before I was elected I was always fascinated by the traffic-calming effect of the snow. Cars are going 20 kilometres an hour in the middle of the street. They turn corners very wide, there aren't others cars trying to pass on the right. And at the time traffic calming was the big issue—there were 300 accidents a year on the Plateau Mont-Royal."

between senior bureaucrats in late 2009. It was one of the regular meetings to prepare for the upcoming borough council session, at which the directors present and defend the contracts they hope to issue, as well as by-laws, amendments and the like that they expect the councillors to pass. "We arrive at the meeting and almost the first words out of Luc's mouth are, 'The Plateau is now Cuba and I'll tell you right away, I'm Castro.'" As was often the case with Ferrandez, he said it with a mix of seriousness and humour, the exact proportions of which weren't necessarily easy to gauge.

Bergeron, who had four years experience dealing with the never simple, rarely transparent, often obdurate, and occasionally deceitful senior bureaucrats of the city and borough, says he put his head in his hands, thinking, "*Tabernak*, what foolishness did he just say."

Such declarations didn't compromise Ferrandez's relations with the directors; on the contrary, his jokes, straight-talk, and energy—not to mention his growing celebrity—endeared him to them. It was essential in getting them to buy into the administration's vision. As Alex Norris says, "He knew that if we wanted to get anything done, we had to be on good terms with the civil service and develop a respectful relationship with them. Luc was very good at keeping them on their toes while being respectful of their expertise."

The fact that Ferrandez often defended the bureaucracy against the Plateau councillors and his own staff wasn't lost on the borough directors and senior staff. Certainly, our relationships with senior borough bureaucrats tended to be more difficult than his, perhaps mine especially.

The City of Montreal is a rigidly hierarchical place, where information is often tightly controlled and channels of communication prescribed. An employee who reports to one *chef de division* would not be expected to communicate with another, let alone a director, without discussion with and approval from his or her superiors—even if the other *chef de division* sat at a desk all of five metres away.

Communication with political staff is even more complicated and delicate. Whereas all borough employees report, ultimately, to the borough director, political employees report to the mayor. The convention is that all communication between the councillors and political staff and bureaucrats be funnelled through the mayor, or the chief of staff, to the borough director, or at very least, the directors of the various departments. Even if it is the most harmless or insignificant of questions, such as how many public trash bins are there scattered around the borough? Do we know how many cars go through a particular intersection on a given day? Is there a reason why no work seems to be proceeding on such-and-such a construction site which is blocking the sidewalk and forcing pedestrians into the street?

Coming from a newsroom culture, abiding by such strictures was entirely alien to me. Why go through three, four or even more people, wasting their time and often waiting for days, for a piece of information that could be easily obtained immediately by simply picking up the phone and calling the staff member who, according to the borough directory, would almost certainly have the information at their fingertips? It seemed not just alien but silly, and for the first weeks of my time at the borough I was incapable of respecting this approach.

My attitude was perhaps simplistic—that we were in this together, political and bureaucratic, and that we should work as a team to improve services and deliver on our campaign promises, rather than as competing interests in a constant process of negotiation—but Cadrin and the other directors saw it otherwise. Having recently gone through the internecine hell of the Falcon years, there was an apprehension that bordered on paranoia, almost a collective PTSD, that made them suspect the worst. They felt I was actively undermining them and their authority, perhaps with ulterior motives.

Certainly, they were not mistaken in assuming that our administration might want to make changes to the senior bureaucracy of the borough. In the words of Richard Ryan, under Falcon, "it was really warfare; everyone was leaving."

One example is particularly telling. A crucial division in the bureaucracy of a borough is that of technical studies. Usually part of the public works or urbanism departments, this is where the engineers and technical agents are to be found and it is the division one deals with for everything from road repairs to installing stop signs to proposing curb extensions to changing a street from two-way to one-way or one-way north to one-way south.

Shortly after my arrival at the borough, I asked the traffic engineer for any traffic counts that were available—the number of vehicles that travelled a street or through an intersection on a given day, broken down, ideally by hour or even by 15-minute period. These are crucial for planning and are measured by a variety of means. Often the speed of the vehicles is measured as well, which provides other useful data. The traffic engineer was candid: she had only been at the borough for three or four months and had yet to come across any traffic counts. I soon learned that in the technical studies division, which at the time counted 15 positions, there had been something like 35 departures in the previous five years. It seemed that as soon as a new employee arrived, they began looking for a new job within the municipal bureaucracy or elsewhere.

Certainly, the Plateau in those years had the reputation as a terrible place to work and experienced great difficulty attracting, let alone keeping, quality staff. One borough employee at the time told the story of being at a party and meeting another woman who also worked somewhere for the city. When the woman found out that my colleague worked at the Plateau, she immediately felt the need to commiserate—before even asking what she did and whether she enjoyed her job. "It was as if I had just told her my dog had died."

I also got on the wrong side of the directors by being too forward when I asked them whether they lived in the Plateau. Relatively few city employees tend to live in the boroughs they work in and in the Plateau at that time it was almost certainly much lower than the average, probably less than 5 percent. This was due to a variety of factors—housing prices, the lure of the suburbs to young families, the fact that the bureaucrat profile isn't really very "Plateau," the ease with which white collar employees within the city can move from job to job and borough to borough. It was apparently a sensitive point among the directors, however.

It was significant because early on I realized that, contrary to the new councillors and political staff, many Plateau employees didn't actually know the borough very well—geographically or otherwise—or seem to feel any real sense of responsibility to it. For them, it was not a home or a mission but just a job, which might have been all one could reasonably expect but which I thought was a pity since I considered it such a special place.

My disregard for hierarchical conventions, combined with the fact that I quickly became friends with several mid-level employees, led to a fair amount of consternation among the directors, who, it was clear early on, valued unquestioning loyalty above competence and, in this way, were unfailingly loyal to each other. Within a few weeks, Cadrin had given Luc a list of employees that I was allowed to talk to. Even if I respected the list, at least for the most part, not many months after that she was urging Luc to fire me.

Luc, however, was happy for me to be something of a destabilizing influence and told me to just continue doing what I was doing. It allowed him to be the good cop—the one who respected protocol, even if he was, in fact, the real force of change and destabilization.

The borough directors had more than enough reason to feel under pressure. In the lead-up to the campaign the team in the Plateau—Luc primarily—had put together a 15-page Excel spreadsheet[19] outlining the dozens, indeed hundreds, of specific changes we proposed bringing to the Plateau. This local platform, brainstormed principally during a two-day retreat at McGill's Thomson House, was now titled "A Cascade of Human-scale Interventions"—and was consistent with the 70-page Projet Montréal program but gave specific examples.

The proposals ran the gamut from new public squares and parks, reserved bus lanes and protected bike paths, to tighter restrictions on deliveries, a tougher noise by-law and, of course, more constraints on car use. Not to forget such small perks as more water fountains, bike racks and park benches, or bigger ones such as a new skatepark, outdoor libraries, public markets. The full platform was never released publicly for fear of generating too many specific expectations. Instead, during the campaign, our pamphlets spoke more generally about

19 For Ferrandez, working in Excel as opposed to Word automatically lent authority to a project or document. As he once told us, with a smile but nonetheless seriously, "A consultant who works in Word can charge $350 per day. If he works in Excel, he can charge $1,500."

things like the need for calmer streets and greener alleys rather than where exactly where and how.

Once in power, however, Luc did not hesitate to share versions of the spreadsheet with Cadrin and the other directors, and began pressing them about what projects might be delivered when.

For our part, we had our own ideas about which initiatives would be easier to implement in the short term and began working on them immediately. Guillaume Cloutier, Christine Gosselin and I had all been assigned areas of responsibility and projects to prioritize when we were hired. Guillaume was to develop a new parking policy for the borough, the aim of which was to generate greater revenue while at the same time eliminating hundreds of spaces in order to make intersections safer and car use less attractive. Christine's main task was more specific: negotiating endless red tape with the central city and unions to get a café-restaurant operating once again in the building perched above the pond in Parc Lafontaine. A vital and attractive destination in the heart of the park in the 1950s and 60s, over the years the restaurant had lost its lustre, becoming a casse-croute and, eventually, a collection of vending machines before closing to the public entirely in the Fotopulos years. My responsibilities were more wide-ranging but certainly no less pressing: traffic-calming, sidewalks, park enlargement and improvement, bike paths and the like—dossiers which for many constituted the essence of Projet Montréal's mission.

At our first meeting with Luc and the councillors on our first day at the office, we went through the list of projects on the spreadsheet and picked out those we felt were the easiest to make happen. Two jumped out: eliminating Rue St-Dominique between boulevard St-Joseph and Laurier, where it ran between Parc Lahaie and Église St-Enfant-Jésus—the fabulous wedding cake church—and getting rid of the parking lot in the middle of Parc Laurier.

In both cases we planned to follow the example of New York City, temporarily closing off these streets and parking lots—as soon as the snow melted—even if we wouldn't be in a position to dig them up and truly transform them for at least a year or two. In the interim, we would paint the asphalt green and encourage park users to appropriate the space.

Naively, we expected there would be little opposition to either project and that afternoon, when I went to speak to residents of a retirement home which had a door on to St-Dominique by the park and who were among its most frequent users, all we got was enthusiasm for the plan. In the weeks following, however, we began running into resistance, not always from whom we had expected, and learned that virtually no project is easy to implement.

The *fabrique* of the church—the local lay members who constitute its governing body—received our proposal politely but were generally opposed to the idea. They appreciated that turning the street in front of the church into a plaza with benches and a fountain which then extended into a revitalized Parc Lahaie would vastly improve the quality of public space. They were concerned, however, about access for hearses and limousines for funerals and weddings, not to mention allowing their aging and dwindling congregation to drive right up to the church door. Happily, the priest quietly liked the plan.

Among many borough employees, however, the project was not at all popular. Our offices were about 75 metres from the park and only a few, senior staff had access to the underground parking in the building. Any other employee who drove to work had to fend for themselves on the surrounding streets. The stretch of St-Dominique between the church and the park provided abundant, free parking which was much used by borough employees, including the traffic engineer whose responsibility it was to handle the closure of the street. She urged us to reconsider, or at least to not block the street off to cars—and parking—until we were ready to excavate it and build the plaza and fountain.[20]

Meanwhile, even if the parking lot in Parc Laurier was little-used and almost completely unnecessary (there was more than enough parking on the surrounding streets), the members of a Golden Age club were very attached to it. For years they had had exclusive use of the top floor of the chalet—it is actually a fairly imposing building—

20 After stalling us on various other projects, more because she didn't agree with the vision of the administration than because they were problematic in terms of conception, the engineer was let go.

to play cards and hold dances and they liked to be able to park directly in front of the building. One member of the club was the mother of Agnès Gruda of *La Presse*; soon enough, Ferrandez and the administration were being accused in the media of picking on old people and not taking into consideration their mobility problems. Not only were we anti-car but anti-seniors as well.

As for our other interventions, to a certain degree we didn't know where to begin. There were so many, they seemed to be equally complicated and pressing, and few would not generate substantial blowback. To help decide which initiatives to prioritize, Luc asked us to constitute what we called *comités aviseurs*—advisory committees—on a variety of subjects. The plan was to make use of what might be called "citizen experts" while also maintaining a regular channel of communication with our supporters and making them understand we still wanted their input even after the team had been elected. "In some areas we didn't have enough depth and I didn't want to do consultations," says Ferrandez. "Often consultation is a hollow exercise because the people who come out react to the ideas you give them but without much thought or expertise. They react according to their interests. I wanted to replace that with citizens who have depth and would meet regularly and really talk things over."

The plan was also meant to speed up the delivery of projects. "My whole approach was to ask for very specific things from the civil service," Ferrandez says. "Speed bumps, curb extensions, park enlargements in precise locations, so that the answer would arrive in two months and not a year."

There was a *comité aviseur* for traffic planning, which I set up and facilitated; one for greening, which Christine was in charge of; another for parking, which Guillaume organized; one for animal control, headed by Piper and one or two others.

The results, however, were mixed at best. Being a political initiative—and because the *comités aviseurs* meetings took place in the evening—we couldn't require borough employees to take part. As a result, frequently, no one was there who might answer basic questions or point out the various technical or financial constraints to a proposal.

Also, in some cases our citizen experts showed little interest beyond their corner of the Plateau or insisted on information we didn't have before venturing an opinion. This became clear at our first meeting of the *comité aviseur* on traffic when we went around the table, asking the participants what they considered the most pressing traffic problem in the borough. The man who lived on rue Christophe-Colomb refused to consider the possibility that there was any issue that could compare with the excess number of cars and trucks—as many as 8,000 per day—which drove past his house. Another would not even venture an opinion until we could provide him with detailed traffic counts of every street and intersection in the borough, which of course we didn't have and would take years to compile.

Depending on its mandate, the *comités aviseurs* stumbled along for anywhere from a few months (a meagre three or four meetings) to perhaps a year and a half (a dozen meetings or more). However long they lasted, the experiment was ultimately considered a failure. "I had the impression that [our supporters and expert citizens] had a lot of solutions," says Ferrandez. "But I realized they didn't have that many." Often, he said, an unworkable or impractical proposal would be put forth, or one that had no hope of resolving a difficult issue, such as a 'residents only' sign to discourage transit traffic on a particular street.

Isabelle Gaudette, the community worker with La Maison d'Aurore and an expert in running consultations, put it best a few years later when she told us, "Citizens are often excellent at identifying problems but nowhere near as good at coming up with solutions."

Chapter 15

WHATEVER THE THOUGHTS OF our *comité aviseur*, our minds were made up about what would become our first major traffic-calming initiative by a woman who came to the public question period of borough council in early 2010. Nathalie Laferté taught at a Cégep on the West Island but lived near l'École Laurier, a primary school on Laurier between Berri and St-Hubert. At the time, a popular route to the eastern downtown for morning commuters was to drive south on de Chateaubriand through Rosemont, then down St-Hubert as far as Laurier. Continuing on St-Hubert at that point wasn't an option—the street is one-way north between Mont-Royal and Laurier. The city had nonetheless made it easy for cars to continue south, by channeling them onto Rue Resther, a narrow residential street 50 metres east. About 5,000 cars per day were going down Resther, five times what is considered tolerable.

Worse, however, were the accidents. Traffic lights were synchronized in such a way that southbound traffic was encouraged to make what might be called an "F1 turn" from St-Hubert onto Laurier and then almost immediately onto Resther—directly in front of the school. Kids, Nathalie Laferté reported, were being hit a regular basis.

I knew the area relatively well and as I sat in the audience listening to the question and Luc's response, a solution presented itself: Laurier was one-way east as of Mentana; why not extend the one-way section so that it started at St-Denis? That way, traffic coming down St-Hubert would have to turn east, away from the school when it reached Laurier.

I pitched the idea to Luc as soon as council ended; he said it was good but didn't go far enough. Laurier should be one-way east from St-Laurent, where it narrowed substantially compared to farther west.

The next day, with maps, pencils and erasers at hand, we studied and discussed it more.

The school was next a metro station which was across from a church and beside a community centre. Huge numbers of pedestrians used the area daily but because the street was so wide—17 metres—and the sidewalks so narrow, it was a hostile, alienating public space that people wanted to flee. Changing Laurier to one-way east, we saw, would not only make the street in front of the school much safer, but offer many other opportunities and benefits. Shrinking the street width to the minimum required for one lane of traffic would allow us to

Before and after. Changing Laurier to one-way east, shrinking the road width, widening the sidewalk and adding trees.

widen the sidewalks substantially, plant trees on both sides, add bike lanes. Best of all, it would allow for the creation of a small *place publique* in front of the metro station.That was the upside. The downside was that channeling the traffic east on Laurier would create a cascade of downstream problems which we would have to devise solutions for in advance. This included more traffic driving around Parc Laurier and then down Christophe-Colomb—already an issue—as well as on other smaller streets which accommodated southbound traffic.

The final plan, announced in June but not implemented for almost a year given all the preparations necessary, involved switching a small stretch of Christophe-Colomb to one-way north from one-way south, thereby rendering it of no interest to transit traffic. For people outside the Plateau, it cemented Ferrandez's reputation as a zealot intent on making life miserable for anyone who made the mistake of driving a car onto or across the Plateau without staying on the major arteries. Many in the Plateau regarded him similarly. Soon enough, however, the benefits of the changes were evident, and outweighed the drawback of having to change one's driving habits and perhaps take a slightly longer route when going home by car.

The Laurier street and school project helped us crystallize our thinking when it came to traffic-calming and traffic-planning. Schools, of course, were top priorities, even if many of them were located on major arteries such as St-Joseph and St-Urbain over which the borough had little jurisdiction. So were parks, given that they were places where children played, old people hung out and, if they were well designed, towards which people from all walks of life made a beeline when the weather was nice. But there were other "pedestrian generators" which had to be taken into consideration, including, most obviously, metro stations, employment hubs and shopping streets (as well as smaller streets leading to shopping streets).

With these criteria, we began planning other interventions. A no-brainer was brought to our attention by a couple of party activists who, along with their children, had posed for a photo used in campaign literature to illustrate that young families didn't have to move to the suburbs, that bringing up kids in central neighbourhoods could be safe and enriching. Their children went to a small public school in the eastern Plateau called St-Louis-de-Gonzague which was bucolically nestled in a corner of Parc Baldwin. Except it wasn't really—the school and its yard were bordered on all four sides by streets. One of these, a stretch of Rue Franchère, was entirely unnecessary; it was all of 60 metres long and separated the school from a church of the same name. Its only real purpose was for parking. Worse, the sidewalk on the school side of the street was only 1 metre wide, too narrow even for a snowplow so children frequently walked in the street, at their peril. We decided to eliminate the street as quickly as possible.

That project led me to a series of studies that Vélo-Quebec had been commissioned to produce, evaluating ways to make walking and cycling to school safer in Montreal. The impetus for these studies was worrying: in the space of two generations across North America, the proportion of children walking or cycling to school to those being driven by their parents had flipped. From a solid majority of kids getting to school under their own steam, to a majority being driven. It varied, of course, from place to place but the trend was constant and one fact jumped out: if a child was hit by a car in the vicinity of a school, it was as likely as not that the driver was the parent of another student, rushing off to work or home to cook dinner.

The school-by-school studies were well done: they provided detailed analysis of existing hazards and mapped out the routes most frequently used by children to get to school. The recommendations, however, were milquetoast—more signage, better marking of crosswalks and the like, perhaps a speed bump or a curb extension. The proposals' mildness and their lack of ambition prompted me to phone the woman at Vélo Québec who had done the study.

Why, in the case of St-Louis-de-Gonzague for instance, had she not proposed eliminating the little stretch of Rue Franchère? I asked.

"I thought about it," she answered, "but I was told it would never happen so I didn't suggest it."

The exchange underscored a disconnect that existed in our relationship with various civil society interest groups. A political administration can usually expect to have groups to both the Left and

Right urging very different policies and interventions. As long as the administration charts a course somewhere between the extremes, it can be presented as a judicious approach. In the Plateau in 2010, however, there were no organized, let alone high-profile groups calling for anything approximately as audacious as what we were prepared to do.

The most prominent such organizations locally, Vélo Québec and the Centre d'écologie urbain, weren't pushing for radical action to reduce car and truck traffic or to provide expanded and safer infrastructure for pedestrians and cyclists. Rather, what they were lobbying for was decidedly unambitious: things like a participatory budget where citizens had a hand in choosing capital expenditure projects in the case of the Centre d'écologie urbain, or, with Vélo-Québec, the right to ride bikes in parks, on the Prince-Arthur pedestrian mall and, of course, the *Mon école à pied, à vélo!* proposals.

While it might have been convenient to have these groups supporting our projects and even calling for bolder action, truth be told, we didn't have much time for them or their leadership. By any measure, they should have been our natural allies but we considered with reason that they had been co-opted by the Fotopulos and Tremblay administrations.

Certainly, Vélo Québec was closely tied to Union Montréal through Michel Labrecque. The fact that it had rented its offices, and its dozens of phone lines, for all of $100 to the party on election day 2009 for its get-out-the-vote operation hadn't done anything to endear itself to us. Beyond that, Luc Ferrandez and the director-general of Vélo-Quebec, Suzanne Lareau, didn't even bother pretending that they didn't detest each other. In this way, it fell to me to cultivate better relations with the organization, usually through dealings with lower-level staffers.

Luc's relations with Dimitri Roussopoulos, the founder and patriarch of Centre d'écologie urbain, were just as difficult, with an element of alpha male competition mixed in. Even if he was nominally no longer the head of the Centre d'écologie urbain, Roussopoulos loomed large in the organization and, in the words of Richard Ryan, "was entirely subservient to Gérald Tremblay."

And, in no small measure, to Helen Fotopulos as well, given that her administration had instituted a participatory budget process in the

Plateau after her election as mayor in 2005, hiring the Centre d'écologie urbain to run it. In theory, there was no denying that involving the borough's citizens to help determine how to spend its capital investment budget was an interesting idea but in application the results were not just underwhelming but bureaucratic and inefficient. At the end of the day, the Plateau had spent about $250,000 to decide how to spend $3.5 million, with the main project being the renovation of a small park which was no better or worse than many other park upgrades done around the city.

Other groups in the Plateau, cultural, social, heritage and the like, had been co-opted to varying degrees by Union and the Fotopulos administration, as is bound to happen over time, especially if, like Union in the Plateau, it could trace its roots back to a grassroots party like the MCM which had emerged from those groups in the first place.

Meanwhile, the only group which had played any sort of role in Projet Montréal's creation was Mont Royal Avenue Verte and by 2010 it had, to all intents and purposes, ceased to exist. This left our administration isolated, yet liberated: we couldn't count on the support of groups which might have been our allies yet we weren't beholden to them either.

Beyond our more ambitious traffic calming initiatives, our street-corner-by-street-corner platform had proposed installing all-way stops at any number of problematic intersections around the borough. Here we ran into the same intransigence that had so frustrated Labrecque.

Quebec's Road Safety Act imposes provincial standards for road design, marking and signage and is as close to a bible as exists for traffic engineers in Quebec. Its prescriptions, however, are generally on a one-size-fits-all basis and don't distinguish a dense urban environment like the Plateau from, say, an industrial park or an entirely rural setting.

As far as stop signs are concerned, the act says they should not be installed any closer than 150 metres to another on the same stretch of street, and no closer than 250 metres to a stop light. The argument is that if they are too close to one another, drivers risk not seeing the closer one because they are focused on that which is more distant.

Stop lights, which are brighter and more dynamic, are even more dangerous in this regard, the theory supposes.

It was this standard which had justified the refusal of the Plateau's technical studies division to install the stop sign at Bernard and Waverly, right by École Lambert-Closse. Waverly, after all, was only 75 metres from both St-Urbain and Esplanade, and there were stop lights at both on Bernard.

The theory, however, was undermined by the facts on the ground just a few hundred metres west in Outremont. There, dating from the era when it was an independent municipality, were all-way stop signs at every intersection along not just Bernard but also St-Viateur, Fairmount and Villeneuve and the accident rate was significantly lower than on our side of Ave du Parc.

In fact, the Road Safety Act's standards regarding stop signs were ignored in many small, wealthier municipalities such as Westmount, Ville Mont-Royal and Côte-St-Luc—and accident numbers showed their streets were much safer than those of the city of Montreal where the standards were rigorously applied.

Labrecque and the Fotopulos administration had finally succeeded in getting stop signs installed along Bernard and St-Viateur a few weeks before the 2009 election but only by the most exceptional of methods: bypassing the borough's own engineers, an outside firm had been hired to do a study greenlighting the installation. In the neighbourhood, it was seen as too little, too late, a desperate attempt by the administration to prove they could impose their authority. It further poisoned relations between the bureaucracy and the mayor and councillors.

Still, the impact was immediate: the vibe of the two streets changed as a healthy hierarchy of users was established and cars deferred to pedestrians and cyclists at every intersection. Not every car or truck came to a full stop, of course, but invariably, they gave the right of way to anyone crossing on foot or on bike.

The consulting engineers had to respect the Road Safety Act, but they had a more nuanced understanding of it. They appreciated that the 150 metres was a standard and not a hard-and-fast rule, and determined it could be overridden if the stop signs were placed as directly as possible in drivers' line of sight.

On Bernard, where curb extensions already existed, this was no problem. On St-Viateur, it meant sticking the stop signs about 1.5 metres out into the street from the sidewalk, protecting them with a planter and the borough undertaking to, in time, build curb extensions around them.

As our administration proposed multiplying the number of stop signs elsewhere in the borough—on streets such as Roy, Marie-Anne, Gilford and the like—this became the new standard. All things being equal, we could install them but rather than costing a thousand dollars or so for a pole, a sign and some paint, we would have to spend anywhere from $100,000 to $800,000 per intersection. This was the cost of demolishing the sidewalk at the corner, excavating it and much of the street, installing new sewers and, in many cases, modifying the geometry of the intersection to ensure proper drainage, and finally pouring the concrete for a new sidewalk with curb extension.

There were, of course, benefits to curb extensions beyond simply providing a place to stick a stop sign. They forced cars and trucks to round corners more carefully, brought the sides of a street closer (and so reduced crossing times), and prevented vehicles from parking too close to the intersection, thus improving visibility for both motorists and pedestrians. Together, these factors made the intersection exponentially safer.

Then there was the greening and beautification element. A few curb extensions had been built around the borough in the previous years. On Bernard, for instance, in an effort to calm traffic *without* installing stop signs; on Gilford at Marquette. But they had been all concrete, perhaps with a bench or garbage can as utilitarian ornamentation.

With Ferrandez as mayor, the order came that as large an area as possible be filled with earth and planted with flowering annuals and other plants and trees by the borough's horticulture division. There was resistance—the workload for the parks' department would be increased, new staff would be required. Ferrandez insisted, and when the first plans were produced with still too much concrete and not enough space for plants, he rejected them, creating friction with Isabelle Cadrin and what we referred to as "the services."

"It was really difficult to begin with," Ferrandez says. "I really wanted to have my hand on the pencil. And it took a very long time before she realized that even though I hadn't studied architecture or design, even though I didn't have a degree or certificate, I knew what I was talking about."

Selling the curb extensions to the population was also a challenge. Some of the first new stop signs installed and curb extensions built were on Villeneuve at Esplanade and Jeanne-Mance. During the 2009 campaign, Alex Norris and Ferrandez had gone door-to-door in the area and residents had complained to them of traffic racing down the street between Ave du Parc and St-Urbain. Stop signs, they agreed, were desirable. Losing parking spaces, however, was a deal breaker for some—even if the parking spaces were, for the most part, illegal given that parking within 5 metres of an intersection is forbidden province-wide.

Norris remembers discussions with residents on the street corner, some of which devolved into heated arguments. In one, he was screamed at and called a "fucking asshole." In time, however, the planted curb extensions became a borough signature and our administration's improvements to it were widely adopted in other boroughs, including some, like St-Léonard, which had virtually nothing in common with the Plateau.

Parking, as a whole, was a major flashpoint in what was portrayed as our "war on cars" and provoked the administration's first crisis. This occurred in late 2010 after the borough announced plans to boost the number of parking metres in the Plateau, and to increase their cost from $2 per hour to $3—matching the cost downtown—while at the same time eliminating hundreds of free parking spots, mostly by enforcing the prohibition of parking too close to an intersection.

The recommendations had been proposed by Guillaume Cloutier's advisory committee, which included the Plateau's merchant associations, and they initially supported the plan. They certainly had good reason to: it promised a financial windfall for them as well as about $2.5 million in much-needed new revenue for the borough. The *Sociétés de développement commerciale*, or SDCs, as the associations are known, had previously been financed by, among other things, subsidies from the borough of $150,000 or so. The new plan would see those subsidies replaced by a 30-percent share of the parking revenue generated on the commercial arteries each SDC represented—an amount which easily eclipsed the subsidies several times over.

For the SDC on Mont-Royal, the borough's biggest and most powerful, the plan would have been especially lucrative and, for a time, seemed like the continuation of charmed relations with Ferrandez. In the months after the election, its director-general Michel Depatie had met the new mayor and been reassured by the fact that his new administration had no intention of pedestrianizing Mont-Royal, even if Projet Montréal had been founded partly on the principle. Ferrandez told him he thought such an initiative would lead to parallel streets nearby, especially Gilford and Marie-Anne, becoming choked with traffic.

Depatie was also happy that the new administration was eager to allow restaurants and bars to rent the parking spots in front of their establishments for the spring and summer in order to erect terrasses on them. It was something the SDC on Mont-Royal had been requesting but hadn't had any success in selling to the borough. "He thought we would never agree to it but we immediately said yes," Ferrandez says.[21] The new parking plan promised to bring Depatie's SDC about $1 million per year to spend on events and activities, even physical infrastructure, and for a few days he sang the plan's praises in radio interviews and the like. Then his members learned its details and called him on the carpet. They didn't like the increased parking costs, which they believed would scare many of their customers away. They were also unhappy with the plan to keep transit traffic on the major arteries and reduce the number of cars using Christophe-Colomb on their way to the eastern downtown. They claimed it would prevent their clients from easily driving to the shops on the stretch of Mont-Royal between St-Denis and Papineau. An emergency general assembly of SDC members was called—all the businesses along the

---

21 "Terrasses sur chaussée" were much less popular with the borough's second biggest SDC, that of Boul. St-Laurent. There, restaurants and bars had been allowed to occupy—for free—about 2/3 of the recently enlarged sidewalk in front of their addresses and wanted to continue to do so but the administration insisted that the sidewalks were for pedestrians.

street are obliged to be part of the association—and Depatie was told to reverse his position or be fired.

He phoned Ferrandez before going public with his new stance. "He told me that he was going to oppose and would attack me publicly," Ferrandez recalls. "He said, 'That's how we do politics. You're the dominant figure so you're the one we're going to attack.'"

The merchants, who had grown used to having a direct line to not only Fotopulos's office but also Tremblay's, phoned up the mayor to urge him to bring the Plateau to heel. Tremblay duly cancelled a central city plan to delegate parking policy and revenue to the boroughs, part of an arrangement to address chronic—and justified—complaints of underfunding, especially from central boroughs.

True to Depatie's word, the merchants went after Ferrandez personally, putting up "Wanted!" posters in their windows and mobilizing their clients against him and the new administration. Their campaign was full-out and all-in and the conflict was eagerly covered, and to a large degree stoked, by the media, not just in Montreal but across the province. Ferrandez quickly became the face of so-called radical, irresponsible political action—as opposed to an example of an elected official simply implementing what he had undertaken to do during the election campaign—and the narrative of the Plateau as a rogue borough, the People's Republic of the Plateau, became entrenched.

With Tremblay's intervention, the parking conflict was resolved after a few ugly weeks of hostilities. Ultimately, there were relatively few changes to the initial plan beyond less revenue and powers for the borough. The bad blood remained, however and through the winter Ferrandez was shouted at, insulted, even spat upon and physically threatened as he went around the Plateau and elsewhere in the city. As *La Presse's* Michelle Ouimet put it, "He was called an ayatollah, a dictator, an ideologue, a reactionary."

On top of that, his girlfriend, who had recently moved in with him, was in the later stages of a difficult pregnancy which kept her bedridden. Exhausted from insomnia and stress, Ferrandez fell sick in the spring and was diagnosed with pericarditis, an inflammation of the lining of the heart, and was ordered by his doctor to take several months off. Richard Ryan, as deputy mayor, filled in, as best he could.

In the office, there was a sense of foreboding. Intensely private despite his gregariousness and *bonhomie*, no one was certain that Luc hadn't had a breakdown or that the wheels weren't coming off our experiment of getting elected on the promise of audacious change and actually delivering it.

I had long felt that an administration which actually fulfilled its electoral undertakings could be successful on that basis. That the communications strategies and triangulation that so often determined an administration's each and every decision might be superfluous if it treated the electorate as adults, effectively saying, "We were elected to do X, Y and Z, we are doing it and if you don't like it, you are free to vote against us next election." An administration with the courage of its convictions.

Luc, Alex and Richard felt similarly and it had been the defining characteristic of the administration in its earliest months. As I would tell people before the election, "Buckle your seatbelts if we're elected in the Plateau." We were emboldened by various factors. On the one hand, there was the nature of the Plateau. Not only did it have a history of being politically progressive but it also had—and still has—the lowest rates of car ownership in Canada along with the highest rates of public and active (walking, cycling etc) transit use. We felt that if we couldn't take public space away from the automobile in the Plateau, it couldn't be done anywhere.

Also, we all had the security of careers we could return to. None of us had gone into politics as a career move or expected that it would lead to anything. Very frequently—far too frequently—the overarching concern of a freshly elected politician is to be re-elected in four years' time. For many, this is the primary consideration from the day they are sworn in, one which determines almost every decision and action, and helps explain the importance accorded to "comms" in so many administrations.

Luc, Alex and I all came from "comms" backgrounds but paid little attention to it once elected. It had the potential to suck up huge amounts of time and energy and we only had four years to really get going on the epic spreadsheet of projects we had drawn up. Still, in the winter and spring of 2011, we were all wondering—to ourselves more than aloud—whether our approach had been naïve, or too headstrong Whether taking on the merchants with their accumulated power and their privileged, often daily contacts with clients—many of whom were our voters—had been foolhardy. Whether our decisive victory little more than a year earlier really had been a vote in favour of our vision or simply a rejection of the other parties.

Even before Luc went on sick leave, there had been signs of fraying. Josée Duplessis, who had never felt fully accepted by the rest of us, had insisted to Luc in the fall of 2010 that we do a sort of workplace group therapy. Her reasons were never clear, or at least never understood by the rest of us.

Certainly, there was something of a hothouse work environment. Under Fotopulos, she, her chief of staff, the political attaché and a secretary had shared a suite of offices while the six councillors had desks in another big room across the hall. When we came to power Luc decided that we would all jam into what had been Fotopulos's suite of offices. Luc had his own miniscule office, while two councillors shared the chief of staff's office and three others crammed into Fotopulos's office. Guillaume and I were put into a windowless room which previously had been home to the photocopier, the stationary cupboard and huge amounts of old files, while Christine worked at a desk in the meeting room. It was crowded, noisy and chaotic—not least of all because we had an open-door policy for citizens, and some of the nuttier ones became regular visitors—but almost invariably good-humoured, fun and productive. But Josée, it seemed, didn't think so. The absence of a secretary also irked her to no end.

We were interviewed separately by the women leading the workplace therapy and then there was a single group session at which most of us said that we didn't know why we were there. That was as far as it went beyond confirming to us that Josée didn't feel the cohesion the rest of us did.

More significantly, Guillaume Cloutier had quit at the very beginning of 2011, not long after the parking crisis had ended in an uneasy truce with the merchants. His reasons for doing so were understandable—UQAM had told him he had strung out completing his master's thesis long enough and it was time, now or never, to finish it. After that, he and his girlfriend, still in their mid-twenties, planned to travel the world. There was nonetheless an inkling that he was perhaps jumping the ship before it went down. He thought so too. "At the time I said to myself, 'It's clear we're not going anywhere,'" Cloutier says a decade later. "I said to myself, 'I don't think we'll get re-elected because there is too much moaning and resistance.'"

The prospect didn't distress him though. Having come out of the contestatory student movement, he says he was simply happy to see a radical politician like Ferrandez push the envelope. "It was 'Fuck you MTQ, fuck you Péladeau, fuck you all that.' Yes, it created controversy, but I didn't mind it. It felt good."

Even if the administration didn't get re-elected, he rationalized, we would have made a few changes, got a few things accomplished, and shown that politics could be done differently.

Chapter 16

THE SAILING DIDN'T GET SMOOTHER in the spring of 2011 when the traffic changes to Ave Laurier and Christophe-Colomb were finally implemented. The public had been well-warned in advance; the announcement had been made almost a year earlier. Still, until the one-way signs were installed and people were forced to actually change their driving habits, it was just theoretical.

Then, all of a sudden, on the morning of May 16th, it became a reality. We found ourselves in the midst of another crisis. Again, it was covered exhaustively by the media, which thrived not just on conflict but also on the directness and colourful quotes provided by Ferrandez.

We had been slow to fully appreciate why much of the media felt so strongly about the traffic changes: both the Radio-Canada building and TVA were in the eastern downtown and many journalists lived in Ahuntsic or Rosemont and used Christophe-Colomb to get to work. One grumpy Radio Canada reporter wrote an opinion piece for *La Presse* portraying Ferrandez as the henchman of gentrification, since he was pushing traffic off the residential streets and onto the arteries. If you lived anywhere in the Plateau, he said, part of your lot in life was to have the residents of the northern boroughs drive down your street on a daily basis. "This case is not fundamentally different from the one in which the Town of Mount Royal fenced off its territory in the 1960s to keep Montrealers out," he wrote. "A ghetto for the rich."

Still, the inconveniences caused to the journalists from Radio-Canada and TVA didn't explain why newspapers in Quebec City, Chicoutimi and Sherbrooke devoted as many column inches as they did to the changes in street direction in the Plateau or as they had to its parking meter prices. Rather, the coverage suggested a culture war between an administration intent on placing constraints on automobile access and a population for whom any constraints constituted an attack on their freedom and way of life.

Traffic engineers had told us that it would take about six months for people to fully adjust to the changes, to develop new patterns, and for us to be able to determine how well the project had succeeded. Until then, we knew we could anticipate congestion on Laurier in front of the park, not to mention a lot of confusion and anger among motorists. We also knew that the public question period before the monthly borough council sessions would be dominated by opponents. There was nothing we could do about that.

Still, the immediate outcry was such that two weeks after the changes were implemented, we decided to hold a public meeting to explain the logic behind them and plead for patience. We initially planned to hold the gathering in a community hall in the basement of the St-Stanislas-de-Kostka church but it soon became clear that the hall would not be large enough and that we would need to use the church itself. With the pews overflowing with more people than the church had probably seen in a generation, the meeting went off the rails as soon as it started.

The sound echoed around the big church and barely anything Ferrandez said was comprehensible. Not that he was allowed to say much between all the booing, the shouting and swearing and at least one man who screamed, "Retournes en Espagne!"—"Go back to Spain!"

When Luc favourably invoked Joseph-Marie Savignac, a local politician of the 1930s, 40s and 50s who, at the dawn of the automobile era, had saved Parc Laurier by keeping the central city from running Christophe-Colomb through it in order to facilitate fluidity, his son, by then quite elderly, rushed the stage. He had misunderstood what Ferrandez was saying and, thinking he was insulting his father's memory, wanted to teach Luc a lesson. A couple of us had to step in between the old man and Luc.

The meeting ended in disarray soon after, happily without any real violence and without Luc backing off on the traffic-calming plan.

If the static we were receiving had only been coming from our adversaries and car owners, on the Plateau and off, it wouldn't have been so bad. But Ferrandez was catching almost as much flak from colleagues within Projet Montréal and its supporters who felt that our administration's approach was ruining the party's chances for future electoral success. Among Luc's most virulent critics within caucus was François Limoges. What Limoges calls his "pure admiration" for Ferrandez the candidate, born from his inspirational *partys de trottoir*, dissipated quickly with Ferrandez the mayor and his shock-and-confrontation approach to implementing projects. "There was a sense that Luc could damage the rest of Projet Montréal, " Limoges says. "Luc was having fun provoking people... and the media only had eyes for him."

Adding to the problem was the fact that Ferrandez frequently didn't attend caucus meetings downtown with Bergeron and the Projet councillors from outside the Plateau, or even city council sessions. If this could be explained by Ferrandez working tirelessly on borough matters—he was often in the office until 9 or 10 PM—it was lost on Limoges and others. "What I found hard, and I'm not the only one, was Luc's progressive loss of interest in the party," Limoges says. "He was taking risks that were quite good gambits for the Plateau but that could do lasting damage to Projet Montréal. I would have liked for him to come and put it on the table and say, 'Okay, we'll talk.' But that discussion never happened."

It was at the caucus meetings where Luc's chair was empty that the criticism of him and the Plateau's approach was the most venomous. "There was a love-hate approach to Luc and the Plateau," says Richard Ryan. "When Luc was there, they loved him, when he spoke. But they were always criticizing him when he wasn't there."

Émilie Thuillier was fast and free with her criticism of Ferrandez when he wasn't there, Ryan remembers. For her part, Thuillier acknowledges that Ferrandez became Projet Montréal's scapegoat both for the population at large, the media, and within caucus. "We had to constantly tell people that if we were elected in Ahuntsic we wouldn't do everything like in the Plateau because Ahuntsic is not the Plateau." It prompted her, she says, to emphasize to voters that she was more than just a representative of Projet Montréal. "I was often just Émilie. People didn't even know what party I was in."

One person who always stood up for Ferrandez and never questioned his approach of bold action was the person most frequently called upon to rein him in: Richard Bergeron. The merchants and Louise Harel had appealed to Bergeron to intervene during the parking crisis while car-owners, Plateau residents and caucus members had urged him to bigfoot Luc on any number of issues, from snow removal and traffic calming to zoning changes. Bergeron always refused, saying that even if he was leader of the party, Ferrandez was mayor of the Plateau and as such, he deferred to him.

Given their differences—and what many saw as a quiet competition between the two men—Bergeron's steadfast support for Ferrandez surprised many in caucus. On some questions, it was based on conviction—"on snow removal Richard would have been happy to go even further than Luc," says Joël Simard-Menard—and, on others, on political expedience. Bergeron saw that often the anger was directed at Luc himself, not Projet Montréal, so steering clear of it meant exposing himself to minimal collateral damage. "The cameras didn't go and seek him out," says Ferrandez. "They came to see me and that was perfectly fine by him."

Having first been elected in the district of De Lorimier, which began at Christophe-Colomb, Bergeron came under pressure to oppose the change in direction of the block between St-Joseph and Laurier. Not least of all, this came from Josée Duplessis and Carl Boileau, who were skittish from the hostile reaction to the move. Bergeron, however, backed up Ferrandez unequivocally, leading to an explicit entente between the two men. "People were urging me to get involved in downtown, even to push Richard out," says Ferrandez. "The deal I had with him was, 'I stay out of your business and you stay out of mine.' And we both kept to that agreement."

Bergeron also had real admiration for Ferrandez's managerial skills. Having witnessed the dysfunctional relations in the Plateau bureaucracy under Helen Fotopulos, not to mention the poisonous ones between bureaucrats and the elected, Bergeron was all the more impressed by the way Ferrandez had taken charge of the borough as mayor. "He was extraordinary as mayor of the Plateau," he says.

Which contributed to Bergeron's surprise when, sometime in the spring of 2011, Luc invited him out for lunch and told him he had had enough. "Luc was fed up. His wife had just given birth. She was walking around with the baby carriage and getting insulted by people on the street," Bergeron recalls. "He says to me, 'Richard, I can't take it anymore. I'm quitting.' No, no, no, Luc. You're not quitting, damn it!"

Bergeron says Ferrandez proposed that he take over running the Plateau. "His plan was that he would transfer the borough mayoralty to me. I said, 'Woah, Luc! That's not how it works! You are elected by universal suffrage. You don't hand over your job to whomever you want. We'd have to go to a by-election and we'd be sure to lose."

Once Ferrandez understood that his quitting would likely result in Projet Montréal losing the mayoralty of the Plateau, he backed off the idea, Bergeron remembers. He says he then told Ferrandez that he had set the tone with his aggressiveness and it was his responsibility to calm things down.

A decade later Ferrandez is speechless when asked about the episode. "Hein!?" he answers. Then, after a long pause, adds, "I have absolutely no memory of that. None whatsoever. Is it a blind spot for me? It would be a pretty big thing to forget."

In many ways it seems unlikely. No Plateau councillors or staff at the time had the slightest suspicion Luc was considering quitting and, even if he always played his cards close to his chest, with his closest collaborators as much as the man in the street, it seems almost inconceivable that he would not have known that his resignation would have prompted a by-election.

There was, however, a third person present who remembers it as clear as day: Joël Simard-Menard, Bergeron's chief of staff. "I understand why Luc has forgotten about it. It was a five-minute discussion. Richard dismissed it straight away. It wasn't a discussion that went on for days and days."

The three men were walking on St-Denis, he says, after a visit to see the new traffic-calming measures. "Luc was tired and burned out and that was why he wanted to quit. But it was also to put Richard in the middle of the chessboard. Luc's idea was, 'Richard, you need more visibility, you need to show that you can manage and lead, and you can bring another leadership style.'"

The discussion ended, never to resume, once Ferrandez understood that a by-election would be inevitable unless he was to resign less than a year before the next general election, which was still two and a half years off.

Spring and early summer in Montreal is always accompanied by a sense of relief. We've survived another winter; we've weathered the storm once again. If the traffic-calming crisis delayed the arrival of that sentiment to our offices by a few weeks in 2011, by the second week of June it was unquestionably in the air with our first unanimously popular initiative, the re-opening of the restaurant in Parc Lafontaine.

In Montreal, boroughs are generally in charge of parks but when it comes to "les grands parcs"—Mont-Royal, Angrignon, Maisonneuve, Bois-de-Liesse, Jarry, Jean-Drapeau and about a dozen others, including Parc Lafontaine—their responsibility only extends to maintenance. Any planning or modifications are decided by the central city.

So when Ferrandez and Plateau director Isabelle Cadrin informed the city that we were planning on reopening the restaurant again, they were essentially told, 'Back off, it's our jurisdiction.' No matter that the borough was willing to pay for the renovations and negotiate with the unions to allow a private, non-profit operator to run it. It was a question of bureaucratic authority. Anyway, they said, they had evaluated the cost of renovating the building and it would be about $7 million, much more than the borough could afford.

After several difficult meetings and some political pressure, however, Ferrandez was able to convince the central city that the work planned was maintenance, not capital investment. "Finally they agreed to it and after that they even went so far as to put money in on a recurring basis."

Despite the borough's still catastrophic financial situation, Cadrin was able to find $600,000 for a bare-bones refreshening of the building. "She was wise and cagey and wasn't going to offer up this money until she was sure it would be spent on a project that she agreed was a good one," says Christine Gosselin.

In charge of the project on the political side, Gosselin went and recruited a sweet couple who at the time were running a café-restaurant in a public building in Parc de la Visitation to set up and run a similar venture in Parc Lafontaine.

By early June, *Espace Lafontaine*, as it was known, was ready to re-open and the project quickly became the administration's first unequivocally popular, unqualified success. The borough imposed a few rules to ensure the restaurant remained accessible—the menu couldn't be too expensive and people were not obliged to order anything to sit at a table—and it quickly became a destination, whether as a place for a relaxed and reasonable lunch or to hold an event in a big, bright and airy room in the middle of a beautiful park.

As a project, the reopening of the restaurant was particularly close to Ferrandez's heart[22]—in a way it hearkened back to his dream of making Montreal, or at least the Plateau, a bit more like Paris, with more attention and love paid to its public spaces—and if he continued to have doubts about remaining mayor, its success likely reinforced his determination to stick with it.

In the following weeks and months, there were a multitude of other initiatives addressing what Ferrandez referred to as "*le désamour*"—loss of love—for public space which had occurred in Quebec, elsewhere in North America and even beyond. As Ferrandez saw it, this was a by-product of the neoliberalism of the preceding decades and, with its celebration of the private and the neglect of the public, contributed to a dangerous social atomization.

"You go to anyone's yard in Brossard or Candiac—you go to my brother's place—it's a little paradise! It's perfectly taken care of," he said in the fall of 2011. "Then you go to the local park, it's like a potato field! It's not normal. Public space is what we have in common. How

---

22 For a micro-manager like Ferrandez it was, in some respects, probably too close to his heart. He, Christine Gosselin and other councillors ate regularly at the restaurant and felt little compunction letting the managers know where they felt the restaurant was falling short.

is it that what we have in common deteriorates so much and then what we have in private is so impeccable?"

The initiatives were an "accumulation of small gestures, street corner by street corner, street by street, alley by alley, that will keep the Plateau beautiful" and, as their impact was felt, gave Ferrandez and the rest of us hope that perhaps our little revolution would succeed. Many of the initiatives were very nuts and bolts, requiring little more than a bit of attention and money. These included new park benches and picnic tables, or new, better play structures for children in neighbourhood parks. The fact that they had often gone years without being fixed or replaced was, as often as not, simply a question of neglect and indifference and a business-as-usual approach to running the borough. With the new administration, however, there was a team of councillors and staff who not only knew the borough intimately but were constantly riding up and down its streets and alleyways and visiting its parks, taking notes and transmitting them to *les services*.

There were other initiatives which required a re-organization of the way the borough did things. In 2010, Ferrandez had insisted on what we called the *bac au sac*—replacing the heavy green recycling bins with transparent plastic bags. It was a controversial move because it forced people to purchase the bags and created more waste. The benefits, however, were numerous: it made it easier for people living in upper-storey units to get their recycling out on the sidewalk, and so increased participation; it reduced the amount of paper and plastic that fell or was blown onto the streets; and it meant that the borough Blue-collar crews could collect the recycling much more quickly and so had time for other tasks, including… picking up litter. It also gave them time to more frequently empty the trash cans on street corners and in parks, the number of which the administration substantially increased, and devote more energy to dealing with the *dépôts sauvages*—the dumping of garbage, whenever, wherever. This was particularly bad at alleyway entrances and in the Milton-Parc/McGill Ghetto neighbourhood. Ferrandez was not alone in wondering why so many students working on advanced degrees in specialized subjects had such difficulty remembering when to put out their garbage.

The tidiness campaign went hand in hand with a greening and

beautification campaign. This wasn't limited to curb extensions, which, given their prohibitive cost, could only be built at perhaps a dozen intersections every year. There was also the campaign to enlarge all the tree squares in the borough which, by the end of the summer of 2011, meant that 1,000 had been increased in size, often substantially. Again, there were multiple benefits to the initiative: more soil and less concrete around the base of the trees lining the borough's streets meant more percolation of rainwater down to the roots of the trees so less watering required by city crews during dry spells. It also reduced the amount of run-off into the storm sewers and thus the risk of overloading the filtration and treatment infrastructure. Finally, it provided space for more flowers and plants.

This "local greening," as Ferrandez called it, was based on a simple principle, he said: "to convey to the pedestrian that he is king." Other aspects of it were directed more towards the borough's children and young families. The alleyways of the Plateau had long been one of its neglected charms. Originally conceived as utilitarian corridors to provide a rear access to the attached multiplexes of the neighbourhood, they had also always served as informal play spaces for generations of Plateau kids, the first outdoor public area into which many young children were allowed to venture alone. As car culture took hold, the alleys became less safe, as residents converted backyards into parking spots or drivers used them as shortcuts.

In the 1980s the city had initiated a short-lived—and expensive—program to enhance various alleys around the Plateau by installing lamp standards and the like but little had been done to limit car use in them. Our plan was both more modest and more ambitious.

To begin with, we moved to block entrances to any alleyways that were routinely used for transit or shortcuts.[23] The public works department was not enthusiastic about this—it meant their access to the alleys would be made more complicated too—but eventually they came around. Then we made the greening of alleyways the main mandate of the borough's Éco-Quartier, which previously had been

---

23 Using an alley for transit or as a shortcut is illegal but it is a very difficult infraction to enforce.

responsible for composting initiatives, flower giveaways and various public education campaigns.

As with the curb extensions, the *ruelles vertes*—green alleys—were slow to get going, but soon became hugely popular, with residents of blocks all over the borough asking that their alley be greened next spring or summer. Unlike the previous city initiative, which involved costly excavation, the laying of power lines and installation of street lamps, greening an alley was relatively inexpensive, especially considering much of the labour was expected to be provided by the residents. In this way, the program was quickly providing a real bang for its buck with as many as a dozen alleys transformed each summer for rarely more than $400,000 or $500,000.

Other public space initiatives were simply a question of modernizing some city facilities. In a little-visited corner of Parc Laurier there was a neglected shuffleboard court as well as horseshoes lawn, neither of which seemed to have been used since the 1970s. We had the borough services remove them and, in their stead, install a pétanque square, some modern exercise equipment, and what were then Montreal's first public outdoor ping-pong tables.

The ping-pong table idea came from a cousin of mine living in Bucharest, who was a keen player of racquet sports. He used to walk across a sketchy park on the way to and from work and was sometimes worried that he might get mugged by street kids who hung out there. When a ping-pong table appeared, however, it became their common ground, as it were, and he soon found himself playing with them, the distrust and apprehension dissipating as a little bit of community was created. If we could do the same in Parc Laurier it would be a step toward one of our fundamental goals, creating a richer, stronger *milieu de vie,* a local environment. As Luc put it in 2011, "You need to run into people who are not of your nationality, who are not of your social level. All these people, this social mix, have to cross paths every day. In the streets, in the parks, on the bicycle paths, in the schoolyards, on the church steps. This is where the great fabric of the city is made."

As with *Espace Lafontaine*, the success of these small initiatives was evident in how the population of the Plateau embraced them, and this gave us hope that perhaps all was not lost for our administration, that perhaps we would actually be re-elected. That our little revolution might even spread beyond the borders of the borough.

Chapter 17

Beyond the borders of the borough, members of Projet Montréal saw things very differently. Future electoral success, it was generally felt, would come from moving towards the middle, and what Ferrandez and his gang were doing in the Plateau wasn't exactly helping in that regard.

An early flare-up came just months after the 2009 election when Joe Magri, the new mayor of Rivière-des-Prairies–Pointe-aux-Trembles (RDP-PAT), resigned for health reasons. The Projet candidate a few months earlier had been a fun, free-spirited woman by the name of Thérèse Deschambault whose life was the stuff of a Harlequin Romance. As a young woman, she had been a Carmelite then a Grey Nun before quitting to start a family. Then, after splitting with her husband and while raising two children on her own, she became a flight attendant, among a multitude of other pastimes, which included painting and swinging. Even if she was little more than a *pôteau*, Deschambault had received almost 20 percent of the vote, a very respectable score for a suburban borough. She wasn't about to run for us again, however: she was over 80 years old and uninterested in a political career.

Projet Montréal's chances in RDP-PAT were not much better six months later, but the party was determined to make a serious run at winning. After all, by-elections tend to be unpredictable at the best of times with the party in power usually faring poorly. So when Martin Dumont, a former staffer in the offices of federal Conservative ministers who had also worked for Union Montréal approached Projet Montréal to be its candidate, Bergeron and others were very interested. He seemed to be a political pro and his offering to run for us suggested that the party was developing mainstream acceptance and credibility. The fact that Union Montréal had turned Dumont down when he proposed running for them didn't concern Bergeron much: that kind of thing happened all the time.

Since there was no ALA in RDP-PAT, it came down to the *conseil de direction* to approve his candidacy, something it did in an 8 to 4 vote. But however solid the support for Dumont's candidacy, those who opposed it weren't about to rally to the decision. Alex Norris, who was the caucus representative on the CD resigned on the spot, storming out of the meeting with Joël Simard-Menard on his heels pleading with him to reconsider.

When Alex reported the events of the meeting to the team back in the Plateau, the rest of the office—except for Josée Duplessis—agreed with his opposition and saw the *conseil de direction*'s support for Dumont's candidacy as a betrayal of the party's essence. We wanted candidates who believed in Projet's vision and values, not political opportunists looking for a vehicle. Especially not if they were former Harper Tories.

Emails flew back and forth and long phone discussions were held with the message to the Plateau essentially being the same: mind your own affairs. By this time, however, the Plateau ALA had been activated and the outcry from the party's strongest base of support was growing impossible to ignore. An emergency meeting was called that evening to discuss the issue at the party's new headquarters on Rue Notre-Dame Ouest, near St-Henri metro station.

The storefront location had been chosen because the rent was reasonable and it was felt that the party had good potential for growth in the boroughs around there—not just Sud-Ouest but also Verdun, Lachine, CDN-NDG, perhaps even LaSalle. A large delegation from the Plateau showed up—councillors, staffers and members of the ALA, by bike and by metro—to meet a clearly grumpy Richard Bergeron and several others.

The meeting was tense and acrimonious, with Bergeron and others questioning the Plateau delegation's presumptuousness in trying to overturn a decision made by a duly elected members of the party. The Plateau's position was less legalistic. Dumont's candidacy, we argued, would paint Projet as a party just like the others, interested in power for power's sake. And one way or another, we continued, Dumont didn't have a chance of winning, so why risk alienating many of our most articulate, fervent and long-time supporters by going with him?

Two of those supporters were present and pressed the case vigorously: Nimâ Machouf, who had been Bergeron's *co-listière* just a few months earlier, and Bruno Dubuc, the neurologist-filmmaker who had made *La fin de néandertal*. Alex Norris had chosen to stay away from the meeting for fear of triggering Bergeron but Christine Gosselin filled his shoes and let loose on the leader, earning his enduring enmity.

Luc Ferrandez was more measured about his disagreement. He said that he opposed Dumont as a choice, but would support Bergeron if he didn't change his mind. The party's new director-general at the time, Carole Dupuis, who had been the candidate for mayor of CDN-NDG the previous November, also questioned the idea's wisdom diplomatically. Recruiting someone who had recently worked in Harper's PMO and for two of his ministers, she said, "might be taking electoral pragmatism a step too far."

The meeting ended with an awkward compromise. Dumont would be told to have his network in RDP-PAT set up a Projet Montréal ALA in the borough. Then, once constituted, it could choose him as its candidate and he could run for the party.

The idea was put to him and soon enough he declined. "He reasoned that he would remain the same persona non grata with or without the process, so he threw in the towel," says Patrick Cigana, who was on the CD at the time. In his stead, the party recruited Colette Paul, who had been a Vision Montréal councillor but at least hadn't worked for Stephen Harper. She finished with 17.5 percent of the vote in an election which saw future Coalition Action Québec minister Chantal Rouleau elected to public office for the first time.

The episode deepened the distrust between Projet's version of *les purs et durs*, represented by Plateau hardliners, and the rest of the party. For many, Projet Montréal was a rare opportunity which allowed Montrealers of all stripes—*indépendentiste* or federalist, anglo, franco or other, leftist, centrist or even a bit right-wing—to embark on a shared political cause, which also happened to be, in the words of Christine Gosselin, "part of an international movement to put cities at the forefront of human development." And while the Plateau saw the Dumont affair as a short-sighted selling-out of Projet's integrity, many in the rest of the party regarded the Plateau's actions as evidence that it was out of touch with the reality in the rest of Montreal. "These guys want to tell us who to run or not to run in RDP-PAT but they couldn't even find their way there," Richard Bergeron is said to have complained.

There was also the impression that the Projet team in the Plateau had been taken over by leftist Québec Solidaire (QS). Certainly, there was evidence for such an impression, above and beyond Nimâ Machouf's outspokenness at that tense meeting held at the party's headquarters. QS had supplied the Plateau campaign with many volunteers as well as supporter lists during the 2009 campaign and ALA meetings were often held in Nimâ and Amir Khadir's warm and spacious living room in their home on Rue St-Hubert.

The Plateau team, however, was conscious that being closely identified with QS wouldn't serve anyone's purpose, in the borough or out. "Amir had to learn that we weren't Québec Solidaire's municipal farm team," remembers Richard Ryan, who helped formed the connective tissue between the two parties. Establishing an appropriate relationship and proximity would take time.

Ultimately, everyone in the party was grateful Martin Dumont didn't end up running for Projet Montréal. In October of 2012 he appeared before the Charbonneau Commission looking into corruption in the construction industry and illegal political financing connected with it and made a series of sensational allegations dating from his time working for Union Montreal between 2004 and 2007.

Among other things, he testified about seeing a Union safe so overflowing with cash that its door couldn't close, about receptionists obliged to count out $850,000 in cash bill by bill, about receiving death threats from construction bosses and about Mayor Gérald Tremblay being present at a meeting where a system of double-bookkeeping was discussed.

Tremblay resigned less than a week after the testimony and Dumont's allegations were seen by many as the last straw. The problem was that Dumont soon acknowledged that some of his testimony was entirely false and when he was called back to account for his lies and inconsistencies, he was disowned by all sides.

The debacle had a major impact on the Commission's credibility and cast an enduring shadow over its work. "The Commission was taken for a ride," Michèle Ouimet of La Presse wrote. "Why didn't [the investigators] check his statements before letting him spill his guts on live TV in front of thousands of viewers? ... There is no doubt that the Commission screwed up."

Projet Montréal's effort to move to the middle didn't just show itself in events and debates. It manifested in new members and few embodied this better than Jimmy Zoubris. Jimmy's family owned a stationary store on Ave du Parc and behind the cash or in the back office, he was a King-of-Kensington figure, a self-appointed unelected mayor for Mile-End and Outremont. He seemed to know everyone: anglo hipsters, francophone intellectuals, the Hasidic community and, of course, any Greeks who remained in the area.

Jimmy might have grown up in Laval and lived there still—he'd been elected as a Laval school commissioner at 19 and went on to serve three mandates—but if there was a local *tête de reseau* it was him. He had worked on campaigns at all levels (municipal, provincial and federal) for candidates of all stripes (MCM, Quebec Liberals, federal Liberals and Conservative) as often as not because they were of Greek origin. But not long after the 2005 election he had begun to lose faith in Gérald Tremblay and Helen Fotopulos. "For them it was more about the photo op than actually getting stuff done," he says. "I felt that Tremblay wasn't delivering so I backed away. Then the whole Park Avenue thing came up."

The "Park Avenue thing" was Tremblay's 2007 proposal to rename the street after former Quebec premier Robert Bourassa. As the most media-savvy, not to mention gregarious, small businessman on the street, Jimmy became the go-to representative for opponents of the initiative. His opposition made his split with Union permanent.

I knew Jimmy because I bought pens and notebooks at his store, and I would often shoot the breeze with him about neighbourhood issues or magazine articles I was working on. We didn't talk much about Ave du Parc's renaming—I never really understood why the passions had run so high over it[24]—but through the controversy I had come to appreciate that Jimmy was a powerbroker in the neighbourhood. So, when in the summer of 2009 it was decided that Alex Norris would be the Projet Montréal candidate in Mile-End, the first person I took him to meet was Jimmy.

I didn't know it at the time, but a few years earlier Jimmy and a couple of other opponents to the Ave du Parc name-change had met with Richard Bergeron with an eye to some sort of political alliance. It hadn't gone well. "It was the first time we had met with people so different from us," remembers Émilie Thuillier, who accompanied Bergeron to the meeting at a Parc Ave restaurant, where every ounce of Zoubris's substantial frame exuded political fixer. "Until then, Projet Montréal was an idealistic party, with lots of intellectuals but pretty much no one who knew anything about politics. It was a culture shock."

The meeting with me and Alex Norris at a café up the street from his store went better. I wasn't after his endorsement for Alex or Projet or any sort of benediction—that was too much to expect from a small businessman who no one had ever seen on a bus or a bike. Rather, I wanted to show him that the area's Projet Montréal candidate was a smart, reasonable guy with good ideas for the neighbourhood. Not someone to go to war against, ideally.

Jimmy seemed impressed with Alex and encouraged to hear that Richard Ryan, who he knew from the neighbourhood, was also on the ticket. He had also warmed to Bergeron, after seeing him in

---

24 As a reporter at the National Assembly during from 1989 to 1993 I had developed a grudging appreciation for Bourassa and his political dexterity. I just always thought Boul. St-Joseph would have been a much better choice of street to rename in his honour given that it connected his childhood neighbourhood in the eastern Plateau with his home of later life in Outremont. It also ran pretty much to the Olympic Stadium, which he might have preferred to forget.

action on various occasions at borough council. "I found him interesting in a quirky way," Zoubris says. "What I always liked about Richard Bergeron was that he didn't just oppose, but always opposed with an idea. He always proposed something else. It wasn't just classic opposition of 'You say white, so I say black.'"

Soon enough, Jimmy was not only urging everyone in the neighbourhood to vote for Projet Montréal but organizing a mid-campaign fundraiser for the party among the merchants of Ave du Parc. It took place in a hall above the Rhodos Bay restaurant and although it was far from the best attended of Projet Montréal fundraisers—there was an early season Canadiens game that night and some of the merchants opted to go to that instead—the party had never seen anything like the cheques it brought in. Instead of donations of $10, $20, or $50, people were giving $250, $500, even $1000. In total, about $8,000 was donated to the party. That evening Richard Bergeron and Joël Simard-Menard fell in love with Jimmy.

While his business was based in the Plateau, Zoubris didn't fit in with the team in the borough. He was wary of our parking and traffic calming measures and thought Ferrandez's anything-but-conciliatory approach was political craziness. Culturally too, he came from another world. He got around by Saab, not bus or bike; he watched (and coached) American football and hockey, rather than going hiking or cross-country skiing; the bars he went to were on Crescent or Bishop Street, not micro-brasseries on Clark or Mont-Royal.

But if this meant he didn't fit in with what was called, both within and without the party, "le clique du Plateau," it made him that much more interesting to Bergeron and others who were intent on expanding the base and making it a bigger-tent party.

"Jimmy was a sort of a canary-in-the-coal mine," Simard-Menard says. He was someone whose reactions provided valuable feedback on how to party was perceived. Because of his contact with the many people who frequented his store, merchants, and those he encountered at bars downtown, he spoke for more than just himself. Even if Jimmy wasn't considered *one of us* in the Plateau, he was appreciated because he was a friendly, generous guy with no pretensions. He and time and respect for everyone. In this way, he became, for a while, one of the most popular people in the party, along with Patrick Cigana, Craig Sauvé and Andréanne Leclerc-Marceau.

The same can't be said for another new face around Projet Montréal during the 2009 to 2013 mandate who worked to give the party a more mainstream image. Joël Simard-Menard had met Guillaume Lavoie while at Cégep in Jonquière. "I knew him as a young Péquiste but he was more Conservative than anything else."

When Simard-Menard was approached to work for Projet Montréal halfway through the 2009 campaign, it was Guillaume Lavoie to whom he turned for advice. "He was my best friend so I asked him, what he thought. He followed municipal politics more than I did. He said it's a party with a future." Conservative or not, Lavoie apparently thought highly enough of Projet Montréal to have voted for the party in 2005, before many of us knew anything about it.

Lavoie, who billed himself as a commentator on international affairs and a public policy analyst, was recruited by Simard-Menard as a facilitator at the first "Lac à l'Épaule" organized by the party, a retreat which took place over a weekend in August 2010 at Cap St-Jacques. About 50 party members were invited—the councillors, staff from Bergeron's office and in the Plateau, employees at the party office on Notre-Dame Ouest, as well as members of the Comité de direction—and that was where most of us first spent any real time with Lavoie.

Initial impressions weren't at all favourable. He struck many as utterly out-of-step with a party which, above all, saw itself as intellectually honest, unpretentious and intent on doing things differently than other parties. There was an overly scrubbed, salesman aspect to him and as he lectured us about Projet Montréal and politics in general, it rubbed us the wrong way. "Everyone in politics is opportunistic in some way," says Richard Ryan. But Lavoie was "opportunist in the bad sense, in the *arriviste* sense. He was very full of himself, very sure of himself, never really listening to people who had other kinds of experience."

Arriviste is also the term Guillaume Cloutier uses to describe Lavoie, dating back to 2004. The two had crossed paths in student politics when both were involved in the *Féderation étudiante universitaire du Québec* for which Lavoie served as vice-president for international affairs. Cloutier remembered the photo Lavoie had posted on the federation website which showed him with an American presidential campaign poster and the caption "Kerry-Lavoie". "Lavoie for VP!" laughs Cloutier.

Lavoie's fascination with American politics manifested itself in another way: when he spoke English, he had a strange Texan drawl as if he had spent too much time studying the speeches of Lyndon Johnson. It was a superficial thing, but it rankled me.

A few months after the "Lac à l'Épaule," as part of a strategic planning process, the party gave Lavoie a contract to do a perception survey on how Projet Montréal was seen by a few dozen opinion makers in Montreal. That study was followed up by similar ones on how people within the party—members of caucus, staff and members—perceived it themselves.

The studies were interesting, if predictable, although it was never clear what purpose they served. They did, however, have the result of bringing Lavoie closer into the orbit of the party and injecting a fresh approach to politics. "He seemed to possess a different analytical capacity," says Richard Bergeron. He knew Lavoie's proximity would make some unhappy—Alex Norris and Craig Sauvé specifically—but it was part of an explicit aim to appeal to a broader swath of Montrealers, for the party to be "representative of all currents. I was pretty fed up with just having Québec Solidaires and the Péquistes."

Lavoie wasn't the only person Simard-Menard brought in to diversify Bergeron's team. He had also hired Catherine Maurice, who had been working for various ministers in Jean Charest's government. to be Bergeron's press attaché. Her Liberal bona fides, he reasoned, would counter-balance and complement his own PQ associations while providing some connection to the party in power in Quebec City.

Despite all the political and borough-level differences, the cohesion of the Projet caucus didn't suffer much at City Hall. Rather, it was boosted by a variety of factors. The most obvious was that its members were almost all new to the game and energized by the challenge of having to learn the ropes together. There was none of the fatigue obvious in the Union or Vision caucuses, where councillors were frequently on their third, fourth or fifth mandate; with the exception of Pierre Gagnier and Pierre Mainville, they were all keeners, imbued with a sense of mission. There was also the fact that Projet Montréal was the *second* opposition and had to work all the harder just to get noticed.

"The role of an opposition is often one of disruption and challenging the narrative of the administration. It was a role that some of us took to with considerable professional pleasure," remembers Alex Norris. "There was a rivalry with Vision Montreal to become the alternative to Union Montreal."

During their first year in council, the Projet Montréal councillors were also faced with a strange incoherence: their party's founder and leader, whom they had caucused with hours earlier, now sat opposite them as part of Tremblay's executive committee. On the one hand, it forced more of the team into the spotlight to pick up the slack which normally would have been borne by the leader of the party. Norris, Thuillier, Limoges, and Gadoury were especially active in this regard.

Bergeron's presence on the executive committee provided other opportunities for the Projet Montréal caucus. Executive committee proceedings in City Hall's Salle Peter McGill are in theory confidential but Bergeron barely paid lip service to that rule. The meetings took place on Wednesday mornings; 48 hours later Bergeron could usually be relied upon to be spill the beans on what took place—the discussions, the dissension—at the Friday morning Projet Montréal caucus. "The fact that he was on the executive committee gave us insights into the administration's thinking and strategy and gave us something of an upper hand at question period," Norris says. "It allowed us to outshine the official opposition and become more noticed. This meant we'd receive more news coverage even though we were the second opposition."

Émilie Thuillier thinks that in making a place for Bergeron on his executive committee, Tremblay had a hidden agenda beyond tapping his urbanism expertise and intellectual energy. "I think Tremblay thought that by taking Richard with him he would kill Projet Montréal," she says.

Bergeron, however, says that Tremblay had long made it clear that he valued the Projet Montréal leader's input on different dossiers.

During the 2005 to 2009 mandate, Tremblay would frequently solicit his advice on various projects, he says, including the centrepiece initiative—an entertainment district called Quartier des Spectacles. Bergeron says he helped convince Tremblay that getting rid of street parking in much of the area would not be disastrous and that the upheaval and inconvenience caused by the transformation of the area would be small price to pay. "The transformation of the city requires sacrifice but it is worth it," he says he told Tremblay and the mayor soon adopted the mantra himself.

Once officially on the executive committee in the next mandate, Bergeron says Tremblay continued to solicit his advice on a wide variety of dossiers. "Tremblay is an intellectual—he likes ideas. He likes a well-made presentation. He likes a well-turned argument. So, I gave my opinion on everything. And we got along well together."

Bergeron dismisses the other members of the executive committee with typical disdain. "Grovelling of the first order. No one would say a thing. When you don't have a backbone, it's easy to not get in trouble," Bergeron laughs. "I was having fun. I knew I was making trouble and I liked it. The rest, they were a gang of sheep."

However high Tremblay's esteem for him might have been, Bergeron failed in pushing through the main dossier he was handed. In the weeks after the 2009 election the Projet leader had convinced Tremblay that the provincial government's plan to rebuild the crumbling Turcot Interchange in a similar manner would be a huge lost opportunity for the city if allowed to proceed. He said the labyrinth of highways and on and off ramps that dominated so much of the Sud-Ouest borough could be built more cheaply and in a far more compact way.

Tremblay bought into the idea and told Bergeron to come up with a counter-proposal. Over the Christmas holidays and throughout the winter of 2010, Bergeron worked intensively with city professionals from the urbanism and transport departments on a new plan. In late April Tremblay and Bergeron unveiled the city's alternative. The new plan was a big roundabout in the sky, similar to interchanges built in Chicago and Shanghai. It would save 160 houses slated for demolition in the province's plan and it wouldn't divide the borough aggressively. Best of all, however, it would free up enough land for a whole new community to be built at the foot of the Falaise St-Jacques, with 8,000 new residences providing homes for 15,000 people.

The new development would "justify any additional costs in terms of tax revenue alone, but also in terms of quality of life," said Tremblay, who Bergeron describes as being "proud as a peacock" at the news conference.

The plan generated a rare consensus at City Hall. After weeks of raising doubts about the proposal, Louise Harel changed her tune entirely: "Now that the proposal is on the table, Quebec City must understand that we in Montreal speak with one voice." Benoit Dorais, the Vision mayor of Le Sud-Ouest, expressed the hope that the wide-ranging support would convince the Ministère des Transports du Québec (MTQ) it was the better plan.

Bergeron's old friend, Florence Junca-Adenot, who had become a go-to for journalists seeking quick expert analysis on urbanism and transport questions, also gave it full-throated support. "For a metropolis like Montreal, it's a project that goes in the direction we have to go in the 21st century," she told *Le Devoir*. "And it allows us to redevelop, almost in the heart of the city, huge spaces with the cliff on one side and the Lachine Canal on the other."

Commentators, meanwhile, were alternately amused and appalled by how utterly Tremblay had come under Bergeron's thrall. "If Gérald Tremblay converts to Richard Bergeron's way of thinking just a little more, we will soon see him smoking cigarettes and running marathons," wrote Yves Boisvert.

Lysiane Gagnon was less light-hearted. "For a long time, Mayor Tremblay allowed himself to be manipulated by greedy contractors and corrupt officials," she raged. "The man has metamorphosed. He has gone from the merchant Right to the trendy Left. He has been manipulated by none other than Richard Bergeron, to whom he has unwisely entrusted the urban planning dossier, even though he had, not without reason, a reputation as a loose cannon and extremist environmentalist."

The MTQ and the Charest government seemed to share Gagnon's opinion. For several weeks they had been downplaying the likelihood that the city's counter-proposal would get much traction or consideration. Transport Minister Julie Boulet told anyone who would listen that the dilapidated state of the interchange meant that it was "five minutes to midnight" and "we don't have the time to start all over again at zero."

Almost as soon as the city's roundabout idea was made public, the province shot it down. Tremblay and Bergeron hadn't put a price-tag on the project so the MTQ quickly did: it would cost at least $6 billion, about double its own plans for the interchange. And since the province was paying for the project, it was up to them to decide. Tremblay, too, felt the Liberal squeeze. He had received a call from Premier Jean Charest, Bergeron maintains, telling him, "You have to choose, Gérald: are you with Bergeron or with us?"

Tremblay returned to the Liberal fold and Bergeron's days on the executive committee were numbered. The MTQ went off to make modifications to their plan, but it was understood they would be relatively minor. In late October Bergeron told the party he would quit the executive committee if he deemed the final version unacceptable.

He tried to walk the threat back in the days after, but just got himself into more trouble when he said, "It's not the MTQ's project that will push me to resign. It will be the mayor's reaction." A day or too later, barely a year after the election, Tremblay kicked Bergeron off the executive committee before he could quit.

The Liberal/Union Montreal fold didn't turn out to be a very good place for Tremblay—or, for that matter, anyone else. During the 2009 municipal election campaign, all the candidates had agreed that a public inquiry was required to shed light on corruption and collusion within the construction industry, especially regarding its relations with elected and public officials.

Although the Charest government resisted an inquiry—instead setting up special police units to look into the problem—it ultimately buckled under pressure and in October 2011 announced the creation of the Charbonneau Commission. In doing so, it sealed Union Montreal's fate.

After a little more than a year—a year of remarkable testimony from a wide cast of witnesses, some reliable, some less so; some forthcoming, some not at all—Tremblay resigned and Union was headed for the scrapheap.

If the months were less tumultuous for Projet Montréal, they were hardly serene. On December 27th, 2010, like a landlord rushing to get a repossession letter out to his tenants before the new year, Pierre Gagnier, the party's *other* borough mayor, quit to sit as an independent. Virtually everyone in the party had known the day would come, that Gagnier's only interest in Projet Montréal was as a political vehicle. Still, it was something of a blow.

Coming just a few weeks after Bergeron was booted from the executive committee, and after the party's hopes the Turcot were quashed for good, Gagnier's departure was discouraging news. For Émilie Thuillier, the other party member elected from Ahuntsic-Cartierville and a true believer, there was also a bit of relief, however. Thuillier had never found Gagnier easy to work with or the least bit interested in making changes in Ahuntsic-Cartierville that reflected Projet Montréal's vision. "I found it easier to be all alone than to have to manage a mayor with whom I did not share the same values," she says. "He realized that he was not in the right gang [and] honestly I found life a bit easier."

Notwithstanding the relief it spelled for Thuillier, Gagnier's departure brought home the fact that the Projet Montréal caucus was shrinking when it should have been growing.

Before long, that would change. Rosemont–La-Petite-Patrie and its mayor François Croteau weren't in the headlines as frequently as the Plateau and its no-holds-barred mayor, but there had been turmoil there too.

Although Ferrandez had lost interest in the pedestrianization of Avenue Mont-Royal, Croteau took up the banner: just a few months after being elected in spring of 2011, he announced that Rue Masson "will be transformed into a vast green public square, to the delight of all."

He also adopted environmental regulations that went beyond anything the Plateau was doing while famously opening the door to let residents—or at least community organizations—keep chickens so as to allow them to collect their own fresh eggs.

In a humiliating defeat for Croteau, Masson's pedestrianization never took place after the street's merchants voted massively against it. He also made some questionable announcements, including a pledge to cap parking meters at $1 per hour in his borough.[25]

Besides having to deal with grumpy merchants, there was friction between Croteau and the councillors. This was perhaps par for the course on a split council with two members from Projet Montréal. But Croteau's biggest problems were with his colleagues from Vision, in particular Pierre Lampron.

Lampron had, of course, expected to be president of the executive committee under Mayor Louise Harel. When that didn't happen, he thought he would apply his managerial expertise to showing Croteau how Rosemont should be run. Lampron "thought he was going to run the borough because 'You [Croteau] are a kiddo and I'm a bigshot from the business world. I'm going to take the lead,'" remembers François Limoges.

Croteau says he also had major differences with the way Harel ran Vision. Notably, he says he objected to being asked to meet with big property developers who gave money to Vision to finance projects they had in his borough. That the party continued to make such requests after the recent scandals was unacceptable and foolish, he felt.

Limoges would often joke with Croteau and say, "When you're ready, come and join us!" Finally, Croteau was ready. He walked into Joël Simard-Menard's office on the ground floor of City Hall to talk about switching teams. Part of the attraction for Croteau to cross the floor was greater exposure in the media, Simard-Menard remembers.

---

25 Low parking meter prices end up hurting merchants since drivers will often occupy a parking place much longer than they might otherwise, denying use of it to other customers. This in turn results in increased congestion and pollution by drivers cruising for an open parking space, a practice which is estimated to account for 30 percent or more of traffic in some urban areas. According to Donald Shoup, widely considered the world expert on parking, the ideal occupancy rate for street parking is 85 percent percent of available spots. If a street tends to exceed that level regularly, its parking meter prices are probably too low; if ocupancy tends to be lower, meter prices might be too high. Masson, with meter rates of $1 per hour, had among the highest occupancy rates in Montreal.

"He saw that Luc [Ferrandez] had a lot of space in the public arena and he wanted as much." Later, the two men met with Bergeron to discuss the idea at their leader's home.

Croteau and Simard-Menard don't agree on when this occurred. Croteau says it was all arranged "a long, long, long time in advance," June or July of 2011. Simard-Menard says it was mid-October. Whatever the case, it was agreed that it would be announced on November 1st, which was the two-year anniversary of the election and shortly before a Projet Montréal fundraising event.

Some members of the Rosemont ALA weren't thrilled with the idea, whether out of skepticism towards Croteau or loyalty and affection for Patrick Cigana. After all, accepting Croteau would effectively rule out Cigana's shot at becoming mayor of Rosemont at the next city-wide vote in 2013. But Cigana himself was pragmatic. "Patrick is a party guy," says Joël Simard-Menard. "He understood exactly the benefit to the party of having Croteau in its ranks."

Chapter 18

CROTEAU'S ARRIVAL BOOSTED our morale and our presence in the media, but it did little to calm tensions between the purists and the pragmatists, between those intent on getting as much done as possible as quickly as possible and those interested in positioning the party as a moderate force before the next election.

A trial run for the election came sooner than most anyone expected when, just a couple of months after Croteau's defection, Vision lost another seat with the resignation of Pierre Lampron in Rosemont. His decision wasn't surprising—he hadn't made the jump into politics to be a simple city councillor, let alone one in opposition—and he had had heart problems requiring a triple bypass shortly after being elected. Quitting was also easy because needed neither the job nor the money. Croteau remembers Lampron looking with amused disdain at the first pay cheque he received as councillor and joking, "Hey! It's my welfare cheque!"

Lampron represented the district of Vieux-Rosemont where my old friend Christine Gosselin had come in second in 2009. Given that she had campaigned hard as well as her continued involvement with the party, it was natural that she be asked whether she wanted to run in the by-election. She wasn't. The candidate ended up being Érika Duchesne, a translator and editor who was the treasurer on the Conseil de direction. She quickly found herself surrounded by an army of volunteers. With the borough now under Projet Montréal's control, and the general election campaign 18 months off, winning the by-election became an imperative and the party threw everything they had at it. "The amount of volunteers we had seemed to out-number the voters. Everyone was all-in," Zoubris remembers.

Despite the abundance of volunteers, it wasn't an easy campaign. The winter, just ending, had seen snow removal in the Plateau make the news every time a few flakes fell. "All you needed was three unhappy people and TVA reporter Yves Poirier was on the case," remembers Christine Gosselin.

The hysteria was fed by Yves Boisvert's column for *La Presse*, published in March under the headline "The commercial agony of the Plateau," in which he described the borough becoming a ghost town because of the administration's parking and snow removal policies. "Hey! Snow removal! Isn't this the ABC's of municipal management in Quebec?" he wrote. "Have you seen how the sidewalks look in the Plateau? If my mother lived there, I'd get her out of the neighborhood."

The following week, after Alex Norris challenged his facts, Boisvert walked the column back. By then, however, François Limoges had gone to a *conseil de direction* meeting and pleaded that Ferrandez be brought to heel. "No party has ever survived a war with the merchants," the minutes report him saying. "It is becoming increasingly difficult to defend Luc Ferrandez's policies."

The conclusion: "It was decided that Richard Bergeron would speak to Luc Ferrandez and ask him not to start any project that might arouse the opposition during the current campaign."

For his part, Ferrandez remembers being told that in Vieux-Rosemont "at every second door people said they wouldn't vote for Projet Montréal because of what we were doing in the Plateau." But if Luc wasn't encouraged to lend a hand in the campaign, the rest of us were, and there were evenings in the spring of 2012 when we trekked up to Rosemont and St-Michel and made calls. Other volunteers came from across the city.

The effort paid off. On April 29th, the party won its first ever by-election by all of 175 votes, edging out the Vision candidate by 2 percent. The sentiment was as much relief as jubilation.

Having two large, adjacent and central boroughs administered in very different ways was good for the party. It demonstrated what we had long argued in the Plateau: there were no one-size-fits-all solutions. "We always had the message that 'Just because we do it in the Plateau doesn't mean we're going to do it anywhere else,'" says

Joël Simard-Menard. Rosemont, and Croteau's different approach, was proof.

Croteau describes his relationship with Ferrandez as a "healthy rivalry" and certainly in many respects it exemplified one of the great virtues of Montreal's borough system: each is a laboratory for different types of projects which, depending on their success, are adopted—or not—by others. The outdoor ping-pong tables were a small-scale example of this; the planted curb extensions, a large-scale example. Croteau says the first time he saw the curb extensions, he went back to the Rosemont borough offices on Iberville and told his staff he wanted them and by the dozen. "It's about inspiring each other, challenging each other," he says.

At times, the rivalry wasn't that healthy. As Limoges says, "the media only saw Luc," and this frustrated Croteau to no end. Ferrandez seemed to take pleasure in rubbing it in. Simard-Menard remembers a TV host asking Luc whether any other borough mayors were doing anything of interest. His response: "I think François Croteau wants to put chickens in his borough." Meanwhile, there were those of us in the Plateau who felt Luc didn't proceed with certain by-law modifications simply because it would appear as if we were imitating Rosemont.

Ferrandez's chronic lateness for meetings—or, simply, his absence—also rankled the team. Simard-Menard remembers one occasion where Luc had finally agreed to come to caucus to present the projects the Plateau was undertaking that year. Croteau and Limoges, he says, intentionally arrived late just to make a point. The unhealthiness percolated down from the protagonists to their teams. In the Plateau we used to laugh at what we called Croteau's "Luc-envy." "The frog who wanted to be bigger than the ox—that was Croteau," says Richard Ryan.

Meanwhile in Rosemont, they regarded our devotion to Ferrandez's leadership as going beyond team spirit. "The first term the team seemed less like a tightly-knit group and more like a cult," says François Limoges. "On our side of the track, it was just weird."

Happily, the caucus and party had a common challenge which overrode these rivalries and tensions: preparing for the upcoming 2013 general election.

Given its democratic nature, the statutes of Projet Montréal require that any candidate who runs for the party be chosen by the members of their local ALA. (If there is no ALA, the *conseil de direction* must approve their candidacy.) This is usually done at a nomination meeting in the months before the election. This presented a problem for keener potential candidates who hoped to start raising money—and their profiles—a year, even two before election day: how to do so if they didn't actually know whether they would end up winning the nomination?

To resolve this issue, the party instituted the concept of *candidats présentis*—prospective candidates who were given the imprimatur of the *conseil de direction* pending nomination by the relevant ALA. This allowed the person some security, if not certainty, while still permitting the members of the ALAs to decide on the candidate.

By early 2012, the *conseil de direction* was approving *candidats présentis* at every monthly meeting. In some cases, these were councillors who had run in 2009 and won; in others, they were candidates who had lost and were eager to give it another go. In still others, they were new arrivals eager to help the party make inroads in areas of the city that so far had proven impenetrable such as LaSalle, or Rivière-des-Prairies–Pointe-aux-Trembles.

At the same time, the party was actively trying to recruit people with profiles in their respective communities, whether geographic or cultural, to become candidates. It wasn't an easy task. Even if Projet Montréal was out-performing Vision in many ways, it was still the "second opposition." "When you are the third party, people often don't return your phone calls or only do so out of respect," remembers Jimmy Zoubris, who was in charge of recruitment along with Joël Simard-Menard and Michel Camus, a mild-mannered epidemiologist who had taken over the presidency of the party from Magda Popeanu.

Anglos remained skeptical of Bergeron, whose English was poor, and Zoubris had no success even among those who had been stalwarts of the progressive municipal Left. With other cultural communities, it was worse. Magda had long appreciated the importance of appealing to them—she was one of the few senior members who had actually lived the immigrant experience. But she hadn't been able to convince

Bergeron to buy in. She would take him to events, she says, and "he would go out and smoke 50 cigarettes in an hour just to get out of there. These communities make up 30 percent of Montrealers, but for him it's enough to say, 'I'm married to a Moroccan woman.' For him it was settled. I said, 'Look, just because you're sleeping with a Moroccan woman doesn't mean you're going to be loved by the communities. You have to do more than that, Richard.'"

Bergeron acknowledges his disdain for this sort of retail politics. "Ethnic pandering, it stinks as far as I'm concerned," he says, noting that it was an issue from the party's earliest days. "Claude Mainville used to say, 'You must adapt your speech to each community.' 'No! I will say exactly the same thing to everyone. You either recognize yourself in what we say, in what we represent, in the ideas we convey. Or you don't recognize yourself.'"

By early 2012, it had become clear that, at the next municipal election, Projet Montréal would likely to be up against a politician who specialized in populist pandering. Even if Gérald Tremblay was refusing to rule out running again in 2013, no one seriously expected him to do so. The Charbonneau Commission was a ticking timebomb with hearings slated in the spring, and there was hushed talk that he had Parkinson's disease or another ailment. Virtually everyone was sure Montreal would have a new mayor before long and the man who had been deftly positioning himself to win the job was former federal Liberal cabinet minister Denis Coderre.

I had first heard his name as a possible successor to Tremblay in late 2009 when Craig Sauvé, already looking forward to the next election, said he had heard rumours that he was interested and would be a formidable foe. I didn't share his concerns. I felt Coderre was out of step with the times; he reminded me of a politician of the 1950s, older than his years, squeezed into a waistcoat and jacket, backslapping and glad-handing his way through a career. I felt a modern electorate would see through the schtick and demand more substance. Reporter Patrick Lagaçé saw something different. In September 2010, while calling Coderre a "shameless self-promoter," he nonetheless said he had developed some respect for him because of his use of social media.

"He remade his image," Lagaçé wrote, "an operation that would have cost him tens of thousands of dollars had he given the mandate to a PR firm... Never underestimate him."

In April 2011, a *La Presse* poll of possible future mayors put Coderre at the top of the list, with 23 percent support. Coderre's genius for building anticipation—even making his election seem an inevitability—was clear. No matter that at the time he was simply an opposition member of Parliament whose short-run in cabinet had been sidelined by the sponsorship inquiry and was increasingly on the outs with his own party.

That party was thrown into disarray by the NDP's Orange Wave in the federal election of the following month, which reduced the Liberals to all of 34 seats. The Orange Wave's success in Quebec, however, gave Projet Montréal hope—and a good idea as to who we might want in charge of our own 2013 election campaign.

Ray Guardia had grown up in NDG, the son of Spanish immigrants. In Cégep and university he had gotten involved with the MCM and the NDP, both of which had strong bases of support in NDG. After graduating from McGill he found himself running the NDP's operations in Quebec. He was the campaign manager when the party elected consumer advocate Phil Edmonston, its first MP in the province, in 1989. After that, he served as the party's national director in Ottawa before coming back, in the summer of 2007, to run Tom Mulcair's by-election campaign in Outremont—the second NDP MP ever to be elected in Quebec. Then, when the party needed a campaign manager in the province in 2011, Guardia got the call.

Jack Layton caught fire in Quebec in that election and the party went from one seat in the province to 59, propelling it into official opposition. Guardia, modest and laid back as he was, became something of a legend. Within the NDP, however, things soured for Guardia following Layton's death in August 2011. Guardia supported fellow Montrealer and long-time NDP backroom player Brian Topp for the leadership of the party rather than Mulcair. When Mulcair won, Guardia was shown the door.

He went to work for the ACTRA union. There he was contacted by Craig Sauvé, who after working as an *attaché politique* for Projet

Montréal from 2009 to 2011, had himself gone to Ottawa on behalf on the NDP after the 2011 federal election.[26] While in Ottawa, Sauvé kept his Montreal apartment and maintained his involvement in Projet Montréal, serving as ALA co-ordinator for the Sud-Ouest much of the time. When it was time for the party to start looking for a campaign director for the 2013 election, he thought of Guardia.

After the ugly ending with the NDP, "I thought I was done with politics," Guardia says. But he met with Patrick Cigana, Jimmy Zoubris and Joël Simard-Menard at party headquarters. His reaction, he says, was "Boy, aren't they nice!" Soon enough he had signed on and started designing the campaign.

Even if it wasn't explicitly stated, it was widely accepted that if Bergeron didn't win in 2013 it would be his last campaign as leader of the party. His third strike, as it were. Efforts had been made to make him a better candidate. He was given a clothing budget to leaven the off-the-rack bureaucrat-special suits he tended to wear. He had tutoring in English on Fridays. Jimmy, Craig, Érika Duchesne and several other party faithful even dressed him up in a Habs jersey and took him to McLean's Pub on Peel St. near the Bell Centre to watch the 2012-13 season opener against the Leafs. Any pay-off was negligible. "He didn't come off warm. He just couldn't," says Zoubris. "It just wasn't Richard Bergeron. It was tough to sell him."

As Ray Guardia eventually pointed out, "You can't run a Jack Layton campaign if you are not Jack Layton." By the late spring 2013, it had been decided that, for better or worse, the strategy for the election that fall would be "Let Richard be Richard."

---

26 He was hired by Hélène LeBlanc who had run as a Projet Montréal borough councillor in the Sud-Ouest in 2009 and was elected MP for LaSalle-Émard in 2011.

Chapter 19

By now, the political landscape in Montreal had been completely redrawn. The Charbonneau Commission had begun hearings in June 2012, taken the summer off and then started in earnest in September. With Martin Dumont's late October testimony implicating Tremblay directly, the mayor's fate was sealed. He retreated to his country house for a few days and then returned to Montreal to announce his resignation on Tuesday, November 6th. He played the victim, as he had before: "This is an unbearable injustice. I never thought I would experience such relentlessness persecution in a society of law. But, one day, justice will be done." Denying Dumont's allegations as well as those made by former Montreal police chief and mayoral candidate Jacques Duchesneau, Tremblay said his resignation was "the ultimate sacrifice, a last act of love in the best interest of Montreal."

Some in the Union camp had been expecting Tremblay's departure for a while; for others it was a surprise. "It was like when you know somebody is dying and you try to get it out of your mind," remembers Helen Fotopulos who, having been elected as Tremblay's *co-listière,* was still in council and on the executive committee. "You say to yourself, 'It will blow over.' That was the tendency. Even if we knew a catastrophe was coming."

Conveniently, the announcement came less than a year before the date set for the 2013 election—three days less—which meant a by-election wouldn't be held to replace him. Instead, city council would elect his successor. Since Union still held a majority in council, it would be up to them to choose as long as they stuck together.

Two councillors who had been anticipating Tremblay's resignation—and manoeuvring to take his place—were CDN-NDG mayor Michael Applebaum, who by then had been named president of the executive committee, and Richard Deschamps, a councillor from LaSalle who was in charge of infrastructure on the executive committee.

Applebaum, with whom Fotopulos used to get rides downtown from the CDN-NDG borough offices, had been "ranting" to her in the weeks leading up to the resignation, she says. "He would always saying things like, 'We're going to get thrown under the bus,' and 'We've got to do something about Tremblay.' So he'd been preparing. It didn't happen overnight."

Not everyone, it seemed, liked the prospect of Applebaum or Deschamps leading the party, and a handful of councillors convinced Fotopulos to throw her hat in the ring. She did so but says she didn't make phone calls or twist arms in the two days between Tremblay's resignation and the Union caucus to choose a successor.

It showed. After a bitter meeting, Fotopulos finished a distant third, with Deschamps edging out Applebaum by five votes for the mayor's job. At this point, Applebaum decided not to play by the agreed-upon rules.

Aware that it was city council which would make the final decision, Applebaum decided he would try to win the mayor's job by seeking support from the opposition as well as any Union councillors who might back him. He quit the presidency of the executive committee and, with a week before council was to meet to decide, began corralling his votes. With Union councillors, his approach was carrot and stick, Fotopulos says. "Michael played a masterful game of making promises, giving people places on the executive, etcetera, to get that vote," she says. There were also threats. "They didn't threaten to break your legs. They threatened to strip you of everything." Fotopulos says she got a series of "if you know what's good for you" phone calls "from the least-expected people." Even her sister, who had served as her campaign manager, was pressured.

With Vision and Projet, it was all carrot. Promising spots on the executive committee and other favours to Vision councillors, negotiations with Harel went smoothly but Applebaum still needed some Projet Montréal support. He went over to party headquarters on November 15th, just before a *conseil de direction* meeting to negotiate with Zoubris and Guardia. "I threw the kitchen sink at him. Six seats on the executive committee, two seats on the STM, everything," says Zoubris, referring to his demands.

They settled for half of that. Deschamps, meanwhile, had refused to meet with the opposition parties personally. He seemed to be banking on Union councillors abiding by the understanding that whoever won their caucus vote would get their support, as well as the fact that Applebaum's shaky command of French would exclude him from consideration by many in opposition.

When the Projet caucus met the next day, few could accept the idea of supporting Applebaum, whether because of his French, a program he had led which would have substantially reduced the budget of various boroughs, including the Plateau, or his take-no-prisoners approach to politics. So the overwhelming majority of the party's 10 votes ended up going to Deschamps.

Applebaum still won by the narrowest of margins, 31 to 29. Since it had been a secret ballot, the new mayor had no way of knowing who had voted for him, and he fulfilled his undertaking to Projet, naming Josée Duplessis and Émilie Thuillier as full members of the executive committee and Érika Duchesne as an associate member.

It was effectively the end of Union Montreal. Applebaum's executive committee had more members from the two opposition parties than from Union, and they occupied the most important positions, including the presidency and the two vice-president roles. But Applebaum's tenure as the great coalition builder would be brief.

With the election looming, there had been an upheaval of a much more minor nature on the Plateau. From the earliest days of our administration, Ferrandez was unhappy with Piper Huggins and Carl Boileau's performance. Part of the problem was office attendance. Piper often wouldn't come in until the late afternoon. "I found that unacceptable," he says. "It wasn't part of the culture of Projet Montréal. You were in a revolution and you were supposed to give 100 percent." Carl's attendance was even less predictable, even after moving virtually across the street from the office.

But it was about more than just putting in the hours. Piper felt a lingering bitterness at having been downgraded from city council candidate during the 2009 campaign and she also resented Luc's insistence that she respect the bureaucracy's hidebound and hierarchical way of doing things. Carl, for his part, felt that his district of De Lorimier was shortchanged in terms of investment while at the same time suffered more than the others from the Ave Laurier/Rue Christophe-Colomb traffic changes.[27] "It made him angry, and that's when he started to be recalcitrant," Ferrandez recalls. "He didn't come to work anymore, he was there one day out of five, then he didn't do anything."

Like Josée Duplessis, his fellow councillor in De Lorimier, Carl tended to be more nervous than the rest of us when it came to our traffic-calming and greening projects. By the summer of 2012, implementation had reached cruising speed. But while the projects were winning over many residents, they left others raging, usually because of lost parking spots.

This was the case with the planted mall protecting the bike path along Rue Rachel as well as the widened sidewalks and plaza out-side Laurier metro and school, a project which became, to a large degree, our showpiece of the mandate. It was the same story with the elimination of Rue Marie-Anne where it crossed Parc Baldwin.

For most of us, it was a no-brainer of a project. Parc Baldwin stretched from Sherbrooke Street almost all the way to Mont-Royal but had various streets running through it, rendering it more dangerous and unattractive to park-goers. We couldn't do much to Rue Rachel but Marie-Anne didn't serve any real purpose except for transit traffic. By the summer of 2012 we had announced we would get rid of the road through the park and were prepared for a bit of blowback. We had enough experience by then to know some opposition was inevitable but also that it would dissipate once the project was complete and the benefits fully apparent to all. A small group of residents opposed our plan, and splitting with the rest of

---

27 This stemmed from his own rigid reading of borough frontiers: Parc Laurier and Laurier metro station which accounted for much of the borough spending between 2009 and 2013 fall both in the Mile-End district even if they are used as much if not more by the residents of De Lorimier.

council, Carl took up their cause. Soon after, he had effectively been expelled from caucus and it was clear he wouldn't run for the party again.

Piper's departure was more complicated. Each district in the Plateau has two councillors, one borough, one city. Borough is the more junior position, doesn't sit at city hall and earns less. Richard Bergeron had always planned to run for council in his home district of St-Jacques in 2013. Normally, as borough councillor for Jeanne-Mance, Piper would be expected to take over Bergeron's spot and graduate to the city council position. It was felt, however, that if one borough councillor deserved promotion, it was Richard Ryan in Mile-End.

Conveniently, Alex Norris, the city councillor for Mile-End, actually lived in Jeanne-Mance, and had for virtually all the 20-plus years he had lived in Montreal. Alex, however, wasn't the least bit interested in changing districts, which needed to happen in order for Ryan to move up a notch. He felt he had invested a great deal of energy in Mile-End and, importantly, that it was a safer bet for his re-election. Convincing him to switch to Jeanne-Mance took several months. I was recruited as an arm-twister, given that I was Alex's oldest and closest friend in the party. Eventually, he agreed but on the condition that Piper not be his borough council running mate. His rationale was reasonable: he felt that having two anglophones running in the same district wouldn't fly. Going unmentioned was the fact that he didn't have any more time for Piper than Luc did. She was not very subtly shown the door.

This meant that all three borough council seats would need to be filled. The Mile-End position was earmarked for a star candidate who was keen to join the team, Marie Plourde. I say star candidate but when Luc first told me he was going to have lunch with her, I had no idea who she was, not having tuned in regularly to Musique Plus, the popular French-language music channel where she worked as a VJ, during the early 1990s. It was Joël Simard-Menard who brought me up to speed. "Daniel, you have to understand—a whole generation of Québécois men were in love with her."

For De Lorimier, Luc liked Marianne Giguère, a geography teacher active in the community who had worked on the 2005 campaign. She had been busy with two young children in 2009 but by 2013 she was ready to get involved again, this time as a candidate. And for Jeanne-Mance, we had set our sights on a cool and somewhat mysterious guy called Fabrice Bosom, whom we encountered when we closed off the entrance to an alleyway to green it. He was an expert in microfinance and had worked in Haiti and elsewhere in the developing world, and seemed like he would be a good fit, both culturally and intellectually.

Christine Gosselin was eager to run again but she was only offered offered the candidacy for mayor of Île-Bizard–Ste-Geneviève. It wasn't completely out-of-left-field—Christine had spent much of her adolescence in that area of the West Island—but it was understood she had virtually no chance of winning.

Perhaps the most interesting local candidacy was that of Mindy Pollak, a young Hasidic woman who wanted to run for us in Outremont, which shares a border with Mile-End.

Her arrival to the party had been slightly convoluted. The congregants of synagogue on the Plateau side of Rue Hutchison, where Mindy lived with her family, wanted to do minor renovations. Some neighbours opposed the idea. It led to an ugly division between the Hasidic and non-Hasidic communities. In reaction, Mindy and a neighbour, Leila Marshy—a writer and filmmaker of Palestinian (and Newfoundland) descent—started up a group called *Les Amis de la rue Hutchison*, calling for understanding.

At a street fair on Rue St-Viateur, Les Amis had a stand. Alex and I wandered by and met Mindy, Mindy's mother, and Leila, whom we had both known for years. A few months later, he phoned Mindy out of the blue. "Alex gave me a call and was like, 'What about running?'" remembers Mindy. "I was like, 'Haha, that's really hilarious.' It was really far-fetched for me to do something like that."

Far-fetched because no Hasidic woman had ever been elected to public office before, anywhere. She didn't, however, give a firm no, and Alex kept calling. He also urged Mindy's mother to be open to the idea when he ran into her in the parking lot outside Canadian Tire. The family went back and forth. "One day my mom would be like, 'Yeah, you know, it could be good. We could change some things,' and the next day she would be 'What a crazy idea. I really don't think you can do it.'"

Finally, she made up her mind to run. "If I can make a difference, how can I say no?" she told her family. Within the community—or communities, given that there are a half dozen Hasidic "courts" or sects—Mindy's decision was controversial. Alex and I were convoked to a meeting with Martin Rosenberg, who as heir to the Rosdev property empire is one of the wealthiest and most influential Hasidim in the country. He lauded Mindy's qualities and said that she might, someday, make a very good councillor—but she was still too young. If Projet Montréal was intent on having a Hasidic candidate, he said, he had several men in mind who would do an excellent job.

We were prepared for this and, only slightly disingenuously, said that there was nothing we could do about it: given that Projet Montréal was a rigorously democratic party, if Mindy wanted to run for the nomination, she could run for the nomination and if the Outremont ALA chose her, then she would be the candidate. Rosenberg got the message.

Chapter 20

FROM LATE 2011, WHEN PEOPLE began to speculate about how the 2013 election might turn out, Richard Bergeron maintained that if it came down to a two-horse race between him and Denis Coderre, he would win. He had the substance, he had the municipal experience, he had the vision; Coderre, for all his bluffing was vulnerable on many fronts. It was a line Bergeron was willing to expound upon to virtually anyone who would listen.

Bergeron was already counting Louise Harel out of running and with reason: under her leadership, Vision had been incapable of getting any traction with the Montreal population and, burdened with substantial debt, appeared to be well on its way to disappearing. Since Croteau's departure, the party had been bleeding councillors to the point that in May 2013, Projet Montréal had, for what it was worth, become the official opposition.

But by the late spring of 2013, even if Vision and Harel didn't look like they would be a deciding factor, it was clear that Bergeron's two-man race wasn't going to happen. Two possible candidates appeared at the end of May, just two weeks after Coderre had finally ended *son striptease* and made his candidacy official. The first was Marcel Côté, an economist and former advisor to both Brian Mulroney and Robert Bourassa as well as candidate for the Union Nationale. According to insider Denis Lessard from *La Presse*, Côté was being recruited by the business community, provincial Liberals, and federal Conservatives to "block the road" to Coderre, who clearly didn't inspire much confidence in corporate boardrooms. Then there was Mélanie Joly, an unknown young woman with an impressive CV and political pedigree—her father was president of the Liberal party's finance committee in the late 1990s and her stepmother a former Liberal minister. Mélanie Joly didn't have a party or a program but, as the director of a PR firm, did have a machine capable of creating buzz for her. According to Bergeron, Joly was put forward in order to hurt his candidacy and the chances of Projet Montréal being elected. "An election with three candidates is random. With four it's a mess. But just the two of us, I beat him," he adds, referring to Coderre.

This comes, of course, with the benefit of hindsight and is eminently debateable even then. Certainly, in mid-June, few people could have predicted what the coming months would bring.

The Charbonneau Commission had been holding hearings throughout the winter and spring with the scale of corruption and rot compounded by virtually each witness. Meanwhile, the *Unité permanente anticorruption* (UPAC), the special police force created in the wake of the revelations of the preceding years, was continuing its arrests and raids. On three occasions it had seized documents at the Côte-des-Neiges–Notre-Dame-de-Grâce borough offices, over which Michael Applebaum had presided before negotiating his way into the top job at City Hall. In mid-January, Applebaum had met with UPAC investigators at his City Hall office and made it appear that everything was business as usual. *Le Devoir*, however, learned that the mayor was under active investigation for questionable zoning changes and variances in his borough, at least one of which involved a mob-related developer.

Finally, at 6 AM on a Monday morning a week before *la Fête nationale*, Applebaum was arrested at his home across from MacDonald Park in Snowden, taken downtown and charged with 14 counts of fraud, corruption, breach of trust and conspiracy. He resigned the next day. More than ever, Montreal was thrown into political crisis.

When Tremblay resigned there had been talk of bringing forward the municipal election or placing the city under trusteeship. Both those options were taken off the table when Applebaum brokered his coalition administration. Now there was yet another discussion of trusteeship for the city but, once again, the provincial government chose not to step in and city council was allowed to choose a replacement. Jimmy Zoubris puts some of this down to Bergeron's calm and reasonable reaction and the fact he didn't try to exploit the situation for political gain. "He jumped on the crisis with a tone that said 'we need to be adults here.' I got a lot of messages from people who would never vote for him, my Conservative friends for example, who said, 'Your guy is looking really good. Like the adult in the room.'"

A week after Applebaum's arrest, council met again and again, the vote was close. This time, Laurent Blanchard, the affable Vision councillor from Hochelaga who had been president of Applebaum's executive committee, edged out Harout Chitilian, a former whiz-kid Union councillor from Ahuntsic who, at 30, had been the youngest city council president in Montreal's history. Even if he wouldn't officially join Équipe Denis Coderre until August, Chitilian was widely regarded as Coderre's candidate whereas Blanchard was the consensus choice of Vision and Projet.

The victory of Blanchard as caretaker mayor, slim as it was, gave the opposition— Projet especially—hope that all was not lost. Still, if Coderre and his allies weren't able to rally support in council, they seemed to have the momentum with the population. Polls from the spring of 2013 showed him ahead of both Bergeron and Harel by a solid 15 percent. His strategy of confidence—winning by making his election appear inevitable—seemed to be bearing fruit.

One Projet Montréal member who wasn't the least bit cheered by Blanchard becoming mayor was Éric-Alan Caldwell. The steady, loyal trooper from Mercier–Hochelaga-Maisonneuve was gearing up for his third run for municipal office and, like Bergeron in his quest for the top job, knew that it would be his last if he didn't win.

In 2009 Caldwell had more than doubled the 2005 vote total for Projet Montréal in Hochelaga, receiving almost 30 percent of the ballots cast. Still, Blanchard had crushed him, winning nearly twice as much support. Vision's decline in the preceding years, however, had convinced him that things might be different in 2013, and that, combined with his calm and constant groundwork, spreading the Projet Montréal gospel in the most deliberate and reasonable way, he might just have a shot at winning.

"At my nomination meeting I was confident," he remembers. Then, on a break in the staff room at the casino where he worked as a croupier, he saw on TV that François Croteau, Projet Montréal's candidate to replace Applebaum, was withdrawing in favour of Blanchard. Caldwell felt his chances vaporize. The added visibility that Blanchard would get as caretaker mayor would surely make him invincible in Hochelaga, he figured. "I am there: a party activist for 8 years. Candidate in 2005, candidate in 2009. And I see it live on TV. Can you understand how unhappy I was?" he asks. "From that moment on I said to myself, 'Oh boy...'"

Luckily for Caldwell, things had barely started.

Applebaum's arrest had dashed one plan that Harel had started cooking up with the interim mayor after Tremblay's resignation: a coalition to unify her nationalist francophone base and his anglo-federalist supporters, a grand marriage of convenience that just might be able to withstand Coderre and Projet. But while Applebaum was gone, it didn't mean such a coalition couldn't happen.

Instead, it would happen with Marcel Côté, the business-friendly federalist. A week after Blanchard was made mayor, Louise Harel announced she wouldn't be running for the job in November. Rather, she and Vision would support Côté, who would run for mayor as an independent.

It was similar to the deal that Harel proposed to Richard Bergeron four years earlier, but here it would be Harel taking the backseat. It was also overdue recognition on her part that her Péquiste past made her unelectable in great swaths of Montreal. "It is an open secret that I have had a lot of difficulty breaking through in the West Island," she said, ignoring the fact that most of the West Island had demerged years before and that, for better or worse, her unpopularity reached deep into other areas of the city.

The move meant the field of mayoral candidates—at least those worthy of media coverage—was reduced to four: three stiff, middle-aged men in suits and one 34-year-old woman. Perhaps unsurprisingly, the young woman wasn't taken very seriously.

In election years in Montreal, there is almost invariably a flurry of activity in the spring and early summer, then a lull of six weeks or so before the pre-campaign gets going in mid-August. This lull allows people a brief vacation, before throwing themselves into the rigours of what amounts to a 10-week, ever more intense race. At least, that's how it's supposed to work.

In reality, parties are always playing catch-up and the lull is used to finish putting things in place before *la rentrée* and the campaign's unofficial start. By early July, Projet Montréal had candidates officially nominated for about half of the 103 elected positions up for grabs, and candidates were lining up for another two dozen. Other than Croteau, none of these were *transfuges* councillors from either Vision or Union—but it was not for lack of trying.

After Tremblay's resignation, Jimmy Zoubris, who was responsible for candidate recruitment, had got on the phone and begun sounding Union councillors out about possibly leaving their sinking ship and signing up with Projet. None showed any interest in coming over.

There was some encouragement when a few familiar faces thought to have disappeared came back, including Craig Sauvé. He returned from Ottawa to run for city councillor in the Sud-Ouest district. Zoubris himself was slated to run in Ville-Marie's Peter-McGill district, which includes the western, more anglophone part of downtown as well as his Bishop and Crescent Street haunts. Meanwhile, Richard Bergeron was to run in his home district of St-Jacques with Janine Krieber—a political scientist at the Royal Military College in St-Jean, not to mention the wife of Stéphane Dion—as his *co-listière*.

Then there were the almost-rans: the recruits we expected to give the party a boost who dropped out. The biggest loss in this category was Marc-Antoine Saumier, a senior salesman with Xerox. What made him interesting was his extra-curricular activities: he was the president of Quebec's LGBT Chamber of Commerce. He was supposed to run in the Ville-Marie district of Sainte-Marie, which includes much of the Gay Village and the Centre-Sud.

But in the late winter of 2013, Saumier dropped out. He hadn't lost faith; he had received a job offer he felt he couldn't refuse. "It was heart-breaking. For him. For us. For everyone," says Patrick Cigana. "He told us, 'I would love to run but I am not guaranteed to win. This job *is* guaranteed,'" remembers Jimmy Zoubris. Bergeron was less understanding. "I guess he's more interested in selling paper than in saving the world," Guardia remembers him saying.

With the party still short of women candidates to be able to claim gender parity, Patrick Cigana determined that Saumier's replacement had to be a woman. It was a thorny issue in the party: everyone agreed that the party needed more women but the Conseil de direction was loath to implement any of the mechanisms that were suggested, whether by reserving certain winnable districts for female candidates, ensuring that there be at least one woman in every contested nomination, or by imposing quotas for female candidates on the ALAs. Eventually Ray Guardia and Patrick Cigana just took matters into their own hands. "We just made it so," remembers Guardia. "We were bombarded with CVs and requests to be candidates and Patrick, in his office—no joke—had a pile of male CVs that we just didn't go through. Meanwhile we were doing everything we could to encourage women to run. We would contact them pro-actively, interview them, encourage them."

For a francophone working-class neighbourhood like Ste-Marie, Cigana felt that a woman with an identifiably French-Canadian name would be ideal. "We needed a name with a lower Scrabble score" than Zoubris or Krieber, he says.

Cigana started working the phone. One of the people he called was Anick Druelle, a long-time member of the Rosemont–La Petite-Patrie ALA, who was a gender equity specialist and well-connected with women's groups in the city. She had been supposed to run in 2009 in Marie-Victorin but pulled out. She wasn't interested in running in 2013 either but suggested Tatiana Fraser who had co-founded and run the Girls Action Foundation.

Cigana spoke to her but despite her abundant qualities and qualifications, her French just wasn't good enough for such a district (to say nothing of her last name). Fraser did, however, have a few suggestions of her own. One of them was a woman who had worked under her at the Girls Action Foundation by the name of Valérie Plante.

At the time, Plante had moved on to a job in communications at a union, the *Alliance du personnel professional et technique de la santé et des services sociaux*, based in Longueuil, and even if she had only been there a couple of years, she was ready for something new. When Cigana phoned her, she was intrigued by the idea.

Another group that Plante was involved in was Groupe Femmes, politique et démocratie (GFPD), a Quebec City non-profit on whose board she served. Its mission was to encourage women to go into politics and support them once they had made the leap. Still, Plante herself had never actively considered running for office. "I never said to myself, 'I'm going to be a politician in life' or 'I'm going to be a city councillor in life,'" she says. "No. It was never a clear goal."

A couple of months before the call from Cigana, however, she had been to a fundraiser for GFPD where she had chatted with Piper Huggins who had spoken to her about Projet Montréal and the role of councillor. Plante says she voted for the party—and Cigana since she lives in Rosemont—in 2009 but only knew the basics about it. "I just knew it was the greenest party, the party that was putting forward the issue of [public] transportation and active transport and that appealed to me."

The conversation with Huggins and then the call from Cigana made Plante want to know more. There was a meeting at party headquarters on Notre-Dame Ouest with Cigana and Ray Guardia, where the two sides felt each other out. There was no mention of a particular district. She took out a membership, and then volunteered to help out at the big pre-election party congress in late May to discuss the program and coming campaign. It was at a UQAM pavilion on Sherbrooke at Bleury. There she accosted the easily identifiable Zoubris. "She knew who I was. She had done her research and read up on the party," he says. "I knew right away she would be good. She had so much energy."

There were more meetings, including one at City Hall with Bergeron and Simard-Menard as well as Cigana and Zoubris. Beyond her name, gender and energy, everyone liked her confidence. "Her laughter was contagious," remembers Ray Guardia who was at the first meeting. "We were immediately determined to put her in a winnable district."

Plante wasn't necessarily overflowing with ideas or knowledge about urbanism but she was obviously progressive with a sense of service towards the community. Anyway, she was the one being recruited by the party and it hardly needed more ideas. The Projet Montréal which Plante says attracted her in particular was the one she saw manifesting itself as she biked through the Plateau. "It's definitely more the approach of neighborhoods, of the city on a human scale. That's really what appealed to me."

The Plateau administration's go-for-broke approach, which was controversial both inside and outside the party, didn't put her off. "I am basically an activist. I was in the feminist movement, I spent my whole twenties going to demonstrations, being super socially involved. So bringing about change that is disruptive is not something that upsets me," she says. "It takes a lot to upset me."

At one point, edging closer to saying yes to each other, Plante visited Cigana at his home in Rosemont, not far from where she lives with her trade-union economist husband and two sons, to discuss the mechanics of running—fundraising, putting together a team, the campaign. Finally, Cigana phoned her and asked if she would like to be Projet Montréal's candidate in Ste-Marie. "Bull's eye," she said.

As a student, Plante had lived in the district and appreciated its challenges. There was much to do to improve the physical space—the main focus of our efforts in the Plateau—but just as much on the social front, where the party's program was less developed. "Planning, design, parks, all that is interesting," Plante says. "But what really interests me is the human aspect. I found that in the Centre-Sud there was both. We can work on improving the living environment but also work on itinerancy, prostitution. It's a neighborhood with a lot of low-income housing and poverty. For me it was obvious that if I went with this party, it was to represent this side, the element of social justice."

Plante was formally nominated after la *Fête nationale* and began campaigning immediately, even though the election was still five months off, going to street parties and community events and the like, getting out there, getting herself known. At the time her only announced opponent was the incumbent Pierre Mainville, who was now running as an independent. As a councillor he was "very ground-level" but old-school, increasingly out-of-step with the changing city, and Plante felt that if she was just as ground-level as he was in her campaigning, she could beat "ce dude là."

Then, barely a week into her campaigning, came the news that led almost everyone, including virtually all of Projet Montréal, to write off her chances: having renounced running for mayor of Montreal, Louise Harel said she would still run for council—but in Ste-Marie, rather than the Maisonneuve–Longue-Pointe district she had represented since 2009.

Harel justified the move by saying that it would allow her to take on whomever was elected mayor at the Ville-Marie borough council, over which the city mayor automatically presides. Conveniently, it also meant she would be running for municipal representation of the same people who had elected her to the National Assembly for over a quarter-century, with crushing majorities.

Another impact of the decision: going into the summer of 2013, no one was betting on Valérie Plante to be elected to council. "It was a bit of a shock," says Cigana. "It had been one of the places we thought was winnable."

Plante's reaction was more to the point. "At that point, I said to myself, 'I'm in deep shit.'"

Chapter 21

IN ENDORSING CÔTÉ, Harel was banking on her nationalist street cred to bring in the votes for the eastern half of the city while the conservative consultant won over federalist and business support.

For his part, Bergeron thought he would win the election on the basis of ideas, two in particular. One was the old favourite, the reason he had started Projet Montréal: the tramway. The second he had been developing for three years, and dubbed *Entrée maritime*. It was a grandiose, ambitious project to redevelop the shoreline of the St. Lawrence from the Old Port to the Jacques-Cartier Bridge, creating a new neighbourhood of 9,000 housing units, a 1.6-kilometre boardwalk and a public transport gondola connecting it all to Île Ste-Hélène and Longueuil. Much of it would be built on a reinforced concrete platform above the railyards which have occupied the shoreline for well over a century; the exodus to the off-island suburbs would be slowed if not completely staunched; and thousands of jobs—27,749 to be exact by Bergeron's calculations—would be created.

Bergeron had unveiled the project a year in advance of the election, at a presentation at the Grande bibliothèque. It generated little media interest at the time, with none of the big daily papers even bothering to send a reporter. Still, Bergeron clung to it, convinced it could be the key to a successful election campaign.

A poll commissioned by the party that summer suggested the tramway and the idea of "providing public access to the banks of the St. Lawrence River" were popular projects. More than anything, however, the poll revealed Montrealers were ashamed and grumpy. When asked to describe their feelings about Montreal and its politics, the most common sentiments were embarrassed (46 percent), angry

(39 percent) and pessimistic (33 percent). Only 1 percent said happy, 1.4 percent proud and 3.4 were confident.

The poll also found that 45 percent of those asked planned to vote for Coderre and more than 50 percent expected he would win the election. There was good news—Bergeron was far ahead of both Côté and Joly with 29 percent against 14 percent and 11 percent respectively—but only 6 percent actually expected him to win.

Drilling deeper the poll found that even if he was firmly in the lead, Coderre was vulnerable on various fronts: he was seen as old-school and his recruitment of so many Union councillors meant that people doubted his capacity to bring meaningful change. Likewise, Côte, at 71, was considered to be too old to become mayor. Tellingly, few people were convinced by the coalition with Harel; for every person who felt it was what Montreal needed, five disagreed.

Bergeron didn't escape severe judgement. If many people polled felt that his experience and his training as an urbanist made him a good choice for mayor, more than twice as many felt he was too dogmatic and his ideas too extreme. Still, to the surprise of all, the poll found that Bergeron was personally more popular than the party. "His positives were higher than the Projet brand at the time," says Guardia. This was put down to the "Ferrandez effect" diminishing support for the party as a whole.

The poll was an important tool in developing the party's election strategy. "The decision was to go big because that was the Projet's brand," says Ray Guardia. "We wanted to excite people about what Montreal could look like." So the *Entrée maritime*, the shoreline redevelopment project, and the tramway would get top billing as well as projects like covering the Ville Marie expressway and levelling the Bonaventure autoroute to create a new neighbourhood.

That Bergeron seemed to be more popular than his party reinforced this approach. "It certainly fed our strategy of 'Montreal is willing to dream because this guy is a dreamer,'" says Guardia.

The long-held party plan to "Go west!" was confirmed by the poll's finding that anglophones were particularly unhappy with the state of the city and unimpressed by Coderre and Côté. Not that the party really had much choice, if it was serious about winning. "It was the mathematical reality of the island," says Guardia. "A question of 'where do we grow?' Obviously Hochelaga but once you get past Hochelaga, there's nothing. We had to enlarge the map to have any hope of winning and the next bit of fertile ground, well, the grumpy anglos were as good a fit as any."

Guardia's own past, growing up in NDG when it was an MCM bastion, made the quest personal. "It made no sense to me historically. How come that is a black hole for Projet?"

Bergeron's apparent popularity, at least vis-à-vis that of the party, also reaffirmed the "Let Richard be Richard" strategy. It was one many of us would question soon enough.

At an event in late August to introduce some of the candidates for the Plateau, Bergeron decided to hold forth on how polarizing Ferrandez was. Half the people he spoke to in the borough thought their mayor was "extraordinary," Bergeron said. The other half, however, despised Luc and said they would never vote for Projet Montréal. It was meant to inspire the Plateau troops to give their all to the campaign but Bergeron's clumsy phrasing got the reporters buzzing.

When they asked him to expand on the remark, Bergeron's attempts to walk it back didn't improve things. "When I said 'fifty-fifty,' that's a figure of speech," he said, before finding firmer ground: "In a three-way fight, if you have 50 percent of the people voting for you, you're well on your way."

Bergeron was really just giving voice to what was conventional wisdom, outside the Plateau. Ferrandez might have done some interesting things in the borough—along the lines of what Bloomberg and Sadik-Khan were doing in New York, Delanoë in Paris, what Jan Gehl prescribed for cities the world over—but he was too abrasive, too confrontational for Quebec. It was widely accepted that he would lose.

Certainly, Patrick Lagacé, Yves Boisvert and most pundits were absolutely convinced of that and told Ferrandez as much, a pessimistic prognosis which rubbed off on him. Luc acknowledges he was far from confident that he would be re-elected and Patrick Cigana says that in the run-up to the 2013 campaign, Ferrandez "always acted as if Projet Montréal would lose the Plateau."

Josée Duplessis also seemed to think we were going down to defeat. After joining the executive committee under Applebaum, she had been made its president when Laurent Blanchard became mayor, thus becoming the second most powerful person in the caretaker administration. It meant we rarely saw her in the office—and that her salary had more than doubled. Still, no one questioned whether she would run with us; after all, she had been nominated again as our candidate in De Lorimier several months earlier. Then, out of the blue in mid-September, she announced that she had decided to leave politics.

The reasons she gave in a letter to *Le Devoir* were noble. "I don't want to cling to power like some professional politicians," she wrote. "It is a mandate to be sought from the population, not a job. I want to see more citizens from diverse backgrounds raise their hands to offer their expertise to the City of Montreal for a term or two. For that to happen, there needs to be healthy turnover."

In the office we took it with many grains of salt. It was pointed out that having spent most of a year on the executive committee, her "transitional allocation," based as it was on her recent salary, would be substantial. Either way, the party, especially the team in the Plateau, was left in the lurch. We didn't have time to call a nomination meeting, but we needed a candidate. So we put feelers out and soon found ourselves settling unanimously on Louise Mainville, who sold herself excellently during her interview. Older than the rest of us by at least 15 years but dynamic and fun, she promised to help win over seniors who tended to mistrust Projet Montréal more than younger demographics while voting in much higher numbers.

There was another last-minute change in the Plateau line-up. When Fabrice Bosom had learned that he would have to win a nomination vote to become the borough candidate in Jeanne-Mance, he petulantly pulled out. Christine Gosselin didn't need to hear the news twice: she immediately asked to run there instead of being the sacrificial *pôteau* in Île-Bizard–Ste-Geneviève.

By the second half of August, things had begun to heat up in the city-wide pre-campaign. Coderre was beginning to go after Joly, suggesting she wasn't a serious candidate by saying she was only in it for the visibility and the exposure. It was a patronizing approach which would appear and re-appear frequently in the campaign and which, combined with his tendency to pompously refer to himself in the third person, almost certainly hurt him in the long run. "One of the things that helped her campaign was the overt sexism of some of her opponents," says one of her advisors. "Coderre in particular. Côté a little as well. They were so dismissive of her." It was, he says, infuriating; until he realized "the more Coderre did that, the more Mélanie was going to get votes."

At a debate well before the official start of the campaign, it was deemed that Joly held her own, even if she offered little in the way of a programme beyond change through youth and was clearly without much of a team.

For his part, Bergeron was unanimously acknowledged to be the candidate best in command of the dossiers—a given since he was the only council incumbent—but couldn't shake his image of a "rigid idealogue" in the words of Michel C. Auger. "You scare me," Joly said to Bergeron during the debate, a remark that clearly resonated.

Earlier in the week Bergeron had made the party's platform public, with 71 proposals over 32 pages—"much more succinct" than the program of fours years earlier, he underlined. The broad objective of the platform was "Do whatever it takes to keep young families in Montreal" and the proposals were diverse: 50,000 new residents and 50 percent fewer parking places downtown in the next decade, municipal tax increases limited to inflation, no more junk food restaurants near schools, no more plastic bullets used by police. Still, Bergeron was characterized as being too obsessed with the tramway, not to mention his new megaproject, the *Entrée maritime*.

Côté, meanwhile, tried to sell himself as a man of solutions but didn't really offer any beyond "good governance." By then his candidacy was already limping, even if he had succeeded in attracting a few high-profile candidates in the West End. Côté had taken a trip to Europe during the summer and been roundly criticized for it. His demeanour during debates and public appearances, sometimes befuddled, consistently vague, didn't help.

That first debate offered a chance for candidates to try out lines of attack and, simply, lines. Going after Coderre, Bergeron said his party ought to be called "Réunion Montréal" because of the abundance of recycled Union councillors in its ranks. It was a remark Bergeron would reuse repeatedly during the campaign even though Coderre quickly figured out how to deflect it effectively. "If they're so bad, why did your party try to recruit so many of them?" he would ask.

The other candidates challenged Bergeron on the cost of his mega-projects, saying the price tags of the tramway and the *Entrée maritime* would shackle future generations with debt. His response: in real dollars, the cost of the tramway was nothing compared with the metro, and the *Entrée maritime*, however transformative, would be less expensive than the DIX30 shopping centre in Brossard. Mayors needed vision and ambition, he said.

The race adhered to this script until the end of September when the campaign got officially underway. At that point, Projet Montréal was the only party to have found candidates for all 103 elected positions in the city and also appeared to have the financial advantage. Fundraising rules had been tightened following the revelations at the Charbonneau Commission and elsewhere and the maximum donation reduced from $1,000 per year to $300. This gave the advantage to grassroots parties with big memberships—of which there was only one. Similarly, the maximum allowable expenditure of the parties during the campaign had been reduced, meaning that they would be ever more dependent on the labour of volunteers and activists—again an advantage for Projet.

So Bergeron had reason to feel confident as some 400 members of the party assembled on a warm and pleasant afternoon for the campaign's official kick-off. The event was being held at the Centre des sciences in the Old Port; airy and bright, chic without being glitzy, it was a world apart from the Centre St-Pierre and a sign that the party had graduated to the big leagues. For a party which had long struggled to get media attention, even more encouraging was the turnout of journalists. Everyone seemed to be there.

"The event was beautiful," remembers Ray Guardia. "Patrick Cigana found a great hall and we packed it. [Former MP and radio host] Jean Lapierre was there and we started chatting. He said he had expected 50 or 60 ragtag hippies with Birkenstocks and dreadlocks, but that the people looked normal."

Everything was going to plan until Bergeron, the headliner, began speaking... and didn't stop. "No one had sat down with Richard and said, 'Here's what you have to do, here's your speech, it can't be more than 15 or 20 minutes,'" says Guardia. "Instead we just gave him the mic and off he went."

The speech-lecture went on for at least 45 minutes, Bergeron oblivious to the crowd's increasing restlessness and the people slipping outside for a cigarette or into a side room to chat among themselves. At one point, Bergeron promised to deliver 37.5 kilometres of tramway for Montreal's 375th birthday in 2017. "There's no one I've contacted who says it's possible in four years. No engineer, no manufacturer, no decision maker at any level. All of them tell me that it is impossible." Still, he assured everyone, he would do it, he would find a way.

"It was classic Richard," says Alex Norris. "The bigger the *scène*, the bigger the gaffe. We watched it fall apart before our eyes."

Guillaume Cloutier had returned from his travels earlier in the year and immediately gone to work in the leader's office for Simard-Ménard. Spending his days—and occasional evenings—at City Hall, he had come to know all the municipal affairs reporters, sometimes leaking them stories and sharing his opposition research with them. He felt he had won several of them over as the campaign approached. After the event, several came up to him and said essentially the same thing: "Man, that was painful. But don't worry, we won't do a hatchet job."

In one excessively long speech, Bergeron had shown that he was fundamentally unchanged from the candidate of 2005 and 2009. His wardrobe might have been fancier, the team around him more professional, but he was still the man who thought he knew everything at the same time as he was utterly heedless—or simply ignorant—of political convention and exigencies. "He was hard to take seriously after that," says Norris.

It was two weeks into the campaign when the first poll was taken. At that point, it was still considered Coderre's race to lose with the real question being whether Bergeron or Côté would come in second and which party would form the opposition. Joly was still being treated by many as a political ingénue, a nice addition to the décor but not a serious threat. She wasn't invited to the first official debate of the campaign; a long article by Brian Myles in *L'actualité* about the race didn't mention her once.

But the QMI poll released on October 7th showed it was too early to count her out. As expected, Coderre was in the lead with 39 percent support. Bergeron was second with 23 percent. But Joly was effectively tied with Côté at 16 to his 17 percent and clearly had wind in her sails. She had only 50-odd candidates running for her, her campaign was seat-of-the-pants with nothing resembling an organization or machine, and her program was vague. Instead of a tramway, she was promising 130 kilometres of dedicated bus lanes, but beyond that, it rarely got more specific than change, real change being required. Still, it seemed to be working on the voters, especially the undecided. Certainly, it was working better than what the other candidates were offering.

The poll sowed the seeds to a new narrative: Projet Montréal had stalled out, Côté and the Coalition were sinking and Joly and her Vrai Changement pour Montréal party were the fresh unknown which could surprise everyone. It was a narrative the next poll would reinforce.

Even if it hadn't been released yet, calls for the QMI poll had been completed when *La Presse* published what was dressed up to be an exposé of improper use of funds by our administration in the Plateau. In what came to be known derisively as *la scandale des tomates*, the paper reported that police were looking into a citizen's complaint that the borough had given $36,000 to a community group, called *Plateau milieu de vie*, "intimately connected to Projet Montréal" to run a summer fruit and vegetable market. No matter that almost all the money was spent on building a shed-kiosk and that it was staffed by volunteer labour with a mandate to offer low-cost, healthy food in the poorest part of the borough, an area considered a "food desert."

For a news cycle or two, our administration was portrayed as rife with self-dealing and cronyism as the Charbonneau Commission was exposing Union and Vision Montréal to have been. "Boy that hurt us," says Ray Guardia. "It took the shine off us and we went into the mud for a week, and it was a critical week." Gradually, however, the facts came out and the story was refuted, including a remarkable disavowal in *La Presse* itself by François Cardinal. In a column headlined "Hit Job", he scolded the bad faith and dishonest journalism of his own colleague, saying "it would be laughable if it were not dramatic" and deploring the fact that it could have an impact on the election.

Many feel it did. Shortly after *la scandale des tomates* broke, polling began for a CROP-Radio-Canada survey. It continued while the Coalition, its desperation growing, was revealed to have used illegal "robo-calls"[28] to cast doubt on the integrity of both Projet Montréal and the Coderre team. "For the three days of the poll, I was all over the place trying to clear Projet Montréal's name," Bergeron recalls. "Every day started the same way: 'So it turns out you are just like the others. We believed in you, Mr. Bergeron, and your party, but you're just like the others.'"

The results were released on October 15th. Coderre was still the frontrunner with 41 percent of the vote but Joly had leapfrogged Bergeron and was now in second-place with 24 percent. The Projet leader had declined to 21 percent while Côté was well behind with 11 percent. It set the tone for the rest of the campaign, especially since it was the last poll to be released. "That poll was really harmful—not so much because we were third but because Joly was second and she had come out of nowhere and had a ridiculously poorly organized campaign," says Guardia. "That was a discouraging moment, and a defining one."

With hindsight, Bergeron is unequivocal: the election was over with that poll. From that point on, he says, Joly got the overwhelmingly majority of the media attention, followed at a distance by Coderre. "They hardly talk about me anymore and Marcel Côté—they didn't talk about him at all."

---

28 Robo-calls—automated calls with recorded messages—are not illegal in and of themselves but if they are commissioned by a party it must be made clear. In this case, Côté claimed the firm carrying out the calls for them "forgot" to identify their client.

As Joly repeated ceaselessly, she was in second-place, the alternative to Coderre. In this way, she had usurped Bergeron as the anti-Coderre. And with a more winning formula. For those who had always found Bergeron rigid or scary, as Joly had, she offered a softer, warmer alternative.

In the boroughs, it was a very different story. Joly's Vrai Changement team was thin, to say the least. In late August she had lost the only candidate she had publicly announced by then and the most credible she would have—Jean Fortier, who had been chairman of the executive committee under Pierre Bourque. (His reason: he didn't want to further split the anti-Coderre vote and felt that Côté was a better bet to beat him.) She had struggled to attract others subsequently and the only moderately known candidate to join her team was Lorraine Pagé, a former union leader who was as famous for shoplifting a pair of gloves from The Bay as she was for fighting the good fight on behalf of the province's teachers.

In total, Vrai Changement only managed to field candidates for 55 of the 103 seats up for grabs by the cut-off date. Where they were running, the presence of a Vrai Changement candidate often shook up the race, just as Joly did at the mayoral level. Their absence from a race also had an effect. In the Plateau, Vrai Changement was only fielding a single candidate, for borough councillor in Mile-End, so the Joly groundswell wasn't a concern to us locally. Even if Luc hadn't been confident going into the campaign, the rest of us were.

Richard Ryan remembers having the distinct feeling that "the wind had changed in our favour" in early 2013. The impact of many of our projects was becoming apparent and every time he was out with Ferrandez—at a meeting, buying lunch, inspecting new curb extensions—Richard remembers people accosting them, but not to complain any more. Instead, it was to congratulate them, thank them, encourage them, and plead with Ferrandez not to lose the election so he could continue the changes to the borough. "Usually you just hear the whiners, but slowly the people who supported him were speaking up," Ryan says.

The emergence of community groups like *Plateau milieu de vie*, which ran a nonprofit fresh food and vegetable market, was also an indication that we were doing something right. These sprung up partly in reaction to the dominant—and negative—media discourse about the Plateau, the administration and the changes we were bringing to the borough. But they were also inspired by the changes themselves. Residents saw what was possible and it stimulated their imaginations and whetted their appetites. This was the case for a plethora of *comités de ruelle*, but also initiatives like *Rue publique* which gave itself the broad mission to "improve the health and safety of Montreal neighbourhoods by reimagining streets and advocating for better use of public spaces."

This ground-level support certainly made me confident about re-election, a confidence which only grew during the campaign with the general lack of enthusiasm for Coderre or Côté and the weakness of their candidates on the Plateau. It was lost on most of the media, however. About two weeks before the election, CBC's Daybreak did a live broadcast from Café Olimpico on St-Viateur which featured a debate between Luc and the Coderre and Côté candidates. I went down to the café and during a pause, found myself chatting with Mike Finnerty, the host whom I had known for years. "You've done some really interesting stuff on the Plateau," he said, "but it's too bad it's all going to come to an end." I told him I wasn't so pessimistic and explained why. He listened politely but it was clear he was convinced we were finished.

Chapter 22

ELECTION DAY 2013 WAS SUNNY for early November, which fuelled our optimism even more. The same dynamic which had contributed to the emergence of supportive community groups also meant that our campaign had never lacked for enthusiastic volunteers and, as usual, never were they so plentiful as on E-Day. At that point, there didn't seem to be any doubt about our re-election on the Plateau. No new city-wide polls had emerged but our own polling showed us with comfortable leads in every district. As the day progressed, the bingo sheets indicated that our supporters were getting out and voting. Contrary to 2009, and then again four years later in 2017, I don't remember any frantic attempts to assure that everyone who indicated that they would vote for us actually went to the polls. The general sentiment of the team was that we weren't going to win the city but the Plateau would remain ours wall-to-wall.

Eventually we all made our way down to the Corona. There was no line-up or crush of people waiting to order beer at the bar but it certainly wasn't empty as election night events so often are for parties when the campaign has not gone as hoped. Relatively early in the evening, Luc and the party's entire slate were declared elected on the Plateau—even if counting was nowhere near complete, the margin of our candidates' leads made it inconceivable that they wouldn't win. As Luc's victory was announced, Guillaume Cloutier turned to where the TV cameras were lined up and gave them the finger with both hands. His message: "You created a parallel reality so big that the world believed it and even we believed it in a way. Then it just didn't happen, goddammit! How could you be so out of touch?"

It wasn't just that we had once again swept the borough, it was the margin of the victory. Everyone had beat their closest competitor by at least 20 percent. In Mile-End, even if she was up against a Vrai Changement candidate as well as ones running with Coderre and Côté, Marie Plourde had won by more than 30 percent. Richard Ryan won by almost 40 percent. As he had anticipated, Alex Norris didn't have such an easy go of it in Jeanne-Mance. Still he beat Piper Huggins, who had ended up running for Côté's Coalition, by 20 percent. Remarkable also was the turnout on the Plateau. Almost 20 percent more people went out and voted in 2013 as they did in 2009, 40 percent more than in 2005. Another by-product of our controversial if generally popular administration was a higher level of civic engagement.

There was a similar trend in Rosemont–La Petite-Patrie where Projet Montréal also scored a decisive wall-to-wall victory. More decisive, as a whole than on the Plateau. Croteau won by 38 percent points. Érika Duchesne more than doubled the scored of her closest opponent, winning by 3,265 votes this time. But the sweetest victory was that of Guillaume Lavoie, running in the least Projet-friendly district against the strongest competition. He won by almost 1,000 votes over former Radio-Canada reporter Françoise Stanton running for Coderre.

Elsewhere, the party made breakthroughs in every direction—Sylvain Ouellet in Villeray–St-Michel–Parc-Extension, Craig Sauvé in the Sud-Ouest, Mindy Pollak in Outremont, among others. Then there were those described as "giant killers" by Éric Alan Caldwell. These included Magda Popeanu who beat Helen Fotopulos, who like so many other Union orphans had ended up running for Coderre.

Both Caldwell and Popeanu were running for the third time and Caldwell's sense of foreboding had not abated during the campaign. Bergeron wasn't popular in Hochelaga. As McQueen had done in both 2009 and 2013, Caldwell had learned to hold the party's brochures a certain way so that the leader's photo wasn't visible. Meanwhile, the question at virtually every door was whether he was with Louise Harel or not. "My girlfriend, who used to go door-to-door with me, used to repeat every night into the pillow, 'You're going to lose, you're going to lose.'"

Still, even if he was up against Laurent Blanchard, who had been unanimously lauded for his steady work as emergency acting mayor, Caldwell campaigned relentlessly. "I worked hard, saying 'Last chance ever!' Still, I was sure I was going to lose." He continued to the bitter end. "I ended my door-to-door campaigning at a friend's house at a quarter to eight saying, 'I just lost six months of my life. Now it's over. This is my third election; this is my third defeat. It's over. Fuck it.' He offered me a beer and a cigarette and I took them."

As the early numbers came in for his district, he was behind Blanchard and thought he wouldn't even bother going to the Corona. "It was my girlfriend who convinced me to go to the rally. On the way I was losing. Then, at some point, it became a tie." Finally, he was ahead and went on to beat Blanchard by almost 7 percent.

Still, if there was one giant who fell in 2013 it was Louise Harel in Sainte-Marie, the district immediately to the west of Caldwell's. Her election in the heart of her fiefdom had been taken as a given—since first being elected in the neighbourhood in 1981 she had never got less than 50 percent of the vote and always more than doubled the total of her closest opponent. But never before had she run on a ticket led by a conservative federalist. Nor had she ever faced a candidate with the energy, enthusiasm and optimism of Valérie Plante.

Projet Montréal didn't invest much in the race in terms of resources or hope. Of much greater concern was getting Bergeron elected in St-Jacques, where he was running against one of Coderre's star recruits, Radio-Canada journalist Philippe Schnobb, and getting Jimmy Zoubris elected in Peter-McGill, the third Ville-Marie district.

Since Harel had announced she would run there, Sainte-Marie was considered "a throwaway, no-chance district" by Projet Montréal, says Oliver Paré, who was the DOC, *directeur de campagne*, for the borough of Ville-Marie during the 2013 campaign.

"There was no world in which she was supposed to beat Louise Harel," he says. "Any resources I got went first to Richard or Janine [Krieber, Bergeron's *colistière*], and then secondarily for Jimmy because we thought we had a shot in Peter-McGill. Val was last on the resource allotment. I was pretty clear with her about it. There was nothing I could do but tell her she needed to bust her ass and that she had no chance unless she went all in. And she responded to that. I asked her to be on the doors every day and she pretty much was."

For his part, it never crossed Bergeron's mind to make an effort to help Plante get elected. "For me, she was the girl who was going to get killed. She was willing to get killed. To me she didn't have a chance there. She couldn't win. Period. No question."

Left essentially on her own, Plante had a core group of four volunteers in her district with whom she would go door-to-door but occasionally found herself alone for the task—something the party discouraged for security reasons. Whether alone or with a volunteer, there were also times when the prospect of another evening of walking the sidewalks and climbing the staircases of Sainte-Marie was almost too much for her to bear, Paré says. "She would bike across the bridge from her work, get home, see her kids and call me in tears, saying 'I don't want to do it tonight. I want to hang out with my kids,'" says Paré. "And I would be like, 'Sorry? Are you *serious*?' I was a prick. I was a jerk. But I felt like I needed to do that in my role as a campaign director."

He adds, "There were definitely breaking points in that campaign where she didn't really understand or know the value of what she was doing, why she was leaving her kids for so long."

Paré, who grew up in NDG, had come to Projet Montréal via Guardia and the NDP, and at one point told Plante that she, like Jack Layton, fit into the mold of the "happy warrior" and "that was her strength—that was what was going to propel her. She liked that and I think she was empowered by that description."

Plante was also fuelled, he says, by blatant sexist condescension of "the two Pierres"—Pierre Mainville and Pierre Paiement, the candidate for Équipe Denis Coderre. Paré remembers a debate in a church basement where the two of them routinely interrupted her, at the same time as they deferred to "the anointed one," Harel, who had shown up to the debate in a fur coat. "It was brutal," he says. "I could see her getting really frustrated. And Louise Harel, everyone would listen as soon as she talked. But Val, she's a young woman, no one had any time for her."

At one point, he says, Mainville, who stands at least 6'4", walked over to Plante and stood towering over her as he expounded on an issue. "Mainville was just very dismissive and shitty towards her, convinced he would win as if it were his right."

This kind of treatment, Paré says, fed Plante's fire. "It was her first entrance into the political realm and she had this feeling, 'Who are these people to tell me I don't have a place?'"

That fire clearly had an impact on the ballot-box. When the district's votes were counted, it wasn't even close: Plante beat Harel by almost 3.5 percent. Meanwhile, next door in Saint-Jacques, it was a nail-biter with Bergeron beating Schnobb by marginal 36 votes. In Peter McGill, Jimmy Zoubris finished fourth of four candidates with less than 16 percent of the votes, Projet's most obvious victim of the Joly surge. "I mailed it in the last three weeks," he says. "I didn't even bother campaigning."

It would take several weeks before the final numbers were confirmed, but several basic facts were obvious as we congregated at the Corona. It was a good night for Projet Montréal. We had doubled the size of our caucus at City Hall from 10 to 20; doubled the number of borough councillors, from four to eight; and doubled the number of boroughs in which we had at least a toehold, from five to 10, out of a total of 18. The party was the official opposition and by a long shot; the Coalition had only elected six councillors to City Hall and Joly's Vrai Changement only four.

Still, it was a bad night for Richard Bergeron. Again, he had come in third-place in the mayoral vote—his share was 25.5 percent, virtually identical to that of 2009. During his speech he acknowledged what we had all taken for granted if he didn't win: that he would not be leading the party into the next election. He even evoked the possibility of not returning to sit in city council and instead leaving Saint-Jacques for Janine Krieber to represent. "We will let you know our decision within 12 days," he said. "I will discuss things with my *colistière*."

It took less than three days. On the Wednesday morning following the Sunday election, he was at a lectern at City Hall surrounded by his new and re-elected councillors, announcing that he would be quitting politics sometime within two years. "This was my third election and it was my last," he said. "I will stay as long as it takes to make sure that Projet Montréal is the real opposition to the Coderre administration, and as long as it takes for all the newly elected officials to be comfortable in their roles. We can imagine between 12 and 24 months. Then I will leave."

Chapter 23

It was an announcement Bergeron says he immediately regretted, or at least questioned. "As I got off the little stage in the big lobby of City Hall, I thought, 'What a mess I just made! What a mistake!'" he recalls.

It wasn't because he lacked a job, a business or a fortune to fall back on. That didn't bother him. Even if "financially I have never been brilliant" he had always got by on his wits and energy. He had no doubt that he would find something interesting and well paid enough. Rather, he realized that he was unlikely to find anything as fun or gratifying to his very healthy ego. The man who had never really wanted to lead the party, who had never seen himself as a politician, had grown attached to the job and the role.

Making matters worse—much worse—no one in the party tried to talk him out of it or urged him to reconsider. On the contrary. "There were people who were only too happy and would have preferred it to be eight months instead of 12 to 24." he says. "I may have stepped on toes without realizing it. I may have dominated too much as the founder, as the leading ideologue, as the leading theorist. Maybe I've offended people over time. I don't know. But still, it never happened that somebody said, 'Maybe you were a little bit quick to quit?' Or 'Can you perhaps reconsider?' Never, never, never. And I didn't like that. I really didn't like that."

Intellectually, Bergeron appreciated that the party needed a new leader before the next election and that, given his personality and his role in creating the party, it would have been near impossible for him to stay on in any capacity but that of leader. Still, as eminently Cartesian and as patently unsentimental as he was, Bergeron couldn't digest the party's eagerness to move on to someone else, even if there was no one waiting in the wings. He couldn't get over the insult or hurt.

It was at the party's *Conseil de direction* meetings every month at the offices on Notre-Dame Ouest where Bergeron says he felt it the most keenly. "Right away finding my replacement was a priority," he remembers. "In an hour-and-a-half meeting, we'd go through all the other points quickly and then the last three-quarters we'd spend talking about my replacement. They were happy to get rid of me. That's how I felt. 'Couldn't you be a little less eager?'"

Even if the subject barely appears in the minutes of the *Conseil de direction* meetings from that period, Patrick Cigana confirms there was "indeed a lot of discussion about his succession." But it wasn't because people wanted him gone as soon as possible, Cigana says. "Rather, because we realized we had a lot of work to do. Since the party had never had a leadership race, that point in the statutes was covered in about one paragraph, and as Joël pointed out to us repeatedly, the devil is in the details when it comes to leadership races."

That said, there was more relief than regret in the party after the announcement. Why members of the party may have reacted the way they did, and why they may not have been as grateful to Bergeron as he would have expected, varies from one person to another. For many, it had simply been an inevitability which had finally come to pass, perhaps an election too late. "We all always had doubts about Richard as a leader," says François Limoges. "Even in 2009."

Then there were those who, having found him remote, cold and a bit superior, simply didn't think he was interested in their displays of gratitude or regret, or were shy about expressing them.

Still others were angry at him for his disdainful attitude during the campaign which had just ended, in particular his scorn for the opinions or advice of others. "Whenever we gave him an idea or tried to suggest something, he was fucking contemptuous," remembers Guillaume Cloutier. "It was kind of like, 'You little staffers with your little ideas. I'm a big academic.' Fucking arrogant."[29]

---

29 I had tasted a bit of that myself while helping coach him for the English debate on CTV. I suggested that he pay homage to the diversity of Montreal by saying that it constitutes one of the city's richest attributes. Bergeron dismissively told me he wouldn't because he didn't agree.

Whatever the case—and for many of us it was a mixture of factors—our collective reaction left Bergeron wounded and unhappy. "No, it wasn't an easy time for me. I thought you all lacked class."

If there was one glimmer of encouragement in his life it came from an unexpected quarter and an unlikely man: Denis Coderre, who showed a willingness to reach across the aisle and entrust Bergeron, along with other councillors elected with other parties, with real responsibilities. A certain amount of this was inevitable if Coderre wanted to get anything done. It is widely accepted that had the 2013 campaign lasted a week or two longer, Mélanie Joly would likely have been elected mayor. In the final two weeks of the campaign, her support kept growing while Coderre's began disintegrating. During the last week, Coderre pretty much disappeared from view, Bergeron remembers. "His team had judged that if he continued to flounder, Joly would become mayor of Montreal."

He ended up winning with just 32 percent of the vote, the lowest share since 1940 when there were only 66,483 voters but nine candidates for mayor. His candidates won only 27 seats in city council, well short of a majority. The day after the vote, Coderre got on the phone and began wooing opposition councillors.

The first he called were those elected with Côté's Coalition, who, he correctly surmised, had little binding them together as a team, and not only because their leader had lost his bid for a council seat. Even if only six Coalition candidates had been elected to city council, three of them were borough mayors. Of these, two were given important portfolios on Coderre's executive committee: Russell Copeman, who was put in charge of housing, urbanism and the *Office de consultation publique*, and Réal Ménard, who was handed environment, sustainable development and *grands parcs*. Elsie Lefebvre, also elected with the Coalition, was made a junior member of the executive committee, while Côté himself was recruited, at an honorary $1/year, as an advisor to the president of the executive committee.

Along with perks handed out to councillors elected with local parties in various boroughs, these moves bought Coderre a degree of loyalty and gave him some breathing room. But his charm offensive didn't end there.

He had frozen Projet Montréal out of what he described as a non-partisan administration but he did have Bergeron in mind for a high-profile task. During the campaign, the Projet Montréal leader had proposed that one of the most overdue initiatives in recent Montreal history be made a priority: covering over the trench that is the Ville-Marie expressway between Rue St-Urbain and Rue Sanguinet, a distance of slightly more than 500 metres.

It was an idea that was unanimously endorsed by the other main candidates and within a few weeks of the election Coderre was suggesting to Bergeron that he oversee the job. Coincidentally enough, Bergeron had got the green light from his caucus to propose the exact same thing to Coderre. "I have never conceived of my role in politics as being to oppose just because I am in opposition," he says.

Coderre was seemingly candid as to why he wanted Bergeron for the job. "I won't beat around the bush: I don't know anyone in my gang who can do it. And I know you'd be good at it," is how Bergeron remembers the conversation going.

Less than three weeks later, Coderre was giving Bergeron another responsibility, that of president of the standing committee overseeing the inspector-general's work. The office of the inspector-general, mandated to "eliminate fraud, waste, corruption and abuse of power" had been one of Coderre's few campaign promises and the commission was created to supervise its work.

Bergeron had also given himself a task: that of preparing a presentation that would be the final word on the benefit tramways offered Montreal. He had been the leading apostle of their re-introduction to the streets of the city for more than a decade and they had been the central plank of Projet's program for three elections. Not without effect—Gérald Tremblay had been seduced enough by the idea to make them the centrepiece of the city's 2008 Plan de transport, which was supposed to determine transportation planning in the city for the following two decades. But since then, nothing substantial had happened. Routes had been proposed, technologies discussed, timelines and financing options alluded to. But no project office had been opened, let alone any excavation undertaken. The disorder and crisis management requirements of Tremblay's last mandate had made sure of that.

But a certain stability had returned to Montreal municipal politics with a new mayor, who many expected to stay in power for multiple mandates. With his presentation, Bergeron hoped to provide the conclusive argument which would prod Coderre into finally moving forward with a modern tramway network.

Bergeron had always put great stock in the power of exhaustively researched and methodically reasoned argument. Indeed, some blamed the recent election defeat on him over-estimating his capacity to appeal to voters' intelligence above their self-interest, political loyalties or emotional responses. But that was Richard and so he set to work.

For the first months of 2014 he was rarely in the opposition offices on the ground floor of City Hall into which the Projet team had moved from the Aquarium nearby. Instead he was at home on de la Gauchetière, preparing three separate documents which would make up the presentation. The first was the 98-slide PowerPoint presentation, with, of course, the script to accompany it. Then there was a 24-page, single-spaced economic and financial analysis of a possible tramway line in Montreal. For this, he chose Boul. St-Laurent, from bottom to top, from Boul. René-Lévesque to Boul. Henri-Bourassa. He estimated that each of its 10 kilometres would cost $40 million to build and attract as many as 125,000 passengers per day. He projected it to be a tremendous cost-benefit success, with a per-trip cost coming in at less than the bus or the metro (and much less than private automobiles). The final document was a catalogue of the 260 modern tramway networks around the globe. During the campaign he had estimated the number at somewhere in the region of 125—fewer, he was to discover, than exist in Europe alone. The message was clear: if cities which most people in Montreal had never even heard about, including a half-dozen in Russia with climates as extreme as ours, could have modern tramways, what were we waiting for? Or, as Bergeron puts it, "It was bulletproof. Someone with these three studies in hand—there's not a word to say. All the answers are there."

Bergeron finally delivered the presentation—it was titled "Move, Enhance, Develop"—to a room of perhaps 75 people at the Phi Centre a few days after *la Fête nationale*. His main goal, he said, was simply to stimulate and raise the level of debate surrounding tramways. But he had another objective. "Seduce. You have to win over the heart, not just the head." To this end, he said he was prepared to give the presentation to pretty much whomever, whenever. "As soon as there are 15 people assured for a presentation, I am available... I'll be happy to take my pilgrim's staff and do this all summer long."

Over the following months he gave the presentation to various groups around the city and felt like he was on his way to accomplishing his mission. But when fall arrived there was one particular audience he hadn't reached. "I got to the point where I thought, 'There's one person left who hasn't seen the conference but should see it, and that's the mayor.'"

So he got in touch with Denis Dolbec, Coderre's chief of staff, and proposed a personal, one-on-one presentation. His offer was accepted and before long Bergeron was entering the mayor's office with a printed version of the study and setting up his laptop. "I thought I was going to spend at least half an hour talking to him about the logic, the economics and the deployment of the modern tramway around the world, " Bergeron says. "But when I start showing it to him, I find he's not interested. He says, 'This is really big. You've worked hard, it's obvious you've worked hard. It seems obvious to me that you're right. You convinced Gérald Tremblay. Why would you be wrong?'"

Still, Coderre said, there was a problem. "You're certainly right, but admit it, this is big for me. I'm going to have a hard time getting this done unless you're on the executive committee. And since you're the leader of the opposition you can't be a member of the executive committee."

Coderre, of course, remembered Bergeron's announcement following the election that he intended to not just step down as leader of Projet Montréal but also to quit politics. And he had picked up on something that few in the party fully appreciated. "He's a politician," Bergeron says. "He knows what politics is. He says to me, 'Richard, between the two of us, you don't want to leave, do you?' Damn! He nails it! Just like that.

"And then he butters me up a little, he says, 'Anyway, Montreal can't afford to lose you. All I ask is that you stay elected. Come join my executive committee.'"

Bergeron didn't require any more convincing but there was a hitch: as determined by provincial law, the executive committee had to have at least seven members but no more than 11. It already had its full complement and Coderre wasn't going to dump someone to make place for Bergeron. "But don't worry," Coderre said with a nonchalance that stunned Bergeron, "we'll just get the law changed."

Bergeron had to break the news to the party. The first person he told was Luc Ferrandez since Bergeron felt he was the only member of caucus capable of taking over Projet's leadership, even on an interim basis. "Objectively, you are the only person who can do this. There is no one else in the party who has the authority to lead it," Bergeron remembers telling Ferrandez.

Luc was flattered but says he had misgivings. His administration was in the midst of controversy once again over parking policy, and Ferrandez anticipated resistance from the rest of caucus. Bergeron also says Luc told him he might not be the best choice because he didn't want to become mayor of Montreal. "I said to him, 'As interim leader you will not be able to be a candidate for the leadership, therefore you can't be candidate for mayor of Montreal.' He said, 'That reassures me.'"

Luc agreed to take over the leadership on an interim basis and even accepted why Bergeron would want to cross the floor to work with Coderre. "Richard said, 'They are in power; we are not. If we want to achieve the things that correspond to our program, I have to go with them. I don't want to leave politics without getting things done for Montreal,'" Ferrandez remembers.

At the time, Coderre was still in his honeymoon phase with an approval rating of 70 percent or higher. As mayor he was smiling and omnipresent, hastening out on a heartbeat from his home or office to the scene of any event generating media attention—a major fire, a sinkhole on a downtown street, mailboxes installed on the edge of a city park—as if his presence alone would remedy the situation. There was a feeling among many—a dread among Projet Montréal members—that he was in power for at least two mandates, possibly more. It was a perception Coderre encouraged, telling people around him, "I will beat Drapeau."

If Ferrandez was understanding of Bergeron's rationale, the caucus as a whole was less indulgent when it was convened on Friday, October 24th to be told the news. Few were convinced when, speaking of Coderre, he said "he's more open than we think." Fewer still when he tried to make his defection appear like he was simply fulfilling his duty. "There is no one in his party capable of achieving anything in urban planning and transport, and it is certain that I will succeed.'"

The perception was that Bergeron had actively solicited a place on Coderre's executive committee while still opposition leader, which many deemed beyond the pale. Bergeron's unspoken resentment of the caucus's lack of gratitude for everything he had done for the party just hardened attitudes.

He had come to the meeting with a resignation letter typed out, but asked caucus to allow him to remain leader for another two weeks, until the party celebrated its 10th anniversary. The idea was greeted skeptically. When he told the caucus that Ferrandez had agreed to be his replacement as interim leader, it was just too much.

Councillor after councillor said their piece, all expressing a sense of betrayal, few indicating any sympathy for his motives or ambition to leave his mark on the city. "Everyone was angry for two reasons," says Ferrandez. "First, that he was leaving [with Coderre] and then that he wanted to appoint his successor because it was not up to him to decide."

It was agreed Bergeron should step down immediately and he was asked to leave while the caucus remained behind in the big light-filled room at the top of the Chaussegros-de-Léry building to decide who would lead the party and how it would deal with Bergeron's departure. He and his press attaché, Catherine Maurice, had asked that it be presented as an amicable parting, that his ascension-defection to Coderre's executive committee be kept under wraps until the 10th anniversary and then spun as if it were happening with the party's blessing.

Many agreed with this but others felt that in the zero-sum world of politics, it would end up being seen as a coup for Coderre. Not just the leader but the actual founder of the opposition—its brain and still, more than anyone else, its public face—rallying to the enemy's side. Eventually, it was agreed that no mention would be made of Bergeron joining Coderre's administration for at least two weeks. In any case, Coderre had only asked Bergeron to sit as an independent, not to actually join his party.

After that was agreed to, the choice of an interim leader was almost anti-climactic. There were only two candidates: Ferrandez and Émilie Thuillier. Émilie says she only ran because she didn't want it to be a coronation for Luc. "It would have been revealing. If I had won the interim, it would have been a real message to Luc."

For his part, Ferrandez told caucus that he was running not because Bergeron had designated him to be his successor but in order to change the focus of the party. He felt less time and energy should be placed on promoting the old hobby horse—the tramway—and more on empowering the boroughs, financially and otherwise, to implement local improvements, street corner by street corner. "The idea was dynamic neighborhoods on a human scale. That's what I wanted to defend."

It was very much the mayor of the Plateau speaking. Even if not everyone agreed with this approach, there was an overwhelming consensus that Ferrandez was the best choice to lead the party, that only he had the authority and stature to succeed Bergeron. He won the vote hands-down—even after he insisted that being interim leader would not automatically render him ineligible to run for the job on a permanent basis. He had decided to keep his options open.

"I was happy with the process, and with the outcome," says Thuillier. "The caucus had chosen Luc so afterwards people could question some things but they couldn't say they didn't choose him."

The announcement of the change in leadership was made the following Monday—very carefully. There was no mention of Bergeron joining the Coderre administration or even of sitting as an independent. Rather, a decade after founding the party, Bergeron said he was ceding the leadership because of "the weight of the years" and because he felt he had "reached certain limits." He hurried from the news conference without answering any questions.

At the conseil general timed to coincide with the 10th anniversary, Bergeron said he was stepping down with a sense of accomplishment.

"It is extraordinary what we have done in the last 10 years. There are 1,500 members of our party today. We have changed the way of doing politics. We have become a new reference, especially in terms of integrity, because from the outset, we said no to certain financing methods. We forced ourselves to do politics with less money, and we showed the population that, yes, it was possible."

The timing of Bergeron's departure was made more poignant by the recent death of party co-founder Claude Mainville, who after moving to the Laurentians in 2006 had found relief for his asthma but in time succumbed to cancer. Bergeron paid homage to his old friend even if they had fallen out of touch, and a moment of silence was observed.

No mention was made of Bergeron joining the Coderre administration, except in whispered conversation among those who already knew. "I'm just waiting for the other shoe to drop," Alex Norris remembers Ray Guardia telling him.

That shoe dropped a week later, by which time Philippe Couillard's government had lifted the limit on the number of members allowed on the executive committee, and Coderre was on the verge of announcing Bergeron's nomination. Leaks to both *La Presse* and *Le Devoir* made clear that Bergeron was pushed toward the exit when it was learned that he was negotiating with Coderre to join his administration.

As news filtered down to the party rank-and-file, Bergeron's departure became caricatured as a sell-out, an opportunistic betrayal. He was about to lose the significant salary boost which came from being leader of the opposition, it was whispered, so he replaced it with the bump that came with a seat on the executive committee.

Bergeron angrily rejects the suggestion that he betrayed the party. "Betrayal? Where is the betrayal? I was the one who had reason to feel betrayed," he says. "I hadn't heard a kind word for a year! On the contrary, you all were smiling ear-to-ear at the prospect of my leaving. In a year I had not had a single sign of appreciation, neither from an elected official, nor from a member, from anyone. Not even from the people closest to me. From Emilie, from Magda, from Patrick Cigana. And on the other side, there was the flatterer..."

Chapter 24

AFTER THE TOUGH YEAR which Bergeron had just gone through, quitting the leadership of Projet Montréal came as a huge, unexpected relief. He has little memory of the showdown with caucus or even the 10th anniversary event two weeks later. He does, however, recall clearly how he felt immediately after the big meeting with caucus. There was no regret or mourning. "When I came home, I felt like I was floating on air. I never would have guessed that that would happen but it felt like 200 pounds had been lifted off my back. I swear. I thought, 'This doesn't make sense. I haven't felt like this in how many years?' That's when I realized the burden I had been carrying."

The relief was soon followed by a sense of exhilarating change, even influence as he found himself once again in a seat at the executive committee table. *Le flatteur* had not given him a "service" or "direction" to be in charge of, such as transport, urbanism or infrastructure, as most members have. Rather, he was made responsible for major projects downtown as well as getting things moving on a tramway system in the city and region, most pressingly on the new Champlain Bridge, upon which construction was due to begin in the coming months.

It was a "horizontal mandate" which required that Bergeron work with staff from various departments without having any real authority over them, but that wasn't an issue, at least not to begin with. Indeed, he could have interpreted such a mandate as to allow him to intervene at executive committee meetings on all and any subject but his cocksure temperament meant that was hardly necessary. In his telling, he picked up where he had left off after being dumped by Tremblay's executive committee four years earlier—eagerly reading all the dossiers which were scheduled to come before the executive committee each week, often involving thousands of pages of documents, and holding forth as he saw fit when subjects came up for discussion.

"I happily ventured into other people's jurisdictions," he says, even if members only expected to answer to Coderre or Pierre Desrochers, the president of the executive committee. "I stuck my nose into the police even if Anie Samson was responsible for them. I pumped up the work Lionel Perez was doing because in my opinion he wasn't getting the recognition he deserved on infrastructure. I stood up to Russell Copeman, and there were a lot of confrontations with Desrochers."

Copeman was a target because he was in charge of urbanism, which of course was Bergeron's specialty and preferred area for pontification. Desrochers, meanwhile, formed an intense enmity for Bergeron after the new recruit convinced Coderre to kill a pet project of Desrochers'—an immense underground parking lot beneath Square Phillips.

When named to Gérald Tremblay's executive committee five years earlier, one of Bergeron's first victories had been to convince the mayor not to build a huge underground parking lot at the Îlot Clark, the plaza near Place des Arts planned as an extension to the Quartier des Spectacles. He had shown that the projected cost of construction and anticipated revenue were both absurdly optimistic. Similarly, with the Square Phillips project, he managed to convince Coderre that there was no shortage of indoor parking in the area and that the project would almost certainly end up being an over-budget white elephant.

"I paid for it though. For three years Pierre Desrochers kept after me," Bergeron says. "But Russell Copeman was my *bête noire*. Russell was always provoking me. And he got me every time. I always picked up the gauntlet that he threw. And that led to some pretty heated arguments."

Sensing that Coderre took pleasure in his challenging, even needling, of other members of the executive committee, Bergeron says he took on the role of provocateur. "He let me speak on everything," Bergeron says of Coderre. He took on Chantal Rouleau when she proudly said she had spent $1 billon one year on maintaining and improving Montreal's water supply and distribution network. "I said,

'Spending a billion dollars, is that in itself something to be proud of? It's as if the minister of health said to his colleagues, 'Ha ha! You're a gang of losers! I spent 50 percent of the Quebec budget!'"

Manon Gauthier, who was in charge of culture, was a favourite target, as she had to defend works of public art which most members around the table had no time for. "I'd say, 'Another horror!' And if there's one thing I know that's worse than contemporary art, *estie*, it's the discourse about contemporary art," he says. "I was poking her and Denis Coderre was happy. He'd say, 'Keep on doing it' even though he had to defend her."

One time, he says, he so demolished the plans for the overhauling of Place Vauquelin beside City Hall that some of the bureaucrats presenting the project with Réal Menard were left on the verge of tears. "What you did there, Richard, it just isn't done," Menard told him. "Even for me it is hurtful what you did."

"What do you want, Réal? I'm obliged to tell the truth," Bergeron says he responded. "This is a very bad project. We don't have the right to let a project like this happen."

The episode revealed a casual, offhand approach to urban design which appalled Bergeron—handing out projects as playthings to elected officials who had no background, knowledge or interest in the field. "Pierre Desrochers is told, 'You have fun with Square Viger.' 'Réal, you have fun with Place Vauquelin.' To each, his toy. As if there is no profession, no skills required for this kind of thing. They think that it is all a game."

The rare former colleague who will speak about Bergeron's time on the executive committee has nothing but good things to say about his input. "His contribution to the debate at the executive committee was next level," says Réal Menard, who sat beside him at the big, round table in Salle Peter McGill. "He was someone who studied the files and asked a lot of questions. Very pertinent questions. And people had to be ready and they had to know their files."

Coderre took Bergeron's opinion seriously—not the case for everyone around the table, Ménard says, confirming, to some degree, Bergeron's assertion that the mayor didn't even bother trying to hide his contempt for some of his underlings.

"Coderre, he didn't like anybody," says Bergeron. "There's only one person he admires and that's Denis Coderre. He has his pawns—Russell Copeman, Pierre Desrochers, Harout Chitilian. Lionel Perez, he's a good plumber. The rest were crap in his eyes."

It was a contempt that Bergeron seemed to share and the impression he gives is that, at least initially, while he was still in Coderre's good graces, he and the mayor were a pair of bros, mocking the other members of the executive committee continually behind their backs, sometimes even to their faces.

Bergeron derides other members of the executive for their sycophancy towards Coderre but he himself may have joined in the fawning. He says that one of the skills he developed to survive and thrive at the orphanage was learning how to kiss up to power. "That was always a concern of mine since I was very young," he says. "Get the adults on your side. Find a way to get the adults on your side. And it always worked."

Later in life, he says he used the technique on employers and others further up the food chain than him, including, apparently, Coderre. It seems to have worked. For a time, Bergeron says that he and the mayor were tight enough that Coderre considered Bergeron might make a good successor, even if he was almost a decade older. "The first two years were fabulous," Bergeron says, recalling a trip back from a function at la Maison Alcan in the mayoral limousine in the fall of 2016. Out of the blue, he says, Coderre said to him, "Look Richard, I may be going into international politics soon, and then you're going to take over, you're going to be mayor."

Bergeron hadn't had any indication previously that Coderre was shopping for a new gig. As far as he knew, he still wanted to surpass Drapeau. "I said, 'Come on Denis! The only job that suits you is secretary-general of the UN and the position has just been handed out.' He said, 'No, there are plenty of other positions and I'm interested in international work.' I said, 'Tell me about it! You're always on a plane, going all over the world.'"

By this time, Bergeron had seen his dream of a modern street-level tramway for Montreal—the mission which prompted him to go into politics in the first place—essentially killed with the announcement that the *Caisse de depot et placement du Québec*, the provincial pension fund, was taking charge of furnishing the metropolitan region with an innovative light-rail system. Known as the REM, it constituted a major paradigm shift in the financing and construction of public transit in the province—as well as an implicit acknowledgement that a project of the scale required was beyond the capacities of the city and the Société de transport de Montréal to implement in a reasonable timeline. After all, how long had Montreal been waiting for the blue line to be extended or the "rapid transit" bus service on Pie-IX to be sorted out?

The province adopted and amended a litany of laws to give the provincial pension fund a virtual carte blanche to implement the project without having to abide by various regulations or accommodate the objections of municipalities and boroughs it passed through. It also provided a variety of financial incentives to make the Caisse's $6-billion-plus investment worthwhile, including a substantial value-added levy on building permits and municipal taxes of properties near REM stations. In this way, once the ooohs and ahhhs following the initial announce of the project subsided, it seemed to many people to be a real-estate play as much as it was a public transit solution. Especially given the fact that the Caisse actually owned many properties in the vicinity of planned stations which would see their value soar.

The announcement that the Caisse would take responsibility for the financing and construction of the project came in the spring of 2015, just a few months after Bergeron was named to the executive committee. The mandate was to provide some sort of light-rail which would cross the new Champlain Bridge from the South Shore and link up to the airport. The city was in turn asked by the Caisse to make a proposal for its preferred type of service, a task which naturally fell to Bergeron.

He proposed a traditional street-level tramway but he knew it was fundamentally flawed. "I had no way to get to the airport in less than an hour," he says. "If you follow the spirit of the tramway, you serve the neighborhoods you're passing through. And if you go through large vacant areas, you take advantage of them to create neighborhoods. With the number of stations that it entailed, it's an hour and eight minutes on the tramway before arriving at the airport from René-Lévesque and Robert-Bourassa."

Bergeron nonetheless got the greenlight from Coderre to pitch the proposal to CDPQ-Infra, the newly-created Caisse subsidiary with the mandate to build the REM, which accepted it with thanks and went off to draw up their own proposal. This was presented to Coderre in the winter-spring of 2016. After seeing it, Coderre called Bergeron into his office. "What CDPQ-Infra proposes is not what you presented to me, " Coderre told Bergeron, "but I would like you to take the time to analyze it. Go see them. If you don't like it, try not to be too obvious about it. Try not to react." Coderre added that he personally found the proposal "extraordinary."

A few days later, Bergeron says he was being accompanied to a meeting with CDPQ-Infra by Denis Dolbec, Coderre's chief of staff, and "a whole delegation to watch over me."

He was immediately impressed by the ambitious scale of the project, including as it did spurs to Ste-Anne-de-Bellevue and Deux-Montagnes. He noticed, however, that the VP of CDPQ-Infra, who was presenting the plan, was tip-toeing around saying that the city's proposal hadn't measured up. Finally Bergeron says he interrupted him. "Stop walking on eggshells. What you've been showing me so far is splendid!" he said. "The only thing that bothers me, that saddens me a little, is that it was not me who came up with the idea."

Leaving the meeting, Dolbec said to him, "We just buried your tramway project, do you realize that?"

"Yes, and I agree. In view of what I have just seen, I agree," Bergeron replied. Finally, he said, an ambitious public transit project with an audacious timeline—the first stretch was forecast to open by the end of 2020. If it wasn't a tramway per se, or even street-level, it was at least light-rail with the capacity to move hundreds of thousands of people every day.

That said, he understood that the plan for automated, driver-less trains effectively ruled out any possibility that the REM would be street-level with its tracks intersecting with roads—and thus crossed by cars, bikes and pedestrians. This in turn made for a huge hurdle in terms of urban integration and accessibility. "But when you only have a hammer in your toolbox, all jobs will will be solved with a hammer."

The REM announcement—and the project itself—divided the Projet Montréal caucus, and the party as a whole, as few other issues had. Some councillors considered it a good if not perfect "intermediate technology"; not exactly a tramway but almost. Others, however, felt it was fundamentally a real-estate play by the Caisse which would only contribute to urban sprawl, not counter it.

This is not to say that the party was particularly united to begin with under Ferrandez's interim-leadership. Even if he had been elected handily to the position, he remained as polarizing as ever as he tried to re-focus the party on plans which emphasized smaller, local changes initiated by empowered boroughs. "I really wanted to recognize the powers of the boroughs and encourage innovation by the boroughs and the transformation of the city street corner by street corner," he says. "But most of the caucus were *en tabernak*. They said, 'What? We are going to get elected with curb extensions and changing one-way streets?'"

Ferrandez was also under fire from many in the caucus for the static that our projects on the Plateau were continuing to generate. Not necessarily expecting to win the 2013 election, Luc had wanted to get as much done as possible beforehand. Once re-elected, we didn't let up at all. This meant inevitable outcry, usually from motorists losing free parking spots. Even if the project was small and the resistance minimal it seemed to always attract media attention because it involved the Plateau and Ferrandez.

When he adamantly refused to slow the pace of change on the Plateau, various councillors from other boroughs again accused Luc of hurting the party's chances to make inroads elsewhere. "I was told that it was sabotage, that I was sabotaging the party," Ferrandez says. "It was very, very aggressive." As during the previous mandate, his most hostile critics were the Rosemont team—François Croteau, François Limoges and Érika Duchesne in particular—but he also says he got friction from new councillors, including Marie-Andrée Mauger in Verdun. "For months I was in a situation where I tried to convince people and often took positions that were ripped apart in the caucus."

Our projects on the Plateau were, in general, more of the same with an emphasis on *more*. One reason we were able to carry out a greater number of projects was increased buy-in from the borough bureaucrats, including new hires in the crucial technical studies division.

Another reason was our discovery of an untapped source of financing for some of our more expensive projects. The way this came about ended up being quite instructive about bureaucratic culture. Towards the end of our first mandate the Conseil regional de l'environnement had created prizes to reward municipalities for projects which encouraged active transport, calmed traffic and improved the quality of public space.

The Plateau was a winner for our work around Laurier school. At the prize ceremony an employee of the Ministère de transport du Québec approached me and explained that the MTQ had funds available for the kinds of projects we were carrying out, and if our application was accepted would pay up to 50 percent of the final bill. She urged us to apply with such fervour that I got the distinct impression that the MTQ was having a problem giving its money away, as too often is the case for these kinds of programs. Soon enough, with Luc's blessing, I had arranged a meeting with four or five members of the technical studies division to plan the preparation of our application.

They all seemed as enthusiastic as I was as we discussed which projects we would apply for, who would draft the technical drawings, who would compose the budget, who might write the proposal and that kind of thing. Then the director of urbanism joined the meeting. He and I had never really clicked. He had always seemed to me the consummate bureaucrat in certain negative ways—one who valued loyalty much more than competence, one whose dedication to serving the city came well behind his dedication to his own career trajectory, one who you never even bothered looking for on a Friday afternoon.

He summarily announced that everyone in his team was far too busy to spend any time on the application, and that it wasn't worth the effort anyway because we would never get the funding. I tried arguing with him but to no avail. The most remarkable thing, however, was that most of his underlings immediately changed their discourse to match that of their boss. Whereas two minutes earlier they had been entirely gung-ho, they now turned on a dime and soberly agreed with the director that everyone had too much on their plate and that it was a lost cause to begin with. So getting up from the table I told the director that I would do the entire application myself and we would see whether we got the money or not.

Sure enough, within six months or so I received word from the MTQ that they would finance half of the $1.3 million or so it would cost us to widen the sidewalks on Avenue Laurier between St-Laurent and St-Denis. It would allow for trees to be planted along that stretch while giving space for the hordes of students and other pedestrians going to and from the metro to walk more than two abreast without anyone having to stray onto the road.

Needless to say, when we got the money, the director was very happy to claim as much of the credit as possible. A year or so later, the same program provided us with more than $1 million for traffic-calming measures, mostly curb extensions, for about five primary schools in the borough.

I was shocked not only that the director had no interest in applying for the funding but that neither he nor anyone in his team were aware of the MTQ program in the first place. I later learned that Rosemont had been applying for and receiving this money for years but had kept quiet about it, not telling other boroughs, so as to have less competition for their projects.

A tragic event in the spring of 2014 empowered the borough to intervene in ways we had long wanted but not previously been allowed. Mathilde Blais was riding a Bixi bike down Rue St-Denis early one sunny Monday morning near the end of April when she was crushed beneath the wheels of a massive six-axle truck carrying a construction crane through an underpass. There had been many cyclists killed by cars and trucks before in Montreal, of course, but the death of Blais, a young speech therapist on her way to work, provoked an outrage and call for change we hadn't seen before.

The accident had occurred under the Canadian Pacific rail tracks which separate the Plateau from Rosemont, and Blais had been crossing into our borough. Ferrandez felt the outrage particularly keenly. Harnessing it, he was on the phone within hours with Coderre's deputies insisting that the Plateau be allowed to introduce measures which before had been the exclusive jurisdiction of the central city.

First and foremost was the right to implement bike lanes on our local and collector streets. It had been a disappointment to learn when we were first elected that the boroughs had no authority over bike lanes on their territory. Rather, it was up to the active transport division downtown to decide where bike paths went. There was a logic behind it—a coherent city-wide network was preferable to 18 different ones and no one liked the idea of a bike path ending abruptly at the border of a borough. At the same time, however, it was at the borough level that staff and councillors best knew the streets that would be good candidates for bike paths, whether because they were already popular with cyclists, were particularly wide or served an area that that needed them. The expectation was that the borough would suggest these streets to the active transport division and it would, in due course, install a bike path if it was judged feasible and useful. The problem was that the active transport division was both short of employees and lethargic, staffed by people who we suspected drove to work and only rode their bikes on Sundays. As a result, in our first mandate we had not succeeded in getting anywhere near as many new bike paths created as hoped.

With the death of Blais, Luc immediately extracted a concession from the central city that permitted the Plateau to draw up and install new bike paths as long as the active transport division deemed the plans safe. Before long, we had added more than 20 kilometres of bike path, effectively doubling the network in the borough.

We also initiated a process to lower speed limits throughout the borough by 10 km/hr—to 30 km/hr on local and collector streets and to 40 km/hr on arteries. It had only been four or five years since they had been reduced to 40 km/hr and 50 km/hr respectively but given the reluctance of police to issue tickets unless a driver was exceeding the speed limit by 20 percent or more, the impact hadn't been as substantial as hoped. In the following years, all boroughs in the city followed suit.

It would have been politically foolish for Coderre to resist acceding to these changes in the aftermath of Blais' death, but the Plateau's eagerness to intervene on its road network clearly irked him. So to limit our capacity to make changes, his administration took a novel if heavy-handed approach: a complete reclassification of Montreal's streets.

The world over, city streets tend to be divided into three categories: local, collector and arterial. Local streets are overwhelmingly residential and the theory goes that the only traffic on them should be vehicles that have a destination there: people who live on the street, their visitors, trades people, deliveries etc. More than 1,500 vehicles per day on a local street is considered too many; ideally it should be much fewer. Collector streets are often shopping streets and are considered busy if they see more than 10,000 vehicles per day. They serve to connect the local and the arterial networks. If you were driving across town, you wouldn't be expected to go the whole way on collectors. Instead, you would use them to transit between local and arterial streets. In this way, if a city's road network were a manual car, collectors would be the second and third gears. Arteries would be the fourth and fifths gears; in a properly designed road network, any trip of any distance in a city should be driven on arterial streets. Arteries often have two traffic lanes in each direction and carry upwards of 25,000 vehicles per day.

This classification system prevails from country to country and continent to continent. When traffic engineers and urbanists from around the world get together, this is the language they speak. In Montreal, in 2014, however, the Coderre administration decided to eliminate the category of collector. In one fell swoop, all collectors were upgraded to arteries, along with many streets which had previously been classified as local but were deemed to have historical significance, or because they had a bus route.

The official reasoning was vague with the reform rolled into an ongoing re-evaluation of the financing of the boroughs. Few in the city had any doubt about the real motive behind the move: it was a power-grab directed primarily against the Plateau. After all, local and collector streets had been under the jurisdiction of boroughs while the central city was in charge of arteries. From one day to the next, the Plateau went from being in charge of 65 percent of its road network to 35 percent while the number of arteries ballooned from 15 to 72.

We received word of this impending reclassification about a month before it was to occur and were appalled by it. It meant that many of the projects we had been elected—and re-elected—to deliver would now be impossible or far more difficult to carry out, since the central city would have to agree to the work. This included things like curb extensions, speed bumps, stop signs—what had become our bread-and-butter. There were also two street closure projects which in all likelihood would be completely derailed. Still, we had a couple of weeks during which we were still in charge so we decided on a quick-strike and rushed through the paperwork. It allowed us to close off what was known as *la bretelle Clark*, a stretch of road beside a popular park which cars tended to take at speed, and only served as a shortcut between Van Horne and Boul. St-Laurent, as well as an 80-metre segment of Rue Gilford between St-Denis and Rivard which we planned to pedestrianize.

If changes to road geometry and configuration were our bread-and-butter, it didn't mean we weren't developing an ever more diversified diet in our repertoire of interventions for the Plateau. Increasingly, our efforts to reverse the undervaluing of public space involved methods that went beyond wider sidewalks and more greenery, trashcans and benches, to include funding activities that would enliven it.

There was the proliferation of small, public markets in various spots around the borough which we encouraged, but perhaps our most famous effort was our outdoor pianos. This was far from a novel idea—they had been installed in cities far and wide for anyone to come and play on and, contrary to the pessimistic expectations of many, had almost been a great success. Pianos, it seemed, didn't attract much vandalism. What's more, accomplished pianists enjoyed playing on mediocre, donated pianos to pedestrian audiences, or for the simple sake of practice. There were a few problems—some neighbours complained of the constant tinkling and one piano on

St-Denis tended to be monopolized by an itinerant who, happily, was a competent piano player. But we tried to move them from place to place around the borough every few weeks and as long as the person contracted to tune them occasionally and ensure that they were protected by a tarp on rainy days did his job, they were a largely headache-free hit.

There were other initiatives—puppet shows in Parc Lafontaine, karaoke in Parc du Portugal, storytelling to kids in Parc Baldwin (sometimes by the councillors or Luc)—which contributed colour, music and life to the borough, especially in the summer.

Meanwhile, the borough's main commercial activities of the summer—the Boul. St-Laurent and Avenue Mont-Royal street fairs—became much more dynamic and interesting. After unsuccessfully waging war on our administration, the SDCs had come under new, more enlightened and collaborative leadership which appreciated that their street fairs should upgrade from sidewalk sales with a few buskers, face painters and balloon twisters, to cultural events during which merchants and their wares spilled out onto the street.

This was particularly true on Boul. St-Laurent where the local merchant association teamed up with Mural Fest to stage a public art event stretching over two weeks. The blank walls of buildings along the artery and on neighbouring streets were transformed by some of the world's top muralists. It quickly began attracting tourists from around the world and was a much better fit for the borough than the other event the street fair tended to team up with: the F1 car race.

In the office, our jobs as Ferrandez's political attachés evolved between the first and second mandates. For me, much less time was required in convincing or cajoling the borough engineers and *agents techniques* to implement the changes we were seeking. In some cases, it was because employees had bought in to our vision. In others it was because new ones who shared it had arrived. Under Ferrandez and borough director Isabelle Cadrin, the Plateau had become a destination borough to work in for many of the more motivated and inspired professionals in the city bureaucracy—not one to flee anymore. So, less holding of the pencil, as Luc would put it, was required.

It didn't mean that we lacked for tasks to fill our time, or that we began to approach the job of political attaché more conventionally, with more focus on communications. One reason for this was because we decided not to renew funding for the borough's Éco-Quartier and instead took over its responsibilities ourselves. The contract to run the Éco-Quartier had always been given to a non-profit organization and we had never felt the borough got good value for $200,000-plus per year it cost. We had also been underwhelmed with the alleys that had been greened; they were excessively timid, with not enough asphalt removed or plants and greenery added.

So Andréanne Leclerc-Marceau took command of the green alleys, while I took charge of a small sideline we had recently asked the Éco-Quartier to set up—a community composting program. There was very little door-to-door collection of compost in Montreal at this time: just a few small "pilot-projects" set up years earlier which hadn't led to the expansion that had been expected. The main reason for this was an absence of treatment facilities and a shortage of political will. Meanwhile, elsewhere in Canada curbside collection had been operating for years; separating organic matter from trash was as much a part of peoples' routine as separating recyclables.

With one of the highest turnover rates among residents in the city, people were moving to the Plateau in droves and phoning up the borough in desperation as they tried to figure out what to do with their organic kitchen waste. Sometimes, we would get calls from people saying that they had been storing their apple cores and potato peels in their freezer for months since moving from Vancouver, Halifax or Toronto and had run out of room. This, combined with local impatience for a borough-wide composting program, led us to experiment with a low-cost, low-tech option involving rotating barrel composters.

It was a Swedish design for which an environmentalist entrepreneur from St-Hilaire had obtained a license to manufacture and sell in North America. Even if the composters looked like WII army surplus, they worked extremely well.Within a few years we had gone from five to 32 to more than 80 composters around the borough with about 2,000 people participating and almost as many on the waiting list to do so.

The composters were very affordable, but they required a certain amount of *suivi* and attention. This amounted to regular visits to make sure all was going well, occasional emptying and sometimes a bit of crisis management when participants didn't follow instructions to chop up their bigger pieces and threw whole watermelons or turkey carcasses into the composters. Still, it was not unpleasant work since it mostly involved biking around the Plateau, talking to residents and keeping an eye on borough operations as a whole.

But as the number of composters multiplied, it began to take up too much of my time so we hired a hugely over-qualified woman called Giuliana Laurent to help run the program, while Andréanne hired a landscape architect assistant to help her with the ever more ambitious and numerous *ruelles vertes*.

It was highly irregular, almost comically unorthodox, for political staff to run such programs. But both required such a combination of activities—dealing with citizens and contractors, managing spreadsheets, as well as actually getting elbow-deep in the muck, whether in planting a *ruelle verte* or emptying a composter—that finding the right municipal employee or even an appropriate job category would have been almost impossible.

Beyond that, the jobs indirectly allowed us privileged contact with the borough's most involved and active residents—those eager to get a group of their neighbours together to transform the alley behind their apartment and those happy to walk their table scraps to a composter three blocks away. As often as not, this contact led to discussions about the party's and administration's vision and other initiatives, so in a way there was a comms component to it, one which was almost certainly as valuable as any number of press releases and news conferences.

The administration's interventions for transforming *le domaine public*—the borough's parks, sidewalks and streets—were also increasingly complemented by regulatory measures to try to ensure the Plateau remained an affordable place for the people who made it the neighbourhood it was, including the immigrants, the artists, and the working and middle-class families who had been here for generations. Ever more frequently, the Plateau was finding itself on lists of the coolest, the hottest, the most vibrant or most liveable neighbourhoods on the planet. This, combined with a renewed appreciation for living in older, more central neighbourhoods—a North America-wide trend—was leading to lower-income residents being squeezed out, a phenomenon that, of course, services such as Airbnb were only aggravating.

We were well aware that many of our efforts to make the borough greener, safer, and healthier were fuelling its gentrification and, in many respects, there was little we could do. The Régie de logement came under provincial jurisdiction and we had no influence over it, no way to give it more teeth or protect tenants more scrupulously. We did work to establish a *régistre des baux*—lease registry—to fight against illegal rent increases but, being optional and not a legal obligation, it never really caught on.

Getting social and affordable housing built was also a huge challenge, requiring complex funding arrangements with the central city, the province and para-public organizations. Since land prices and constructions costs are significantly higher in the Plateau than, say, Pointe-aux-Trembles or Pierrefonds, these "partners" often preferred to develop projects elsewhere. Up against the market—one which was pushing real estate prices higher everywhere—our capacity to counteract it was minimal.

Still, there were some meaningful moves made, usually thanks to pressure from Richard Ryan for whom housing was especially close to the heart and who became the party's expert on the issue. Right off the bat, we had refused to consider easy zoning changes for properties which developers had acquired, often at bargain basement prices, from religious orders. These tended to be zoned *communautaire* with the developers planning to get them rezoned as residential or commercial. Our logic was that they had been built with community money—the $2 put into the collection plate on Sunday, the widow's bequest or the tax breaks that churches always benefit from—and so they shouldn't be privatized. This sometimes led to old church buildings sitting empty and bitter disputes with developers, but it helped prevent speculation as well as the transformation of at least several convents and the like into luxury condo complexes.[30]

We also adopted an "inclusion policy" which required that any new building projects of five units or more in the borough had to either include social or affordable units or contribute to a fund which would help build these elsewhere. Within a few years, most other central boroughs had adopted similar policies and, in time, the central city followed suit but with a by-law and even more ambitious objectives.

In an effort to protect the Plateau's artists, we took a different tack. With the decline of the textile industry in Montreal, tens of thousands of square feet of industrial space became available at very reasonable rents in what's known as the St-Viateur East Area. Gradually, many of these were occupied by artists with short-term leases. Then, as the area became trendier—thanks in part to the artists themselves—deeper-pocketed businesses in the high-tech and knowledge sector began moving in and the value of the buildings and the rents they could charge soared. The artists were increasingly pushed out.

After a Toronto-based real estate income trust bought two almost identical 11-storey buildings for $37 million each—after one of them had been sold for $8 million three years earlier—we imposed a radical horizontal re-zoning. It effectively limited who the new owners could rent space to unless they agreed to put a substantial amount of their buildings aside for artists to occupy at reasonable rates. It wasn't perfect but it allowed many of the painters, sculptors, dancers and other artists and artisans who had helped make the Plateau special to stay in the neighbourhood.

30 In one case several notaries and other professionals, who had bought a small convent on Boul. St-Joseph near Parc Laurier hoping to transform it into luxurious homes for themselves, grew so frustrated at not being able to have the zoning changed to residential that they formed their own church and claimed to be living there communally as generations of nuns had done before them. The court was not convinced.

Chapter 25

As we entered the second half of our second mandate, I began to think it was time to do something else, maybe something completely new, or old-new, and go back to journalism and writing. Plateau operations were stable and running smoothly. I was starting to feel that, as enjoyable as it was, I had biked around the borough enough for one lifetime.

The *bureau des élus* was as fun a place to work as ever. Happily, us attachés were no longer stuck in the windowless old photocopy room. Instead, we had a big bright space adjacent to Luc's office and the relationships between us were excellent. As a councillor Louise Mainville had proven to be a bit of a bust, rarely in the office and certainly not the dynamic engaged elder she had sold herself as. Still, as a colleague, she was pleasant and the energy and dedication of Marianne Giguère ensured that the De Lorimier district didn't suffer. Marie Plourde was lots of fun to work with; the fact that she and Luc had become a couple didn't complicate office dynamics much at all, and not only because Luc was spending most of the week at City Hall as interim-leader of the party.

If there were tensions between councillors, it was between my old friends Alex Norris and Christine Gosselin who both represented the Jeanne-Mance district. Things had started off well enough between them but as the mandate wore on their strong personalities clashed and, occasionally, I found myself having to choose sides.

But my desire to do something different didn't have anything to do with that, Nor was it related to the fact that, even if the borough bureaucracy was ever more collaborative, I still didn't much enjoy dealing with the directors. Rather, it was more a sentiment that I had done my work, contributed what I had to contribute in getting the Plateau moving in the right direction. It was time to move on. Certainly, neither the pay nor the pension provided much incentive to stay on.

So in early 2016 I told Luc that if, after the next municipal election in the fall of 2017, it was more or less status quo—Coderre still the mayor, Projet Montréal still the opposition—I wouldn't be sticking around. I had no doubt whatsoever that we would win the Plateau and Rosemont again, perhaps another borough or two, maybe even three. Still, unless things were *really* different, I felt I had done my time.

By then Ferrandez had made a more momentous decision: he would not seek the leadership of Projet Montréal on a permanent basis. In parallel to trying to shift the focus of the party away from the tramway and other big-ticket projects, Luc had tried to give it a boost by enticing well-known Montrealers to join the party, whether as prospective candidates—perhaps even for the leadership—or as employees. He calculated that without Bergeron around, without his questioning of 9/11 and his often suffocating, know-it-all manner, moderates were more likely to come aboard and give it momentum.

To say that the results were mixed would be generous; they were closer to an abject failure, at least for those Ferrandez tried to interest in becoming candidates. There was good reason for their reticence. Even if Coderre had been elected with only 32 percent of the vote, his smiling omnipresence and grandiose promises—as well as the unifying image he had won by recruiting political opponents to his team—had boosted his approval to over 70 percent two years after his election. In contrast, Projet Montréal looked like a lost cause. Beyond that, an election was still two years off. For anyone seriously contemplating running for municipal office, that was an eternity. There was no reason to commit for at least a year.

Ferrandez was more successful when it came to attracting people if he had a pay cheque to offer them. Even then, however, it didn't come without some turbulence. A few days after he had become interim leader, Sue Montgomery and a fellow journalist from the *Toronto Star* created the hashtag #BeenRapedNeverReported and it went viral. Alex Norris and I had known Sue for years and we told him she could be a high-visibility hire as a political attaché in the opposition offices at City Hall. The interview didn't go well. "I was unable to get one sentence from her about municipal politics," Ferrandez remembers. "She had no idea and no interest in whatever issue I was talking to her about."

Ferrandez also went after Glenn Castanheira, who at the time was running the merchant association SDC du Boul. St-Laurent, and had nurtured its willingness to collaborate with the borough and forged the Mural Fest partnership. Castanheira agreed to become a political attaché responsible for economic development but at a steep price. Not only was he paid almost 50 percent more than other political attachés in the office but Luc agreed to support his candidacy when he determined he had had enough of being Plateau mayor. When the rest of us on the Plateau team learned of this, we were outraged. Castanheira certainly had the goods. Unlike the rest of us, he had roots in the Plateau. His family owned Rotisserie Coco-Rico, a popular Portuguese chicken restaurant on St-Laurent. He was perfectly trilingual and sure of himself to the point of cockiness. The problem was that pretty much no one but Luc could stand him. We were convinced he was only interested in the party as a political vehicle. One by one we trooped into Luc's office to tell him we wouldn't back him on that particular undertaking.

Glenn was still promoted as a big catch: the opposition offices held a press conference[31] touting his arrival, and Luc promised that Glenn would be allowed to speak his mind publicly. "He can say what he wants. If he contradicts me publicly, it won't be a problem. It's not like it will be the first time!"

Castanheira was put in charge of developing policy on "business, tourism and events." For bigger picture economic development policy, Ferrandez hired left-wing economist Ianik Marcil on a six-month contract.

Luc also hired two urbanists as *attachés politiques*—Jérôme Vaillancourt, a former Quebec City councillor and co-founder of the environmental group Vivre en Ville, and Andréanne Maltais-Tremblay,

---

31 Guillaume Cloutier's reaction to the party promoting the hiring of a political attaché to the extent Projet did with Glenn: "C'était whack en crisse."

who at the time was a sustainable transportion advisor at the MTQ. All these hires generated questions from the team in the opposition offices at City Hall, including Patrick Cigana who Luc had brought downtown from the party offices, feeling he needed a change. "He wanted to turn the *cabinet* into a think-tank," he says. "Think tanks write reports but do they win elections?"

As a veteran of the Plateau, Guillaume Cloutier understood better than others Luc's aim: to break the mold of traditional politics while redefining Projet Montréal. "He wanted to upend the way politics was done, he wanted to score big with big ideas, big projects, big conferences, big shows. Everything had to be big, all the time. It had to be *fucking* big."

There were a few small successes. Ferrandez got a fair amount of attention for his proposal to overhaul Rue Ste-Catherine, and for his scathing criticism of the Royalmount megamall planned for construction near the intersection of the Décarie and the Métropolitain. Relatively quickly, however, he began to lose heart, says Cloutier, at least about his own prospects for being the leader the party required to win City Hall. His enthusiasm "lasted a few months, maximum four, five months. Then, at a certain point, he just got discouraged, really discouraged. He saw that our office wasn't about to create this platform for him, these fireworks that he wanted to impress Montrealers. But that kind of thing will never happen because no one gives a shit what the opposition thinks. That's life. It's just like that."

Beyond discouraging people from signing up with the party, Coderre's popularity also helped convince two councillors to abandon it while Ferrandez was interim-leader. Or at least that's how it looked. The reality was more complicated.

The first to go was Marc-André Gadoury, the roguish councillor for the Étienne-Desmarteau district in Rosemont. He quit to join the mayor's team in early August, 2015, at a time when he and everyone else were expected to be on vacation. He framed his defection as a way to get things done for his constituents. "Now I will just knock on the door of Mr. Coderre with my suggestions and they will be heard," he said. "I won't have to do it by asking a question at city council." At the time he was caucus leader—the equivalent of the whip in council. His defection was reported as a major blow to the party and suggestions by his former colleagues that Gadoury was doing it for opportunistic or financial reasons fell flat when Coderre pointed out that he wasn't getting a spot on the executive committee or any other perk for making the move. It was actually causing him to lose salary.

Gadoury was followed—half-way—a few weeks later by Érika Duchesne, from the district next to his of Vieux-Rosemont. She quit the Projet Montréal caucus to sit initially as an independent, then joined Coderre's team six months later.

In both cases, Gadoury says, their departures had more to do with the dynamics of the Rosemont team than Coderre or the direction Projet Montréal was headed in. "It never clicked between Érika and Croteau," he says, adding that within weeks of her by-election victory in April 2012 she stopped coming into the office. Both felt excluded from any real decision-making role and insulted that Croteau insisted on being present at any meeting that they had with bureaucrats. The only tasks they were ever given, Gadoury says, were to tell community groups that they were getting their budgets cut.

Gadoury, who had never hidden his own ambition to be mayor of Rosemont—if not Montreal—says the final straw for him came in mid-2015 when Croteau told the team he was planning to run for borough mayor again in 2017. He had previously said he would only serve two mandates. He also says Ferrandez would have just segued into the Projet Montréal leadership on a full-time basis had he and Duchesne not quit the party. "There never would have been a race if we had stayed," he says.

If that was the case, or even if it played a role, unsurprisingly Ferrandez didn't mention it when he announced he wouldn't seek the job permanently at the end of January 2016. He made the announcement in a 40-minute speech wrapping up a party congress, a speech during which he alternately excoriated Denis Coderre and vaunted the virtues of Projet Montréal.

Coderre, he began, was a "giant with feet of clay" whose honeymoon with the Montreal public was over. Endless press conferences, promises and reassurances couldn't hide the fact that Coderre had "an at-best approximate knowledge of the city's operations" coupled with a complete "absence of vision, absence of ambition for Montreal."

Making matters worse, Coderre was anything but the team player he had promised to be. "He is an imposter in regard to his promises of working together, to forming partnerships, to extending a hand. He never does it," Ferrandez said.

This meant that, for all the mayor's bluster, he was vulnerable, and could be beaten in 2017. But Ferrandez wasn't the person to do it. Luc said he was too easy to caricature as an extremist. "I don't want to give to Mr. Coderre the last card that he might play. I don't want to let him come off as a man of the middle ground by portraying me every day as someone who is too radical. And perhaps I am a little."

Projet Montréal wasn't anywhere near as fringe as its opponents made out, he said, and it needed a leader to convey that, "a person recognized for their openness, their flexibility and suppleness, their capacity to listen." In his speech, Ferrandez made it sound like that person would be found within the party ranks, and urged those who thought they didn't quite measure up, who thought they might be lacking in experience, or knowledge of certain fields such as urbanism or transport, to think again. They would have the support of a team without equal in expertise regarding all things Montreal. "Projet Montréal is a fabulous tool," he said.

Given that Ferrandez was addressing a gathering of the faithful, it is entirely understandable that he would suggest that the new leader might be found among them. If he actually thought so, however, it was only out of despair at generating any interest among people outside the party.

In the time that he was interim leader Ferrandez met with dozens of people in an effort to convince them to consider running for the leadership. These included predictable choices such as Steven Guilbeault, who was still at Équiterre and still flirting with the idea running for office, student leader Gabriel Nadeau-Dubois who was known to be interested in entering politics at the provincial level, and Karel Mayrand of the David Suzuki Foundation. It also included Dominique Anglade, who at the time had quit the Coalition Avenir Québec but not yet joined the Quebec Liberals. Then there were the people from the private sector—lawyer Kim Thomassin, pollster Jean-Marc Léger, entrepreneur/investor Alexandre Taillefer, Daniel Langlois, a founder of Softimage and philanthropist, as well as Marie Élaine Farley, the president of Bixi.

Ferrandez says that at certain periods when he was interim leader, he was spending more than half of his time trying to recruit someone to replace him. His motivation, oddly enough, was Mario Dumont and the Action Démocratique du Québec. At different moments in its short history, the party had led the Liberals and the PQ in the polls. "But it never went anywhere because he was never able to recruit strong people," says Ferrandez.

By early 2016, however, it didn't look like Ferrandez was going to have any more luck than Dumont in attracting heavy hitters to his party so he was beginning to look more seriously within party ranks. The most obvious prospect—"*le plus ministrable*" as they say—was Guillaume Lavoie. After his election in late 2013, Lavoie had thrown himself into his duties as a councillor, exuding competence and ambition in equal parts. From his position on the finance commission he impressed some of the city's most experienced bureaucrats. Lavoie also quickly became one of the most visible Projet Montréal councillors, happy to alternately wax indignant or praise effusively, as the situation required, on almost any subject, in front of any microphone.

This energy and ambition, combined with his oratorical skills and the fact that he had more than one or two ties and jackets in his closet and could coordinate his colours, convinced Ferrandez for a time that Lavoie was the best person to lead the party. "Luc was very, very warm to the idea of Guillaume Lavoie," remembers Ray Guardia. "His lens was, 'Guillaume is a politician. He's a machine. And that's what we need.'"

Chapter 26

In his speech announcing he wouldn't be running for the party leadership, Ferrandez had singled out Lavoie for special mention along with a few other caucus members. He lauded Lavoie's exhaustive analysis of the city budget, just as he praised Richard Ryan's expertise in housing, François Croteau's study of snow removal operations, Christine Gosselin and Sterling Downey for their dedication to "animal management," Marie Plourde and Anne-Marie Sigouin for heritage and Sylvain Ouellet "because he is good in everything."

Most councillors, however, didn't merit a mention. This included one who was already planning to run for the leadership. After knocking off Louise Harel in Ste-Marie a little more than two years earlier, Valérie Plante had done little to distinguish herself. She wasn't closely associated with distinct issues or projects, nor did she display a silver-tongued way-with-words or theatrical flair that made her stand out either in caucus debates or in council. She wasn't considered a disappointment by any means—not at all. Rather, she was seen as a rookie councillor finding her way in what was a complex new world, one who was well-liked by her colleagues for her spirit and fun energy.

"We all got along more or less even though we would fight and debate," says Mindy Pollak, nostalgic for the collegiality of the caucus in that mandate. "The vibe was very, 'This is who we are, we are a family and we are here for each other.' It was awesome." As a borough councillor, Pollak didn't sit at City Hall, where sessions would often go late into the evening. Afterwards, a gang of Projet councillors and staff went out for a drink, often on the *terrasse* of Brasseur de Montréal by the Gare Viger. They included Richard Ryan, and a rotating cast of others, including staff such Guillaume Cloutier, Marie-Êve Gagnon, and Joël Simard-Menard. Valérie was almost always among them. Discussion regularly revolved around party matters and, of course, the leadership.

It was during these conversations that Plante first had the idea that she might run for the leadership. "One thing which struck me immediately was the degree to which whenever there was discussion about who might be leader, males names were always mentioned. Always, always, always," she remembers. If the name of a woman was mentioned, it was only after a long list of men. "It started to aggravate me, to bug me."

One of the first people in the party she discussed the idea with was Patrick Cigana. He remembers her saying that she would run for the leadership if only to prevent it from being a race between three White men. "She said she would drop out after the first round. I asked her, 'What if you are in second place? Will you still drop out?'" Cigana credits Plante's husband, union economist Pierre-Antoine Harvey, with convincing her to throw herself into the race completely if she were it enter it at all. "He said to her, 'It doesn't sound like you, planning to drop out even before the start of the race.'"

The reaction of some of her drinking partners at Brasseur de Montréal also stoked her determination. They were convinced she was only doing it to raise her profile, whether for a boost to provincial or federal politics in due course or an eventual seat on the executive committee. No one suspected she was really serious about winning—or so deluded that she thought she might. "For me it was a positioning campaign and I didn't take it seriously," says Guillaume Cloutier. "I was kind of like, 'We all know what you're doing is positioning. But that's cool! It's good! It's fun! Go girl!' And it pissed her off." He adds: "Nobody took it seriously. She was the girl who came out drinking with us. The coolest councillor with the staff and someone we didn't see as an authority figure at all."

Plante had been down this road not many months earlier. And if others around the table didn't fully appreciate it, she understood that in politics, especially municipal politics, anything can happen and the smart money is often not that smart. Her unexpected victory in Sainte-Marie was proof of that. "It was her debut into the political realm and everyone else is saying that it is impossible. Then she wins," says Oliver Paré. "It snowballed. Her decision to run for the leadership soon after was similar in the sense that she went, 'Who is there to tell me that I can't do this? Who is to say no? Who is to say that it's impossible?'"

Another factor that seems to have played a role in convincing Plante to run for the leadership—and one that certainly helped her win it—was her appointment to the board of the Broadbent Institute, a left-wing think-tank set up by the former NDP leader to "champion progressive change" by, among other things, "the training of a new generation of leaders."

In the spring of 2014, the board had an opening and it was determined that the new member should be a woman from Quebec. Rick Smith, the head of the institute, contacted Ray Guardia to ask him to suggest someone. He ended up suggesting Valérie. "I thought she would benefit from being in a room with people who viewed the room through a certain ideological prism," says Guardia. "I thought it would be good for someone like her who had all the right stuff. I thought she would get something out of it. She will meet Ed Broadbent. She will meet people who have spent a lifetime, thinking about inequality, thinking about social change." She also met people who ended up running her leadership campaign. "The Broadbent opened up a whole network to me and gave me confidence in myself," Plante says.

Plante had made up her mind to run at least two months before Ferrandez announced that he wouldn't be a candidate. By then she had called up other women in the party, including Émilie Thuillier and Marie Plourde, to sound them out about their intentions. None had indicated an interest in running. Plante remembers thinking that if Ferrandez were to seek the leadership "I wouldn't have a chance at winning. But there has to be a woman who runs for the leadership of my party. If not it would be just too sad."

By then Guardia had patched things up with Tom Mulcair and moved back to Ottawa to be the NDP leader's chief of staff. He was still one of the first people Plante told of her decision, and on a trip back to Montreal he met her for a coffee on Rue St-Hubert near the old bus station. "She was just asking for advice," Guardia says. He told her that the first thing to do would be to get a campaign team together. "You need a campaign manager and they're going to work full-time so you might have to pay them. You are probably going to have to do some fundraising. And you're going to need a comms person."

For those tasks Valérie decided to call on her new network from the Broadbent Institute—in particular, Willy Blomme, an Institute employee in Montreal, and Rim Mohsen, a consultant and activist involved with groups such as Québec Inclusif and the World Social Forum.

The party had been discussing the parameters and timing of the leadership race since shortly after Bergeron announced he would be stepping down, but it was only after Ferrandez announced that he wouldn't be a candidate that they got down to it in earnest. Eventually, at the May meeting of the Conseil de direction, it was decided that the race would officially begin on Labour Day with the vote to be held three months later on December 4th.

After his January announcement, Ferrandez kept up his schedule of coffees and lunches with people that he or others in the party thought might be a good fit. It was to no avail. Increasingly he seemed to believe what he had suggested in the speech: that the new leader would come from inside the party, if only because no one with any profile outside the party was interested. If that were the case, he assumed that it would be Guillaume Lavoie as did the great majority of caucus. "I found that he was a hard worker and that he conveyed an image which we didn't really have at Projet Montréal," Ferrandez says. "He was serious, he was meticulous."

As 2016 wore on, however, Ferrandez began to share the opinion of most of the rest of the Plateau *bureau des élus*—that the new leader of Projet Montréal should be anybody but Lavoie. This, he says, was due to conflicts with him over a dossier which was almost as divisive and contentious within Projet Montréal as the REM: what was known as "the sharing economy"—most specifically Uber and Airbnb—and its consequences for Montrealers.

Lavoie espoused a neo-liberal, free market philosophy and for him these enterprises represented the future—not one that was simply inevitable but one which was desirable. Alex Norris and Richard Ryan, in particular, saw things very differently. The impact of Airbnb was already being felt keenly on the Plateau, with increasing numbers of rental units being used for that purpose—as many as 5,000 at certain periods, 8 percent of the total housing stock in the borough. This meant that many renters found themselves pushed out of their homes and the Plateau, as a whole, while the fabric of the neighbourhood suffered from, among other things, increased noise and tidiness complaints about partying tourists. Meanwhile, the threat that Uber and other ride-hailing services posed to the taxi industry and public transport, was a concern city-wide.

Norris says that whenever he heard Lavoie talk about these businesses, he felt he was listening to a lobbyist, while Ferrandez found Lavoie's attitude to the taxi industry and its drivers—Uber's first victims—particularly disturbing. "He made out that they were all swindlers who didn't pay their taxes, that they all had five taxi permits and made others work for them like slaves. Even though the statistics showed something else."

Many drivers had bought their taxi permits from others for upwards of $100,000 even if the initial cost of the permits had been a tiny fraction of that amount. Saying that for many drivers their permits were their pensions, Ferrandez opposed any solution which didn't recognize their market value. Lavoie, meanwhile, said the city should buy back the permits for no more than what they had originally cost. "I said, 'That is ridiculous. You are sending thousands of people into poverty. You can't do that.'"

Ferrandez was also increasingly put off by the contempt and disdain Lavoie showed for other peoples' opinions when they didn't agree with him. "He was disrespectful. He had no consideration for what anyone else had to say. It was almost insulting," Ferrandez says. Lavoie would tell people, "You are suffering from a deficit of information," he says. "Which is a way of saying, 'You don't know what you are talking about.'"

As someone who has never shied away from doing his research, Ferrandez found that on subjects such as self-driving vehicles, which Lavoie thought would completely transform urban transportation within a few years, the Rosemont councillor made himself out to be much more of an expert than he was. While in Paris, Ferrandez had done the preliminary work towards a doctorate on the adoption of radical innovative technologies from the laboratory to the marketplace. "And I told him, 'Innovations which can be launched in three years just don't exist. Especially a product like self-driving cars.'"

As autumn approached, and the campaign officially got underway, only one candidate has formally declared their intention to run for the leadership: François Limoges, who had announced his interest in mid-May. We all expected Guillaume Lavoie and Valérie Plante to jump into the race soon enough, but many of us were impatient for another option—especially those of us adamantly opposed to Lavoie. This option eventually extended beyond the caucus to Justine McIntyre, the Pierrefonds councillor who inherited the reins of Mélanie Joly's party Vrai Changement pour Montréal. Vrai Changement didn't seem to be going anywhere. After maintaining throughout the 2013 campaign that she was on the Montreal municipal scene to stay, Joly was gone within a year to a career in federal politics. Her successor as Vrai Changement leader was Lorraine Pagé who herself barely lasted a year before leaving the party to sit, first as an independent, then join Équipe Coderre. By early 2016, it was McIntyre's turn to lead the party and its caucus of three, including herself.

To the surprise of many, the earnest piano teacher from south-western Ontario, who had come to McGill to study music and never left, quickly became one of the city council's most effective voices. To the extent that by September, at least two seasoned observers of city politics felt that she should set her sights beyond being leader of what at best looked like it might be a spoiler party in the next election and instead think about taking over the main opposition.

Campbell Stuart and Ricardo Hrtschan were both former suburban mayors who ended up at the law firm of Colby Monet and discovered their shared interest in municipal politics. Neither of them liked Denis Coderre and both had been impressed by McIntyre's plucky performance in city council. The two men invited her to a meeting one day, ushered her into their nicest boardroom and pitched her on the idea of running for the leadership of Projet Montréal. Neither man had anything to do with the party but in their minds, she was a good fit to be its new leader. McIntyre was surprised, flattered and intrigued. When Stuart and Hrtschan offered to broker a meeting with Ferrandez, she agreed. "I think that they were looking for a way from behind the scenes to point Projet Montréal in a direction where it would stand a good chance of winning against Coderre," said McIntyre.

When Luc heard the idea, he was just as intrigued as McIntyre had been. Before long, on September 14th, he was visiting the Colby Monet offices himself to meet McIntyre. The two were soon left alone, sitting across a boardroom table from each other. McIntyre says she admired Ferrandez "tremendously, his fire and passion," and the meeting went well. Both were thinking bigger than simply McIntyre running for the leadership. They saw a full-on merger of their two parties. "Everyone found me too radical and the party's image too radical, and Projet Montréal was just focused on the Plateau and Rosemont," says Ferrandez. "I wanted to make a leap and go recruit someone in an unlikely area, the West. Justine seemed to have a greater openness which would allow us to attract more than just the NDP and Quebec Solidaire." McIntyre, however, had a condition that would be difficult to meet: even if its caucus and membership were a fraction of the size of those of Projet Montréal, she didn't want Vrai Changement absorbed into the main opposition. She insisted that the two parties come together and create something completely new, "a new entity," a new brand. If Ferrandez saw a problem with that, he didn't allow it to derail the discussion. For his part, he said he had but one condition: that if she became leader she "wouldn't touch the Plateau."

When they parted, Luc said he was going to phone Valérie Plante immediately and ask her to not to run. He told McIntyre he thought he would be able to convince her. "We left the meeting feeling as if we were on the same page and really wanted this to work," McIntyre says. "And then he called Valérie and, from my understanding, all hell broke loose. She didn't take it well at all. He had underestimated how deep her engagement was. He just thought that she was somebody who had put her name in the hat, a decent candidate but not very strong. He really underestimated her."

In the Plateau, we all tended to underestimate Valérie and had the same attitude to her candidacy as Guillaume Cloutier: it wasn't very serious, likely more about positioning for down the road and, anyway, she didn't have the stuff to beat either Lavoie or Coderre.

Valérie had begun reaching out to people in the Plateau since at least the spring, when she and a dozen or so other Projet councillors had gone over to Christine Gosselin's home on Rue Boyer in Rosemont. At the end of the evening, Plante brought up the leadership contest. "It would be a real drag if it ends up just guys," Marianne Giguère remembers Valérie saying as she reiterated her determination to run. "You will support me, right?" Gosselin said she would like to but didn't really know where Plante stood on many issues. She asked her what her vision was for the city. Valérie didn't answer directly, instead simply replying, "Don't worry, I have ideas." Giguère pressed the point but still Plante didn't talk specifics. "Trust me," was her line. "She didn't have anything to propose," Giguère remembers.

Most of us very much liked Plante, even if we didn't think she was up to the task of being party leader. But there was at least one person in the Plateau caucus who had no time for her at all. Louise Mainville was both impressed by Guillaume Lavoie and viscerally put off by Valérie. "Louise couldn't stand her," says Ferrandez. "She didn't like the way she was always munching on vegetables during caucus. She said she lacked respect for people, that she only smiled at people who had power, that she was the opposite of a real feminist." The hostility of Mainville—and later, Christine Gosselin—towards Valérie, underlined an odd tendency: whereas outside the Plateau many of her strongest, early supporters within the party were women, in the Plateau the only people who ending up opposing her candidacy were women.

It would still, however, be several weeks before anyone in the Plateau got behind Plante's candidacy. The fact that Ferrandez and others weren't rushing to rally behind her didn't bother her, she says. "He didn't take me seriously. But hey, I've been there. It doesn't bug me."

But when Ferrandez asked her to not to run and instead get behind McIntyre, "that did hurt," Plante says and she made her feelings known. Even after McIntyre phoned Plante up herself and tried to repair some of the damage, it was clear Valérie now saw her as an enemy. As McIntyre wrote in an email to Hrtschan, "Valérie Plante was shocked that Luc would even ask her; frankly it was clumsy and hasty and now I will have her against me, even if I phoned her afterwards to repair the damage."

Still, it wasn't enough to give McIntyre and Ferrandez second thoughts. "I meet my caucus on Monday to present this merger proposition," McIntyre goes on to say in the email. "I've thought about it, and I think it is worth going for." She added: "Guillaume Lavoie also seems locked & loaded to kick off his campaign. In his most intimate fantasies, he already imagines himself mayor of Montreal."

That Monday, however, Lavoie announced just the opposite. In a Facebook post, he wrote that after a great deal of thought, he had made "a difficult choice" and decided not to run for the party's leadership. "In the context of my very young family, it is the choice which imposes itself at this time," he wrote. In the Plateau, we received the news with a great deal of skepticism. We were under the impression that Lavoie and his supporters had been selling memberships for months and it wasn't as if his "very young family" hadn't been around then. We immediately suspected some sort of ruse and that Lavoie would be back; after all, the deadline for entering the race was still almost a month away.

Two days later, Valérie made it official and entered the race formally; like Limoges she announced her candidacy alone, without any councillor colleagues pledging support by her side. She did, however, outline what would be the important themes of her campaign: transport, housing and food security. And she made her first campaign announcement: as mayor she would find a way to ensure that any company doing business with the city paid all employees at least $15 per hour.

Chapter 27

In late September city council held its regular monthly meeting. By then, rumours that McIntyre might be a candidate in the leadership race were beginning to get around and a number of Projet councillors approached her. "They came up to me and grabbed me by the elbow and pulled me to the side to say, 'Justine, if you are even thinking about it, do it, I will support you, I will go out and get signatures for you.'" Unsurprisingly, the prospect of her candidacy seemed to especially excite councillors like Peter McQueen and Magda Popeanu, from boroughs with a lot of anglophones and where Vrai Changement had done well.

McIntyre and Ferrandez had met again once or twice since the lawyer's office to further plan things out and during a break in council, they went for a walk. Luc suggested that the best way to launch her candidacy would be with him at her side, unequivocally endorsing her. Convention required the interim leader stay neutral, but he said he was prepared to resign from the position. Before that, Ferrandez faced a not-insignificant hurdle: convincing the party to change a crucial internal rule. Party statutes required that all candidates be a party member for at least 90 days before a leadership vote. He took the idea first to caucus on October 7th. He said that for a party which wanted to show openness, attract new blood and expand into new areas of the city, the rules governing the leadership race were too restrictive. He didn't need to hold out the carrot of Projet Montréal merging, or even absorbing Vrai Changement, a party which had finished in second-place three years earlier—the media had got wind of the discussions a few days earlier.

After a long, stormy meeting during which Lavoie and Ouellet vigorously opposed the change, the caucus eventually agreed that the 90-day requirement should be lifted; a candidate only had to be a member at the moment of filing their papers. They also agreed to extend the deadline to entering the race an extra week, to October 22nd. The caucus's proposal was then taken to a *Conseil de direction* meeting a few days later. It was no less stormy,[32] with François Limoges continuing to rail against the loosening of the rules. Still, the proposed changes were endorsed by a vote of 12 to one and everything seemed to be falling into place.

By this time, Luc had already convinced most of us in the Plateau's *bureau des élus* that Justine was the best way to stop Guillaume Lavoie from winning the leadership and maybe even to get Projet elected city-wide. With his abundant powers of persuasion, he also convinced my colleague Sébastien Parent-Durand that he should take a leave of absence from his job as an *attaché politique* and run Justine's campaign. A meeting with Justine was organized for the next morning at Laïka, a café on St-Laurent.

At the meeting, Alex Norris, Sébastien and I heard about Justine's insistence on changing the name of the party. This, coupled with the fact that still no other members of the Vrai Changement caucus had agreed to come over yet, gave us pause. But it was really when Sébastien started making calls to various *militants* in the party to ask them what they thought about the idea that things began to fall apart. One of the first he called was Josée Vanasse, a straight-talking political veteran who had run Amir Khadir's constituency office and later been the Projet campaign director on the Plateau for the 2013 election. "Who the fuck is Justine McIntyre?" was her reaction. Pascal MacDuff, who as a teenager had been behind the unionization of the first McDonalds in North America before going on to a career as a flight attendant and,

---

32 Gérald McNichols Tétreault, an urbanist and architect with no roots in the party but who had expressed an interest in leading it, was invited to the meeting, as were François Limoges and Valérie Plante. He was so put off by the "*mépris*" and lack of respect on display, that he decided then and there not to run. When the meeting broke up he phoned McIntyre and suggested she not run either, calling the party "savage" and "ungovernable." She put it down to his lack of familiarity with political meetings.

in his spare time, one of Projet's most valued volunteers, was similarly unimpressed. After a few more conversations of the sort, Sébastien began to suspect the whole idea was crazy. "I knew we were headed to the slaughterhouse," he remembers. He left the café to take a long walk.

Ferrandez, for his part, was going in and out of Laïka to make his own calls—and receiving similar feedback, which he duly reported to McIntyre. "People within the party are very wary of an outsider," he would tell her. "Over the course of the day his confidence in my ability to win the leadership race eroded," McIntyre remembers. Eventually, Parent-Durand, still on his walk, called up Ferrandez and said he was out. He just didn't think he could make it happen. Ferrandez accepted the news with equanimity; he felt the same way himself. It was time to pull the plug on the whole undertaking.

McIntyre says she was "devastated, just devastated" when Luc told her it wasn't going to work. She took the train home to Pierrefonds-Roxboro and phoned him. "I couldn't accept it. I called him again and said, 'Luc, it has to work. This is Romeo and Juliette, this is the impossible romance, it's the beautiful story that everybody is waiting to hear. Everyone is so fed up with Denis Coderre. He is so conflictual, so confrontational. And here is a beautiful story of two parties coming together because they share mutual values. Coming together for the greater good. We have to make this work.' He said, 'I agree with you, but it's just not going to work.'"

Parent-Durand, meanwhile, had two tasks. The first was to write a communiqué that the party and McIntyre would issue jointly in which each graciously said, in essence, "Thanks, but no thanks." The second was to get on board the Valérie Plante campaign. There was a new urgency. A day earlier Lavoie had announced that he was going to run for the leadership of Projet Montréal after all. He said he had withdrawn initially because a member of his family had had a health scare. It turned out to be unfounded, he said, so he was back in—and with force. Surrounding him at the press conference where he announced his candidacy were about a dozen Projet Montréal councillors, including heavy weights such as the mayor of Rosemont, François Croteau, Magda Popeanu and Sylvain Ouellet.

On the Plateau, we felt our skepticism had been validated, our distrust of Lavoie confirmed, and so we jumped on Plante's campaign, newly energized. Richard Ryan had never been a big fan of the Justine idea and had been the first to sign up. "Justine was still in the picture but it was dragging on and I finally told Seb, 'Fuck off, count me out. Me, I'm supporting Valérie.'"

The rest of us followed in short order. The morning after he wrote the communiqué, Sébastien phoned up Willy Blomme, Valérie's DOC, to tell her our office was overwhelmingly behind her and would do whatever we could to help Plante win. This led to daily calls between the two to discuss any developments in the race, brainstorm on strategy and plan announcements. Neither Blomme nor Rim Mohsen, Plante's comms person, had a real understanding of how the city worked—what was a central city responsibility, what the boroughs took care of, the level of control City Hall could exercise over, say, the *Société de transport de Montréal*—and Parent-Durand coached them on that. It was something he was more than happy to do. "There was really the feeling that it was a case of life or death for the party," he remembers.

One of his important contributions was to help develop policies which would appeal to Projet members while also being realistic. That is where the $15/hr proposal was borderline. The minimum wage is, of course, a provincial jurisdiction and while it sounds easy to say that the city should require all its suppliers and subcontractors to pay their staff that amount, assuring compliance would add yet another level of bureaucracy to an institution already choked by paperwork and rules. In this way, Plante's early announcements had been seen as weak, whereas Lavoie had always projected a good understanding of the municipal apparatus. This was what appealed to Sylvain Ouellet, one of Lavoie's strongest supporters in caucus. "Guillaume was very interested in how the city worked," he says, adding that being on the finance commission allowed him to explore since it examined the spending of all the city's services.

Parent-Durand worked with Blomme and Mohsen to develop policies on animal control—pitbulls had been in the news a lot—and, with Richard Ryan, on housing, based on the social-and-affordable inclusion guidelines of the Plateau. Gradually, "we took the lead in dictating the narrative of the leadership race," says Parent-Durand. This might have been due to a certain complacency in the Lavoie camp which felt that the solid support from caucus would allow him to cruise to an easy and decisive victory; that however fine-tuned his understanding of the city was, he didn't have to propose much in the way of ideas or policy.

Still, however important the lead in the narrative might be, the absence of endorsements from any colleagues was a real weakness at the start of Plante's campaign, as it was for François Limoges. Plante had announced her candidacy on September 21st, but by the time Lavoie jumped in with half the caucus at his side three weeks later not a single councillor had yet endorsed her. Desperate to show that she had some backing, her team urged Craig Sauvé to announce. If there is one councillor within Projet Montréal who sees politics—whether federal, provincial or municipal—through a left-right prism, it is Sauvé and he knew from the start that he wasn't going to back Lavoie. When he had heard of the *bloc* of councillors who were planning to come out for Lavoie on October 11th, he had phoned several of them and "tried my damnedest to get them to refrain from adding their support." To no avail. "Guillaume was obviously a big problem because he is a conservative. A progressive conservative, let's say. A nationalist, progressive conservative but I thought that the party would split into two under his leadership," Sauvé says. "I was trying to find a star left-wing candidate. I wanted us to take a turn to the Left on social economic principles, egalitarian thinking, economic justice thinking."

When his—and everyone else's—efforts to recruit a star failed, "I boarded the Valérie bus. Simple as that," says Sauvé. He wanted to wait before making a public declaration of support, however. "I had told myself to be smart, use my experience from previous NDP leadership races and hold off a bit. Take my time, don't show colours. Wait and see." Still, he understood her need for momentum and so on October 14th, Sauvé became the first councillor to support her. He was joined by Michel Camus, the former party president, and Naïri Khandjian, who had briefly worked for the party and been a candidate in St-Laurent in 2013.

It wasn't much, but it was a start. Within a week, half of the Projet councillors on the Plateau—Richard Ryan, Alex Norris and Marianne

Giguère would also publicly declare their support. By then they were already well into that *incontournable* of 21st century politics, their social media campaigns in support of Plante. Ever since the 2009 election, the team had used Facebook to communicate directly with our supporters, without being mediated by the *Journal de Montréal* or *The Gazette*. Each had their distinct style and while it was often exhausting dealing with the comments and questions, it was hugely useful for communicating our vision and the rationale behind different projects.

Alex specialized in thorough, reasoned arguments and brought this to a post about why he was supporting Valérie. It was a study in elegant evisceration; without mentioning Lavoie at all, he managed to make it as much about him as it was about Plante. "Valérie is in politics as a matter of conviction—not to pursue a carefully plotted career plan," he wrote, praising her dedication to sustainable urbanism, social justice, affordable housing and the like, "because she believes in it."

"Her goal isn't simply to win arguments," he went on. "She is tolerant of differences of opinion and welcomes debate…I believe voters today are seeking authenticity in politicians. People want to support someone who is approachable, compassionate, open-minded, fair, determined and competent. Someone who will truly do politics differently."

Norris and Lavoie had locked horns in the past. This post, gloves-off even if no straightforward punch was thrown, set the stage for what was to be bitter campaign, with Alex the bad guy and very happy to play the role.

Perhaps for that reason, Plante's campaign kept him at arm's length and didn't involve him in any of the sessions where we worked on policy, prepared announcements, discussed strategy or coached Valérie for the big debate that took place on October 30th. I was invited to several of those and they were enjoyable evenings, a half-dozen of us, evenly split between NDPers and Projet people from the Plateau. But although Norris wasn't at those sessions, he wasn't idle. Rather, he was concentrating on the task which would really make the difference to whether Plante or Lavoie[33] became the new leader

33 Even if he had been the first to declare his candidacy—by four months—François Limoges' campaign never seemed to get out of first gear.

of Projet Montréal : signing up new members who could reliably be depended on to get out and vote for Valérie when the time came.

On a regular basis, as with any political party, councillors and staff were asked to work the phones, email and/or Facebook to raise money from members or sympathizers or sell them tickets to the annual fundraiser cocktail. It was a chore people tended to put off until a few days before the end of the calendar year or the weekend before the cocktail. This was a similar exercise but there was no leaving it to the last minute—to vote in the leadership race a person had to have been a member for at least 30 days, which meant we had to sign up as many people as possible before November 4th.

The party had had about 1,000 paid-up members in mid-2016 and the aim of Valérie's campaign was to sign up at least as many again. We suspected that the Lavoie campaign had been selling memberships for months but probably didn't feel a great urgency, given its overwhelming support in caucus. On the Plateau, we had all swung into action as soon as we decided to back Valérie and no one more so than Alex and Richard Ryan. From his days as a journalist and his years on the Plateau and, as a councillor, Alex had a large network which he contacted systematically and persuasively.

His sell was not subtle: Guillaume Lavoie was a right-wing opportunist and if he won the leadership, the unique, lefty green grassroots party that Projet Montréal had always been would soon be but a memory. Anyone who supported the party or simply appreciated its presence on the municipal scene should support Valérie Plante, he argued. For his part Richard Ryan worked on his contacts in Québec Solidaire and what he would always refer to as "*le milieu*," community groups. "I would tell them: 'I have never asked you for anything. Now I am. Projet Montréal is at a point in its history which is super important. We need you.'"

Coverage of the campaign was pretty patchy; the US election campaign was drawing to a close and even if everyone was confident Hillary Clinton would pull it off, the simple fact that Trump was a candidate—and making a race of it—was obsessing the media, not to mention the world at large. To give some exposure to *our* race Parent-Durand collaborated with a journalist from *Ricochet*, at the time a fairly new left-wing website, to produce an article which came out in late October. It was headlined "Guillaume Lavoie: the smiling right comes to Projet Montréal" and painted a devastating portrait of the candidate, so neo-liberal he was almost a libertarian, ready to sign over the city to developers (and, of course, Uber) and detailing his association with various bugbears of the Left including the Tories, the CAQ, the ADQ, and the right-wing *Institut économique de Montréal.* Norris and others forwarded it freely and it brought in more new members while helping to convince many of those who hadn't needed a leadership campaign to join Projet Montréal that Lavoie was an existential threat to the party.

Conservatively, Parent-Durand estimates that our *bureau des élus* signed up at least 300 new members directly and that Alex was responsible for half of them. Richard Ryan signed up his share as well with many of his contacts themselves recruiting for Valérie. I know I signed up about 30 or 40 and wasn't delicate about twisting my friends' arms to get them to join. As interim leader Ferrandez couldn't be seen to take a side but that didn't stop him from pushing the limits. Before the campaign started Lavoie had asked him for a meeting and the two men had taken a walk in Parc Lafontaine. "He said to me, 'Do I have your support?'" Ferrandez recalls. "I said, 'No, I will not be supporting anyone.' He said, 'So you promise you will be neutral?' I said, 'Yes, I promise to be neutral.'"

Still, staying officially neutral didn't prevent Ferrandez from sending out an appeal to people who tended to like his Facebook posts—there were hundreds—urging them to join the party and vote for Valérie. His note was sent to directly to people by Messenger, allowing him to argue that he was not taking a public position, and, like Norris's post, it never mentioned Lavoie. But it didn't make any reference to him either, instead simply saying that Valérie "would guarantee that Projet Montréal was inspired by progressive values" and that she was up against people who wanted to make the party grow by moving it to the Right.

Luc likely brought in about 75 new members and convinced many more old-timers, lots of whom wished he would have run for the leadership, to support Valérie.

Within the office, two councillors didn't show their hands until late in the race. Even if she was in a relationship with Ferrandez, Marie

Plourde remained unconvinced by Valérie until fairly late in November. By the time she announced, François Limoges had dropped out and thrown his support behind Lavoie who, he said, represented the best chance to beat Coderre. Plourde praised Lavoie also but said she was backing Plante for the same reason. "In my eyes this woman is the antidote to the soulless and shallow administration of Denis Coderre."

Christine Gosselin's decision to support Lavoie was a more complicated calculation—if only because she was backing someone the rest of the office were demonizing daily. She was close to Guillaume Cloutier who, even if he himself was solidly in Plante's camp, felt that the Plateau should not support Valérie *en bloc*. Ever the political strategist, he argued that if the Plateau overwhelmingly backed Plante but Lavoie won, relations afterwards would be all the more tense. The Machiavellian reasoning was good. I, however, explained things differently. Based on my friendship of a quarter-century with Christine, I suspected that she just couldn't countenance a woman less brilliant than herself leading the party but could tolerate yet another man.

She explains her support by saying she simply felt Lavoie would make a better leader for the party. "We only had two choices. I knew he was imperfect but I saw him as collaborative and rational, with a real interest in public service," she says. "I had never heard Valérie say a single interesting thing. Except that she was a glass-ceiling breaker. I didn't think she had the strength to champion a vision through adversity."

Whatever the case, it created a slightly weird atmosphere in the office, given that in general we were so in step with each other on such questions. But it was a weird month in general. Trump, of course, had been elected and Leonard Cohen had died.[34] These were distractions enough to push the leadership race into the background for many.

---

34 Cohen's death led to one of the gestures I was more proud of during my time working for the Plateau. Lhasa de Sela's death had been announced a day or two before my first day of employment for the borough and I reported to work urging the Plateau to recognize her somehow, given that Lhasa had adopted the neighbourhood and been such a presence in it. I learned very quickly how ill-suited the borough was for such an acknowledgement. Even getting a few lines onto the borough's web page was hugely complicated. So when Cohen died I simply told Luc I would be otherwise occupied that day on a little guerilla

Street sign erected in front of Cohen's Montreal house following his death.

There had only been the one debate in late October and during it Plante had held her own—if partly by acknowledging that she wasn't the smooth, polished orator that Lavoie and Limoges were. "There is the smoke and mirrors, and there is the work on the ground," she said at one point. Instead, most of the campaign was indeed "work on the ground," given the limited media coverage. Meetings with different ALAs, Facebook posts including videos, one-to-one convincing of councillors and others in the party who were still undecided.

When there were events at which Plante had to perform—giving a speech, answering questions in front of a crowd, doing an interview—her rate of improvement was a huge encouragement to her supporters, especially those who had only rallied behind her because she wasn't

---

gesture of recognition. With the help of a graphic designer friend, a print shop, my step-son and a ladder we repurposed a street sign in front of Cohen's house into a little homage to him which, happily, the public works department didn't remove for several years.

Lavoie. "She improved at a pretty spectacular rate. From one occasion to the next," remembers Parent-Durand.

Émilie Thuillier, a respected and veteran voice-of-reason within the party, publicly announced her support for Plante in mid-November, an endorsement which sent the message that it wasn't just the Plateau and the party's leftists who backed Valérie. "For me it wasn't anybody-but-Guillaume" says Thuillier. "But I didn't see what Guillaume could bring against Coderre...I didn't see much value added. That said, Valérie was starting from way behind."

Still, as voting day approached, even if she was getting closer to making it a real race, Plante's team knew it needed an announcement to grab people's imagination, ideally one involving public transport. Over the previous two years, as the party had distanced itself from Bergeron and thus the tramway, more thought had been given to other public transport options, including a diagonal metro line extending northeast from downtown towards Montreal North. On October 22nd, as Sébastien Parent-Durand, Pascal MacDuff and Willy Blomme sat around Blomme's dining room table with a Saturday night's supply of beer, discussing what might make for a good public transport announcement, they hatched their own version of the line. They mapped out stations, what major institutions should be served, and discussed what colour it should be. They decided on red.

MacDuff, who is good with computer design and graphics, went home to work on the visuals. Over the following hours he sent them various mock-ups and suggested they go with pink, a nod to the fact that the proposal was coming from the woman in the race. By Monday morning, the idea was given a huge spread in *La Presse*, with a long interview with Valérie hitting all the right talking points and MacDuff's graphic prominently displayed.

After two days of advance voting at the Projet Montréal offices, the majority of members cast their ballots on at the Théâtre Olympia on December 4th, a sunny Sunday. The atmosphere was an odd mix of festive and tense after a campaign which, though superficially friendly, had seen its share of ugliness and low blows. "We were cheap. It has to be admitted," says Parent-Durand.

Clumps of members gathered amongst themselves, the groupings usually determined by which candidate they supported and from which borough they hailed. Certain councillors and activists studiously avoided each other or made the briefest of polite small talk as they waited to cast their ballots or, later, for the results to be announced.

Before coming down to the Olympia, those of us who had recruited for Valérie spent an hour or two contacting the new members we had brought in to remind them to vote. Seeing so many of them lining up to vote was encouraging but Richard Ryan still didn't think Valérie would be the next party leader. "I was certain she was going to lose. I had it in my head. And I had convinced Alex, 'Guillaume will win and we will join him on stage. Afterwards, we will make up our minds. Whether we resign, whether we run again or not, whether we create a new party, whatever. But we get up on stage and we are gallant.'"

Projet Montréal had 2,884 paid-up members eligible to vote in the leadership race and 1,923 of them did, precisely two-thirds. After counting and recounting the ballots—a lengthy ordeal which just increased the tension in the room—the results were finally announced as afternoon turned into evening: Plante 998 votes, Lavoie 919, with six spoiled ballots. 52 percent to 48 percent.

There was a moment of stunned silence and then a mixture of cheers and groans. As the shock subsided and upbeat music began filtering out of the speakers, Valérie's team huddled while Lavoie and campaign organizer Joël Simard-Menard left the theatre hastily. Meanwhile Richard Ryan and Marianne Giguère went around the floor of the Olympia, urging all councillors, whomever they had supported, to join Valérie when she ascended the stage in a show of party unity if not real solidarity.

It was a long and awkward few minutes. Many adamantly refused to go, at least initially. Peter McQueen gave Richard Ryan the finger and then swore at a CDN-NDG *militant*—who, like him, had supported Lavoie—when she suggested he be gracious. Finally most councillors made their way up on stage but smiling for several was too great an ask. "I was really depressed when leaving," remembers Sylvain Ouellet. Only a pep talk from Patrick Cigana, who gave him a lift home, made him think that perhaps all was not lost. As an employee of the party at City Hall, Cigana had been discreet during the leadership race but he told Ouellet he voted for Plante for one reason and one reason only: like Thuillier, he thought she stood a better chance of beating Coderre.

"His analysis was that Coderre was like your old uncle at the party who makes you embarrassed. Who makes dumb jokes, hams it up, makes people laugh but makes you ashamed. On the other side, Guillaume is your other uncle, who is doing a doctorate in literature and smokes a pipe...You're not necessarily embarrassed by him but you don't necessarily want to hang out with him. Then there is Valérie, she's not one or the other."

In her victory speech, Plante concentrated on the failings and shortcomings of the Coderre administration while extolling the qualities of Projet Montréal. She made little reference to the deep divisions in the party that the leadership race had exposed and aggravated except to say, "Together and only together will we win Montreal in 2017."

Even if he left the Olympia in a huff, Lavoie also made the right noises about putting the campaign in the past. "There were two camps, now there is just one at Projet Montréal," he tweeted. "Congratulations to Valérie Plante!"

No one in the party, however, was under the illusion that the healing would be easy. A substantial majority of councillors had supported one candidate; a very small majority of the members—two-thirds of whom had signed up in the previous weeks—had supported another. And it was the members who decided. At best, caucus meetings would be very tense; at worst, councillors might walk, and the party might split.

Chapter 28

THE DAY AFTER THE VOTE, Plante met with Guillaume Cloutier at a café on St-Denis in the Quartier Latin to plan the coming days. Cloutier had taken over as chief of staff when Lavoie entered the race and Joël Simard-Menard had taken a leave of absence to become his campaign manager. Even if Cloutier and Marie-Ève Gagnon, the opposition's communications director, had both been relatively discreet about it, they had supported Valérie from early on in the campaign despite her inexperience. "Guillaume, we knew he was more talented in traditional political terms. He was the best for rhetoric and verbal jousting," says Cloutier. They wanted a hard-working, structured leader and knew Lavoie would deliver in that regard. "But our hearts weren't in it, and quite frankly we were scared of Guillaume. You don't want to work for a boss who is a little dictator."

At the café, Plante broke the news to Cloutier that Gagnon was going to be her chief of staff. Plante, he said, framed it as a decision based on gender more than anything—she wanted a woman. "I protested a little because you kind of have to." They also tried to plan out the caucus meeting to take place that week even if they quite quickly realized that it would be impossible to know what to expect. It would be best, they determined, to simply let people say their piece, let them *vider le coeur*. And it would be very good if Alex Norris not attend.

The meeting took place in a big room in the grand if slightly tattered Lucien Saulnier building on the other side of Place Vauquelin from City Hall. Tables were arrayed in a large rectangle with seating for 30 or 40 people. At one end sat Valérie with Richard Ryan, the caucus president. At the other end sat Guillaume Lavoie with his supporters filling the chairs beside him and, indeed, around most of the table.

Valérie's relatively small rump of supporters were squeezed around a corner of the table beside her, big windows looking out over the downtown at our backs.

There were, essentially, two items on the agenda: Valérie had to impose her leadership on what was an overwhelmingly disgruntled caucus, and that caucus, or at least the disgruntled element, had to be allowed to vent. One by one they did, holding little back. The outrage and indignation of those who spoke first spurring on those who had the floor later. "It was very, very uncomfortable," remembers Marie Plourde.

"There was a general feeling that things had not been done fairly," says Christine Gosselin. "That Guillaume Lavoie had been gratuitously bad-mouthed in a way that you don't do to your own. That what had been said about him was beyond the pale of what you say about someone in your own party, that it hadn't been a sporting fight."

There was, of course, the article in *Ricochet*, which had been picked up by *Le Devoir* and other media, as well as the letter from Luc. Both were invoked as evidence that Valérie's camp had not played by the rules. Worse, perhaps, were the phone calls that had been made to members, in which they were urged to vote for Valérie because Guillaume would transform the party into something unrecognizable. Some of these calls had been reported back to Lavoie's camp; a disproportionate number seemed to have been made by Alex.

Cloutier says that during this meeting he began dividing Lavoie's supporters into one of two categories: the hardliners and the cynics. The hardliners, which included Sylvain Ouellet, Magda Popeanu and Marie-Andrée Mauger, were councillors he thought might leave the party. "The cynics were more, 'Ok, fine, I accept the result but it was a damn bad choice. You're no good and it's going to all go to hell but so be it,'" he says. "They were those who wouldn't necessarily put up daily resistance, throwing sand in the works and making threats to quit. They would just be there and cynical. But at the end of the day, you'd be able to reason with them." The cynics outnumbered the hardliners, he calculated with relief. And even if people were complaining bitterly and angrily, well, as long as everyone is talking rather than walking out and slamming the door, it was a good thing.

Christine Gosselin, who says she was actually slightly relieved by the results—"I didn't see anything in Valérie I could get behind but I was also a bit terrified by Lavoie"—was one of the more subdued speakers. She remembers telling Plante that "she needed to consider why she won, how she won and thanks to whom she won."

Throughout, Plante was a model of level-headed firmness, neither defensive nor aggressive, acknowledging people's hurt and anger but not apologizing for it. Affirming her leadership calmly but not insistently, she said what happened had happened, and the party had to move forward; the real adversary was Denis Coderre, not each other, and in 11 months Projet Montréal had an election to win.

If anything, Richard Ryan, who had to preside over the meeting while also being an object of wrath for many of his colleagues—he was, after all, part of the Plateau clique who were seen to have stolen it for Valérie—was more flustered than the new leader. At one point, Valérie took his hand under the table and squeezed it, a message of "be strong, be calm." "It was during that meeting that all her human qualities showed themselves," Ryan says.

The worst was yet to come. Finally, it was Lavoie's turn to speak. If his tweet had suggested that he was ready to put the leadership battle in the past and move forward, every word he uttered, every gesture he made indicated otherwise. "Guillaume began talking and he was scathing," remembers Ferrandez, who was on the receiving end of much of his venom. "He was aggressive to the point of not being able to speak. His jaw was trembling."

Stabbing the air with his finger, Lavoie berated those of us who had doubted the sincerity of his motives when he said he wasn't running in order to take care of his family, only to enter the race a few weeks later. "I am not a vengeful person but I don't wish for any of you to run into my wife on the sidewalk," he said, not for the first time.

Then, in what amounted to his finale, he stared first at Richard Ryan, and then at me—if only because I was regularly considered a proxy for my absent friend Alex Norris— and pulled out a line I thought I recognized from a Dirty Harry or an Arnold Schwarzenegger movie: "You fuckers are dead to me." In English. And then a second time in case we hadn't caught it the first. "You fuckers are dead to me."

A few days later, Guillaume Cloutier went into the opposition offices at City Hall to find Joël Simard-Menard, Lavoie's campaign manager, packing up his own things and intent on negotiating his departure. Among his conditions was one that concerned Lavoie and the seating arrangement in city council. Lavoie wanted his desk moved as far away from Valérie's as possible. The demand—as well as the fact that he had his old friend make it for him, rather than making it himself—was a sign of things to come. "After Guillaume's defeat, he didn't speak to me nor look at me for six months," Plante remembers. "I would pass by him, and I'd say, 'Hello, hello everyone!' and he wouldn't answer.'"

She wasn't alone. "A month or two beforehand, I was trotting the guy out constantly to comment on this or that, giving quotes to the journalists," says Cloutier. "Then all of a sudden, flakkk! Nothing. The guy won't say a word to me. The professional relationship is finished. From that moment on, he played the victim. He stopped talking to everyone. Even people who had supported him."

Lavoie didn't quit the caucus or party or threaten to do so. Instead, he was hoping for a mass defection which he would be part of, says Sylvain Ouellet. "He would have liked it if there were a bunch of us who just slammed the door. It came very, very close. In the two or three weeks following the race, it came very close to imploding." Two factors prevented this from occurring. One was Lavoie's sulky, sore-loser attitude, not even talking to councillors who had supported him. "For weeks he kept up the vengeful, aggressive tone," says Ferrandez. "And at a certain point, people just unplugged. There was no more support for Guillaume in the caucus."

The other factor was François Limoges. "Limoges was one of the first to rally," says Cloutier. "Right away he went to see Valérie and said to her, 'I will work to get people onside.' He really helped out a lot."

Ouellet was harder to win over. Plante had run into him a day or two after winning the leadership and tried to engage him. "I just didn't want to talk to her," recalls Ouellet. "I was still unhappy about the result and she took me by the arm and she said to me, 'We need to talk' and I said, 'Another time.'" A while later she appealed to him—and his vanity—again. "She said to me, 'You are really important to the party.'" At the same time, he felt that Lavoie was asking a lot in his expectation that long-time members would abandon a party they had spent years helping to build. "You don't renounce your political party that easily. There were people who had given a great deal, who had been there for a really long time...for whom do you have more loyalty? Guillaume or the party?" Ouellet says. "If I stayed it wasn't because of Guillaume or Valérie. It was, 'Hey fuck *ostie*! I have spent ten years of my life building this party. I am not just going to abandon it just like that.'"

Cloutier says that had Lavoie taken a completely different tack and rallied in the same way Limoges and others later did, he could have had his pick of positions—in the opposition and then later in the administration. Plante was very aware of the old political maxim, 'Keep your friends close and your enemies closer' and, in fact, turned out to be better at applying the second part than the first. Lavoie, Cloutier says, could easily have become president of the executive committee had he accepted Valérie's victory. "She would have given him whatever he asked for."

Even if it was still very much a longshot, by the end of 2016 it was becoming less and less inconceivable that Projet Montréal might actually form the next administration and its new leader win the right to name the next executive committee and its president. This was not because of any surge in Plante or the party's popularity. Rather, it was because Montreal was undeniably souring on the mayor it had elected three years earlier. If the city's honeymoon with the mayor was over by January 2016, as Luc Ferrandez had argued in his speech to the Projet Montréal congress, by January 2017 a definite chill had set into the relationship. This was made abundantly clear when, invited onto the Bell Centre ice to award a prize at the end of the World Junior's hockey tournament, Coderre was lustily booed.

The factors behind the disenchantment were many. There was his tendency to improvise—banning pitbulls and *calèches* without any serious study to cite as evidence, deciding that bars should be allowed to remain open all night. There was his high-handed authoritarian streak, often involving the police. These ranged from banal—his telling an officer, "You you work for me!" when he was asked to keep moving because his selfie-taking with admirers was blocking an emergency passage way—to much more serious, as when he asked the chief of police to spy on journalist Patrick Lagaçé who had been tipped off that Coderre had cancelled a $444 traffic ticket he had been issued.

More substantially, there were his priorities and projects, which were increasingly seen to be less about improving life for Montrealers and more about bettering his chances for re-election while helping out his buddies and indulging his fancies. In a year he had dubbed "the year of public transport" his administration's budget cuts had actually forced the STM to reduce service. Meanwhile, Coderre seemed to be endlessly jetting off somewhere—Japan, Argentina, France, Italy, Haiti, all over the U.S.—often on questionable endeavours. There was his administration's decision to cut 1,000 trees on Île Ste-Hélène to create an enormous, $30 million amphitheatre for very occasional use by major music festivals, all of which seemed to be run by Evenko, owned by le Groupe CH and controlled by Geoff Molson, a friend of the mayor's. There was, of course, baseball, whether professional—in Coderre's obsession to ensure that the Expos returned to Montreal—or amateur, by creating a fund of $11 million to renovate diamonds around the city. This, despite the fact that it was a declining, space-intensive sport, whose average fan was in his late fifties.

And there were the various projects planned for the city's 375th anniversary, which conveniently happened to fall in an election year and which Coderre hoped would propel him to re-election on a frothy wave of celebration. These included lighting up the Pont Jacques-Cartier at a cost of $40 million and almost $4 million for granite stumps and benches installed in Parc Mont-Royal. Not to mention the plans to hold a rodeo—not exactly a Montreal tradition but so what?—and another car race, this one electric, this one in the heart of downtown.

All the projects and events were beginning to generate static for the mayor by early 2017 and a certain grumpiness among Montrealers. Which didn't do much for the mayor's own mood, already bad thanks to problems in his personal life. His university-age son was being investigated for credit card fraud—an investigation which stemmed from a call made by Coderre to the police chief—and his marriage was on the rocks. He had given up exercising after the death of radio host Jean Lapierre, who he used to listen to while on his exercise bike, and had had a case of severe prostatitis which caused him discomfort and rendered him chronically cranky. "In 2017 he wasn't feeling it. He was going through the motions but he didn't have the flame he had in the other years," is how one former aide put it. "Detestable, detestable," is Bergeron's less diplomatic way of describing Coderre that year. "It was the Coderre show as usual. But Coderre was always in a bad mood. Even in a good mood he was liable to explode but now, he didn't even smile, ever."

The media, which Coderre had always placed a premium on cultivating, also smelled blood, and because of the Lagaçé affair as well as simple fatigue and familiarity with his schtick, began to go after him more. "All the journalists, feeling that he was vulnerable, would provoke him," remembers Bergeron. "And he was always responding like a jerk. No more the jovial big guy from before. He was always in a bad mood."

Coderre's woes were enough to give some confidence to the team coalescing around Valérie in early 2017 and, as winter advanced, other reasons to be encouraged emerged. Focus groups indicated that Valérie scored well against Coderre, even if she remained largely unknown by the population at large. It was for the same reasons which had motivated Thuillier and Cigana to support Plante in the leadership race: she contrasted well with Coderre, offering hopefulness and a fresh, collaborative, non-threatening style against his bluster and authoritarianism.

There was a creeping optimism developing within Projet. The polls might still be putting the party behind by 20 percent or more, but the new leader—and just how different she was from both Bergeron and Ferrandez—seemed to be rubbing off in a good way. Plante may not have been as intellectually imposing, but she was also much less polarizing, even frightening than those who had gone before. Perhaps brilliance, ideas and vision had always been over-rated in the party? "It was a bit ridiculous but we were like, 'Hey wow! 20 percent in the circumstances, it's not that bad!'" remembers Guillaume Cloutier. "For lots of people, progressivism wasn't about leftist ideas or environmental ideas. Progressivism was about having someone who is smiling, dynamic, open, who wants to shake things up."

In this way, even if no one made the connection, Valérie was shaping up to be the Mélanie Joly of 2017, but in her case backed up by a structured, hungry party with a solid program and an army of supporters. "Mélanie Joly, Christ, she didn't have anything," Cloutier continues. "She didn't have a party, no infrastructure. Had she run with us, she would have won."

As it looked increasingly likely to be a two-person race, Plante against Coderre, Projet Montréal against Équipe Denis Coderre, and with Coderre constantly alienating people, well, the picture just got rosier. Not only would Projet get the votes of our supporters but also those of people who wanted anybody but Coderre, a potentially very large pool of Montrealers that was only growing. "We weren't unhappy with the set-up," says Cloutier. "Not at all."

To win a head-to-head race for mayor of Montréal was one challenge—and not a small one—but the party would also have to win control of more boroughs. That is where I decided to concentrate my efforts. After our decisive victory in 2013, virtually no one in the Plateau doubted our re-election for 2017. Our projects were more and more popular, generating less and less controversy. On at least two occasions, we were shocked in the *bureau des élus* when new bike lanes eliminating dozens of parking spots didn't cause any blowback, let alone media hysteria.

In my mind, the only question was by how much the majorities in the Plateau would increase; I figured that any electoral energy and expertise that I had to offer might be of better use elsewhere. So while there was still snow on the ground, I told Luc and my colleagues that I would work the campaign in another borough and after that, who knew? The Orange Line strategy for the party's growth was still a valid one, and I was torn between two big boroughs where there was lots of room for the party to grow: Côte-des-Neiges–Notre-Dame-de-Grâce, that old bastion of the MCM where Projet only held two of five council seats; and Villeray–St-Michel–Parc-Extension (VSMPE), where we had only one of four.

I was more drawn to VSMPE, or at least parts of it. The district of Parc-Extension intrigued me. One of the poorest, most diverse and densely populated neighbourhoods in all of Canada, it had been neglected and needed love. Most of its population, however, was too busy just getting by, not to mention marginalized from the mainstream political culture, to demand change. It had one of the lowest election participation rates in the city—30 percent lower than Villeray, the district next door, 40 percent lower than Outremont, the district literally on the other side of the tracks—and its councillor was the type of politician for whom term limits were invented. Years earlier, Mary Deros had obtained something for her community we were in awe of in Mile-End and elsewhere in the Plateau—a pedestrian-level crossing over the Canadian Pacific rail tracks between Parc Ex and Jarry Park[35]—but since then, she had been MIA. She seemed to consider bike lanes a socialist conspiracy.

I was also uncomfortable with the fact that the kind of public space changes we were implementing in the Plateau—greening and traffic-calming around parks and schools and, yes, bike lanes—seemed to be either the harbinger or the result of gentrification. I felt there was a moral and political duty to bring, or at least offer, these kind of improvements to areas where public space was especially important given the density of the neighbourhood. Much more so than in the Plateau—let alone Outremont or Ville-Mont-Royal—the population of Parc Ex tended to live cheek by jowl, with families of five or more people regularly crammed into small dilapidated apartments plagued by bedbugs, roaches, mold and the like.[36] I also had a person I thought would make the perfect candidate—a progressive academic with a Greek last name who spoke not just excellent French and English but also Hindi and Urdu. Someone who could be a bridge between the different cultural groups in the area while championing our vision.

---

35 Since early in our first mandate on the Plateau we had been pushing for similar level crossings at various spots between our borough and Rosemont but had been shut down by CP despite the fact that hundreds of people crossed the tracks illegally each day between the two boroughs. Eventually, we appealed to the Office national des transports to arbitrate the dispute.

36 Parc Ex has a population density that's more than *five times* Montreal's average and 50 percent higher than the Plateau, which itself is considered a very densely populated for a largely low-rise neighbourhood.

As a district, Villeray was also interesting. Between 2013 and 2016 I had collaborated a fair amount with its councillor, Elsie Lefebvre, in her efforts to make the intersections of her neighbourhood safer by getting all-way stop signs installed. A sovereigntist above all and popular in her district, Elsie had been elected with Vision under Louise Harel and then with the Coalition of Marcel Côté, even though her district voted Projet Montréal at the borough and city-mayor levels. Elsie very much liked what we were doing for the Plateau and wanted to bring those kinds of changes to Villeray. I had helped Elsie write various briefs to submit to her services and in this way, she and I had become almost friends. I, along with many others in the party, tried to recruit her to switch over to Projet Montréal. I thought that if she could be convinced to run for mayor of the borough, it would be a fun campaign to work on.[37] VSMPE was also closer to home for me; I wouldn't have to bike across the mountain to get there.

Things were up in the air with the VSMPE ALA, however. The co-ordinator spent half his time in Sept-Îles where he worked as an advisor for the Naskapi and his wife had just given birth to their fourth child; the election seemed to be the last thing on his mind. Meanwhile, in Parc-Ex some of the local Projet activists, who tended to also be housing activists, were understandably wary of a Plateaunik with a penchant for curb extensions and dreams of getting new Quebecers to embrace cycling as a healthy and cheap means of transport. They were also keen on finding a South Asian woman candidate who actually lived in the district.

As a borough, Côte-des-Neiges–Notre-Dame-de-Grâce interested me less even if, as a middle-class anglo, it was perhaps a better cultural fit for me, at least the NDG half of it. It too needed a good mayoral candidate, ideally one with some name recognition. Again, the idea of Sue Montgomery surfaced. Alex Norris and I sounded her out but she was not interested; she had tried to win the NDP nomination for the

---

37 Nathalie Goulet, our candidate for mayor in 2013 had done well, falling short by barely 2 percent, but had decided to run as councillor in her home district borough of Ahuntsic.

2015 federal election and lost. That, she told us, was enough for her. Anyway, she told us, she disliked Peter McQueen so much that if she were to run municipally, she'd prefer to run against him. The other possible candidate who seemed to be circling around was Kevin Copps, who had been Coderre's candidate for mayor of the borough in 2013 and finished fourth of four. Even if he was a nice guy, I wasn't particularly interested in campaigning for someone who, just the election before, had run for the enemy and whose political calling card was the fact that his sister Sheila had been a federal Liberal minister.

Then Valérie phoned up Sue to ask her to go out for coffee. When she got the call, Montgomery told her what she had told Alex and me: thanks but no thanks, my experience trying to win the NDP nomination was enough, I'm not interested.

Plante heard her out and then twisted her arm. Just come for coffee, she said, and Sue agreed. They met and got along well, both being warm, outgoing and quick to joke and laugh. And, of course, strong feminists. Valérie appealed to that, making running for mayor of CDN-NDG sound like a calling, even a duty, and soon enough Sue agreed to give it a shot. On one condition: she be allowed to speak her mind on issues she considered important. Valérie agreed.

The timing was good for Sue. She had recently left a comms job with the National Inquiry into Missing and Murdered Aboriginal Women and Girls and seemed keen for something very different. Plunging into this new world that she was utterly unfamiliar with, Sue was eager that I work with her, on the campaign and afterwards if she was to win. Even if we had only seen each other perhaps four or five times in the preceding 20 years—almost invariably at parties of mutual friends—we picked up where we left off and understood each other well. So as summer approached, I made up my mind—I would work the campaign in CDN-NDG and hope to help produce the same results there as the MCM had achieved 31 years earlier.

Elsewhere along the Orange Line, things were falling into place as well. In the Plateau and Rosemont, as in 2013, there were only minor changes to the teams, and really only to fill the holes left by the departures of Marc-André Gadoury and Érika Duchesne who had joined Équipe

Coderre, as well as Louise Mainville. Not for the last time, it would turn out, would a borough councillor from the Plateau—in this case Christine Gosselin—run as a city councillor in Rosemont because it was the easiest way to rise a rank. Both François Croteau and Luc Ferrandez decided to seek third mandates. in Ahuntsic–Cartierville the steady and solid Émilie Thuillier had decided to run for the job of borough mayor. She was inspired by Valérie's rise and reassured by it. Winning the borough mayoralty under the leadership of Bergeron or Ferrandez would have been several degrees harder. "Valérie, she impressed me so much," she says. "There are people like that who with each rung that they climb are transformed by every new challenge. That is how it was with Valérie."

So as summer approached, a fairly solid team seemed to be coming together, in spite of the fact that we didn't have the star candidates we'd often dreamed of, never seemed able to attract, but always managed to live without.

Chapter 29

A PASSION OF RICHARD BERGERON'S, which he never spoke about much within Projet Montréal, is car racing, in particular Formula 1. He went to his first Canadian Grand Prix race at the Mosport track outside Toronto in the mid-1970s and since the race moved to Île Notre-Dame a few years later, he hasn't missed a single one. His friends and family know not to disturb him or walk in front of the television when a race, or even the qualifying sessions are being broadcast. He can talk for hours about different drivers and teams, race strategy on tracks around the world, technological advances over the years and, of course, specific races that took place decades ago. It is not a subject to bring up with him unless you are prepared for long-haul listening.

So when Denis Coderre first told his executive committee that he wanted to bring a *second* major car race to Montreal, this one electric and roaring through downtown streets, Bergeron was all over the idea. "I was the first to say, 'Wow! Fantastic.'" Bergeron remembers. "No one was against the idea. With Denis Coderre, it's not in your interest to be against his ideas." But Bergeron was the most enthusiastic. "I reacted immediately, 'We must absolutely do it.'"

Given his knowledge of car racing and his responsibility for the downtown, Bergeron was put in charge of overseeing the planning of the course. By late 2016, it had been decided it would take place in the streets of Bergeron's own district. It would greatly inconvenience many of his voters for weeks given the set-up and dismantling time required, but that was the cost of throwing a good party. Bergeron—and Coderre—didn't understand that most Montrealers couldn't care less about car racing, indeed most found it annoying, and many didn't understand why a 375th anniversary was such a big deal. "I didn't take it seriously enough," Bergeron says. "I was intellectually lazy. I am angry with myself because part of the failure of the operation is my fault because I was the most enthusiastic, and I was also the local councillor."

As public resistance to the race increased, so did Coderre's already ill humor. He had been planning to surf to re-election on a non-campaign campaign, with the minimum of posters and advertising, not much of a program or platform, and little in the way of announcements or promises. The strategy was to basically coast on the warm feelings and festivities of an anniversary no one anywhere seemed to have ever bothered celebrating before. Increasingly, success seemed unlikely.

Since earlier in the year, Bergeron had observed that Coderre was souring on him, treating him with the same disdain accorded most of the other members of the executive committee. "The situation degraded. Gradually my position deteriorated. I ended up realizing that I was in the shit as well," he says. Still, that didn't stop him from pitching an audacious plan for their collective re-election. It was an open secret within the executive committee that its president, Pierre Desrochers, the former Imperial Oil executive, had had enough and was calling it quits after one mandate. Bergeron knew just the man to replace him, and not as a simple lieutenant but almost as an equal partner. Himself.

It was an interesting idea which would have let Coderre do what he liked and was good at—bask in the attention of the media, travel the world, shake hands and slap backs—while someone with a head for details, an intimate knowledge of the city and a clear roadmap for its evolution really ran the shop. Politically, it held a definite appeal as well—the founder and chief visionary of the opposition party running side-by-side with the incumbent. It could be something of a dream-team. So in late May, Bergeron asked Denis Dolbec out for lunch. "When you speak to the chief of staff, it is as if you are speaking to the mayor," says Bergeron. "I told him, 'I dare make this proposal because if you walk in the street, of all the city council, there are only two names which are known to people: Coderre and Bergeron.' I said, 'The two names together and on the same ticket.' I said, 'I dare to make this proposal because I feel I am worth 5 percent in municipal politics.

I don't think my head is too swollen in saying I am worth 5 percent.'" Bergeron also proposed that he write a brief platform for the team. "I was clear. 'We don't have a program. We have a platform. Ten points. Or if 10 is too many, then just 5. Everything would be based on the credibility of the Coderre-Bergeron tandem.'" Dolbec said he would talk to Coderre and give Bergeron news.

Returning to City Hall, Étienne Coutu, the political attaché who had followed Bergeron over to Coderre's team, asked Dolbec how the lunch had gone. "The only thing he stopped short of asking for was to be mayor of Montreal in place of Denis Coderre," Dolbec answered. "Who does he take himself for?" Within a few minutes, Coutu had reported this back to Bergeron. Still Bergeron hoped Coderre would see the wisdom in the plan. When, a few weeks later, Dolbec still hadn't got back to him and Bergeron learned that Desrochers, who wasn't event running for re-election, was in charge of writing a program for Équipe Denis Coderre, "I had my answer." Coderre and Dolbec still thought they would win the election easily, he says; what would a 5-percent Bergeron bump matter?

When Bergeron told Dolbec that the only municipal politicians with any name recognition in Montreal were him and Coderre, he may have been exaggerating things but not by much. Winning the leadership race had got Valérie Plante a brief flurry of attention, including a long, flattering profile by Nathalie Petrowski, but she was still unknown by most Montrealers as spring turned into summer. By then Guillaume Cloutier was already well into planning out the campaign in terms of announcements. He had studied the two previous elections meticulously—the point the media engaged and began following it closely, the point most people made up their minds—and he had begun mapping out a possible arc for the campaign.

People slowly began getting interested in the campaign as of mid-August, he determined, but through *la rentrée* until mid-September or so, they were never more than half interested. During that period, it was just a question of getting on peoples' radars. "It is more about, '*Allo*! We exist!' So it is more stunts, nothing much in terms of substance." Then, for about a month, it was the classic core of the campaign:

announcement after announcement, lots of canvassing, polling and promises, with, invariably, the candidates' debates and prompt, intelligent reaction to unanticipated news of the day. By mid-October, most people would have made up their minds, and the last two weeks depended on whether we were ahead or trailing. If it was the former, says Cloutier, "It's the time where you make announcements like, 'We're going to name someone from the other team to the executive committee,' 'We'll be transparent.' You do feel-good things and you show that you will bring people together. You show that you are above the *mêlée*, you show leadership." If it was the latter, you did whatever you could to reverse the trend, whether with more announcements or by going negative.

By April, Cloutier had begun work on a calendar of announcements for the six weeks of the campaign from mid-September on, with a pair of large sheets of construction paper covered in Post-its, each of which referred to a fact sheet with an outline of the issue and the essence of the position the party would take: "homelessness," "Hippodrome—family neighbourhood," "St. Lawrence River," "end of partisanship," etc.

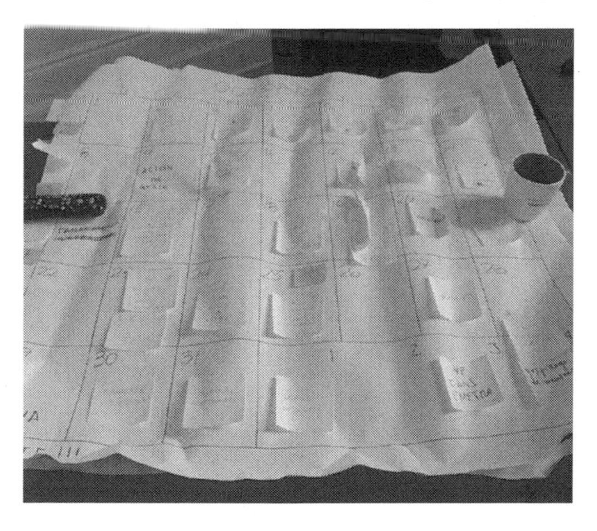

Campaign calendar covered in Post-it notes.

For the "stunt" part of the operation—the "*Allo*! We exist!" pre-campaign from mid-August to mid-September—the party knew it needed something professional and called on Upperkut, a Plateau-based "multi-platform creation agency." The party had $20,000 to spend and it was agreed that that the centrepiece of the campaign would be a short, animated video called "Kône-o-rama" which poked fun at all the roadworks blocking the streets of Montreal. There would be a few other elements including a poster of Valérie meant to boost her profile, but it was expected that the playful video, which featured Plante playing a Pac-Man-like game on her phone, would generate all the buzz as it was shared from user to user on social media.

Sometime in late June, Cloutier and Marie Depelteau-Paquette visited the Upperkut offices in the basement of Église St-Jean-Baptiste to see what the agency had come up with. It had taken two photo shoots to come up with an image of Plante which made everyone happy and the agency had tried it out with a whole bunch of taglines. "There were like two walls at Upperkut covered with a shitload of slogans," says Cloutier. "We were told, 'Ok, we will start by showing you those we rejected and then we'll show you those we kept.' And *l'homme de la situation* was among those that had been rejected and me and Marie Depelteau, we said, 'No, that's the one we want!'"

Before long, they were presenting the proposed campaign at a meeting of caucus and staff. Reactions were mixed. There were those of us who loved it immediately: the absence of the party's usual earnestness, the way Valérie's crossed arms and wry smile underscored the teasing tagline, the combination of humour and seriousness. Others, however, feared it would set people off, that it was too provocative. "Anne-Marie Sigouin [city councillor for Saint-Paul–Émard–Saint-Henri-Ouest] was like, 'We can't, no! Na na na, it will provoke reactions,'" remembers Cloutier. "And I was like, 'That is exactly what we want, Anne-Marie! That's what we want! Yes!'"

Sure enough, the reaction was immediate, overwhelmingly positive and abundant—especially since the party initially only printed three of the super-sized posters and put just one up on a construction site on Rue Alexandre-de-Sève in the Centre-Sud. "There was one poster. One poster!" says Cloutier. "Everyone is convinced they saw it somewhere but unfortunately, no, there was only one poster!"

The plan had initially been to rent billboard space at two or three strategic locations around the city but given that the Plateau was in year seven of litigation to ban billboards in the borough, Cloutier nixed the idea. The attention the poster generated in the media eventually began to cause some concern. "It got so much traction that we began to freak out," Cloutier says. "At one point we called them up and said, 'We have to put up a couple more.' But it was maximum five and maybe one in English in NDG."

It was a case—not the first in advertising—of the echo being much, much louder than the sound itself, and needless to say, the "Kône-o-rama" video disappeared without a trace. Still, it was mission accomplished—Plante was being talked about, around water-coolers, in cafés and bars and around dinner tables. Suddenly, the city was intrigued.

At the same time, things were going from bad to worse with Coderre, and the campaign hadn't even begun. The Formula E race had been held on the last weekend in July and was a total bust, to the extent that Coderre refused to say how many tickets had been sold—making matters that much worse. Meanwhile, other over-priced and ill-conceived 375th anniversary gimmicks continued to generate the exact opposite effect from that which the mayor and his team had hoped for. The concrete stumps on Mont-Royal, for example, were "the gift which keeps on giving," in the words of Alex Norris, who gleefully denounced them to journalists at any occasion possible.

Unsurprisingly, Coderre's mood continued to degenerate. In early September, the mayor's team organized a media event around the Ville-Marie candidates—including Bergeron, Cathy Wong, and Pierre Mainville, now running for Coderre—depositing the official paperwork to be candidates at borough electoral offices on Rue St-Jacques. Coderre was late and grew incensed when he arrived to see Bergeron pleasantly chatting with journalists who had shown up. "What did you say to them?" he angrily demanded of Bergeron after first scolding the reporters. "Whoa, whoa, whoa, Denis," Bergeron replied. "Let's calm down. There is nothing serious and it is you who are late." "You have no business talking to the media," Coderre snapped at him.

"I wanted to walk away then and there," remembers Bergeron. "I had seen Coderre being nasty and vulgar with others. But here he was being nasty and vulgar with me."

Bergeron had his own reasons for being extremely unhappy during this period. In the preceding months, his wife Amina, who Projet Montréal members knew as the sweet and gentle counterbalance to Bergeron's brilliant but rough edges, was diagnosed with early-onset Alzheimer's while still in her fifties. It had resulted in her losing her job and the couple would have to fight to get her a pension. It was more than enough to make for an *annus horribilis* on its own, without having an election campaign go utterly off the rails.

Before the Formula E race, Bergeron had spent hours and hours going door-to-door in his district, trying to sell the race to irritated residents, giving them complimentary tickets, free bus and metro passes and coupons for parking outside the affected area. He felt he had done his quota and told anyone who would listen he wasn't going to do any more during the campaign. "The summer is going by and I am really angry. We have our executive committee meetings and I am even more arrogant," he remembers.

"You are doing door-to-door?" Bergeron says he would ask his colleagues. "Yes? That's excellent that it's getting done. Me, I don't have the time. I'm just too busy."

"Too busy doing what?"

"Twiddling my thumbs," he would reply. "I knew it would get to the ears of Denis Coderre."

Eventually it did, and Coderre accosted him at an event. "You are going to do door-to-door!" he ordered. A few days later, Bergeron got a call from Catherine Maurice, who had become Coderre's main media person after also crossing the floor from Projet Montréal. The two had a very good relationship and when he told her he still wasn't doing any door-to-door, she said her father, who got along well with Bergeron, wanted the experience of going door-to-door with a politician.

"I accept doing door-to-door with your father," Bergeron told Maurice. "But tell Denis Coderre to go and eat shit."

By this time, Bergeron, along with growing numbers of Montrealers, was doubting whether Coderre would win. Even if he did, Bergeron certainly didn't expect to find himself with a seat at the executive committee table. With about 10 days to go in the campaign, Bergeron ran into Jimmy Zoubris at a campaign event involving candidates from the different parties. "Richard, you know that you are losing?" Zoubris had asked him. "If you only knew how little I give a damn! I don't give a damn! So what!" Bergeron had answered.

Two days later, he says, he decided to drop out of the campaign, withdraw his candidacy, just quit. "I don't care whether I am elected or not. I have had my fill. That's it. Finished," he remembers venting to Étienne , 319. "I hadn't thought about it at all beyond that. I just wasn't able to handle his bad mood, his vulgarity and his constant self-centredness," he says, referring to Coderre.

Coutu, ever calm, ever good-natured and ever loyal to Bergeron, was able to convince him to stick it out for a few more days and even to play an active role in what was the last great act of desperation of the Coderre campaign: a press conference where various *transfuges* to the administration were trotted out to sing its praises. And attack Projet Montréal.

In this way, Bergeron was soon standing shoulder to shoulder with Russell Copeman denouncing the party he had founded for having become "radical" and drifting over to the "extreme Left." "With Projet Montréal, in my opinion, it is the end for investment in downtown," he said.

The virulence of his words shocked many in the party while confirming two basic facts: the Coderre team was panicking, and Bergeron, well, good riddance.

Compared to the acrimonious choppiness of the Coderre campaign, the Projet Montréal campaign appeared to be a study in good-humoured seamlessness. The success of the *L'homme de la situation* meme had set the tone and the campaign proceeded according to the calendar and script drafted months before by Cloutier. As had been the case during the leadership campaign, Valérie Plante seemed to improve from day to day, event to event. Calmer, more in command of the issues, and always the same smile and hearty laugh.

That laugh was what Bergeron had first remarked about her

when she was elected in 2013. "For everyone she was just the girl who laughed loudly. In fact, we always knew if she was in the borough offices because you would hear loud laughter." As a new councillor, she would often buttonhole him at the office, soliciting the ideas, the learning, the wisdom of the party founder. "There were times when I sought to escape because I knew it would always be the same thing. She had everything to learn and I would often spend half an hour explaining really basic things to her. And I found it heavy going. I didn't tell her she should figure it out on her own but that is what I thought. I would say, 'I have been with you for half an hour. I have another meeting and I am going to be late.'"

Even before he resigned as party leader, Bergeron feels that Plante resented his chumminess with Coderre, especially in meetings when all the Ville-Marie councillors got together to discuss the upcoming borough council. "I think she was angry at me from that point on because I spent less time helping her fulfill her role and more time helping the mayor be a good mayor."

When she was elected party leader, he was as astonished as anyone. "It was written in the sky that it would be Guillaume Lavoie." And now here she was, "the girl who laughed loudly,' looking ever more likely to win the job he had so long sought for himself.

Below the surface, of course, things at Projet Montréal were not as perfectly well-oiled and choreographed as they might have seemed. As in 2013, Luc Ferrandez had essentially been locked in the closet and not let out beyond the Plateau's borders for most of the campaign. "In general, the idea was 'Valérie, Valérie, Valérie.' We didn't want it to be the image of the Plateau,'" Ferrandez says. He didn't disagree with the strategy, especially when Coderre, ever more rattled at the prospect of losing, took to saying that the election of Projet Montréal would result in an "administration Ferrandez-Plante".

Nonetheless, because of his grasp of the municipal machinery, including the budget, Ferrandez says he was called regularly by Marie-Êve Gagnon to test out lines and give his advice on announcements and undertakings. "Valérie had no experience. None whatsoever," he says. "Marie-Êve would call me every day to ask 'Can we say this? Can we say that? There was no knowledge of the budgets. There was no knowledge of the programmes. 'Is this our responsibility or that of the provincial government?'"

Ferrandez describes it as a "flexible campaign, quick but not very deep" which was "young, dynamic, nothing-to-lose because we thought we wouldn't win." Even if it was hugely successful, at least against a grumpy opponent whose heart was clearly elsewhere and who had alienated much of his team, he says he didn't much like it as a campaign. "The campaign seemed to be driven by slogans. Sometimes Marie-Ève would call me up to ask, 'Luc, do you have a slogan for this or that thing?' or 'What slogan can we use today?' It wasn't very planned out. It ran off energy that was renewed each day."

Certainly, the campaign's fixation on orange cones seemed an odd one to some Projet members, many of whom hoped for increased constraints on private car ownership and mobility in order to prioritize public and active transport, including more bike and reserved bus lanes. Ferrandez also questioned the "More Welcome. Less tax." proposal, which would reimburse the Welcome Tax for families buying their first home. It suggested less tax overall, he felt, something which had populist appeal but which the city could ill afford.

Still, most in the party were judging the campaign less on the substance of the announcements and more on how they were being received by the public and the media—and in that regard there was nothing to complain about, especially as Valérie's poll numbers kept rising and the word "wave" was being whispered, with growing excitement.

Increasingly, while going door-to-door, candidates were running into effusive enthusiasm for Valérie. In districts as different as NDG and Hochelaga, Peter McQueen and Eric Alan Caldwell had adjusted the way they folded the party leaflets. No longer did they do everything to hide the face of their leader. Just the contrary. Valérie was front and centre. "On the ground, it was crazy. I really felt it," says Caldwell. "Something was happening."

He compares it to the surges in popularity that Jack Layton inspired in 2011 and that propelled Justin Trudeau four years later. "I lived it with Valérie Plante. There was enthusiasm, confidence, momentum, positivity. There was an electric atmosphere. It was the only time in my life that I felt that—a palpable political groundswell. It was an incredible feeling."

There was only one moment in the campaign when things seemed to teeter. It was in mid-October and if Plante was clearly gaining, no polls had put her in the lead yet. Then, after two years of consultation and debate, the National Assembly voted in Bill 62, "An Act to foster adherence to State religious neutrality." Decreeing that public servants would be prohibited from not only wearing certain visible religious symbols but also from offering services to people wearing niqabs and burkas, the mayoral candidates were called upon to react to the law.

Coderre, understanding that the law was aimed at pleasing "the regions" and that it would be highly controversial in Montreal, denounced it immediately, something that many of us in Projet Montréal expected Valérie to do also, if only because women from diverse backgrounds seemed to be targeted by it. Instead, she equivocated and, if anything, seemed to support the law. For what seemed to be a long news cycle, a bunch of us—generally anglophone and more sensitive to how badly such a line would play in the English and cultural communities—besieged the central campaign with phone calls, texts and emails saying Valérie had to nuance her position or risk writing off big swaths of the city. Happily, Valérie modified her stance without making it appear a reversal in time for the evening newscasts and the next day's papers. From that point on, the swell we had all been feeling gathered force, becoming a wave cresting at just the right moment.

There were those who were slow to accept that it was really happening. Christine Gosselin remembers talking to Luc Ferrandez with two weeks to go and him saying that he still didn't think Valérie had much of a chance. "I told him, 'No! Even the old people are telling me that they hate Coderre and are going to vote for Valérie,'" she remembers. "I was terrified."

Sylvain Ouellet was even more pessimistic. His doubts about Plante's leadership hadn't dissipated, nor his bitterness at how the leadership campaign had turned out. He hadn't been tempted when, during the summer, Guillaume Lavoie sounded him out about possibly running along with him and Justine McIntyre and whoever else might be convinced to defect from Projet Montréal. The initiative amounted to nothing and Lavoie eventually quit rather than run again for Projet or run for Coderre as many expected him to. Meanwhile, after being unable to negotiate a "non-aggression pact" with Projet Montréal, McIntyre ended up running for mayor of Pierrefonds-Roxboro with a much-reduced slate of 20 candidates. Ouellet appreciated that the absence of a third option was very good news for Projet Montréal and had observed the signs of discord, even panic in the Coderre camp. Still, he says he was "super-pessimistic throughout the whole campaign" and even thought he would lose his seat. Then he actually began talking to citizens. "Throughout the campaign I hadn't really done any door-to-door. I didn't have the time and it was complicated with my family to get free," he says. "Then I finally insisted to the mother of my children, 'It's the last week. I want to give all I have to give. I want to be at the metro stations first thing in the morning.' And people were saying, 'Valérie? Okay, oui! Coderre, I just can't stand him anymore.' There were lots of people saying that, and not my typical electorate. They were really disgusted by Coderre."

By then, it was almost election day and soon enough Ouellet would find himself onstage at the Corona, his margin of victory having gone from .26 percent to 18.42 percent, from 23 votes to 1,555. Added gratification: Coderre's candidate was Érika Duchesne, the Projet *transfuge* from Rosemont who had decided to run in her home district which she had deemed a safer bet.

Chapter 30

A FUN FACTOID EMERGED from the 2017 election: no one who had ever won a seat with Projet Montréal had ever failed to keep it in the subsequent election—as long as they were still a candidate for the party. The flipside: with just one exception, no one who had ever left the party to run with another team had managed to hold onto their seat.[38] Duchesne, Marc-André Gadoury and Richard Bergeron all went down to defeat and by substantial margins. Bergeron had watched the results come in with Amina, a brother, and sister-in-law. Once he saw that *la fille qui riait fort* was going to beat the man who so many had been convinced would be in the job for decades, "I prayed to the heavens not to be elected," he said. "To find myself in opposition against Projet Montréal would have made no sense."

The steady growth of Projet Montréal—from one seat on city council to 10 to 20 and now to 33, a majority, if razor thin—coupled with the fact that Montrealers seemed to appreciate the service its councillors provided once elected, suggested a certain inevitability to the party's progress. It was so controlled, so organic that certain optimists—or at least, me—predicted that, after our 2017 victory, we were in power for the long haul. That our chances of winning again in 2021 were almost unparalleled, especially given that with his defeat, Coderre had promptly resigned and so his party, now the opposition, had lost any glue holding it together. I felt that as long as we did a reasonable job of running the city, applying the

38 The exception was Ahuntsic mayor Pierre Gagnier, for whom Projet Montréal was never anything more than a party of convenience and who left it after barely a year; he was later re-elected with Coderre.

lessons we had learned in the Plateau and Rosemont both on a city-wide basis and in the eight new boroughs we now controlled, the odds of remaining in power for multiple mandates were excellent.

My ebullient confidence wouldn't last long. A few days after the election, the councillors and senior staff, floating back down to earth, gathered for the first caucus meeting of the new administration. Appropriately, it was held in the same room at the Centre St-Pierre in which the party had been founded. The cast was almost completely different—Émilie Thuillier was the only person to attend both gatherings—but the one was the clear result of the other, 13 years and one week earlier.

The agenda was light. Mostly thank-yous and congratulations with the real business of the day being a short briefing on how the executive committee would be composed. There was no mystery as to who would be its president: Plante had announced a few days before the vote that Benoit Dorais—not Luc Ferrandez as Coderre had been warning—would get the job. Beyond that, parity was important and the mayor-elect was serious about including members of the opposition; her office was already talking to certain of the more palatable councillors elected with Coderre to gauge their interest. A certain regional representation was important but newly elected borough mayors would be expected to concentrate on that job—none of them would be getting the nod. For everyone else, chief of staff Marie-Ève Gagnon said that if they hadn't received a phone call by the following Sunday evening, then they could assume they were not going to be on the executive committee.

It was a tight but not impossible timeline. The meeting soon broke up with everyone going off into the Centre-Sud sunlight. The unseasonably warm weather which had characterized the autumn had returned and our spirits remained high.

Some of us, however, were a bit troubled by something our new mayor had said. In her short address to caucus, she had been emphatic about not owing anything to anyone. No one, she seemed to say, should expect any payback for their loyalty or support. It was perhaps something she had to say, establishing for the record that she wouldn't be playing favourites or letting warm and fuzzy feelings get in the way of building an executive committee of the best and most competent councillors. After all, the divisive leadership campaign that brought her to this place wasn't even a year in the past. So maybe what was troubling was the way she said it, as if she really believed it, as if she were firmly convinced that it was entirely her doing that she or any of us were here at all. Was the collaborative, collegial approach we had expected to apply under Mayor Valérie, where everyone, whether executive committee member or simple attaché, had a voice around the table, just a dream? Would her administration become like so many others, where her office made virtually all the decisions, issued directives and expected everyone to fall into line?

From my limited vantage point, the initial signs weren't encouraging. At the next caucus meeting, a post-mortem of the campaign was on the agenda and I anticipated a frank discussion of the sort that had traditionally taken place around the caucus table. I put up my hand to speak and after lauding the general excellence of the campaign, I brought up the Law 62 misstep, suggesting that the communications director should have listened more quickly to those of us who objected to Valérie's conciliatory stance. At the first hint of criticism, Valérie glared at me. It was a look I might have expected if she had caught me slashing her bike tire. At that moment it was clear that, now that we were in power, the culture of caucus meetings was going to change.

The naming of the executive committee also suggested things weren't going to play out as many of us hoped. In the first place, it turned out to take much longer than promised, in particular because members of the opposition weren't jumping with the expected alacrity at the opportunity. This was particularly true for Cathy Wong, the new councillor for the downtown Peter-McGill district, whom the administration prized because of her openness and because she would add some *diversité* to an otherwise extremely White, European caucus. Valérie, however, was still unhappy that Wong had even run with Coderre instead of Projet and angry that she had released private text exchanges between the two during the campaign; she insisted that Wong publicly renounce Équipe Coderre if she was to join—something Wong refused to do.

In the end the only opposition member who could be tempted onto the executive committee was Verdun mayor Jean-François Parenteau, previously the owner of an orthopedics supply store, who was an easy sell largely thanks to his friendship with Benoit Dorais. He didn't do much for the diversity or parity goals. "It was complicated to close things with the opposition, and that delayed everything a bit because it was like a puzzle," says Guillaume Cloutier.

The upshot of all this, however, was that virtually no one in Projet had been called by the Sunday night and many councillors hoping to be offered a seat were driven to distraction with anxiety. All the more so because Valérie's team didn't even bother telling people that the process was taking longer than expected. Richard Ryan, who at least wanted to be offered the housing position given that he was the party's acknowledged expert on the issue, was so afraid of rejection that he ended up writing an email saying he didn't want the job. Others, including François Limoges and Alex Norris, were similarly fraught.

In the end, the choice of councillors seemed to be heavily influenced by the desire to keep Plante's former enemies close. Magda Popeanu and Sylvain Ouellet, two of Lavoie's most fervent supporters, were named the vice-presidents of the executive committee while Alex Norris, Craig Sauvé and Marianne Giguère all experienced and very competent councillors who had supported Valérie in the leadership, were only given associate member positions.

Luc Ferrandez was the only member of council who supported Plante to be accorded a full position and even then it didn't come easily. Christine Gosselin, who was the obvious choice for the culture position given her erudition and multilingualism, was asked by Marie-Ève Gagnon what might be a good job for Luc. They didn't feel they could give him a major portfolio such as transport, housing, or public security because his vision was too uncompromising. Neither could they give him too junior a job either. When Gosselin said *grands parcs* would be perfect for Ferrandez, Gagnon was elated, Gosselin recalls. It would keep Luc busy and out of the mayor's hair. "Valérie was intimidated by the Plateau," Gosselin says. "And so she marginalized it."

By this time, I was trying to do just the opposite—export the Plateau revolution to Côte-des-Neiges–Notre-Dame-de-Grâce. Eighteen months earlier, I had told Luc that I was going to quit if it was status quo after the election; it was very definitely not. So I shelved my plans of returning to writing or doing something entirely new to remain a city employee—but not in the Plateau.

During the campaign I had discussed with Sue Montgomery the idea of becoming her chief of staff if she were to win. I told her the job interested me as long as we approached things the way we had under Ferrandez when first elected in 2009: a focus on delivering the projects we had spoken about during the campaign—safer streets around schools and parks, better cycling infrastructure, rejuvenating neglected commercial arteries, cracking down on negligent slumlords—with relatively little attention to "comms." I wanted the councillors and Sue herself to be autonomous, not relying on me or the political attachés we would hire to answer their emails, write speeches for them or in any way hold their hands.

Like so many in the party, Sue was a huge fan of Luc and what we had accomplished in two mandates in the Plateau, and she signed onto that approach immediately. So I handed in my resignation for the Plateau and soon enough Sue and I were preparing for the transition in CDN-NDG. It was a very different borough than the Plateau had been in 2009. Not only did it not have a deficit but it had an almost embarrassing surplus—something in the order of $20 million.[39] It also had fairly stable leadership in a borough director who had been in the job for almost a decade. What the borough seemed to lack entirely was vision and direction.

Ever since the borough system was first created, CDN-NDG had voted for the winning side city-wide and its mayors had always found themselves with major responsibilities on the executive committee which sucked up the lion's share of their time. Often, they were only in the borough for a day or two per week so a steady-as-she-goes approach to running thing prevailed. Almost no creative initiatives were undertaken. Instead, there was a general indifference to, and slow decay of, municipal assets, whether it was parks, city buildings

39 Confusingly, Magda Popeanu adamantly refused to call it a surplus or be pleased about its existence. She insisted on calling it a "deficit of services" on the premise that the borough had been negligent in not spending the money on any number of things that she considered lacking in the borough.

or commercial arteries. Only road and sidewalk repair seemed a genuine priority and then it was almost invariably exactly as before.

One of our first meetings was a pro-forma transition conversation with the outgoing mayor Russell Copeman. He had been genuinely shocked to lose; he had thought that even if Coderre went down to defeat he would survive. Losing to Sue made it that much worse, given her poor command of the issues, and of French, as well as her cheap shots and teasing during their debates. He was patently unhelpful in the meeting, answering "NLMP" several times to different questions. We had to get him to explain after he first pulled it out. "No. Longer. My. Problem," he answered. When I asked if he ever met with the borough's *chefs-de-divisions*, architects or engineers, he was almost aghast. Why would he do a thing like that? He just dealt with the directors and most often just with the borough director, Stéphane Plante.

Our first meeting with Stéphane was pleasant in comparison—and certainly much better that what we expected. Sue and I had heard complaints about his combativeness. We had also observed him at borough council where he took up much more space than directors tended to and acted almost like a member of Copeman's team rather than a disengaged public servant. There was also the fact that he had been the borough director when Michael Applebaum had been mayor of the borough, and on the take of developers, pushing through zoning changes in return for kickbacks. One senior employee in the urbanism department had been jailed for his involvement while another committed suicide after being grilling by police. My take was that Stéphane had either turned a blind eye to what police referred to as a "stratagem of corruption" or was so disconnected from what was really going on in his borough offices that he had no idea it was happening. Damned if he knew, damned if he didn't; either way, I felt, he should probably be gotten rid of and a fresh start undertaken with a new director. Sue agreed.

At that meeting, however, and at others to follow, Stéphane had good answers to all our questions about the Applebaum affair and displayed a knowledge of the borough and familiarity with all its operations that dwarfed anyone else's. That he was a sophisticated and well-read man who appreciated what Projet Montréal was all about just made things better. Sue felt likewise and we began to think that perhaps we had been a bit hasty in determining that he should be fired. I candidly asked other directors in the city of Montreal who had had dealings with Stéphane what they thought about him. Their reviews were unfailingly positive. Finally, firing someone who has always received enthusiastic performance evaluations is—rightfully—a complicated and often costly affair.

All this, along with the fact that we didn't have a replacement candidate waiting in the wings, was more than enough to convince us that we should try and make a go of it with Stéphane.

Elsewhere in the city, Projet Montréal mayors and councillors in other newly conquered boroughs were also coming to terms with power. For some, it went more smoothly than others. In Ahuntsic-Cartierville and Mercier–Hochelaga-Maisonneuve both Émilie Thuillier and Pierre Lessard-Blais seemed to take the reins naturally and authoritatively. In Lachine as well, where Maja Vodanovic had been a borough councillor already for four years, she was able to slide into the role of mayor without much complication In Outremont, Philipe Tomlinson was also able to take charge with minimum bumpiness.

Meanwhile, in Villeray–St. Michel–Parc-Extension things went off the rails almost immediately. The two Projet Montréal councillors elected with Giuliana Fumagalli—Sylvain Ouellet and Rosannie Filato—both found themselves with heavy responsibilities on the executive committee and were hardly in a position to help her adjust to being borough mayor even if they had wanted to. And Fumagalli needed help, lots of it. As one person who worked with her said, "She has zero skills in any aspect of management: budget and finance, personnel, project management, planning."

If there was any effort to try to make a fresh start of it between Giuliana and Projet Montréal after the election, it didn't go far. She proposed "a whole bunch of names" for her chief of staff. "Everybody we submitted was always refused," she says. "And they kept giving me names of people that I was refusing because I didn't trust them. I didn't trust Projet Montréal because I felt I had been backstabbed by them." She also didn't much trust the borough director who, at their first meeting, had told her straight up that he was good friends with her predecessor, Anie Samson. "My reaction was, 'Well, fuck, then go cry with her and leave your job.'"[40]

Eventually, Fumagalli and the party agreed on a chief of staff—a woman who had worked as a political attaché for Benoit Dorais in Le Sud-Ouest—but she left within a couple of months. Then Patrick Cigana was convinced to take the job. During the campaign he had set up and run the central polling operation for the party, based out of a sprawling and grungy former massage parlour on de Maisonneuve East. It was very successful and cost-efficient in terms of collecting data, winning over voters and identifying important issues in specific districts as its staff performed various functions—polling, canvassing, even focus-grouping. It was a surprise to many then that Cigana didn't end up with a job in the mayor's office. When it was announced, however, that he would be in charge of reining in Giuliana and structuring her administration, there was great relief both that a position had been found for him and that such a reliable person was in the job. But he too was gone after barely two months.

Within two months of that, Fumagalli had lost yet another chief of staff and was being ordered to work from home after members of her political staff and the borough civil service brought allegations of psychological harassment against her. The party had dispatched various councillors and other borough mayors to talk with Fumagalli, to try and coach her, try to make her understand the limits of her powers and what she could demand of the borough employees—and in what kind of language. Among others, Émilie Thuillier, Maja Vodanovic, Christine Gosselin and Sophie Thiébaut had answered the call and done their best. Even Helen Fotopulos tried to mentor her after they ended up sitting beside each other at an event. "I met with her many times to try and help her," says Maja. "She

40 Samson seems to have been determined not to make things easy for Fumagalli herself. "I arrived and I had no office furniture—there was nothing—and Anie had put everything in the shredder, emptied out all the offices... That was the context of my arrival. Everything was fucked up...I had the *fonctionnaires* against me, I had the party against me and then I had my base, the activists against me."

didn't listen and she didn't understand her role and she didn't want help because she thought she knew best."

Valérie's office initiated a mediation process but it didn't produce any better results than the coaching and mentoring. In August, after new allegations of harassment came to light, Fumagalli was expelled from the Projet Montréal caucus. "I was overwhelmed," Fumagalli says about that period. "I didn't understand how things worked."

Overwhelmed, not understanding how things work—it's a state that new administrations find themselves in all the time. And, after 2017, it applied at City Hall as much as it did in many of the boroughs now controlled by Projet Montréal. This was the case for certain members of the executive committee as much as it was for staff. "There were lots of people who were just fucking panicking in front of their responsibilities," says Guillaume Cloutier. "Then there was a caucus full of lefty *militants* who were always in opposition and all they knew how to do was complain, complain, complain."

Cloutier, who still saw himself as a relative newcomer, was surprised to realize that he was considered by others as something of a wizened old pro who could counsel them on how to deal with difficult directors and the like. It would have been great, he says, if it had been possible to press pause for a few weeks as everyone settled into their new roles but that, of course, is not how it works. Making things particularly complicated in Montreal is that, within a few weeks of being elected, new administrations, both at the borough and city level, are required to table and adopt the next year's budget. The fruit of months of work, it is unrealistic for a new administration to hope to significantly modify the budget, even if it was drawn up by a predecessor with diametrically opposed priorities.

In this way Valérie Plante and Benoit Dorais soon found themselves tabling a budget inconsistent with the Projet Montréal campaign promise not to raise taxes above the rate of inflation. That the increase was split between the usual property tax, a water tax and local borough hikes didn't convince anybody, even within the party. This gave the new administration its first black eye with the media and taxpayers at large although it wasn't its first controversy.

That had come within a couple weeks of being sworn into office when a Projet candidate who had run unsuccessfully for mayor of Montréal Nord turned on Plante and the party, accusing them of, among other things, systemic racism. Along with Sue Montgomery, Balarama Holness was one of the star recruits of Projet's 2017 campaign. He was all the more interesting for his background: few ever would have expected a former professional football player to run for Projet Montréal. A downtown resident, it was initially thought he might run in Peter-McGill or even as Plante's *co-listière* in Sainte-Marie. He wanted to run for a mayoralty, however, and so Holness chose Montréal-Nord, where the party still didn't have a candidate when he signed on in late spring. Not the best idea, as it turned out.

Denis Coderre's home borough and stronghold, Holness never had a serious chance in Montréal-Nord—he ended up winning 33 percent of the vote while Coderre's candidate won twice that. But the reason he lost, Holness maintained, was because Projet had abandoned him during the campaign. The posters were late, his campaign wasn't provided an office and "Valérie Plante only came to see us two or three times." He added: "They use candidates of colour to their advantage and then toss us aside when no longer convenient... The Whites close the door behind them when it comes time to distribute positions of power."

However questionable his allegations, they underscored an important fact: Projet was still an extremely White party, and with White councillors occupying almost all the seats that might be considered likely bets, the party would have to find a way to ensure greater diversity in its caucus.

That however, was a problem for down the road. In the meantime, the administration had a city to run... and transform.

One of the few members of the executive committee who was not overwhelmed with his new responsibilities, according to Cloutier, was Luc Ferrandez. Luc was very happy to have been given *Grands parcs* but says he would also have liked "a bigger role in urbanism." As it was, urbanism, along with transport, went to the cautious Éric Alan Caldwell. The two responsibilities were, at least to begin with, too much for Caldwell and soon Ferrandez was getting his wish. "Marie-Ève Gagnon didn't know how to manage a cabinet so she was running in the corridor asking me, 'Luc, can you take care of Sainte-Catherine Street?' 'Luc, can you take care of the Royal Victoria?' 'Luc, can you take care of Square Phillips?' Without asking Eric."

Fortunately, along with being cautious, Caldwell was easy-going and didn't mind Luc being handed some of his most high-profile projects as long as he was kept informed. As in the Plateau eight years earlier, Ferrandez wanted to do everything, immediately. In some cases, this worked out. He had the plans for Sainte-Catherine Street and Square Phillips redrawn dramatically to include wider sidewalks, the pedestrianization of McGill College and the planting of dozens and dozens of new trees. In the case of Rue Sainte-Catherine he had the city urbanists and architects work over Christmas so the call for tenders could be issued before the big contractors' workbooks got too full to take on such a major project.

But in the case of the plan to close Voie Camillien-Houde across the mountain to transit traffic it didn't work out, not at all. In the *bureau des élus* in the Plateau, we had long harboured dreams that the road could be eliminated, or at least reduced substantially in width, possibly made into a parkway. We knew that the building of the road in the 1950s had been hugely controversial with the mountain considered by many Montrealers a sacred place. Even the mayor after whom it was named had questioned its construction while Frederick Law Olmstead, the designer of Parc Mont-Royal, would certainly not have approved, we were quite certain. Then the death, just before the election, of a young sport cyclist who, racing down Camillien-Houde, had crashed into a car doing a U-turn halfway up prompted calls for something to be done. Ferrandez had an idea of what to do and, finding himself in charge of *Grands parcs*, quickly had a plan drawn up.

It was not released, however, at a carefully planned news conference with compelling visuals and a convincing *argumentaire*. Instead the plan came out in a *Commission des finances* hearing in early February where the 2018 spending planned for the *Grands parcs* department was being scrutinized. The mayor's office was blindsided by the project. "Luc worked on it with his services but hadn't shared it," says Cloutier.

"Normally, the way it works is you develop a game plan, then you present it at a meeting with the mairesse. There are modifications, then communications get involved, and then you put the plan into action."

The backlash was immediate and intense, especially on the western side of the city. It was driven by a crowd, it seemed to me, who liked the pleasant drive across the mountain to get their bagels on the weekend, perhaps make a stop at Schwartz's or Wilensky's or to buy their socks and underwear from Schreter's. There were calls for consultations, which Luc maintained were unnecessary: the Office de consultation publique de Montréal had discussed the idea a decade earlier and about three-quarters of the respondents had backed the idea.

But the opposition smelled blood. Left without a focus or really even a reason to exist after Coderre's humiliating defeat and subsequent resignation, it had renamed itself Ensemble Montréal and was now led by Lionel Perez. When groups such as Les Amis de la Montagne also came out against the plan, the administration got cold feet. The question, it was announced, would be referred to the Office de consultation publique de Montréal again; the definite closure planned for the spring of 2018 would only be a pilot project. If Ferrandez hadn't understood it already, he did then. This was not an administration which would follow the example he'd set in the Plateau, implementing its program come hell or high water, whatever public opinion of the moment might feel. Pinning its re-election hopes on a satisfied if silent majority expressing its support rather than bowing to the outcry of *les grandes gueules* each time a project proved controversial. "I thought that on day two we would close Camillien-Houde," Ferrandez says. "Then when I saw there wouldn't even be question about it, it was an early wake-up call."

Ferrandez says that, within weeks of the election, Plante had told him that the most important thing for her was being re-elected in 2021, not necessarily delivering on the party platform. He says she framed it in terms not of ego or ambition but of her feminism. "I want to prove that a woman can do the job as well as a man," he remembers her telling him. She was also upfront with him about resenting the attraction he still held for the media. On one occasion, he recalls her coming back from an interview at Radio-Canada, and she was furious. "Guess what they spoke to me about?" she said to him. "You!" He assumed it was because he had said or done something to put the mayor or the party in hot water, but she said no. The Rad-Can people had been saying good things about Ferrandez and she was unhappy that he was still capturing the imagination and attention of the media more than she was. "It really showed what a beginner she was. That she would even admit that to me," Ferrandez says.

After the Camillien-Houde debacle, Cloutier says that the mayor's office determined that greater control would have to be exercised over the executive committee members and caucus. "Some will say excessively but it was it was really just—Christ, when you have an idea which is a little out there, work on it present it, get it approved." Many did indeed bristle at the excessive control, especially when they would get texts or calls telling them to take down a Facebook post or comment which the cabinet felt went too far. Many began to feel that the party of ideas and debate which they had joined and helped to build was being strangled, or at least transformed into a party where the leader's office insisted on calling all the shots. A model which might work for *Équipe Denis Coderre* or any other party built around an individual and interested in power largely for power's sake, but not for a grassroots party like Projet Montréal.

Certainly, by mid-2018 there was uneasiness at the way party caucus meetings evolved under a Projet Montréal in power. Frequently, Plante and much of the executive committee were absent. If the mayor did show up, it was for only 45 minutes or so. "The Projet Montréal caucus from before 2017 was not what we had," says Christian Arsenault, who had been a liaison agent for the party before being elected. "Caucus was basically being treated as a means for cabinet to give us lines and information and that was it. Few questions being asked, no votes being taken. It was beginning to frustrate a lot of us and worry us." Cloutier says that even people in the mayor's office were surprised at Valérie's limited tolerance for dissent or even debate, whether on Facebook or in caucus. "For a super-friendly woman, you would normally expect a much more consensus-driven, friendly approach to caucus management," he says, adding that senior staff urged her to be more solicitous of and attentive to caucus, or at least to go through the motions. "But that is not what happened, not at all." Asked why that might have been the case, he says he has no explanation.

Others have their theories. Ferrandez puts it down to her character and a desire to show that she could be as iron-fisted as any male mayor. "Her vision was, 'I am a woman and I have to prove that I can be considered as a full-power mayor.' She is ambitious and she is determined to impose her power." Some feel it is more complicated, that the bold can-do self-confidence that propelled her rise from city council candidate, who no one thought had a chance, to mayor in less than five years suddenly ran out. That suddenly, in power, she felt insecure and perceived any questioning from within as a challenge to her authority. Plante herself says that the leadership campaign was the most difficult race for her for reasons which are similar. "Because you fight with your brothers and sisters, your colleagues. And when they tell you, 'I'm not choosing you, I'm going with the other,' it hurts. So you question yourself, 'What is it I lack?' or whatever. It is really difficult. The whole leadership campaign, I found it difficult. Very, very, very difficult."

It was during the leadership campaign, she says, "that I developed my shell. After that I was pretty much bullet-proof." But each time Plante took dissent by caucus members personally, each time she lost her temper when circumstances didn't justify it, or left a meeting in tears, it left people wondering whether she had truly become bullet-proof enough.

All this, however, was internal. In terms of actually doing its job—managing the city, delivering on its election promises and implementing the party's vision—there were relatively few complaints from within caucus, other than from Ferrandez who, as usual, felt that things weren't moving far enough, fast enough and certainly not with the urgency that the climate crisis required.

This was despite the fact that many of the administration's early big announcements involved projects pushed forward by Ferrandez. There were of course the redrawn Ste-Catherine and Square Phillips projects—with the not negligible addition of a pedestrianized McGill College added to the mix. There was also the creation of what one day will become Canada's largest urban park, *le Grand Parc de l'Ouest*, through the stitching together of more than 3,000 hectares—that is 5,600 football fields—of greenspace, some already public, some agricultural, some unbuilt and slated for suburban development, in the West Island and on Île-Bizard. Of particular interest to us in Côte-de-Neiges–Notre-Dame-de-Grâce was the announcement of the *Parc de la Falaise*, a ribbon of land along the three-kilometre escarpment which formed the border between our borough and Sud-ouest. The MCM had planned to turn the land, which is a unique micro-climate, into a park before they lost power in 1994. Since then it had continued to be used for what had been its traditional vocation since the 1800s—a dump.

Announcements in other areas showed that the administration was serious about delivering on what its members expected and what it had undertaken to do during the campaign. Almost immediately upon taking office, the administration ordered 300 new hybrid buses and not much later began work on having an ultra-modern underground garage built in Rosemont; more buses, after all, require more garage space. Similar bold moves were made to enable the city to fulfil its goal of 12,000 new social and affordable housing units by the end of 2021, whether by acquiring existing buildings, land for new constructions or just getting projects happening.

While some initiatives, such as the Réseau express vélo, took longer to get going because they were entirely new and required extensive planning, others required little more than a simple vote in council. These included the scrapping of the Formule E race and the controversial P-6 bylaw, which had curtailed the right to protest, as well as the opening up of *Commission de sécurité publique* (CSP) hearings and the requirement to hold a minimum of 10 public meetings per year. Previously the CSP, which is responsible for police oversight, had only met in camera, and sometimes not even twice a year, even if that was the minimum required by provincial law.

The boroughs, meanwhile, undertook their own projects. For the Plateau and Rosemont, it was business as usual, though with added vigour and improved collaboration from the central city. Since 2016 Croteau had grown less cautious about traffic-calming and other public space initiatives, perhaps because he had noticed that, on the other side of the tracks, all the new stop signs, speed bumps and bike paths only seemed to make Ferrandez more popular. Meanwhile, among many other initiatives, the Plateau moved forward with two major protected bike lane projects, one on Rue Clark, the other on Ave des Pins, each of which would add dozens of trees and other plantings to streets almost devoid of greenery.

The new boroughs which came under Projet Montréal's control in 2017 didn't of course, benefit from any such momentum. Not only were the new administrations required to get up to speed with how their boroughs were run and, usually, begin the slow job of trying to change the bureaucratic culture, but we had to develop projects to get into the pipeline so that they might begin to happen as quickly as possible. As we had learned in the Plateau, a four-year mandate is not very much time if your aim is to transform a borough, however modestly. And in most boroughs, there was much to transform.

Certainly, this was the case in Côte-des-Neiges–Notre-Dame-de-Grâce. Most of the borough had been laid out and built a crucial 20 to 60 years after more central neighbourhoods, whether in Ville-Marie, St-Henri, le Plateau, or much of Rosemont and Villeray. Whereas the development of those neighbourhoods took place largely between the 1870s and the 1920s, a great deal of CDN-NDG was built after WWll, when the car had become king. Although this meant that the sewer and water lines were generally in better condition, the sidewalks tended to be narrower and the streets wider. In much of the borough, sidewalks were built only four feet wide, not even 1.3 metres, barely enough room for two people to pass or walk abreast. And almost completely absent in the borough were any buffers of grass and trees between the sidewalks and the street as are found so frequently in Rosemont, Villeray and elsewhere. Meanwhile, with wider streets come faster cars, no matter the speed limit.

So, as in the Plateau we decided to begin our traffic-calming projects around schools. Soon enough, with the help of an urbanist friend from Projet who was hired on a $5,000 contract, we had over $1 million in MTQ funding promised for projects around a half-dozen schools in the borough. From there we moved on to a variety of other initiatives. Bike lanes, of course, including a protected link across a very inhospitable bridge spanning the Décarie expressway, and lots of bike parking. The enlarging of Loyola Park by more than 6,000 square metres (just a bit more than one football field, but still). Better equipment in other parks, including new basketball courts. The revitalization of various commercial arteries, including Sherbrooke and Somerled, whether by relaxed zoning when it came to restaurants and upgrades in street furniture and maintenance, or, in the case of Queen Mary, wider sidewalks, calmed traffic and a public square outside the very busy Snowdon metro station.

We also tried to push forward two main "*projets structurants,*" big-ticket initiatives which would require the collaboration of the central city and which would have a marked impact even beyond the borough. The most pressing was the Empress Theatre on Sherbrooke St. Formerly known as Cinema V, the handsome and sprawling Egyptian Revival building had been owned by the city for more than two decades and in that time become a case in point of municipal incompetence. Successive administrations had promised to do something with it and then been defeated by the complexity and cost of the task. We began developing our own project, ideally involving space for arts and community groups, a performance space and housing on upper floors as well as a microbrewery to give life to a neglected stretch of Sherbrooke while taking advantage of the fabulous location across from Girouard Park.

A more left-field project, but one which could pay just as significant dividends, was a plan I developed for a new public market on the south side of Jean-Talon Ouest between Victoria and the Décarie. A new neighbourhood of mostly highrises called The Triangle was taking shape on the north side of Jean-Talon with 3,000 housing units already built or in the works. In the longer term, there was also a new much bigger residential community planned for the site of the old Hippodrome just on the other side of the Décarie. It was expected to be home to more than 20,000 people eventually. Then there were the dense, diverse and underserved communities just to the south, across the CP rail tracks. I felt that a big, bright public food market—a Jean-Talon market *ouest,* if more multi-ethnic and less tony—could do very well in the area, allowing residents to buy their traditional products side-by-side while permitting them not to be beholden to the IGA, the Maxi or the Walmart nearby. Designed well, it could become as much a place for social and cultural exchange as for commercial transactions. It would also add life to an otherwise hostile and disagreeable stretch of Jean-Talon dominated by car dealerships, factory outlets, warehouses and sprawling parking lots.

Still, nothing ever happens quickly enough with the city—I used to joke that there is geologic time and then, only slightly less slow, there is municipal time. And elected officials are as impatient for change as the rest of us. There were other problems as well. I had expected Sue Montgomery to be a little like Luc Ferrandez or other councillors I had worked with and throw herself into the job, curious as to how the city worked. Anything but. It quickly became apparent quite that she liked the idea of being mayor but not the actual work itself. "She was not interested in the job. She didn't like the job," says Christian Arseneault. "For the better part of the first year, she constantly said out loud that she hated the job. She said a number of times that she wanted to quit."

Knowing Sue's sarcastic humor as I did, I took those comments with a grain of salt and thought that she would grow into the post, if more slowly than hoped. I put some of this down to her poor French, and perhaps not being able to follow the discussion in meetings very well. Being immersed in a French environment would change that I hoped, as would regular French lessons with one of the attachés politiques we hired. Still, it was quickly apparent that she wasn't developing the interest in the work that the job required if she was to do it remotely well. She wasn't reading her files, whether it was the *sommaires décisionnels* for the items which were to be voted on at council or the various reports and documents which make up the daily paperwork of running the city. And the monthly city council meetings just bored her to the point where she was openly contemptuous of the proceedings. If she was good at what is called "*représentation*"—meeting with citizens and community groups at different events—because of her warm and fun nature, her capacity for extemporaneous public speaking was slow to improve.

The directors at the borough, used to a straighter and more serious mayor, were surprised and perturbed by Sue's attitude. This was not helped by her chronic lateness to meetings—perhaps the only characteristic she shared with Ferrandez—nor when, after meetings where she spent her time buried in her iPad, they saw that she had been tweeting away on subjects completely unrelated to borough business. "She spent entire meetings on social media without paying attention to what was being said by her team or her staff and frankly that didn't change at any point," says Christian Arseneault.

Gradually, I came to understand why friends who knew Sue better that Alex or I did, including her husband and brother-in-law, had been skeptical of our plans to recruit her for mayor. The fact is, however, in 2017 as in 2013 and 2009, we hadn't looked beyond election day when recruiting candidates. We looked for people who shared our vision and who the population would be inspired to vote for. We rarely asked ourselves whether they would make good councillors or mayors, or had the managerial skills, even inclination, to call the shots in a complex bureaucracy. And the less good our chances in a particular borough, the less those questions mattered. That said, in politics as in sports and other domains, it is often hard to know. Someone who looks great on paper can turn out to be a bust while someone who doesn't inspire much in the way of expectations can end up a very happy surprise. By the summer and fall of 2018, many of us in the party were beginning to accept that Sue was in the bust category.

The summer of 2018 in Montreal was scorching hot, with one heatwave after another. For anyone reluctant to believe what we were being told ad nauseum, it confirmed the fact that climate change was very much upon us. Imbued with a sense of urgency, Ferrandez assembled a loose group of Projet Montréal boroughs to collectively urge the administration to take bolder action. We drew up a list of proposals built around substantially reducing the space devoted to cars in the downtown and central neighbourhoods. This included the creation of more bike paths, more pedestrianization and the planting of thousands of trees to counter the heat island effect caused by asphalt and concrete covering so much of the city. We also proposed the elimination of all free parking in the central areas of the city and higher taxes on private parking lots. This measure would not only have reduced private car use but provided a new revenue stream for a city that was far too dependent on property taxes, so we thought it might hold some appeal for Benoit Dorais, who at the time was putting together the first budget which was truly a Projet Montréal creation.

However hot the summer, the proposals received a frosty reception from Plante and Dorais, not unlike the one given a caucus committee which had been created to identify measures by which the city could reduce its greenhouse gas output. Shortly after it proposed decisive action, the committee was dissolved.

A few months earlier, Ferrandez had threatened to resign over the administration's willingness to change the greenspace zoning of a golf course in Anjou to industrial in order to accommodate a British company which claimed it wanted to build a manufacturing plant for solar panels on the site. The project had the backing of the city's economic development department because the company said it would invest $1.8 billion in the project and create as many as 1,000 jobs. Ferrandez, however, coveted the golf course—the last remaining greenspace of significant size between Parc Maisonneuve and Pointe-aux-Trembles—for a *Grand parc de l'est.* The proposal to change the zoning of the green space was that much more absurd for the fact that there were dozens, indeed hundreds of acres of disused, available land nearby already zoned industrial. Eventually, between Ferrandez's opposition and the revelation that the promoter was more huckster than globetrotting investor with access to billions, the project fell apart. Still, it left Ferrandez questioning how long he might last in an administration he felt was too soft. "I knew that if a second situation like that arose, I would leave," he says.

Christine Gosselin, my other friend and former colleague who was now on the executive committee, was also finding it rough going, if for very different reasons. She had been put in charge of the complex culture department which was in the midst of a difficult overhaul. As with the other neophyte members of the executive committee, she found herself with very little back-up in the early months, expected to figure it out the best she could. "I was thrown into the deep end with no support," she says. The mayor's office "never communicated any orientations, only expressing displeasure when something hit the media." Displeasure even about how she dressed. Gosselin says that during one executive committee meeting, part of which was live-streamed, she received a text from Marie-Êve Gagnon telling her to sit up straight and pull up her blouse—she was showing too much cleavage. She did so, but as the meeting dragged on, she reverted to slumping in her chair again. She got another message telling her the same thing from Gagnon, this time adding that she was writing on behalf of the mayor.

Of all portfolios on the executive committee, culture requires the most *réprésentation* and Christine was regularly going to three events or more per day, often in the evening—conferences, vernissages, opening nights, awards ceremonies. She says it was "overwhelming for a sincere non-bullshitter like myself," all the more so since people at these events would regularly buttonhole her to tell her how she should be doing her job and what she and the administration in general were doing wrong. Reports began filtering back to the mayor's office of Christine blowing up at people at public events. Her occasional outbursts around the office also shocked staff and colleagues; one secretary had already quit and another was on the verge of doing so. "I was afraid of finding myself with a harassment complaint to deal with," says a member of Plante's inner circle. There were "personnel in my office in tears, regularly. Bureaucrats wouldn't listen to her anymore, it was so intense."

On March 29th, 2019, her birthday and exactly ten years to the day since she had first met with Patrick Cigana and he had immediately urged her to run for Projet Montréal, Christine was asked to make herself available for a meeting with Valérie as of 4:30 PM. She had suspected something was up for a while; she had been trying to meet with Benoît Dorais for a few weeks but he had been avoiding her. Finally, at 7 PM she was called into the mayor's splendid office where she found Valérie and Marie-Êve Gagnon sipping on white wine. Plante broke the news to her; she wasn't being shuffled to a new responsibility on the executive committee, she was being kicked off it entirely. When Christine asked why, Valérie replied, "You don't manage your services well, and I am giving your dossier to an excellent manager." Christine asked who and was told culture dossier was going to Magda Popeanu who until then had been responsible for housing. At that point, Christine says she broke out laughing, convinced there was another explanation; around the executive committee table, Magda was known to be as overwhelmed as anyone. "I regret not being given a real chance," Gosselin says. "The reason it hit me so hard was that after fifteen months of incredibly tough slogging I was finally getting somewhere. I felt really badly used."

Justified or not, there was a heavy-handedness to Christine's firing which shocked many in the party. She had long been one of Projet's most devoted and energetic members and her social life had grown to include many she had met through the party, whether councillors, staff or volunteers. For those worried that the Plante administration might be straying from—even betraying—Projet's heritage, it was an ominous sign.

Another was soon to come. Ferrandez's frustrations had increased with the administration's reluctance to come out unequivocally against two major land development schemes. One was the massive Royalmount office and hotel complex, also known as the 15-40 because it was to be located where Highway 15 met the 40, and was being built by the same property developers who had built Brossard's DIX30 megamall. The other was the proposal to build a new baseball stadium, surrounded by condo towers, on federal land near the Peel Bassin, in order to provide a downtown home to which the late, lamented Expos might return.

Both projects were anathema to the great majority of party members, in particular the 15-40 project against which Ferrandez had crusaded when it was first announced. "People were writing to me saying that the project was going against the essence of Projet Montréal," he says. There was little the city could do to stop it—it was to be built entirely in Ville Mont-Royal—but Ferrandez wanted Plante to "go to war against the project" by refusing to make access to the hard-to-get-to site easier, whether by car or public transport. It was not something the mayor was willing to do. "I refuse to look like a socialist in front of the Chamber of Commerce," Ferrandez said she told him. "That was the end of the argument." The city ended up simply negotiating for more housing to be included in the project.

The proposal for a new baseball stadium split the executive committee when it was brought up for discussion. Everyone agreed that no city money should go into the project. For those who opposed it, it was largely an opportunity-cost debate: the federal land, on which the city had first right of refusal in acquiring, would be better used for a new high-density, low-rise residential neighbourhood with social and affordable housing—or any number of other projects, Ferrandez and others argued. The city already had a stadium, Éric Alan Caldwell reminded his colleagues. Others, however, said it would be "political suicide" to give any indication that the administration wasn't entirely committed to building it. "They were all piece-of-shit projects," says Ferrandez. "Anjou, baseball, 15-40—they were shit and everyone knew they were shit but they just didn't want to admit it because they were scared of losing votes."

It was only after councillors discussed the stadium in caucus, and the scale of the opposition—especially from Sophie Thiébaut and Craig Sauvé, in whose district the land is located—became clear, that the administration's position grew lukewarm. By then Ferrandez was edging towards the door. When devastating floods hit the Montreal region in late April, he wrote a Facebook tirade that began with a phrase that was soon being immortalized on T-shirts. "Fuck you, *nous autres*," he wrote. "We all know we shouldn't build in flood zones [...] We all know what we should and shouldn't do—and we have for a long time. But we are, citizens and elected representatives alike, spoiled brats. So this morning, to everyone: fuck you. We fully deserve all the unhappiness that befalls us and the much greater unhappiness for which we are laying the groundwork—out of cowardice—for our children." He went on to enumerate a long list of things Quebecers continued to do even if they knew better, including "constructing two stadiums."

As usual for his posts, it was soon on the way to generating hundreds of likes and dozens of comments. Then the call came from Plante and soon the post had been taken down. "We spoke, he apologized," she told reporters. At that point, it was only a matter of time. Barely two weeks later, Ferrandez was writing another long Facebook post, this one announcing that he was quitting politics. While lauding the administration for its "environmental balance-sheet," he said it wasn't going nearly far enough. Banning single-use plastics and home-heating oil was all very well, as was buying new hybrid buses and protecting green space, he wrote. Then he launched into a long list of what should also be being done, including taxing parking, taxing driving into the downtown, taxing garbage, taxing foreign investment and taxing meat. Until such steps were taken, he said he would suffer from imposter syndrome. "I have the impression I am hoodwinking citizens in having them believe that we are collectively taking all the measures necessary to slow down the rhythm of destruction of our planet." For good measure, he attacked the idea of the 15-40 and a new baseball stadium again. "Incapable of influencing the mairesse (as well as the president and members of the executive committee) as to the seriousness of the situation and the measures we need to take, I have chosen to not remain part of this team."

Ferrandez stressed the fact, however, that Plante "is more representative of the population than I have ever been" and had a responsibility he didn't have: ensuring that Projet Montréal was elected again in 2021. "I do not want to weaken her leadership or work with another team. On the contrary I hope that Projet Montréal remains strong and united and wins the next election." Two years later he stands by that decision. "I didn't want to make Projet Montréal like the PQ. I didn't want to form a group of resistors who would remain within the party but try to render illegitimate certain decisions."

An hour before posting the announcement on Facebook, Ferrandez had phoned Plante to give her a heads-up. She didn't plead with him to reconsider. That didn't surprise Ferrandez; he knew that his departure, even if it would be mourned by many in the party, would be welcomed as a relief in the mayor's office, whose strategy for managing him, as Marie-Ève Gagnon had admitted to Christine Gosselin, was "to work him like a dog and keep him in the closet." Plante did, however, try to convince him to hold off pressing "post" for a day or two. Council was sitting and she didn't want his announcement to overshadow a declaration she was due to make.

I didn't know it then, but my own days working for the party were numbered as well. As we arrived at a year in power, Sue would increasingly say that she didn't "feel in control." I gently suggested she read her files more diligently and concentrate more in meetings to retain more information. She would often ask the same questions from one week to another, frustrating the directors. As one put it, "She is interested in nothing and she learns nothing. Which is inevitable because if you don't take an interest in something, you are not going to understand it." Eventually, however, she seemed to determine that it was my fault as her chief of staff and say that she wanted someone who was more focused on taking care of her. We both knew I wasn't that person but she said she desperately wanted me to stay on in charge of getting our projects for the borough happening. So a new position was created for me—special advisor in charge of projects. I was to be paid the same amount as before. "It's not a demotion," Sue wrote me. "Look at the bright side. You won't have to deal with Magda and Peter." As her new chief of staff, she hired the 27-year-old daughter of a former *Gazette* colleague. Annalisa Harris had been a federal Liberal activist since her teens—her grandfather was a Liberal senator—and she had been working with a Trudeau minister in Ottawa but had been fired for some undisclosed reason.

At the team's first meeting with her, Harris announced, "I have only one job and that is to ensure that Sue is happy." I had always seen my job as delivering on the undertakings we made during the election campaign, I said, so maybe we would be complementary. That optimism persisted when, after I told her I wasn't very interested in comms or press releases, she told me she was very, very interested in them. It diminished when she told me that she felt no hurry for our administration to fulfil our promises to make cycling safer in the borough with more bike paths and the like: having the noisy NDG cyclists' association angry at us would make us more popular with car drivers, she reasoned.

After working alongside Harris for three weeks, during which time Sue was almost completely absent from the office though not on vacation, I took a week off. The day I returned, Annalisa asked to meet me in the late afternoon, later changing the time to 11 AM the next morning and insisting that I cancel a long-planned meeting with our public works director. When I got to the office and discovered that Annalisa had instructed the political attachés to stay home that morning, I suspected what was up and began packing my bags. When the HR person showed up with a dour face at the stroke of 11 AM my suspicions were confirmed. Sue literally read from notes that Harris had prepared for her as she fired me. When I suggested we might talk as adults, even as people who had known each other for three decades and might be described as friends, her response also came from the notes: "I don't think that would be useful," she said.

Like that, my adventure working for the city, working to transform it for the better, was over. Like Christine, I felt betrayed and used. But like Bergeron, I also felt a tremendous lightness and relief that it was no longer my responsibility to find solutions for problems which on the surface seemed so simple but ended up so complex; to implement projects everyone agreed should happen but for which there were only endless obstacles.

The brutal circumstances of my departure, which led my filing a complaint at *la Commission des normes de travail*, greatly complicated my relationship with Projet Montréal, to which I was still very attached and to which I had devoted a decade of energy and enthusiasm. Things got simpler a few months later, however. Convinced she knew how to deal with senior bureaucrats and staff, Annalisa Harris had continued her humourless and heavy-handed ways and soon found herself facing formal complaints of psychological harassment from Stéphane Plante as well as a political attaché. Valérie Plante's office tried to mediate the disputes, by negotiating Annalisa's transfer to another job. "I went to see Annalisa," says Guillaume Cloutier. "She sits down and tells me, 'I have control over Sue. Sue is crazy but I am able to control her. So what are you offering me?' That is what she told me, word for word."

Guillaume proposed that Annalisa accept a job with the party; she insisted on a position in Valérie's office, Cloutier says. That was the end of the discussion. When Sue chose to stand by Harris, Valérie expelled her from the Projet Montréal caucus.

Epilogue

It is entirely normal that, over the course of a mandate, the size of an administration's caucus will fluctuate. New members will often be added through recruiting from other parties, as was the case with Cathy Wong, who eventually left Ensemble Montréal—the remains of Équipe Denis Coderre—to join Projet. Others might arrive thanks to by-elections, as did Caroline Bourgeois, who was elected mayor of Rivière-des-Prairies–Pointe-aux-Trembles under Projet's banner in December, 2018. Then there are those who will leave, usually due to a disaggreement over a particular project or policy. Halfway through Valérie Plante's mandate, Jimmy Zoubris, who had been hired as a senior advisor to deal with the anglo and business communities while also working as a behind-the-scenes fixer and disciplinarian, was confident about being able to bring over any number of councillors from a demoralized, rudderless Ensemble Montréal. They would come over in time as the election approached, he assured people. It would be a slow, death-by-a-thousand-cuts for the opposition. That never materialized. Instead, Projet Montréal was the party which continued to bleed. It wasn't because of projects or policies, however, let alone what had provoked defection after defection at Vision and Union in their later years: the undeniable realization that the ship was going down due to corruption and rot.

On the contrary, Projet Montréal had remained impeccably scandal-free, but for the fact that Benoit Dorais was prone to driving way over the speed limit and getting nabbed for it. Beyond that, the administration had continued to deliver admirably on its promises and its vision. Thousands of young families had been spared the welcome tax, hundreds of intersections had been made more safe, a network of bike paths "worthy of the name"—the Réseau express vélo—was being built, tens of millions of dollars had been made available to boroughs to upgrade their parks, more greenspace was acquired and protected by the city in those three years than had been by the previous three administrations, a person could apply for simple permits online, the 311 operators were answering calls more quickly. The list went on.

The administration also responded with agility and humanity to the Covid pandemic, pedestrianizing a handful of commercial arteries—including, finally, Mont-Royal—around the city to minimize close contact on sidewalks while opening up hundreds of beds in emergency shelters, including the old Royal Vic hospital and the Hôtel Place Dupuis, for the city's homeless and vulnerable population. After coming to terms with the initial wave, the city's public health department became a model for contact tracing, keeping subsequent outbreaks low. And economically, Montreal proved as resilient as any city, anywhere.

Rather, Projet Montréal lost councillors—three in December 2020—through the administration's poor management of caucus, its human resources. The first to go went the most discreetly. Rosannie Filato was considered a star in the party, going straight onto the executive committee after being elected in 2017. A lawyer, she had been responsible for public security since March 2019 but had grown increasingly frustrated by not being included in decision-making and instead just being handed positions and lines by Plante's office. Like most caucus and party members, she was sympathetic to the idea of reallocating resources from the police to social service units better equipped to deal with people in crisis situations—what amounted to a thoughtful "defunding" of the police. When the 2021 city budget was drawn up, however, she wasn't consulted and the police were attributed an increase much higher than the average, a position she had to defend. Rarely, if ever, has a government minister of official quit because their department was given *more* funds than they hoped, but in Filato's case it was at least partly to blame. She quit the executive committee if not the caucus, saying she wanted to devote the rest of the mandate to serving the citizens of Villeray. She also announced she would not be running again.

The next to go was Christian Arseneault, in many ways the best of the bunch left in Côte-des-Neiges–Notre-Dame-de-Grâce. He had been growing increasingly disgruntled for a while. In 2019, he had expressed concerns that new plans for the western arm of the Pink Line showed it running through the Sud-Ouest to Lachine rather than through southern NDG, as originally sketched. "And we got smacked down by the mayor. She didn't like the fact that we sounded like we were complaining." Things came to a head with the decision to name the REM station in Griffintown, a traditionally Irish part of town, after Bernard Landry—a sovereigntist associated by many, correctly or not, with ethnic intolerance. It was a concern shared by many in the caucus, in particular the anglos and those from the Sud-Ouest and Verdun. The call to name the station after Landry, however, had been made personally by Plante, and she didn't appreciate it being challenged. "We were basically treated like traitors by Valérie," Arseneault says. "We were made out to be undermining her authority, that we were disrespecting her. It was absolutely insane. Absolutely insane."

He adds: "Was she under a lot of stress? Yes. Was it an abject failure of leadership within the party? Also yes. We had been having discussions about the lack of real debate, lack of a real role for caucus and then we tried to bring something up in caucus and we got beat down hard." Not long afterwards, he said in a comment on the Facebook page of the United Irish Societies of Montreal that he "respectfully disagreed" with the decision. It wasn't appreciated by the cabinet. When, a couple of weeks after that, he went on Facebook again and publicly admitted that he never voted for Sue Montgomery in the 2017 election because he had never felt she was up to the job, the cabinet decided he need to be punished and he lost his place on a commission, along with the prestige and salary bump that came with it. It didn't matter that Montgomery had been expelled from caucus almost a year earlier and was well on her way to becoming the most irksome thorn in the mayor's side. "I really put my neck out for the administration. I was really on the front line when all the stuff came out about Sue," he says. "The experience threw into sharper relief the extent to which it was becoming a one-way street in terms of the mayor always asking us to take the punches for her even though there was no mechanism for disagreement."

Arseneault calculated that with "the shitshow" that continued to surround Sue's expulsion—the tribunal complaints, injunctions and lawsuits that were flying—Projet Montréal wasn't going to be much of a calling card in his western NDG district. Certainly, he didn't feel he needed the party any more than it needed him. So he quit to sit as an independent. He was followed a week later by Christine Gosselin, who also quit, guns blazing. She had still not digested being dumped from the executive committee almost two years earlier, and she had been up front with many of us about her plans to serve her revenge cold, when it would hurt Plante the most. In early 2020 she had even proposed to some of us founding another green, left-wing municipal party, an idea I thought was just nutty. Finally, when a court judgement came down criticizing the Plante administration's handling of the Montgomery affair, Christine had an excuse which allowed her to make it appear that she was resigning on a question of higher principle. "I am opposed to the values and behaviour of the major of Montreal, principally in terms of her management of human resources," she wrote. "I consider her leadership to be retrograde and authoritarian."

Like Luc, Christine sang the praises of the party and its vision, saying "I wish to all my colleague councillors continued success with their remarkable work." Still, her door-slam of a departure was calculated to do the administration damage in the lead-up to the election. When I pointed out this incoherence to her, she told me she was doing it because she loved the party and wanted to save it.

The flurry of resignations cost Projet Montréal its majority in city council. It also sounded an alarm bell that, at precisely the wrong time, with an election less than a year away, things were starting to go sideways. A group of about half a dozen moderate councillors, those known to be real team players[41], and representing boroughs from around the city, got together and wrote a letter to Valérie urging greater openness and tolerance of dissent and more inclusion

41 These included Richard Ryan, Pierre Lessard-Blais, Marianne Giguère and Sophie Mauzerolle, who had been elected as Valérie's co-listière. Councillors considered to be squeaky wheels, as it were, were not invited to join the initiative.

of caucus in decision-making. To some, it seemed as if history might be repeating itself.

A factor which former MCM councillors invoke when asked to explain the demise of a party which once seemed so vital and entrenched, which many had expected to become a fixture on the Montreal municipal scene for decades, even generations, was that it stopped listening to caucus, at least those elements of caucus who dared dissent. "The administration was bureaucratized very quickly," says Sam Boskey, who was elected for the party in 1982 but left within a couple years of Jean Doré becoming mayor. "Access to the inner circle—Doré and the executive committee—was very difficult and restricted, even for the heads of the standing commissions that were set up by the administration." Those who stuck with the party much longer, such as Helen Fotopulos, don't disagree. Fotopulos had run for the party in 1978 and in 1986 became a political attaché in Doré's office, "the only other" as she puts it. With hindsight, she says, the administration "listened too much to bureaucrats," not challenging them enough on their way of doing things or what they maintained was possible or needed to be done. "When left-wing parties come into power, they often have a great deal of trouble adjusting to having power," she adds.

The party structure of Projet Montréal also sounded similar concerns as those expressed by caucus. Under a dynamic new president, Guedwig Bernier, "a council of the wise" including Patrick Cigana and Michel Camus had been created in the fall of 2020, and it lets its worry be known. Certainly, the party itself—as distinct from the administration—has a role to play. In different post-mortems of the MCM, a recurring theme is that after its resounding victory in 1986, the party structure withered. Gradually abandoning its oversight role, and its responsibility to be a conduit between members and the administration, it increasingly became a rubber stamp for the mayor's office. Projet Montréal can't yet be accused of having done so; at its spring 2021 congress, members passed at least one resolution that made the administration distinctly uncomfortable—a proposal that would see some police patrol without a firearm. The party also called for a review of Montreal police financing. Still, it is always a risk for a party in power that the party structure becomes what amounts to a PR asset for the administration as opposed to a compass, a monitor and, if necessary, a corrective device.

To neither caucus nor the party did Valérie or her office offer an explicit *mea culpa* beyond saying things would change. Nor were any changes made to staff considered to be responsible for the situation. Still, councillors feel that the message was understood and that in the months following things did change and greater consideration was paid to their points of view.

If so, it was overdue. Political parties are invariably approximations: people with similar but not identical views on any number of issues join together to advance an agenda broadly reflecting their shared vision and values. No one expects absolute uniformity of ideas—even those in the opposition or the media whose business it may be to point out inconsistencies or contradictions. Indeed, divergent views, as long as they are not on issues central to a party's *raison d'être*—say, in the case of Projet Montréal, the need for more and better public and active transportation options, the importance of investing in greenspace and parks, and the urgent imperative to contain urban sprawl through human-scale densification on the island—are a sign of healthiness within a party. They are nonetheless often inconvenient to party leadership, especially when it is called upon to account for the divergent views by the opposition or the media. Rarely, however, does tolerating dissent within a party ever hurt it as much as does not tolerating it. And there are those within Projet Montréal who not only want more tolerance, but want Plante to clearly articulate that the party is one where differences of opinion are part of its DNA. That way there would be no point for the opposition or the media to try to make a big deal out of small discrepancies or disagreements.

There are other lessons from the MCM to be learned, pitfalls to be avoided. Six months before the 1986 municipal election, it was obvious to everyone in Montreal the Drapeau era was over, that his Civic Party was done for, and that the MCM would be elected. This led to a deluge of opportunists without real roots in the party signing on and, in many cases, winning nominations to be city council candidates. Their attachment to the MCM's program and vision was often questionable and their loyalty to Jean Doré, seen to be their meal ticket to electoral success, overrode all else. Once he was knocked from power by Pierre Bourque in 1994, the party was left rudderless and was soon overtaken by discord and dissension, in time turning from tragedy to the farce that François Limoges watched from a ringside seat in the late 1990s.

Projet Montréal's victory in 2017 was anything but a foregone conclusion. Still, even if it is generally accepted that, as Guillaume Cloutier puts it, "Valérie without the party doesn't win; the party without Valérie doesn't win," some members are concerned about Projet becoming too focused on its leader. A leader putting their stamp on a party is entirely normal; but confusing themselves *for* the party is much more problematic, especially when it is a party that existed long before they joined it and was a collective grassroots endeavour of hundreds of idea-driven members. As one borough mayor who asked not to be named put it, "The biggest mistake Valérie makes is that she speaks in 'Je.' 'Je fais ci. Je, je, je, je.' And that excludes everybody else and it gives her less power because people don't identify with 'Je.' And not 'mon administration.' I hate that. It should always be 'nous.' Never say 'je' because 'je' excludes." Luc Ferrandez echoes the sentiment while being more to the point: "The reason why I handed in my resignation was because I saw that. I saw it becoming Équipe Valérie Plante."

Of course, a cult of personality requires both the persona and people to buy in to it. If one could be said to be developing within Projet Montréal, it is not necessarily the exclusive doing of Plante and her entourage. Still, her tendency to promote councillors who do the most cheerleading and the least questioning and criticizing has caused dismay to some in caucus as well as party members outside it. "The bar of sycophancy is so high," says Christine Gosselin, decrying the naming of one particular councillor to the executive committee "for being an Olympic quality suck-ass."

Denis Coderre's striptease reveal of his mayoral candidacy in 2021 was, mercifully, shorter than his announcement for the 2013 race. He made it official on a broadcast of *Tout le monde en parle* at the end of March, surprising approximately no one. He had released a book a week earlier entitled *Retrouver Montréal*. The book was presented as his vision for the city, even if it turned out to have been written by a committee of six people, including at least two executives of public relations firms.

If *Retrouver Montréal* constituted a program for his candidacy, it could be seen as progress on his 2013 and 2017 campaigns when he ran on little more than his bluster and the network he had built during his many years in federal politics. Still, many of the ideas he put forth left us confused. He had ridiculed the Pink Line proposal throughout the 2017 campaign but here he was, four years later, calling for not only a very similar diagonal metro line to Montréal-Nord and beyond but also suggesting that the Yellow Line be run underneath Ave du Parc and Acadie up past Marché Centrale. Not to mention, on the South Shore from Longueuil a dozen kilometres south to La Prairie. These were just some of his public transportation proposals. He also called for more bike paths while questioning the new network of bike lanes being built on St-Denis and, suggesting that density can only be achieved with high-rise apartment towers, called for developers to be allowed to build higher than Mont-Royal.

It certainly wasn't the strength of his arguments which convinced the caucus of *Ensemble Montréal* to acclaim him as their new leader in place of Lionel Perez, who had kept the chair warm since 2017. Rather, it was the narrative that Coderre was a changed man—not only had he lost more than 100 pounds, but he had learned how to be humble. And most of all, it was the absence of anyone else to lead the party. After the 2017 defeat, Coderre was as disliked as Valérie Plante within *Ensemble Montréal*, widely blamed for having blown the campaign and ruined a good thing for all of them. Over the following three years, however, no one stepped up to take over the party, even if after the provincial Liberals lost to the CAQ in 2018, it was hoped a former cabinet minister or two might be tempted to take a run at it. For his part, interim leader Lionel Perez had set his sights on unseating Sue Montgomery as mayor of CDN-NDG; like many others, he didn't feel that as an Orthodox Jew, he stood much of a chance city-wide.

Coderre's return to the municipal politics scene did cost the Plante administration a junior member of the executive committee when Hadrien Parizeau, who had been elected with Coderre, returned to the *Ensemble Montréal* fold. He had been brought in to the Projet Montréal orbit by Rosannie Filato when the two began seeing each other romantically, so it was not entirely a surprise when he left the party after she departed from the executive committee and announced she wouldn't be running again.

It wasn't entirely a surprise either when Guillaume Lavoie announced that he would be running alongside Coderre in 2021. It was, however, seen as a big comedown. Richard Bergeron says that when he was leader of Projet Montréal, new candidates were almost uniformly grateful when their offer to run for the party was given the green light. "They would always say, 'Thank you, thank you for having accepted me." With Lavoie it was different. "Guillaume always said to me 'You're really lucky I accepted to be a candidate for you. Are you aware of all the premiers who asked me? Are you aware of the number of times I have said no in politics? Are you aware of how much potential I have in politics?' That was Guillaume's line."

Along with that arrogance, came a prickliness. When Bergeron announced to the Projet Montréal caucus in 2014 that he was stepping down as party leader, Lavoie got wind of it and went and knocked on Bergeron's front door. "I have heard rumours," Bergeron remembers him asking. "I'd like an explanation." Bergeron welcomed him in and confirmed that the rumours were true and began to explain his reasoning. "At one point he stood up and said, 'Mr. Bergeron, I will never speak to you again. This is the worst betrayal of my life. And he walked away."

For the next three years, as the two men served out the rest of the 2013 to 2017 mandate, Bergeron says, "Guillaume did not speak to me. He did not greet me. When I saw him, I used to take pleasure in saying, in a loud voice, 'Hello Guillaume!' I did it on purpose. But he would pretend not to hear me. I wanted to tell him every time, 'But what a childish attitude! Don't you understand anything? You see me as an enemy? I don't see anyone here as an enemy. Any political party. We greet each other, we work together."

Then, in early January 2021, Bergeron received an email from Lavoie. Bergeron says it was ostensibly to send condolences about Amina's condition which Lavoie said he had just heard about. Still,

Bergeron was suspicious because of the timing. There was an election less than a year off and people were beginning to position themselves. It was a foregone conclusion already that Denis Coderre would be running, and Lavoie had already been in the media indicating that he too was interested in running. He didn't want to run with Coderre, however; he was interested in the top job and, anyway, "Guillaume knows very well who Coderre is. Coderre only takes people who say yes. He would have to be a yes-man."

For his part, Bergeron was also eager to get back in the game. He still had a lot to contribute to the city, he felt, but had been completely frozen out by Projet Montréal since the election. Whether because of his original sin in crossing the floor to Coderre in 2014 or his caricaturing of his former party as "radical" and "extreme *gauche*" in the panicked last days of the 2017 campaign, it had been made clear to him that he was *persona non grata*. A few days after the election, Valérie had rebuffed an overture he had made, with unseemly haste, to offer his services to the new administration. Then, 18 months later, she was said to have personally nixed the idea of him being invited to a big party in the Old Port to celebrate Projet Montréal's 15th anniversary. Maybe, Bergeron thought, he could collaborate with Lavoie on a third option. Neither Projet Montréal nor Coderre, something between the two. There was a some back and forth. Then Lavoie went quiet.

Around the same time, Lavoie was also negotiating with Justine McIntyre about taking over Vrai Changement pour Montréal. She had kept the party alive for five years, investing more time, energy and heart into it than she probably should have, but was ready to let it go and put it behind her. She had moved to Hochelaga from Pierrefonds-Roxboro and was doing an MBA at the HEC, a business school in Montreal; she was on a new chapter of her life. Still, she wanted to leave the party in good hands.

Lavoie had originally approached McIntyre in the summer of 2020 to tell her he wanted to take over the party. "He said to me, 'I am not going to use the term 'hostile takeover' but I do want to take it over,'" she remembers. "And I said, 'But you just did use the term 'hostile takeover!' He was very adamant that this was what he wanted to do."

Then, she says, he fell into a "cycle of over-analysis"—what she deems his political Achilles heel—and a reluctance to go with his gut feelings or take a leap into the unknown. In January 2021, McIntyre again met with Lavoie to discuss his taking over Vrai Changement. "My understanding was that he was still engaged and he was still interested and I wanted to facilitate that. I thought, if he wants to take over the party, I'm not going to stand in his way." McIntyre had even recruited Christian Arseneault, a friend and fan of Lavoie's, to urge him to take over Vrai Changement. Lavoie, however, was more interested in discussing the idea of him and McIntyre both running for Coderre. "I said no. I said I was not there to talk about opportunities with potential candidates who have not yet announced themselves."

That was pretty much it for Vrai Changement. In mid-March, McIntyre and the other members who remained agreed to pull the plug on the party. Lavoie, for his part, was still undecided, however. In early April, the weather still cool, Richard Bergeron says he spent three hours on the rooftop terrasse of the building where Lavoie lives in Villeray discussing the idea of "a third way." Bergeron would have liked to put the old team again together—him, Joël Simard-Menard, Catherine Maurice and Guillaume Lavoie—but he knew it was too late. The opportunity had passed. "If you had reacted in February, we could have made something happen," Bergeron says he told Lavoie. "Now it is too late."

By then, other former Projet Montréal councillors and candidates, exiled from the party of their own choosing or not, had founded their own parties or were on their way to doing so. Giuliana Fumagalli created Quartiers Montréal as her re-election vehicle in Villeray–St-Michel–Parc-Extension, and Sue Montgomery created her own for Côte-des-Neiges–Notre-Dame-de-Grâce team called Courage. (Fumagalli says she phoned up Montgomery to talk about joining forces but didn't get any indication of interest.) Meanwhile, in May, Balarama Holness announced the creation of Mouvement Montréal.

Few people were giving any of the new parties much chance of electing anyone to council in November, or surviving long enough to fight another election, or, one day, taking power. But then again, back in 2005, there hadn't been too many people willing to bet on Projet Montréal and Richard Bergeron either.

Going into the 2021 election, the party is not just alive, its base solid and its bank account healthy, but its chances are pretty good. Even if it was well behind in the spring polls, the party has been there before and emerged victorious, against the same opponent. The fact that, despite the creation of Quartiers, Courage, and Mouvement, it still looks likely to be a two-party race also means there will be fewer variables. And likely more default votes for Projet. Coderre, after all, has always generated as many negative feelings as positive, and for all his makeover and new-found modesty, seemed, in the spring pre-campaign, to be as prone to improvisation and and ill humour as ever.

Whatever happens, Projet is almost certain to hold onto at least a few boroughs, including the Plateau, where it seems, indeed, to have become the natural ruling party. Transforming the city, one initiative, one experiment, one project at a time. Elsewhere, it will have left its mark. "Even if Projet Montréal loses the next election, it's too late," a city of Montreal director who has served under Tremblay, Applebaum, Coderre and Plante said to me. "In 20 years' time, people will recognize that the four years of Projet Montréal were the moment when the city of Montréal moved into the 21st century. In this sense, you have done something important. If Projet Montréal returns to power, so much the better, because it can continue. But if it doesn't happen, there's no going back."

As to what will become of the two men most responsible for the success of Projet Montreal, as to whether there will be any "going back" for Richard Bergeron and Luc Ferrandez, it is anybody's guess.

Ferrandez's departure left many expecting a return to politics some day, whether at the municipal, provincial or federal level but he is not in any hurry. "If I return to politics, it will be like a storm," he says. "I'm not going to try and be nice. It will be because the world will be at the edge of a crisis and we'll be ready for radical changes." In the meantime, he will continue doing radio commentary on 98.5 FM and, not being shut in a closet for the campaign, may ironically end up a greater asset to the party in 2021 than he was in 2017 or 2013. "Being outside of the party, apart and at some safe distance, I want Projet Montréal to be re-elected, and maybe someday it will evolve into the kind of team we had in the Plateau. Maybe Montreal will be the kind of city that is able to do things like that."

Bergeron's main gig these days is also radio commentary but not so much of it and of a much less political nature. In his home on Rue de la Gauchetière near the corner of Hôtel de Ville, almost in the shadow of City Hall, he happily admits he would jump back into municipal politics in a heartbeat, that he misses it intensely. He lives alone now—Amina is being taken care of by her family back in Morocco and his children have their own lives and their own homes. His phone doesn't ring very often and he enjoys visitors, debate and discussion—a pleasure of which the pandemic deprived him. Even if he says he only recognizes his Projet Montréal "*plus ou moins*" he is immensely proud of being the founder and, in his words, "principal idea-generator, facilitator and builder" of the party. "It was for me an incredibly rich experience," he says. He made a bad decision, if only because he hoped to get his tramway built and leave his mark on a city he loves, and then compounded it with some over-the-top remarks in the heat of an election campaign. But he feels he has done his time in the wilderness and that he still has something to offer. To Montreal at very least, if not Projet Montréal.

ACKNOWLEDGEMENTS

Given that it's part journalism and part memoir, this book doesn't fit neatly into any particular category. But as much as anything, it is an oral history of Projet Montréal and the world of Montreal municipal politics in which the party has come to play such an important role.

In this way, it could not have been written without dozens of people being generous with their time and their memories. First and foremost among these is Richard Bergeron, whose candour and willingness to talk were disarming and touching. I was never close to Richard when he was leader of the party but he didn't hesitate when I asked him for an interview nor suggest any conditions. One interview turned into five day-long interviews spread over more than a year—more than 20 hours worth, as well as many emails. As forthcoming about his failings and mistakes as about his brilliance and *bon coups*, getting to know Richard was probably the greatest pleasure of writing this book. Heartfelt thanks to him, along with the hope that he soon gets the recognition he deserves from both the city and the party.

Patrick Cigana, Émilie Thuillier, Guillaume Cloutier and Magda Popeanu were similarly accessible and generous with their time and recollections. Much thanks to each of them as well.

Then there are Luc Ferrandez, Christine Gosselin, Alex Norris and Richard Ryan, among others. Interviewing friends can be tricky; if any bridges are burnt, I hope they are gently singed. They were all accommodating and I extend my gratitude to them as to everyone I interviewed, whether I ended up quoting them or not.

Thanks are also due to my very tolerant and flexible editors, David Murray at Éditions Écosociété and Carmine Starnino at Véhicule Press, as well as my old friend François Émond, architect, for giving me the keys to the jungle where I spent many peaceful weekends writing this book. Final thanks to Catherine for her even greater tolerance of me as I wrote the book, which I dedicate to my father Clyde and my brother Richard. Writers both, and inspirations too.

POLITICAL PARTIES

Montreal Citizens Movement (MCM)—a municipal party with similar ambitions created three decades earlier and in power from 1986 to 1994.

Vision Montréal—a party created in 1994 as the political vehicle for Pierre Bourque, mayor of Montreal from November 1994 until November 2001. Led subsequently by Benoit Labonté and Louise Harel. Dissolved in April 2014.

Union des citoyens et citoyennes de l'île de Montréal (UCCIM)—a party created in 2001 out of what remained of the MCM and an alliance of suburban mayors who were seeing their municipalities forcibly merged into the city of Montreal. Elected to power in Nov. 2001 and re-elected in 2005 and 2009 under Mayor Gérald Tremblay.

Québec Solidaire—Quebec's most established left-wing provincial party. Elected its first member to the National Assembly in 2008 in the riding of Mercier, which covers most of Plateau-Mont-Royal, and has held it since. Traditionally a close ally of Projet Montréal.

Projet Montréal—a municipal political party found in Montreal in 2004 to push for better public transit, better infrastructure for pedestrians and cyclists, greener communities and less urban sprawl.

Union—the new name for UCCIM as of May 2007. Dissolved in May 2013 after a series of corruption scandals.

Coalition Montréal—a party created in 2013 in support of the candidacy of Marcel Côté. Endorsed by Louise Harel and Vision Montréal in the election that November. Dissolved after the election of 2017 saw only one candidate win his seat.

Vrai Changement pour Montréal—a party created in 2013 in support of the candidacy of Mélanie Joly. Dissolved in 2021.

LIST OF CHARACTERS

Michael Applebaum—interim-mayor of Montreal after resignation of Gérald Tremblay in 2012; later charged, convicted and imprisoned for corruption.

Richard Bergeron—the principal founder of Projet Montréal and leader from 2004 to 2014.

Patrick Cigana—early Projet Montréal activist and the party's director-general from 2011 to 2015.

Guillaume Cloutier—the DOC for the 2009 race on the Plateau who later became a political attaché and the DOC for the city-wide 2017 race. Valérie Plante's deputy chief-of-staff.

Denis Coderre—former federal MP elected mayor of Montreal in 2013 at the head of a team made up largely of former Union Montréal councillors.

Marcel Côté—economist, businessman and former advisor to premiers and prime ministers recruited to run for mayor in 2013 by federalists and conservatives who were uneasy with the prospect of Denis Coderre being elected.

François Croteau—elected mayor of Rosemont–La Petite-Patrie for Vision Montréal in 2009; crossed the floor to Projet Montréal two years later.

Luc Ferrandez—elected mayor of the borough of Plateau-Mont-Royal for Projet Montréal in 2009 and one of the party's most visible and controversial figures until he quit politics in 2019.

Helen Fotopulos—early MCM activist who later became attaché to mayor Jean Doré and was elected city councillor for Mile End in 1994. Served as the Plateau's first borough mayor, from 2005 until

2009. Longtime member of the executive committee for, among other things, culture.

Giuliana Fumagalli—Postal worker who was elected Projet Montréal mayor of Villeray-St. Michel-Parc-Extension in 2017 despite difficult relations with party. Expelled from caucus in 2018.

Christine Gosselin—political attaché on the Plateau from 2009 to 2013 and later borough councillor there. In 2017 elected to city council in Rosemont becoming the executive committee member responsible for culture.

Amir Khadir—Medical doctor and leftist activist who in 2008 became Québec Solidaire's first candidate to be elected to the National Assembly. Represented the riding of Mercier until he stepped down in 2018.

Janine Krieber—political scientist and former Projet Montréal official who ran as Richard Bergeron's *co-listière* in 2013.

Guillaume Lavoie—ran for leadership of Projet Montréal with the support of most of his fellow councillors but lost narrowly.

François Limoges—Early Projet Montréal member and activist who represented the Rosemont–La Petite-Patrie district of St-Édouard from 2009 until 2021.

Claude Mainville—the other main founder of the Projet Montréal. Never elected and had little to do with the party after 2006.

Justine McIntyre—pianist and teacher who was elected to city council in the borough of Pierrefonds-Roxboro in 2013 for Vrai Changement pour Montréal. Later led the party.

Alex Norris—longtime Montreal *Gazette* reporter elected to city council on the Plateau in 2009. Represented the district of Mile-End until 2013 and Jeanne-Mance since.

Marie-France Pinard—micro-biologist, hardline left-wing activist and founder, along with her partner Claude Mainville, Richard Bergeron and a few others, of Projet Montréal. Not active in the party since 2006.

Valérie Plante—city councillor elected leader of Projet Montréal in 2016 and then mayor of Montreal less than a year later.

Magda Popeanu—early party activist and candidate. Served as Projet Montréal's president from 2006 until 2010. Elected to city council in 2013.

Richard Ryan—social worker and Projet Montréal activist who was elected as borough councillor for Mile-End in 2009 and later served as the district's city councillor from 2013 until 2021.

Craig Sauvé—Early Projet Montréal activist with strong ties to the NDP. Elected city councillor in the Sud-Ouest borough in 2013.

Joël Simard-Menard—longtime a member of the Parti Québecois, who became the first political professional hired by Projet Montréal. Richard Bergeron's chief-of-staff from 2009 to 2014. Close friend of Guillaume Lavoie.

Émilie Thuillier—early Projet Montréal activist and the party's first employee. Elected to city council in 2009.

Jimmy Zoubris—small businessman from Mile-End who became active in Projet Montréal in 2009. Party fixer, backroom organizer and unsuccessful candidate in 2013 who persistently tried to push the party to the centre.

TERMS

ALA (Association locale d'arrondissement)—Projet Montréal's equivalent of a riding association; responsible for fundraising and candidate selection in each borough while generating policy proposals.

Bureau des élus—the political office within a borough, made up of the mayor, the councillors and their political employees.

Co-listier/co-listière—the running mate of a party leader for city council; if the party leader is elected mayor, the co-listier/co-listière occupies the council seat.

Cas de quartier ("neighbour case")—or any issue or problem raised by a resident and brought to the attention of the borough mayor or councillor for resolution.

DOC—the campaign director, whether at a borough or city-wide level. In a borough race, often the only paid position in the party's campaign machinery.

Conseil de direction ("board of directors")—the main governing body of Projet Montréal on which sit a variety of rank-and-file members as well as the party leader and a representative of caucus.

Pôteau (literally, a "post")—a candidate who has no chance of winning and doesn't put much effort into the campaign.

Candidats présentis—prospective candidates who have been approved to run for the nomination but have not yet won it.

INDEX